Urban Violence in the Middle East

Space and Place

Bodily, geographic and architectural sites are embedded with cultural knowledge and social value. This series provides ethnographically rich analyses of the cultural organization and meanings of these sites of space, architecture, landscape and places of the body. Contributions examine the symbolic meanings of space and place, the cultural and historical processes involved in their construction and contestation, and how they communicate with wider political, religious, social and economic institutions.

Volume 1
Berlin, Alexanderplatz: Transforming Place in a Unified Germany
Gisa Weszkalnys

Volume 2
Cultural Diversity in Russian Cities: The Urban Landscape in the post-Soviet Era
Edited by Cordula Gdaniec

Volume 3
Settling for Less: The Planned Resettlement of Israel's Negev Bedouin
Steven C. Dinero

Volume 4
Contested Mediterranean Spaces: Ethnographic Essays in Honour of Charles Tilly
Maria Kousis, Tom Selwyn, and David Clark

Volume 5
Ernst L. Freud, Architect: The Case of the Modern Bourgeois Home
Volker M. Welter

Volume 6
Extreme Heritage Management: The Practices and Policies of Densely Populated Islands
Edited by Godfrey Baldacchino

Volume 7
Images of Power and the Power of Images: Control, Ownership, and Public Space
Edited by Judith Kapferer

Volume 8
Performing Place, Practising Memories: Aboriginal Australians, Hippies and the State
Rosita Henry

Volume 9
Post-Cosmopolitan Cities: Explorations of Urban Coexistence
Edited by Caroline Humphrey and Vera Skvirskaja

Volume 10
Places of Pain: Forced Displacement, Popular Memory and Trans-local Identities in Bosnian War-torn Communities
Hariz Halilovich

Volume 11
Narrating Victimhood: Gender, Religion and the Making of Place in Post-War Croatia
Michaela Schäuble

Volume 12
Power and Architecture: The Construction of Capitals and the Politics of Space
Edited by Michael Minkenberg

Volume 13
Bloom and Bust: Urban Landscapes in the East since German Reunification
Edited by Gwyneth Cliver and Carrie Smith-Prei

Volume 14
Urban Violence in the Middle East: Changing Cityscapes in the Transition from Empire to Nation State
Edited by Ulrike Freitag, Nelida Fuccaro, Claudia Ghrawi and Nora Lafi

Urban Violence in the Middle East

Changing Cityscapes in the Transition from Empire to Nation State

❖• •❖

Edited by
Ulrike Freitag, Nelida Fuccaro,
Claudia Ghrawi and Nora Lafi

berghahn
NEW YORK • OXFORD
www.berghahnbooks.com

First published in 2015 by
Berghahn Books
www.berghahnbooks.com

©2015, 2020 Ulrike Freitag, Nelida Fuccaro, Claudia Ghrawi and Nora Lafi
First paperback edition published in 2020

All rights reserved. Except for the quotation of short passages
for the purposes of criticism and review, no part of this book
may be reproduced in any form or by any means, electronic or
mechanical, including photocopying, recording, or any information
storage and retrieval system now known or to be invented,
without written permission of the publisher.

Library of Congress Cataloging-in-Publication Data
Urban violence in the Middle East : changing cityscapes in the transition from empire to nation state / edited by Ulrike Freitag, Nelida Fuccaro, Claudia Ghrawi and Nora Lafi.
    pages cm -- (Space and place ; volume 14)
    Includes bibliographical references.
    ISBN 978-1-78238-583-7 (hardback) -- ISBN 978-1-78238-584-4 (ebook)
    1. Urban violence--Middle East--History. 2. Sociology, Urban--Middle East--History. 3. City and town life--Middle East--History. 4. Community life--Middle East--History. 5. Political culture--Middle East--History. 6. Petroleum industry and trade--Social aspects--Middle East--History. 7. Social change--Middle East--History. 8. Middle East--Social conditions. 9. Middle East--Politics and government. 10. Middle East--Colonial influence. I. Freitag, Ulrike. II. Fuccaro, Nelida. III. Lafi, Nora. IV. Ghrawi, Claudia.
    HN656.Z9V587 2015
    303.60956--dc23
                                                                    2014033530

British Library Cataloguing in Publication Data
A catalogue record for this book is available from the British Library

Printed on acid-free paper

ISBN: 978-1-78238-583-7 hardback
ISBN: 978-1-78920-829-0 paperback
ISBN: 978-1-78238-584-4 ebook

This book was published as part of the 2nd DFG/AHRB collaborative projects
(PAK 566, FR 1004/10-1).

Contents

List of Figures   vii

Acknowledgements   ix

Introduction   1
Claudia Ghrawi, Fatemeh Masjedi, Nelida Fuccaro and Ulrike Freitag

Part I. Managing and Employing Violence

Chapter 1. Mapping and Scaling Urban Violence: The 1800 Insurrection in Cairo   29
Nora Lafi

Chapter 2. A Capital Challenge: Managing Violence and Disorders in Late Ottoman Istanbul   52
Noémi Lévy-Aksu

Chapter 3. Gendered Obscenity: Women's Tongues, Men's Phalluses and the State's Fist in the Making of Urban Norm in Interwar Egypt   70
Hanan Hammad

Part II. Symbolic Politics of Violence

Chapter 4. Urban Violence, the Muharram Processions and the Transformation of Iranian Urban Society: The Case of Dezful   91
Reza Masoudi Nejad

Chapter 5. Symbolic Politics and Urban Violence in Late Ottoman Jeddah   111
Ulrike Freitag

Part III. Communal Violence and its Discontents

Chapter 6. The 1850 Uprising in Aleppo: Reconsidering the Explanatory Power of Sectarian Argumentations   141
Feras Krimsti

Chapter 7. The City as a Stage for a Violent Spectacle: The Massacres of Armenians in Istanbul in 1895–96   164
    Florian Riedler

Chapter 8. Transforming the Holy City: From Communal Clashes to Urban Violence, the Nebi Musa Riots in 1920   179
    Roberto Mazza

Part IV. Oil Cities: Spatiality and Violence

Chapter 9. On Lines and Fences: Labour, Community and Violence in an Oil City   197
    Rasmus Christian Elling

Chapter 10. Reading Oil as Urban Violence: Kirkuk and its Oil Conurbation, 1927–58   222
    Nelida Fuccaro

Chapter 11. Structural and Physical Violence in Saudi Arabian Oil Towns, 1953–56   243
    Claudia Ghrawi

Afterword. Urban Injustice, Urban Violence and the Revolution: Reflections on Cairo   265
    Khaled Adham

Notes on Contributors   287

Selected Bibliography   289

Index   309

Figures

Figure 1.1. Map of Cairo, 1800.	30
Figure 1.2. Shaykh al-Bakri Neighbourhood, 1800.	34
Figure 1.3. Mapping Violence in Cairo, 1800.	46
Figure 4.1. A public procession at a cemetery in Dezful on the day of Ashura.	95
Figure 4.2. The traditional boroughs and the Heydari–Neʿmati division in Dezful (1920s).	97
Figure 4.3. The traditional division of the Ashura procession and the major procession routes in Dezful.	99
Figure 4.4. The main routes of processions in Dezful since the 1950s.	106
Figure 4.5. The procession of Ashura morning, when all city quarters run their processions to Rud-band Shrine. Dezful, 2006.	107
Figure 4.6. Extending the border between Heydari and Neʿmati quarters through the modern city. Dezful, 1990s.	108
Figure 5.1. Carsten Niebuhr, sketch of the city of Jeddah.	117
Figure 5.2. Map of Jeddah, 1851, drawn after an Ottoman map of 1851.	119
Figure 5.3. Map of Jeddah, 1880/81, drawn after an Ottoman map of 1880/81.	120
Figure 10.1. Kirkuk's pipelines and oil stations, 1952.	225
Figure 10.2. Kurdish worker in Kirkuk oilfields, 1945.	227
Figure 10.3. British Indian soldier guarding an oil well in Kirkuk Fields, 1945.	232
Figure 11.1. The spatial organization of Dhahran, 1965.	246
Figure 12.1. The route of the main demonstration to Midan al-Tahrir on 25 January 2011.	270

Figure 12.2. Street celebrations in 2010 for the national football team's winning of the African Cup of Nations. 273

Figure 12.3. Dreamland. 275

Figure 12.4. The transformation of Manshiyyat Nasr into an upscale district in the first draft of Cairo Vision 2050. 277

Figure 12.5. Midan al-Tahrir as an urban theatre during the revolution. 280

Acknowledgements

This book presents some of the results of collective deliberations on urban violence in the Middle East by a group of researchers: Rasmus Elling, Ulrike Freitag, Nelida Fuccaro, Claudia Ghrawi, Nora Lafi and Fatemeh Masjedi. We collaborated between 2011 and 2013 as part of a German–British research project sponsored by the German Research Council (DFG) and the Arts and Humanities Research Council (AHRC) as part of PAK 566, FR 1004/10-1. We are grateful for their support of the project, which allowed for intensive conversations amongst and between the editors and the contributors of this book, and which has led to its publication. Through this process the two research groups – based at Zentrum Moderner Orient, Berlin, and the School of Oriental and African Studies, London – were able to develop a common understanding of urban violence. Many colleagues and staff at both institutions encouraged the project and provided the necessary logistical support during our activities, for which we would like to express our thanks.

The chapters in this volume are based on some of these conversations. They are a first attempt to bring together in a more systematic way general theoretical literature on urban violence as a means of contestation with Middle Eastern case studies. We are grateful to the publishers, Berghahn Books, for their unequivocal support of the project, and to the anonymous reviewers for their comments which urged us to push our reflections further than we might otherwise have dared.

In the course of the three years' work on the project, and of editing this book, we were very happy to be supported by outstanding student assistants without whose help the group's activities, the conference and the editing of this book would not have been possible. Nushin Atmaca, Jihan Akrawi, Semra Kertal, Yasser Mehanna, Layla Safta-Zecheria, Patrick Winkelhorst and Christoph Rother, as well as, in the later phases of editing, Christian Kübler and Teresa Schlögl, were of invaluable help, while Mitch Cohen gracefully and often at short notice was willing to improve the English of our texts. We also thank Melody Mosavat for drawing the maps for the contributions by Lafi, Freitag and Ghrawi.

Editing a book with Arabic, Ottoman and Persian spellings, as well as various European language renderings of personal and place names, always presents a challenge. We have opted for a simplified system of transliteration which follows the IJMES style, unless the names are part of quotations.

The editors
Berlin, January 2014

Introduction

CLAUDIA GHRAWI, FATEMEH MASJEDI, NELIDA FUCCARO AND ULRIKE FREITAG

This book was conceived in mid-2010 as a response to a perceived gap in scholarly reflections on different forms and expressions of urban violence in the history of the Middle East from the late eighteenth until the mid-twentieth century. While urban violence has recently become a vibrant field of study in other regions, and has increasingly been understood as an extreme but not exceptional expression of political and social contention, we felt that scholarship on the Middle East differed. There, urban violence was often seen as a sign of the violent nature of the region's societies or as an expression of confessional or ethnic factionalism. We thus aimed to bring together contributions that would show a variety of contexts in which urban violence could develop, erupt or be suppressed and avoided, discuss the actors and institutions involved in these processes, and reflect on these events in the context of more general theories and debates. We thereby get away from the 'hysterical mainstream [that] locates the sources of violence in or emanating from the region in Islam(ism) or attributes it to some half-baked but remarkably persistent cultural explanations (tribalism, ancient hatreds, cycles of violence, etc.)'.[1]

In addition, we were wondering about the impact of the transition from empires (the Ottoman and Qajar) to nation states in the region, a process that was heavily 'moderated' by European powers, which after the First World War experienced a last apex of imperial expansion in the Arab Middle East in the form of the mandates system.[2] As it turned out, the modernizing and centralizing reforms undertaken by the Ottoman and the Qajar empires since the mid-nineteenth century provided for a more gradual transition between the two forms of state than we had initially assumed. What turned out to be more important than the form assumed by the state were processes and degrees of centralization and urbanization, as well as, from the early twentieth century on, of industrialization.

Hence, the contributions in this volume aim at understanding the crucial relationship between political and social protest, the evolution of the urban public sphere, and the physical expansion of urban centres. Urban violence is understood here as one particular ritual of power and a ploy for popular and state legitimacy in the context of street politics.[3] Besides instances of ritualization in both public ceremonial and ritual performances, it can be used to make political claims that cannot be realized in other ways or can serve the at times dramatic and theatrical enforcement of the rule of law. The chapters also investigate in different ways how episodes of violence relate to the transformation of the physical landscape of the city and to changes in the specific settings of popular contestation and state action. They also examine how these changes reflected wider trends across the region as well as European and Western influences.

While the majority of contributions in this volume are written by historians, they are influenced by strands of historical analysis that make strong use of sociological concepts, most prominently those advanced by Charles Tilly and William H. Sewell, Jr. In the spirit of these scholars, they treat events of urban violence in modern Middle Eastern history as an expression of contentious politics and as 'both the outcomes of structural ruptures and the causes of sequences of cultural and political change that lead to new structural configurations'.[4] Furthermore, the contributions to this volume do not deal with episodes of cataclysmic violence such as war or large-scale massacres. Instead, they analyse more common violent events performed by both individuals and groups that can be explained as part and parcel of the 'systemic and stabilising' violence of the everyday, to use David Nirenberg's words.[5] Finally, the focus on public violence largely implies that, at least for most of the historical contributions, the historical gender segregation is replicated in the historical narrative, since often women either did not participate in the events actively or are not mentioned in the records available to the historian, except as victims (e.g. chapters by Lafi, Krimsti, Freitag) or a potential moral danger (e.g. the brothels mentioned in Lévy-Aksu's chapter). Thus, their very prominent appearance in Hammad's chapter mirrors two aspects, namely their increased public role by the 1950s, and the fact that the state increasingly involved itself in censoring the everyday life of its subjects and hence started to concern itself with the policing of abusive language among neighbours.

The Iranian and Arab Uprisings, Urban Violence and the Modern State

The volume thus contributes to theoretical as well as empirical debates that have already informed the study of violence in other parts of the world, and it destroys the myth of the Middle East as a region marked by particularly violent eruptions, for instance of a communal nature. It does so by integrating its history into more universal processes of urban change and political negotiation. Writing about the past, however, cannot be divorced from the present. This lesson was brought home in particularly poignant terms when the so-called Arab Spring emerged in early 2011 while preparations for this volume were in full swing. The wave of uprisings that spread in North Africa and the Middle East was preceded by Iran's 'Green Movement',[6] which erupted as a series of protests against the second term in office of the Iranian President Mahmoud Ahmadinejad in June 2009. In all these cases, the movements did not erupt overnight.

These events sparked a new scholarly interest in the societies of the Middle East, which for decades were perceived as being caught in a hopeless political stalemate. The urban centres of the uprisings, such as Azadi Square and Enqelab Square in Tehran, Tahrir Square in Cairo and University Square in Sanʿa became symbols of the struggle between citizens and state power. We argue that the historical case studies in this volume can contribute significantly to a better understanding of the processes of the recent past and present, and highlight continuities and ruptures in the urban social formation.

A closer look at Middle Eastern cities reveals that until early 2011 they were not dormant at all. To start with Iran, a trend that Asef Bayat terms 'post-Islamic' became visible by the early 1990s. On the one hand, the new mayor of Tehran allowed the symbols of the Islamic revolution, such as photographs of martyrs and revolution leaders, to become less prominent on the streets of Tehran. They were replaced by commercial billboards, and the construction of inner city highways and shopping malls followed an American model rather than the archetypes of the 'ideal Islamic city' embodied by Qom and Kerbela, which had been propagated after the Islamic Revolution. New parks and recreational facilities built by the municipality provided spaces for men and women to mingle, and music and art added to the changing urban culture and introduced new ways of being young and Muslim at the same time. This contributed to a new youth culture among college students, male and female, and especially women's and students' movements, laying the foundations for the Green Movement of 2009 with its large female component.[7]

The Green Movement itself, which started as a contestation of the Iranian elections, came to signify the struggle for civic rights beyond an Islamic agenda. It was driven by students, youth, religious intellectuals, professionals and state employees, including women, and gave the important signal that large segments of Iranian society demanded fundamental political change. This has to be seen against the background of a young population, 70 per cent of whom were under the age of thirty-five. The Iranian state answered the movement with harsh violence. Many activists and participants were arrested, tortured, killed or disappeared.[8]

Similarly, what started in early 2011 with a young Tunisian's desperate act of self-immolation in front of a governorate building in the provincial Tunisian town of Sidi Bouzid, with the murder of a young blogger by policemen in an Internet cafe in Alexandria, with demonstrations against fake parliamentary elections in Cairo and with schoolchildren spraying anti-regime graffiti in the Syrian provincial city of Derʿa (to name only some events and places),[9] had begun to unravel long before. The 'Arab Spring' uprisings in North Africa and the Middle East advanced, unnoticed by most observers, from outside the marble-clad centres of the political elites and the sparkling meeting places of the new urban bourgeoisie. They had their origins in the suburbs and provincial towns, where a rapidly growing population has struggled for the fulfilment of basic needs, where large-scale modernization projects in conjunction with the privatization of many basic services had neglected the rights of the poor and the disenfranchised majority, and where state-patronized factionalism has fuelled dissatisfaction amongst those who were denied participation in the opportunities of economic liberalization. The protests that erupted in early 2011 could draw on discrete movements with specific concerns that had started to form earlier, such as initiatives concerned with the environment in Cairo. These movements at times reflected economic or political grievances and at others expressed localized political concerns.[10] Besides these connections to earlier mobilizations, the uprisings of 2011 were ignited by events of exemplary everyday violence that demonstrated the powerlessness of the people vis-à-vis unjust and brutal governments, quite closely comparable to the Iranian Green Movement.

The mobilization that followed these initial events was eased by various communication and social networks that not only connected local communities with each other, but also linked towns and cities on national and regional levels. Hence, spontaneous public articulation of enragement against despotism, corruption and social neglect in urbanized areas quickly gained a more organized form that aimed at the urban centres of state power. When the wave of protest reached the capitals and other major cities of the respective states, a wider spectrum of the population embraced the movement for civic empowerment and began to challenge the current social, economic and political orders. Activists, intellectuals and common folk alike seized the opportunity to take political change into their own hands by claiming their ownership of both the city and the socio-political transitions incubated in the urban sphere.[11] Spontaneous concerts in the squares and parks of Tunis, symbolic 'cleaning' sessions and street painting in Cairo, and the procession of the revolutionary flag through the boulevards and alleyways of Homs and Damascus demonstrated a unified and determined public that governments could no longer ignore.[12] In cities where no obvious public spaces for assembly and demonstration existed, as in Bahrain, these were spontaneously created, as testified to by the protesters' camp on Pearl Roundabout in Manama. Even under the most oppressive circumstances, protesters were remarkably inventive when it came to leaving their mark where it could be noticed, as illustrated by the dyeing of water in public fountains in Damascus.[13]

Yet, already at an early stage of the uprisings, it became clear that they also were marked by a notable degree of violence. For instance, Egypt's peaceful political spring in January 2011 was interrupted by a 'day of rage' during which protesters in Giza, Suez, Alexandria and other cities fought street battles with violence-prone police forces, smashed windows and set fire to or attempted the siege of police stations, municipal buildings and National Democratic Party headquarters, throwing stones and Molotov cocktails.[14] It was Charles Tilly who suggested analysing such outbursts of violence as a universal, albeit extreme, means of putting forward collective claims in any given society and time. Tilly also emphasized that 'above a very small scale, collective violence almost always involves governments as monitors, claimants, objects of claims, or third parties of claims'.[15]

The crucial role played by the 'modern' state in the definition, sanctioning and monopolization of violence has been observed by, amongst others, Fernando Coronil and Julie Skurski, who came to the conclusion that 'any definition of violence already assumes a partial standpoint sustained by violent relations'.[16] In the process of building centralized and professionalized state administrations, governments in all parts of the world were increasingly able to use their institutional leverage to define violent and criminal or deviant behaviour and to forestall such action on the behalf of public security, but also as a response to challenges against their own legitimacy. The latter has been termed the state's external and internal monopoly over legitimate use of force, however debated the boundaries of legitimacy might be. Whilst external military action does not fall within this volume's focus, internal policing in the preventive and intervening sense is central for the assertiveness of the modernizing state[17] and thus for our inquiries. State policing became most apparent in the urban context, where new forms of governance and modern infrastructures were first introduced. The three contributions in Part I of this volume by Lafi, Lévy-Aksu and Hammad on 'Managing and Employing Violence' discuss the pivotal role played by the late Ottoman state and by European and modern state administrations in Middle Eastern cities from the late eighteenth until the early twentieth century. However, the processes of industrialization and urbanization at times outpaced those of state building and the modernization of the state apparatus, sometimes leading to cases in which external powers intervened in policing or the state took recourse to the military for internal repression.[18] This is demonstrated in detail in the three contributions in Part IV on oil cities (Elling, Fuccaro and Ghrawi).

The urban character of violent struggle has even farther-reaching implications. For example, most of the Arab uprisings in 2011 and since have shown that the lines of confrontation by no means always run exclusively between governments and people. Different groups and factions within the urban community may enter temporary or permanent alliances and exert violence against each other in their struggle for the reallocation of power or resources. During the uprisings in Egypt and Tunisia, the spontaneous formation of street and quarter groups defending their local urban spaces against police raids as well as against opportunist marauding might well serve as an example.[19] Similarly, the formation of youth gangs joining in the protest as well as using the occasion for looting resembles the violent crowds described by Krimsti, Riedler and Mazza in Part III. These chapters, which cover the period from 1850 to 1920, point to a number of continuities as well as to many ruptures in the development of collective action in the urban context. For example, present-day rioters could often build on new types of sociability, such as football clubs or political organizations, in addition to the new media such as Facebook and Twitter, through which they could mobilize much more quickly in the vastly expanded modern urban spaces.

In some cases, the symbolic dimension of violent behaviour must be emphasized. Thus, rioters attacked symbolic sites as well as their guardians, as in the case of the aforementioned torching of Cairo's headquarters of the National Democratic Party, which supported President Mubarak's regime, and in the attacks on more than ninety police stations all over Egypt. The symbolic significance of the choice of targets and occasions for the deployment of violent protest is also highly visible in the fatal clashes between supporters of soccer teams closely identified with the opposed regime, on the one hand, and protesters on the other.[20] For their part, governments at times chose to retaliate against protesters with excessive force that aimed at discouraging others to follow their example as much as at stigmatizing protestors as outlaws and expelling them from the regime's 'goodwill', such as in the attacks on the protesters in Tahrir Square or in the Syrian town of Derʿa, the torture of children who had decorated the walls of their school with graffiti demanding regime change. The symbolism of these violent acts transmits their socio-political message in a way that was heard and understood by all conflicting parties in the respective context. It further seems to multiply the coercive power of violent behaviour by those who lack other resources to make their voice heard, as will be discussed later in this introduction. Some of the historical case studies in this volume, such as the articles by Ulrike Freitag, Reza Masoudi Nejad and Florian Riedler, examine symbolic uses of extreme violence by states and protesters during events of seemingly irrational outrage and killing, or during outbreaks of (ritualized periodic) violence between neighbourhood communities. These authors' examination of an anti-Armenian pogrom also draws attention to the complexities of sectarian violence, which have been a marked feature of the Arab uprisings. The contributors to Part III, on 'Communal Violence and its Discontents', develop this topic further.

Another aspect of the violence witnessed during the 'Arab Spring' can be linked to specific spatial structures and distribution of power and resources that seem to be characteristic for the evolution of the 'modern' nation state and that paralleled processes of economic integration into world markets and rapid urban growth. In Part IV, the link between 'Spatiality and Violence' is explored in three contributions by Elling, Fuccaro and Ghrawi, who look at the specific setting of twentieth-century oil cities in the context of nascent nation states, and discuss ethnic segregation and social control in the light of economic growth and parallel underdevelopment. Khaled Adham follows a similar path of inquiry in his chapter on contemporary Cairo, in which he discusses the recent uprisings in connection to their interrelation with neo-liberal economic conversion and urban planning. He demonstrates how those people whom government officials and their business cronies had expelled to the margins of the city and had excluded from access to decent living space chose to stage their demands for justice in the heart of the city and at the centre of power, namely Tahrir Square, with its direct access to the surrounding government buildings. The four contributions thus add a structural argument to the notion of the city as a 'stage' for protest.

Why Urban Violence?

While Riedler's aforementioned article demonstrates how the imperial capital of Istanbul, as a capital city, provided an ideal stage both for a national and an international audience on which to play out (in extremely violent terms) the Ottoman-Armenian conflict, many of the case studies in this volume consider violent incidents in secondary and provincial cities. Thus, it was the provincial towns of Sidi Bou Zid and Derʿa that sparked the uprisings in Tunisia and Syria respectively. It seems that the usually emphasized characteristics of the city – such as a developed infrastructure, a wide social stratification and the quality and diversity of urban lifestyles[21] – did not necessarily play key roles in the outbreak of the uprisings, although they seem to have helped to accelerate the events once the protests reached the regional towns and cities. This raises the question of why cities matter and how we conceive of urbanity.

Obviously, the focus on cities is not self-explanatory, given the widespread occurrence of rural rebellions and uprisings in Middle Eastern as well as, indeed, in global history.[22] Still, the Arab Spring protests started in densely populated and rapidly expanding environments that can be qualified at least as 'urbanized'. Mirroring this urban focus, the case studies in this volume are likewise concerned with a variety of cities and towns that range from cosmopolitan Cairo and Jerusalem in the nineteenth century to embryonic forms of industrial settlements that were only beginning to develop into larger urban formations during the second half of the twentieth century. Certainly, the role of cities has increased with the dramatic urbanization processes since the nineteenth century, but most notably in the second half of the twentieth century, in much of the Middle East. Furthermore, these have caused an increased blurring of the urban–rural divide through phenomena such as the 'urbanization of the countryside' and the 'ruralization' of the cities, thus highlighting connections that can be found in earlier periods as well, albeit in different forms. One such earlier form is the entanglement of urban tax-farmers and the rural hinterland of cities through webs of tax raising, credit provision, access to markets and manufacturing through contracts.[23]

Since we contend that there are certain specificities to urban violence, we cannot avoid the basic question: What do we mean by 'urban'? Furthermore, the Arab Spring uprisings evolved in varying manners, but all witnessed various forms of violence at some stage. If we consider such fundamental divisions as between systemic or state violence, ritual and everyday violence, cataclysmic violence and violent protest, and if we bear in mind the multiple levels of conflict that might be fought out in a violent event, violence becomes an immensely complex concept that needs to be defined with reference to the urban sphere, on the one hand, and to the historical transitions discussed in this volume, on the other.

To begin with, the urban sphere in this book's context is portrayed as 'a site, an arena where larger social, economic, or cultural processes are worked out'.[24] Yet, this site is not static, but is itself undergoing a constant process of transformation in which changing visions of society are reified in the material and organizational surface of the city as much as in the social practices that evolve in the urban sphere. The basic idea that socio-spatial relationships are 'an inherent part of societal development' was formulated in the second half of the twentieth century by neo-Marxist thinkers who linked transitions of and within the urban sphere to larger changes in industrial capitalism and the world economy.[25] In his influential work *The Production of Space* (1974), Henri Lefebvre suggested that social practices in the urban sphere either reinforce or alter a given socio-political order. By arguing that the modern urban space is the product of capitalist modes of production and thus 'structures' capitalist order, makes it concrete and – consequently – reproduces it through everyday practices and routines, Lefebvre claimed that alternative interpretations and utilizations of space can challenge and alter the prevailing socio-political system.[26]

Lefebvre's writings on the relationships among the capitalist mode of production, urbanization and revolutionary change must be read in the context of his own experiences with the Parisian uprisings of 1968; they thus strongly reflect intellectual thought and urban experience of the late twentieth century.[27] Yet, they certainly were an inspiration for what became known as the 'spatial turn' in social and cultural sciences four decades ago.[28] The turn towards a stronger reflection of space in historical analysis was prepared by thinkers such as William H. Sewell, Jr. who conceptualized processes of historical transition in the wider theoretical framework of structuralism. Sewell emphasized the 'strong reproductive bias built into structures', which leads to 'powerful continuities of social relations' but also makes it 'possible to explain the paths followed in episodes of social change'.[29] Later, he used his concept of structure to define space as 'a constituent aspect of contentious politics'.[30] In this sense, the ability to control, utilize, transcend, imagine or reinvent space and hence to reproduce or transform social order is put into effect in 'the ways that spatial constraints are turned to advantage in political and social struggle and the ways that such struggles can restructure the meanings, uses, and strategic valence of space'.[31] Thus, the built environment and the social and communication networks of the city become essential conditions, but also issues of social mobilization. 'In providing a site for alternative forms of political organization and action, cities offer a number of spatial and social resources', argued Fran Tonkiss in 2005.[32] Among these resources she recognized were: first, the public space in itself and therefore 'the informal spatial infrastructure for political action and association'; second, information and mobilization networks, 'from dense transport networks and a concentration of press and broadcast media, to the informal communications technology of bill-sticking and graffiti'; third, 'social networks that support pressure groups' including 'crucial sites for a politics of assembly, collectivity, spontaneity, and for spatial expressions of solidarity'; and finally, 'identities, ideologies and "lifestyles" … which provide *the critical mass* to locate politics in space'.[33] Hence, the urban sphere is a physical as well as cognitive intermediary in contentious politics, as it provides the means for mobilization, serves as a rallying point for collective identities and allows for collective practices that are able to challenge spatial and socio-political structures. Furthermore, it is the space in which most institutions representing the state are located, and hence is where state actions as well as actions against the state are played out most effectively. In addition, and given the specific structures of the rural and urban economy in Middle Eastern history, many key economic players (such as landowners) and institutions (such as banks, industries and trade) have been mostly urban-based, adding to the attractiveness of the city as a theatre for protest and violence, as discussed in the chapters by Riedler and Adham, among others.

Clearly, the urban level of analysis brings to the foreground the historical processes 'at stake', the conflicts that arise around reproducing and transforming structures of all kinds and at all scales – from the street, the neighbourhood and the quarter to the city, the state and the whole region. The contributions in this volume analyse the resort to violence as one possible means of partaking in these conflicts. As Norbert Elias has argued, violent behaviour is, regardless of the time and place, a normal part of human emotional affects. Yet, the acceptance of the use of violence in relations between individuals or groups has changed over time. Whereas violent brawls and struggles between smaller competing socio-political entities used to be the norm where no regulating central power existed, the development of the centralized and institutionally differentiated state led to a growing regulation of violent behaviour.[34] As Coronil and Skurski have reasoned for the context of the 'modern' state, violence 'is associated with acts of transgression and aggression against central values, [but] it is also present in the mechanisms that preserve order and legality and in the practices that seek to institute new visions of society'.[35] Their observation that 'in the context of political violence, violence appears as a tool wielded in the pursuit of power'[36] should be emphasized here. Ussama Makdisi has drawn our attention to the intricate link of the Ottoman modernization process and the employment of violence by the state in Lebanon and Syria, notably in the forceful suppression of the 1860 massacres. Persecuting the perpetrators of crimes against Christians, the Ottoman authorities reflected an image of justice and tolerance that was central to defining the Empire as 'modern', particularly in the eyes of the Great Powers.[37] One of the topics that feature in a significant number of chapters in this volume is that of the exercise of state violence as an intricate part of the process of building a 'modern' state, both in the imperial and the post-imperial period.

The Role of Violence in Contentious Politics

Violence constitutes a kind of coercive power in conflicts in *all* times and is mobilized by governments and subjects alike. The employment of violence follows the logic of resorting to existing power resources in a conflict. It can be the chosen long-term strategy in conflicts in which the rebelling party lacks many supporters, internal cohesion or legitimacy, or simply the adequate resources for large-scale mobilization. Especially in the case of suicide bombings, the violent act aims at equilibrating the inferior number or strength of those who make a stand against a superior opponent.[38] Yet, in many cases, the turn from peaceful to violent behaviour seems to happen spontaneously or as an ad hoc decision that does not reflect any discernible long-term strategy. Violence is indeed often employed by subaltern actors in the absence of other available resources and as a means for self-empowerment. In her work on religious rioting in sixteenth-century France, Natalie Zemon Davis identified cases of 'folk justice' in which groups of individuals from various social backgrounds employed violence against 'idolaters' in order to enforce traditional law or social values and norms because the authorities were either unable or unwilling to do so.[39] Edward Palmer Thompson analysed bread riots in eighteenth-century England as a means to warn authorities of popular discontent and to pressure them for action or to start a bargaining process between starving people and authorities.[40] Even what looks like irrational and excessive violence follows this logic. 'Violence is explained not in terms of how crazy, hungry or sexually frustrated the violent people are (though they may sometimes have such characteristics), but in terms of the goals of their actions and in terms of the roles and patterns of behaviour allowed by their culture.'[41]

Charles Tilly has suggested that repertoires of (violent) contention changed with the emergence of a centralized state and a capitalized economy in more recent history. Analysing conflict in Great Britain between 1750 and 1830, Tilly asserted that, with the emergence of an 'increasingly powerful and demanding state', the repertoire of contention likewise gained new forms that were better suited to placing demands.[42] Contentious action in the eighteenth century, he observed, evolved largely around local issues and nearby objects, and was employed either directly or relied on 'a local patron or authority who might represent [people's] interest, redress their grievances, fulfill his own obligation, or at least authorize them to act' and further 'included a good deal of ceremonial, street theater deployment of strong visual symbols and destruction of symbolically charged objects'.[43] The street as a theatre for 'abstract forms of symbolically constructed violence – targeting persons and communities by exposing them to humiliation'[44] is one possible entry into the problematic of urban violence in Middle Eastern cities, and is taken up by a number of authors in this volume. Such forms of contention, Tilly argues further, were replaced in the nineteenth century by new forms of mass action that could occur in different places while addressing the same national issues. The socio-political and physical transformation of the urban sphere played a crucial role in this change of repertoires. 'Voluntary associations formed, especially among the middle classes, to promote self-help, recreation, education, moral reform, and political action' while 'pubs and coffee houses became increasingly important gathering places and bases for special-interest associations'.[45]

This applied to Middle Eastern cities as well. Edmond Burke III was among the first who encouraged a study of shifting repertoires of urban protest in the transition from reforming Ottoman and Qajar empires to the Young Turks and Persian revolutions of 1908 and 1906 respectively, and the evolving nation states.[46] For the nineteenth century, Burke evoked a symbolic world and the existence of a predefined 'ritual drama' that unfolds in the urban theatre. In the context of nationalism and secularly based social movements in the twentieth century, 'the old repertoire of collective action, based on the gathering of the crowd at the mosque, solemn processions to the seat of government, and the presentation of petitions to the authorities faded out everywhere' and were exchanged for new styles of collective action like strikes and boycotts.[47] In a similar approach, Sami Zubaida analysed forms of popular organization and mobilization in the major cities of the Ottoman Empire and its successor nation states, retracing the transformation from 'traditional' urban politics that evolved in the urban quarters and around ulema, urban notables, and *futuwwat*, into a 'political modernity' that enacted more inclusive political units and increasingly targeted the centres of state power.[48]

Contentious Politics in Middle Eastern Cities

Covering a time range from the late eighteenth century to the 1960s and encompassing a geographical space from contemporary Egypt and Turkey to Iran and Saudi Arabia, this book aims at further developing an urban perspective on the politics of contention and specifically on the occurrence of violence in the transformation process from the Ottoman and Qajar empires into nascent nation states, highlighting the diversity of actors, forms and spatial dimensions of urban violence. The transformations in question were not just political transitions, but were at times also preceded, and at others accompanied, by wider processes of urban modernization. This process can be traced to the middle of the nineteenth century, although it certainly accelerated in the twentieth century and needs to be put in the context of the cities in question. Urban modernization came in different guises: from administrative reforms starting in the Ottoman Tanzimat from the 1850s, the subsequent improvement of old and the introduction of new infrastructure (water supply, street lighting), new types of policing, all the way to the major reshaping of the urban space through massive building projects and efforts at town planning.[49] In more recent times, considerable rural to urban migration and the rapid expansion of cities also need to be considered, again occurring at different times in different places, but taking on a particular dynamic after the 1940s.[50] These processes resulted in the socio-political and physical transformation of cityscapes, as well as in new spatialities of injustice.

In this volume, the changing cityscapes are presented from two complementary perspectives. Some of the authors depict how transitory processes in Middle Eastern history, such as the late imperial administrative reforms and growing economic activity by foreign countries in the Ottoman Empire, unbalanced the existing socio-economic conditions and accentuated older or created new lines of urban conflict. It is in this constellation, for example, that confessional and ethnic identities came to be regarded and used as a major factor in conflict and mobilization. Urban violence, then, might be understood as a practice employed by resident communities and governments to establish a new socio-economic equilibrium, as illustrated in the chapters by Feras Krimsti, Florian Riedler and Ulrike Freitag. Other authors, such as Reza Masoudi Nejad and Claudia Ghrawi, interpret urban violence as a means to overcome spatial restrictions and their social implications and, with them, to challenge whole socio-political systems.

As we will see, analysing violent events and their actors at different scales (the street, the neighbourhood, the city quarter, the municipality, the empire or the nation state) is essential in order to grasp the dynamics of urban violence. This approach informs most contributions to this volume, although it is demonstrated most explicitly in Nora Lafi's chapter on mapping and scaling urban violence in the 1800 insurrection in Cairo. A number of chapters (Lafi, Freitag, Fuccaro, Ghrawi) pay attention to how new spaces of urban contention were created inside the city and in its immediate hinterland, and how they were chosen and used as sites of violent confrontation by different actors. The salience of space, urbanization and urban planning becomes clear in a number of contributions, most notably in the chapters dealing with oil urbanization and political unrest.

The chapters are grouped in four thematic parts that share similar argumentative approaches and thus invite the comparison of case studies and results. The first, 'Managing and Employing Violence', includes contributions that consider how different state administrations employed or sanctioned violence in order to exercise and maintained their authority in the urban arena. These include a European imperial power, namely, the French in Egypt, the late Ottoman imperial government, and the modern Egyptian state that emerged after the First World War. Nora Lafi's contribution discusses in detail the topography of violence in Cairo under the French military occupation of the city. She focuses on a specific episode of unrest, namely the revolt staged in 1800 against French rule. Her article discusses forms of repression and terror as methods of governance in an environment where local political alliances were of crucial importance for the occupying power. Lafi shows how rebellious notables mobilized urban factions in order to foment unrest. She also focuses on the different articulations of violence, from unrest on the street to clashes between regular armies. Thus, she suggests the need for a typology of urban violence that can better conceptualize the different forms that it takes in urban spaces.

An understanding of late Ottoman urban society through definitions of order, disorder and criminality is at the heart of Noémi Lévy-Aksu's chapter, which discusses Istanbul under Hamidian rule. Lévy-Aksu examines how processes such as classifying violence and instituting a new type of police force helped to bring the issue of violence and public disorder to the attention of the authorities in a more systematic manner. She also demonstrates how the press popularized violent crimes as acts directed against public order and not just against individuals. In doing so, Lévy-Aksu highlights the extent to which the Ottoman state, with its new instruments of urban control (censuses, police and press), was able (or indeed unable) to control violations of public order. Its upkeep was central to the legitimization of the state, which therefore concentrated on disturbances of what came to be considered the 'public order', rather than crimes against individuals.

While Lévy-Aksu depicts the last years of imperial rule, Hanan Hammad's chapter is squarely set in interwar Egypt, a nation state in the making under British tutelage. While the contributions of both Lafi and Aksu take more of a macro-perspective, Hammad starts from below. She examines how women use explicit sexual language as a 'weapon of the weak' in the working-class environment of al-Mahalla al-Kubra. As a number of cases involving such language were taken to court, the state (represented by the various bureaucrats involved in these cases) contributed to defining not only appropriate and inappropriate language, but also gender and social hierarchies. In criminalizing the use of offensive language and public sexual gestures, the state conformed to the dominant middle-class values of the ruling *effendiyya*. In addition, Hammad's discussion of state intervention in cases of mutual, sexually explicit recrimination shows the extension of the power of the government in regulating social, often neighbourly relations. In addition to the different degrees and methods of state involvement in violent acts, which was to some extent congruous with the transition from empire to nation state, these three chapters in Part I also demonstrate how different analytical scales help to make sense of instances of urban violence. While this is at the heart of Lafi's approach, Hammad, taking the bottom-up perspective, also shows how very trivial local incidents could demand a state response in order to define social order. These definitions are, as discussed above, central to Lévy-Aksu's contribution.

Part II, on 'Symbolic Politics of Violence', explores the theme of symbolic politics in two different settings: the first is in the context of a prominent Shiite religious ritual, namely the Muharram procession in the Iranian city of Dezful, and the second regards an attack on consuls and Christians in the Red Sea port town of Jeddah.[51] In the first chapter, Reza Masoudi Nejad presents the traditional annual Muharram processions organized by the quarters of Dezful to symbolize the competition between two rival urban factions, Heydari and Neʿmati, in the late Qajar and early Pahlavi period. While this rivalry had a long, religiously grounded history in a number of cities in Western Iran, Masoudi Nejad traces its transformation in the 1940s into a competition between landlords vying for the control of different neighbourhoods. The processions had long served to channel aggression and violence. Masoudi Nejad argues that, in the context of political transformation in the 1940s, urban crowds in some of Dezful's quarters started to use the processions as a way to express their resentment against the very same landlords who organized them.⁵² This ended with the land reform of the 1950s, which eliminated the problem by transforming the political and social position of traditional landowners.

The Dezful case illustrates how urban rituals could both contain and channel aggression, but also provided a potential outlet for contingent violence. The second chapter in this part, Ulrike Freitag's article on the 1858 massacre in Jeddah, shows how extreme violence was used consciously: by the urban crowd to express grievances otherwise suppressed by the Ottoman state, but also by the state itself (and even more so by the European powers whose subjects were killed during the incident) to punish the suspected and real culprits in order to deter a repetition of the bloodshed. The symbolism held also for those who were attacked in what might have seemed to contemporaries like a recurrence of communal violence elsewhere in the Empire: Christians, no matter whether they had European or Ottoman nationality, had come to be identified locally with the imperial powers, which were feared for their economic prowess and military might. Thus the killing of Christians by the urban crowd, which had been incited by local notables, took on a symbolic meaning beyond the elimination of immediate competitors in the lucrative overseas trade. Freitag investigates the spaces in which the violence was staged, and shows how, by the end of the nineteenth century, both urban change and shifts in international power relations had made a recurrence of such events far less likely. Both chapters in the section highlight the importance of urban spaces for the course of events. In Masoudi Nejad's chapter, this pertains to the routes chosen by the Muharram processions, in Freitag's contribution to the spatial proximity of port, market, government and consular buildings, which greatly facilitated the rapid mobilization and escalation of violence.

The chapters in Part III on 'Communal Violence and its Discontents' review prominent cases of sectarian violence, thereby scrutinizing the validity of monocausal explanations that tend to emphasize intercommunal tensions as causes for violence. In his chapter on the 1850 riot in Aleppo, Feras Krimsti challenges the seemingly obvious idea of a Muslim attack on Christian neighbourhoods. He asks what the language employed in contemporaries' writings betrays about the idea of a clash between Christian and Muslim inhabitants, and afterwards compares these accounts with the actual spatial setting of the riot. Krimsti's textual and spatial analyses reveal the degree to which religious confrontation was evoked by contemporary narratives, and traces the events back to the emergence of Aleppo's Christians as key economic and political actors in the city's history. He thus convincingly argues that the attacks targeted the symbols of this socio-economic rise more than the Aleppine

Christian communities in general. Once again, the symbolic dimension of communal violence becomes quite evident.[53]

Writing about the massacres of Armenians in Istanbul in 1895–96, Florian Riedler follows a similar approach, making use of a spatial analysis of urban socio-economic structures to explain the extraordinary and unprecedented violence against the Armenian inhabitants of Ottoman Istanbul. Besides showing that the city provided a 'stage' that allowed Armenian nationalists and the Ottoman government to convey their respective political message far beyond the immediate witnesses and parties involved, Riedler succeeds in deconstructing larger categories of actors such as 'Muslims' or 'Armenians' by developing a more differentiated picture of the effects and interdependencies of urban violence at the micro-level of the city. He points out that it was mainly poor Armenian migrant workers who were attacked and killed during the massacres. Not only were they living in the centre of events, which made their neighbourhood an easily accessible and thus logical option for the attack, they were also exposed to the discriminatory administrative practices of the municipal government concerned with unwelcome migrants who entered into competition with other urban groups in the local labour market.

In both chapters, a spatial examination of the violent events and their urban settings negates the idea of a direct confrontation between distinctly divided Christian or Armenian and Muslim communities. Although certain neighbourhoods of both Aleppo and Istanbul were known to be inhabited by Christian or Armenian majorities and others by Muslim majorities, these communities did not live in strict separation, but rather formed residential clusters in what we would nowadays call multi-ethnic and multi-religious cityscapes. Furthermore, spatial divisions were determined not only by ethnic or religious belonging, but also by occupation, social status, and by the necessity to lodge newly arrived migrant groups in the process of urban expansion. This also applies to the chapter by Roberto Mazza on the transformation of Jerusalem and the Nebi Musa Riots of 1920. Far from being a 'confessionalized' city, Mazza argues, nineteenth-century Jerusalem showed the pattern of shared spaces, inhabited by both Muslims and Christians. Violent intercommunal strife was in fact exceptional, as relations between the communities were mediated by a system of urban politics that gravitated around the Ottoman governor and a few urban notables. This changed only with the growing confrontation between Arabs and Zionists at the beginning of the twentieth century, which introduced violence as part of the local political vocabulary. Mazza shows how, in this period, intercommunal violence became organized into events, following a distinctive script and rituals, and with a specific spatial logic. What Mazza defines as 'structured violence' was further reinforced by the new conceptualization of urban space operated by the British mandatory administration, which promoted a particularistic vision of the city with confessionalized spatial divisions. The three contributions in Part III suggest that the focus on religious and ethnic explanations of intercommunal violence seems to be either the result of a biased reconstruction of events (Krimsti) or of purposeful political mobilization (Riedler, Mazza). Further, the causes of violent strife can be found in the shaking of socio-economic foundations of urban coexistence by administrative and economic reform, immigration into cities and the exclusionist practices that accompanied the advancement of nationalist political agendas.

While most of the chapters in this volume examine urban violence in naturally 'grown' but now transforming cities, the chapters in the last thematic section, Part IV on 'Oil Cities: Spatiality and Violence', use the mainly planned and heavily industrialized oil conurbation as their analytical point of departure. Oil cities and their hinterlands present a rich empirical field for testing the dynamics of structural violence and violent protest, thereby offering a different insight into the politics of violent contention at the historical juncture of oil industrialization in the context of consolidating nation states. The widespread perception of violent unrest as a struggle between a 'colonizing' foreign company and a 'native population' is explicitly challenged in Rasmus Elling's chapter on violent struggle in the Iranian oil city of Abadan during the Second World War. Revisiting the image of Abadan as a 'dual city', Elling concentrates on an understudied and seemingly 'banal' incident of violence between local and Indian residents. He argues that the city offered multiple spaces for violent confrontation as a result of the various ethnic and religious groups living in Abadan. In his case study, Elling shows that violence was not only an oppressive means of control and coercion employed by the company in the pursuit of economic interests, but was also embedded in the urban 'everyday politics' that structured relations between the different labour forces employed in the oil industry. Elling concludes that 'social processes and political structures that shape modernity were and are often moulded and sustained by violence and coercion'.

Taking a different yet complementary approach, Nelida Fuccaro investigates how the oil industry in Iraq generated 'multiple histories of violence' in Kirkuk and its oil conurbation in the period of the Hashemite monarchy. Fuccaro examines forms of structural and physical violence, and shows their interconnections as they became an integral part of new urban geographies and disciplines of industrial production under the aegis of oil. She analyses how the creation of new and differential urban spaces paralleled the deployment of mechanisms of surveillance and control, in turn triggering the mobilization of different violent actors, from policemen and tribal leaders to labour activists. The oil industry, she argues, created spatial, social and political 'orders of difference' that became most manifest in a variety of violent urban landscapes, culminating in the explosion of labour unrest after the Second World War. By the 1950s, oil-related violence was increasingly directed against the Iraqi government, given the increasing association of the oil company with the Hashemite regime.

Claudia Ghrawi pursues a similar line of argument in her chapter on structural and physical violence in Saudi Arabian oil towns between 1953 and 1956. In the emergent oil towns, she contends, structural suppression of the Saudi labour force was violently and deliberately advanced by the state, thus driving the oil workers struggle for better working and living conditions towards a more and more explicit confrontation between state and subjects. This confrontation contributed as well in shaping the physical setting of the growing oil conurbation. Ghrawi demonstrates the interdependence of structural violence, violent threats and the actual deployment of physical violence. Structural inequality and repression, and the use of downright force on the side of the state, occasionally prompted oil workers to resort to physical violence against spatial and other representations of the opposed order. These attacks are read as having at times been effective attempts to re-enter the bargaining process when non-violent means had proved unsuccessful. Buttressed by the replacement of traditional local forms of personal rule with a gradually more impersonal and centralized government, physical violence became, at least temporarily, a frequently employed resource in conflict resolution between the government and Saudi oil workers.

The contributions dealing with oil cities suggest that the interplay between structural and physical forms of violence and oil urbanization is far more complex than interpretations that portray violence as being a result of straightforward confrontation between oil companies and the labour force. Violence as an urban phenomenon in the context of oil development involved a number of actors, often reflecting various ethnic and religious divisions among the workforce living in and around the oil cities. Structural and physical violence thereby complemented each other as modes of 'oppression' and 'insurrection' in the context of the functioning of corporate power and the parallel building or consolidation of the modern nation state. Here, the use of force became a decisive means of contention.

In lieu of a conclusion, Khaled Adham's Afterword on social injustice and revolution in contemporary Cairo redraws the analytical link to the

Arab Spring of 2011, and accentuates the significance of urban physical structures for collective claims by arguing that the Egyptian revolution was not only played out in specific urban places, but was also a result of what he calls the 'spatiality of social injustice'. As in the case of oil towns, the urban planning process in Cairo was driven by profit considerations as much as by the aim to build hierarchies and displays of the power of corporate or state agents into the urban sphere and make them absolute and permanent. In both scenarios, the subaltern urban population became marginalized and isolated from the wealth and prestige accumulated in the city. Yet, these marginalized individuals found their rallying point in the manifest symbols of their inferior position in society and could turn them into a resource for mobilization. Given the widespread nature of the type of urban planning discussed by Adham, this chapter speaks to concerns that extend far beyond modern Middle Eastern cities.

In most chapters of this book, urban violence emerges as one of the means of contention that aims at changing the balance of power between conflicting parties. Violent conflict is often preceded by the violation of a prevalent order by peaceful means, most notably in assembling and staging demonstrations in places strongly controlled by the authorities (Fuccaro, Ghrawi and Adham) or in a ritualized manner by crossing the invisible but nevertheless absolute lines of social or political relevance (Masoudi Nejad). In other words, such 'violations' are answered by physical violence against attempts to mobilize power resources to change the power equilibrium by challenging the city's social, ethnic or religious geography or by the sheer power of the united mass. In the modern city, be it the mid-twentieth-century oil conurbation or contemporary Cairo, this violent answer became institutionalized and built into the structure of urban governance in the form of a permanent threat of force, facilitated by urban planning that allowed for more control through the spatial layout, with wide streets and open spaces, and by greater state policing ability. This type of increased state control, which can be considered a feature of political modernity, can be traced back to the modernizing reforms of the nineteenth century. Lévy-Aksu's article provides clearer definitions of deviance and of measures for the better surveillance and control of the urban sphere, while Hammad traces them to the level of neighbourhood and individual relations by considering cases brought to court in order to censure particular behaviours deemed 'dangerous' or 'deviant'. Lafi and Elling, on the other hand, show that the process of implementing surveillance and control, especially when foreign actors or corporate interests were involved, was accompanied by a remarkable degree of violent resistance, as well as everyday violence by and between social, ethnic and religious factions of the urban population.

Clearly, the expansion of state control did not pass unchallenged. Rather, violence could at times take the form of the last resort by people not otherwise involved in the decision-making processes as a means to rebalance the lost social, economic or political equilibrium. This was often done under the rubric of restoring the 'traditional' order, as Freitag's chronologically early case study shows. Here subaltern violence is used conservatively and thus takes part in the (attempted) reproduction or reinstitution of local structures that were challenged by the modernizing empire/state (Krimsti, Masoudi Nejad). In other cases, governments or urban administrations themselves might take the (informal) lead in a violent confrontation between conflicting parties in order to further the imposition of their national or imperial visions (Lafi, Riedler, Mazza). In a contrasting manner, the intent to overcome traditional divides and to create a more inclusive urban geography can be marked by the urban community's symbolic abolition of violence (Masoudi Nejad).

As the chapters in this volume show, the phenomenon of urban violence as a particular type of contentious politics is rather complex. Yet, in comparison with the discussion of urban violence in a range of sociological and social science literature that seeks to explain its occurrence elsewhere, its occurrence in Middle Eastern cities does not represent an exception. In the modern Middle East, as in Europe and indeed elsewhere, violence has been a latent historical feature of local communities and local and state institutions under pressure as a consequence of political, social and economic change. Its latent presence in society is nothing specifically Middle Eastern, even though the forms of its manifestations and the frequency of its eruptions might differ from society to society. What the contributions to this volume suggest is the relevance of regionally specific processes of urban modernization, often under the impact of foreign actors and spanning both the imperial age and the establishment of the modern Middle Eastern states, in determining particular forms of violent contention as well as specific practices of conflict resolution within Middle Eastern cities.

Notes

1. L. Khalili. 2013. 'Thinking about Violence', *International Journal of Middle East Studies* 45, 791.
2. The designation of Persia as a 'Qajar Empire' after 1856–57 is a matter of debate; see F. Kashani-Sabet. 2002. *Frontier Fiction: Shaping the Iranian Nation, 1804–1946*, London: I.B. Tauris, 143.

3. For more on street politics, see A. Bayat. 1997. *Street Politics: Poor People's Movements in Iran*, New York: University of Columbia Press.
4. S. Tarrow. 1996. 'The People's Two Rhythms: Charles Tilly and the Study of Contentious Politics', *Comparative Studies in Society and History* 38(3), 588.
5. D. Nirenberg. 1996. *Communities of Violence: Persecution of Minorities in the Middle Ages*, Princeton, NJ: Princeton University Press, 13.
6. N. Hashemi and D. Postel (eds). 2010. *The People Reloaded: The Green Movement and the Struggle for Iran's Future*, Brooklyn: Melvin House; H. Dabashi. 2011. *The Green Movement in Iran*, New Brunswick: Transaction Publishers.
7. A. Bayat. 2013. 'Post-Islamism at Large', and 'The Making of Post-Islamist Iran', in A. Bayat (ed.), *Post-Islamism: The Changing Faces of Political Islam*, Oxford: Oxford University Press, 7–9 and 39–43 respectively.
8. Dabashi, *The Green Movement*, 43–46, 66–70.
9. S. Poisson. 2013. 'Les Mobilisations Discrètes des Mouvements Environnementalistes au Caire', *Confluences Méditerranée* 85(2), 129–40.
10. Karine Bennafla stresses this transformational aspect of the cities: K. Bennafla. 2013. 'Avant-propos', in K. Bennafla (ed.), *Villes Arabes: Conflits et Protestations*, Paris: L'Harmattan, 9–16.
11. As David Harvey put it, 'the right to the city is ... far more than a right of individual access to the resources that the city embodies: it is a right to change ourselves by changing the city more after our heart's desire': D. Harvey. 2003. 'The Right to the City', *International Journal of Urban and Regional Research* 27(4), 939.
12. A Middle Eastern perspective on the role of the public in contentious political processes can be found in: S. Shamy (ed.). 2009. *Publics, Politics, and Participation: Locating the Public Sphere in the Middle East and North Africa*, New York: Social Sciences Research Council.
13. C. Bank. 2012. 'Al-Thawra al-Suriyya...Ikhtilat al-Dam bi-'l-Fann', *Deutsche Welle*, 27 March, retrieved 23 September 2013 from http://dw.de/p/14Sm2.
14. M. El-Ghobashy. 2012. 'The Praxis of the Egyptian Revolution', *Middle East Research and Information Project* 258(1–7), retrieved 13 September 2013 from http://www.merip.org/mer/mer258/praxis-egyptian-revolution.
15. C. Tilly. 2003. *The Politics of Collective Violence*, Cambridge: Cambridge University Press, 9–10.
16. F. Coronil and J. Skurski. 2006. 'States of Violence and the Violence of States', in F. Coronil and J. Skurski (eds), *States of Violence*, Ann Arbor: University of Michigan Press, 9.
17. See for example W. Reinhard. 2000. *Geschichte der Staatsgewalt: Eine vergleichende Verfassungsgeschichte Europas von den Anfängen bis zur Gegenwart*, second edition, Munich: C.H. Beck, 363–70.
18. Reinhard accordingly regards the use of the military for internal repression and the absence of a functioning state police as symptoms of a weak state: ibid., 363.

19. D. Zayed and S. El Madany. 2011. 'Egypt Vigilantes Defend Home as Police Disappears', *Reuters*, 29 January, retrieved 13 September 2013 from http://www.reuters.com/article/2011/01/29/us-egypt-vigilante-trib-idUSTRE70S3AZ20110129.
20. D. Tuastad. 2013. 'From Football Riot to Revolution: The Political Role of Football in the Arab World', *Soccer & Society* 14(1), 1–13.
21. J. Abu Lughod. 1969. 'Varieties of Urban Experience: Contrast, Coexistence and Coalescence in Cairo', in I.M. Lapidus (ed.), *Middle Eastern Cities*, Berkeley and Los Angeles: University of California Press, 159–87.
22. P. von Sievers. 1988. 'Rural Uprisings as Political Movements in Colonial Algeria, 1851–1914', in E. Burke III, E. Abrahamian and I.M. Lapidus (eds), *Islam, Politics, and Social Movements*, Berkeley and Los Angeles: University of California Press, 39–59. For an early comparative volume, see R.P. Weller and S.E. Guggenheim (eds). 1982. *Power and Protest in the Countryside: Studies of Rural Unrest in Asia, Europe, and Latin America*, Durham NC: Duke University Press.
23. H. Kuroki. 1999. 'The 1850 Aleppo Disturbance Reconsidered', in M. Koehbach (ed.), *Acta Viennensia Ottomanica*, Vienna: Institut für Orientalistik, 221–33.
24. A. King. 1989. 'Culture, Space and Representation: Problems of Methodology in Urban Studies', in Research Project 'Urbanism and Islam' and The Middle Eastern Culture Center in Japan (eds), *Proceedings of the International Conference on Urbanism and Islam (ICUIT)*, Supplement, Tokyo, 341.
25. Ibid., 342–43.
26. H. Lefebvre. 1974. *La Production de l'Espace*, Paris: Anthropos.
27. For a new appraisal of Henri Lefebvre's works *Le Droit à la Ville* (1968) and *La Révolution urbaine* (1970) in the light of urban uprisings of the last decade, see D. Harvey. 2012. *Rebel Cities: From the Right to the City to the Urban Revolution*, London and New York: Verso.
28. D. Bocquet. 2012. 'Henri Lefebvre und der Begriff der Urbanisierung ohne Urbanität: Deutung eines missverstandenen Begriffs aus heutiger Sicht', *Informationen zur Modernen Stadtgeschichte* 2012(2), 41–47; M. Löw. 2008. *Die Eigenlogik der Städte*, Frankfurt am Main: Suhrkamp, 37.
29. W.H. Sewell, Jr. 1992. 'A Theory of Structure: Duality, Agency, and Transformation', *American Journal of Sociology* 98(1), 16.
30. W.H. Sewell, Jr. 2001. 'Space in Contentious Politics', in R. Aminzade et al. (eds), *Silence and Voice in the Study of Contentious Politics*, Cambridge: Cambridge University Press, 51–52.
31. Sewell, 'Space in Contentious Politics', 55.
32. F. Tonkiss. 2005. *Space, the City and Social Theory*, Cambridge: Polity Press, 65.
33. Ibid. Italics set by the authors of this Introduction.
34. N. Elias. 1976. *Über den Prozess der Zivilisation*, vol. 1, Frankfurt am Main: Suhrkamp, 263–65, 278–79.

35. Coronil and Skurski, 'States of Violence', 9.
36. Ibid., 1.
37. U. Makdisi. 2002. 'Rethinking Ottoman Imperialism: Modernity, Violence and the Cultural Logic of Ottoman Reform', in J. Hanssen, T. Philipp and S. Weber (eds), *The Empire in the City: Arab Provincial Capitals in the Late Ottoman Empire*, Beirut and Würzburg: Ergon Verlag, 37.
38. W. Pearlman. 2011. *Violence, Nonviolence, and the Palestinian National Movement*, Cambridge: Cambridge University Press.
39. N. Zemon Davis. 1973. 'The Rites of Violence: Religious Riot in Sixteenth-Century France', *Past & Present* 59, 63, 83.
40. E.P. Thompson. 1971. 'The Moral Economy of the English Crowd in the Eighteenth Century', *Past & Present* 50, 122–23.
41. Zemon Davis, 'The Rites of Violence', 90.
42. C. Tilly. 1993. 'Contentious Repertoires in Great Britain, 1758–1834', *Social Science History* 17(2), 273.
43. Ibid., 271–72.
44. G. Ajimer. 2000. 'The Idiom of Violence in Imaginary and Discourse', in G. Ajimer and J. Abbink (eds), *Meanings of Violence: A Cross-Cultural Perspective*, Oxford and New York: Berg, 9.
45. Tilly, 'Contentious Repertoires', 274.
46. E. Burke, III. 1986. 'Towards a History of Urban Collective Action in the Middle East: Continuities and Change 1750–1980', in K. Brown et al. (eds), *État, Ville et Mouvements Sociaux au Maghreb at au Moyen-Orient: Urban Crisis and Social Movement in the Middle East*, Proceedings of the C.N.R.S.-E.S.R.C. Symposium, Paris, May 23–27, Paris: Editions L'Harmattan, 42–56.
47. Burke, 'Towards a History of Urban Collective Action', 46, 49.
48. S. Zubaida. 2008. 'Urban Social Movements, 1750–1950', in P. Sluglett (ed.), *The Urban Social History of the Middle East 1750–1950*, Syracuse and New York: Syracuse University Press, 224–53.
49. M. Maʿoz. 1966. 'Syrian Urban Politics in the Tanzimat Period between 1840 and 1861', *Bulletin of the School of Oriental and African Studies* 29(2), 277–301. For a recent discussion of the process of reform in the Ottoman Arab province of Jerusalem, see J. Büssow. 2011. *Hamidian Palestine: Politics and Society in the District of Jerusalem 1872–1908*, Leiden: Brill, 41–82.
50. On urbanization and modernization, see B. Hourcade. 2008. 'The Demography of Cities and the Expansion of Urban Space', in P. Sluglett (ed.), *The Urban Social History of the Middle East, 1750–1950*, 154–81. On past and present planning and urban development in some Middle Eastern cities, see Y. Elsheshtawy. 2004. *Planning Middle Eastern Cities: An Urban Kaleidoscope in a Globalising World*, London and New York: Routledge.
51. For a discussion of symbolic politics, see, e.g., T. Mergel. 2002. 'Überlegungen zu einer Kulturgeschichte der Politik', *Geschichte und Gesellschaft* 28, 574–606.

52. On rituals and violence, see P. van der Veer. 1996. 'Riots and Rituals: The Construction of Violence and Public Space in Hindu Nationalism', in P.R. Brass (ed.), *Riots and Pogroms*, New York and London: Macmillan Press, 154–76.
53. See the plea for an approach that is sensitive to historic specificities and takes into account a multitude of factors culminating in communal (or 'ethnic' or 'nationalist', and by extension also 'confessional') violence in R. Brubaker and D. Laitin. 1998. 'Ethnic and Nationalist Violence', *Annual Review of Sociology* 24, 423–52.

Part I

Managing and Employing Violence

❖· Chapter 1 ·❖

Mapping and Scaling Urban Violence

The 1800 Insurrection in Cairo

NORA LAFI

The study of urban violence has become one of the most active fields of research relating to understanding the anthropological grounds of violence in general. The link between violent acts and urban space is also increasingly recognized as a crucial entry to an understanding of the general functioning of societies.[1] Studies of urban violence are developing in the context of recent theoretical elaborations on the very nature of violence, which have changed the general point of view on the question.[2] The influence of the work of Charles Tilly, who argues that violence, far from being an abnormal expression outside of the functioning of societies, is instead part of their very nature, has been key in orienting studies of social movements and in stimulating the development of a new approach to the history of urban violence.[3]

The object of the present chapter is to examine, in the light of such questions, what happened in Cairo during revolts against French occupation. The chapter illustrates how violence is both the expression of potentialities existing in the normal organization of society, sparked by a change in their usual control and canalization, and the result of the interaction between local stakes and a specific geopolitical context. The example of the Cairo revolts of 1798 and 1800, against French occupation by Bonaparte and his troops,[4] is taken here as an occasion to underline the entanglement of scales in the sparking of violent events, from the street to international geopolitics and from urban factions to regular armies, and to put on a map the most relevant elements explaining how space is not only a setting for violence, or a stake of fights, but also an element full of socially and politically constructed meanings.

Figure 1.1. Map of Cairo, 1800. SHAT, Carte du Caire LII-128-0001-H.

French Occupation and Urban Order

In 1800, the second Cairo revolt against French occupation and its repression was one of the most violent events the city has ever experienced. On this occasion, various forces and factions clashed with French troops, in the context of Ottoman attempts to finally challenge the French seizure of the Ottoman province of Egypt. Various scales of conflict were involved, from Mediterranean geostrategy all the way down to the level of the city, neighbourhoods, streets and even houses. The object of this study is to discuss the urban dimension of violence and in particular to analyse the articulation between the urban space and the various forces and scales involved. The aim is to trace not only the nature and changing patterns of urban violence in various urban contexts, but also to better understand how, even in the case of an event with international implications, violence relates to the anthropological features of urban territories at the level of the street. For this purpose, information for this chapter has been taken from various chronicles and archival resources,[5] with the aim of collecting spatialized data about the events at various scales in order to progressively map all relevant information. The insurrection is seen here as a unique occasion to reflect on the interaction of different scales of conflict and stakes at the very moment when new conditions were impacting on the whole Arab world. The aim is also to trace, from the perspective of urban historical anthropology, how old forms of violence, pertaining to the traditional clash of factions in the streets of an Arab Ottoman city in the context of a rupture of the imperial *pax ottomana*, and new forms, relating to the impact of foreign occupation and warfare, and to the challenge to Ottoman imperial belonging, mixed and interacted.

From the start, the French occupation challenged the Ottoman 'old regime' urban order, which was based upon the neighbourhood as the basic unit of governance, and on guilds, markets and the power of notables. The latter were responsible for the everyday administration of the city and were the interlocutors of the Ottoman authorities. Such authorities, furthermore, should not be seen as merely extraneous to the city, but rather as part of a network of connivance with local notables and sometimes local factions. This urban *pax ottomana* resulted in (and was the result of) a fragile and constantly negotiated balance between factions and in the intimate entanglement of scales and positions between the local and the imperial.[6] It was also the result of a constant canalization of possible violent eruptions: the potential violence of factions or of gangs of young men came under the supervision of notables, and how it was dealt with on a daily basis was part of the local networks of urban patronage. Only in extreme circumstances did the imperial authorities have to intervene.

Mapping and scaling the disorder of the revolts against French occupation is impossible without having this complex situation in mind: Ottoman Cairo before the occupation was a city in which notables were both rooted in their neighbourhoods and part of the imperial networks of governance. The Ottomans did not just have a military presence in the city, with soldiers of various origins but, more importantly, their power was the expression of a negotiated balance with local notables and factions, who themselves controlled plebeian groups and canalized their potential violence. This urban feature of the Ottoman old regime was generally efficient in keeping order, but was also sometimes fragile because it was built upon the dominance of one faction against another, or of a coalition of pro-Ottoman factions against others, that, in turn, were subject to the temptation of becoming involved in anti-Ottoman foreign enterprises or of using plebeian agitation and violence for political ends.

This feature, although generally dealt with by negotiation and the exchange of favours, was always a potential source of trouble and became even more so on occasions when anti-Ottoman spies tried to reverse the hierarchy of factions. Just as agents of the Republic of Venice in seventeenth- and eighteenth-century Balkan towns used local factional leaders to challenge Ottoman imperial authority, so French and British agents began to act in this way at the turn of the nineteenth century in Arab cities of the empire. A typical example of disorder in towns of the

Ottoman old regime was when a faction revolted against the pro-Ottoman dominant faction with the help of external anti-Ottoman elements (foreign or dissident). Here, again, the entanglement of scale between the local and the geostrategic was significant, but the arrival of new kinds of international stakes resulted in the emergence of a new situation, of which Cairo was the first theatre. This kind of data needs to be considered when analysing the anti-French revolts, since the French built their dominance over the occupied city of Cairo on the empowerment of a local faction that was a rival to the one the Ottomans had used as their local go-between. Urban violence in times of international troubles is also the expression of, and is expressed by, a movement of local factions. These factions, furthermore, were the aggregation of both notables (often nobles) and their clientele, always with a component of mob and young gang members. They controlled the territory of their neighbourhood. Each neighbourhood in this old regime had its own entrance, which was closed at night. At the top of the local hierarchy of the neighbourhood was a local shaykh, who was in charge of public order.

The French challenged this situation, first with the military goal of better control of the city, but also with the aim of challenging the existing social order and the whole urban dimension of the symbol of power. The French occupation troops' order to dismantle the entrance gates between neighbourhoods and even doors at the entrance of streets and dead ends[7] was also the expression of the foreign occupier's choice not to delegate the public order at the street level to the previous system, even if there was a change of dominant faction. For the French, the main method of security enforcement was armed patrols and not the nightly closure of the neighbourhoods under the responsibility of local notables (during the day, all passages were controlled by a *bawwab*, a guard of the door, a figure who was part of the system of urban government and at the same time held a position of trust among the local population). In a very symbolic demonstration, the French army had all the doors amassed for public display in Ezbekiyye Square. They then dismantled them and recycled the wood and the metal.[8] This opposition to the old urban order was also an expression of the difficulty the French had in dealing with local notables beyond the limited horizon of those who were prepared to collaborate with them, the faction they empowered.

As the French were about to enter Cairo during the summer of 1798 after the Ottoman retreat from the city,[9] many shaykhs, mostly those of the dominant pro-Ottoman factions, fled the city, including al-Jabarti, the member of the city council in charge of the daily writing of the civic chronicle. Bonaparte, in a negotiation that was a kind of recognition of their power, then managed to convince many of them to return to the town. The French general tried to build a relationship with a faction of notables. But 'Umar Makram, the *naqib al-ashraf*, that is, the most prominent figure of the caste of urban nobles and, in the Cairo form of the Ottoman old regime, the person in charge of urban governance, decided to stay in exile.[10] He had been the only prominent figure to call on the Cairo population, over whom he had a certain authority as chief of the noble faction and moral chief of the urban administration, to resist French occupation.[11] But the French, even if they represented a revolutionary government, did not intend at all to bring about social revolution to Egypt by promoting a kind of plebeian power against the nobles; so they regarded the support of the shaykhs as crucial.

These early events are important when it comes to understanding the later role of factions in urban violence and the link between shaykhs and violent elements of the crowd. The *naqib al-ashraf* being absent, the French started to look for a possible replacement. As the al-Jabarti chronicle tells us, after many conflicts with Shaykh Sharqawi, who was the first choice of the French but proved reluctant to act as their frontman – he refused, for example, in a very symbolic move, to wear the French tricolour revolutionary *cocarde* – the French turned to Shaykh al-Bakri. He belonged to one of the most prominent Cairo families and was head of one of the most important noble factions. He controlled a neighbourhood (figure 1.2) and a certain number of clients and possibly elements of the crowd. Bonaparte made him the new *naqib al-ashraf*. In other words, the general used the old system for his own purposes, counting on the shaykh's capacity to control the urban crowd and its potential violent outbreaks. The French also made use of local rivalries between factions, al-Bakri being the archrival of Makram. The occupiers played one faction off against another, but always within the same social game of factions made up of noble notables, clients and gang members. This introduced new components in the quest for a mapping and scaling process of social and political realities: like the Ottomans and Mamluks, when the imperial power was embedded in such games among local factions, the French also used the same method to deepen their grip on the city, and in that way linked the scale of local factionalism to the geostrategic scale of their fight against Ottoman and local Egyptian resistance to occupation.

In this balance of power, there are also spatial elements at play, since the territorial base of the new dominant faction is not the same as that of the evicted faction. There is also no doubt that Ottoman agents and British spies played the same game with other factions and shaykhs to counter this move by Bonaparte. Al-Bakri had tried to obtain the office of *naqib al-ashraf* in the 1770s, but allegations of homosexuality and

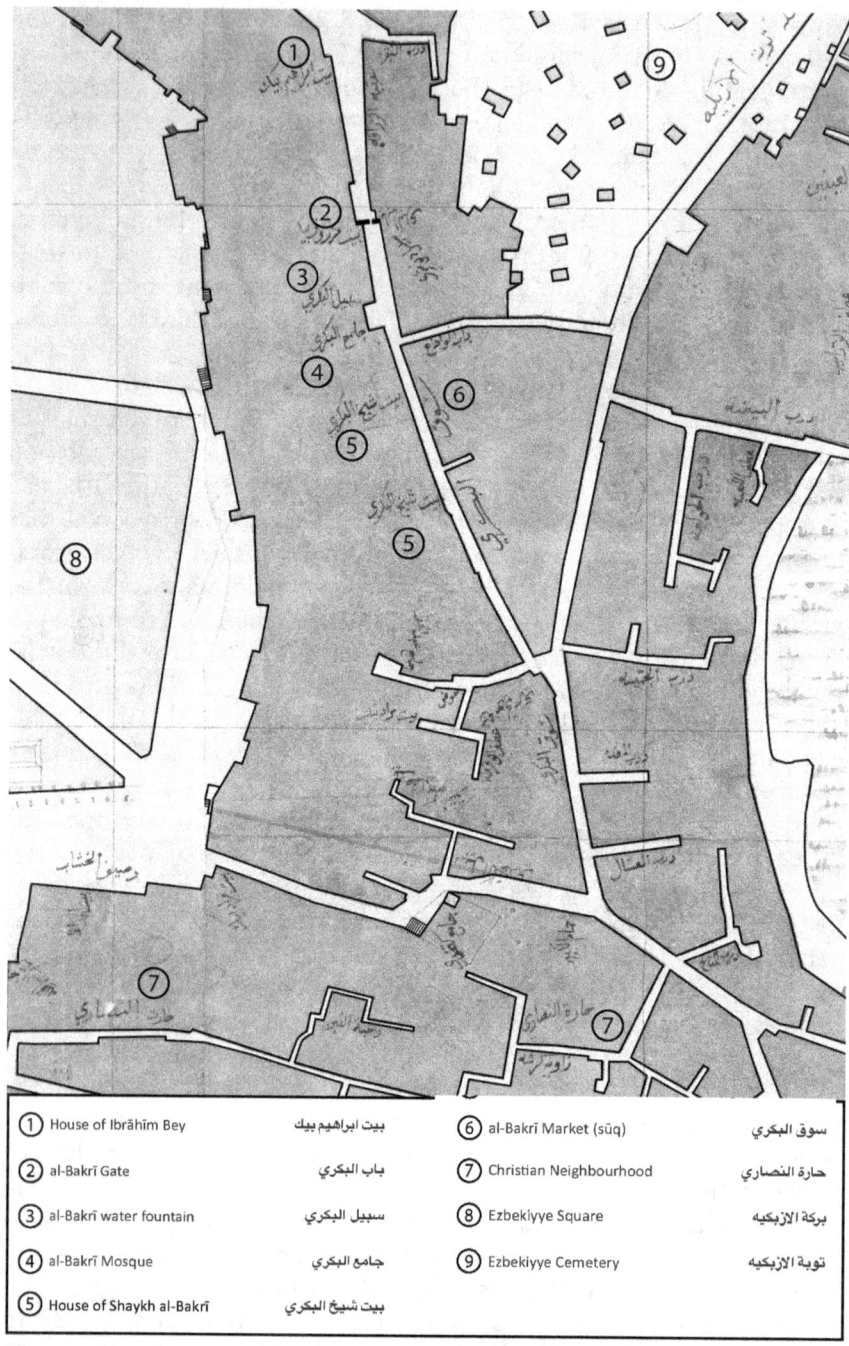

Figure 1.2. Shaykh al-Bakri Neighbourhood (Ezbekiyye Square), 1800. Extracted from SHAT, Carte du Caire LII-128-0001-H.

alcoholism spread by Makram had prevented him from reaching this goal.[12] In Cairo, moral reputation and rumours were political weapons. By appointing al-Bakri, the French were using their power of influence in the rivalry among factions. This also had an effect on the map of neighbourhoods, since each faction had its own spatial position. Scale and map matter here. And of course, the development of events only accentuated this situation.

With the absence of the chiefs of the pro-Ottoman faction, the French, far from promoting any revolutionary municipal or democratic system,[13] in fact confirmed the existing Ottoman system, itself based upon a medieval heritage, simply using the factional rivalry to reinforce their control of the city and its social space. The Ottomans had done the same on several occasions: they shifted their choice of the factions, on whom they built their power in order to solve a crisis.[14] They would do so again with the restoration, Makram being finally reinstated at the end of the period of French occupation.[15]

All chronicles show that once in charge, al-Bakri employed the same methods and social codes as his predecessor. His house became the new headquarters of the urban governance administration, just as the house of his predecessor was the place where the council of notables met. But with this shift in power and alliances, the political map of the city changed: a new neighbourhood became the centre of local governance, while the previous dominant one became the social stronghold of the potential opposition. An example of the relationship between the occupiers and this situation is instructive: a French officer, Poussielègue, was in charge of the supervision of the al-Bakri urban governance institution and watched over al-Bakri's shoulder on every decision he made. This might be the first occurrence of colonial supervision of an Arab administration.

The First Cairo Revolt and the Logics of Factional Violence

It was against this background that the first Cairo revolt exploded in October 1798.[16] At first glance, this revolt seems to be a popular one, a sign of the Cairo population's spontaneous discontent with French occupation. In his chronicle, Al-Jabarti indeed shows great contempt for what he sees as the violent revolt of a populace, who not only attacked the occupying forces, but also the very order of things – that is, the urban social order of the city being ruled by the caste of its noble notables.[17] The chronicle by Nicolas Turk also underlines that those in revolt belonged to the lower classes of the population.[18] What seems to shock the chroniclers is that the crowd acted outside of the social scheme in which popular elements obey signals provided by the notables. And this revolt was indeed marked by violent episodes. Symbols of the social domination of the notables were destroyed. Popular factions, in other words elements of the crowd acting outside of the traditional network of members of a faction headed by a notable, acted violently against the noble factions guilty of collaboration with the occupiers, in the context of the betrayal of one of the most prominent notables, al-Bakri, who had agreed to work with the French.

Here, we see violence that exists continually in society, but usually canalized, being unleashed in the specific context of the breaking of the negotiated social consensus. The geography of this revolt recalls the map André Raymond proposed in his study of popular movements in the previous decades.[19] But violence was of course not totally spontaneous. Agents and provocateurs, as well as Ottomans and British spies, are known to have been active, as reports of the French secret service and of Kléber himself confirm.[20] The map of this highly political revolt fits with the one of social disorders in the city during the previous decades. Obviously, however, new stakes were at play. The interaction between the local at the street level and the geopolitical, in the form of the more or less spontaneous revolt of young local delinquents interacting with international spies, outside of the usual social system of canalization of violence, is a novel element.

The situation was even more complex: it seems that even in this new form of revolt, which appears to short-circuit the power of the notables with a direct interaction between the scale of international politics and street violence, there was a dimension of influence of urban notables who played 'dirty' – that is, who broke the codes of their social milieu for the sake of the fight against occupation. Al-Jabarti indeed also invokes other urban figures acting in the course of events of the first Cairo revolt.[21] In this hypothesis, a plebeian faction was manipulated by an urban notable of a faction rivalling the one in power.[22] However, against such a shocking eruption of violence, which affects the social order, the consensus of notables is quickly re-established, as al-Jabarti states in his chronicle.

Many shaykhs who had been critical of Bakri's collaboration now joined forces with him. In his study of these events, Livingston has illustrated how, during the revolt, the shaykhs then went back to their respective streets and closed them with improvised barricades. The French, who had previously tried to open up the old regime's spatial and social order, accepted this measure, which helped to stop the spread of the popular revolt.[23] Confronted with social and physical danger, notables used their spatial bases to create separate cells within the city. The city space, when confronted with popular violence, ceased to function as a unit. In a context of violence, only separation could stop its spread, through a reinstatement of old-regime features of spatial and social control.

This revolt is also an occasion for the historian to uncover mediations among shaykhs and caste solidarity. In his home, Al-Bakri imprisoned shaykhs whom the French suspected of being accessories to the revolt. By keeping them under guard in his own house, he protected them against immediate punishment by the French and rebuilt networks of social support among his peers, in spite of faction rivalry.[24] In this way, he tried to demonstrate the importance of his position as protector in adversity.

But here Bonaparte made what might be considered the biggest mistake of his Cairo occupation: he had these shaykhs arrested and executed in spite of the protection that his own ally among the notables had given them. He thereby undermined the very authority of his protégé and enacted an institutional violence that was an insult to the codes of the very social milieu he was trying to uphold. In violently violating a strong social code, he lost all hope of securing any efficient old-regime-style mediation.

Only Shaykh Sadat, the representative of one of the most prominent noble families in Cairo, saved his neck, because of his rank. After Bonaparte cut the very branch on which he was sitting, that is, the legitimacy of an allied faction, French domination of the city was possible only by generalizing violence and extending the military grip on space. With the failure of the revolt, but most of all with the consequences of its repression, a new map of violence was inaugurated in Cairo. Popular violence lost part of its link with the network of governance by the notables, and the very milieu of notables lost every hope of mediation with the French: only a generalization of violence as a tool of occupation could secure lasting French control over the city. Of course, all later attempts by the French to convince Makram to return to Cairo and accept the position of mediator proved to be in vain.[25]

The Second Cairo Revolt: Violence, Factions and the Challenge to the Social Order

This context, and also the evolution of French–British–Ottoman relations, explains the nature of the second Cairo revolt, which illustrates yet another modality of violent eruption in a city. Only a few weeks after the January 1800 agreement on the French evacuation of Egypt, and in the context of its difficult implementation, and even before Nasif Pasha, the general of the Ottoman army which was to attack the city a few days later, had called on the urban population to rise against the French,[26] the second Cairo revolt began. It started with a violent incident in the city, which was both an urban street fight and a fight between the soldiers of two armies; of course it is possible that the strife was deliberately provoked.[27] On 3 March 1800 (*12 ventôse an 8*; *Shawwal 7, 1214H*), a fight between a group of French soldiers and a group of Ottoman soldiers left two French dead (one, according to al-Jabarti[28]). The Ottoman soldiers then barricaded themselves in the al-Jamaliyya neighbourhood, blocking the streets, possibly with the help of inhabitants, while the whole city, at the news of the incident, 'closed itself', as Nicolas Turk writes.[29] What is to be noted is that the al-Jamaliyya neighbourhood was that of a faction hostile to the French and to the factions they gave power to. Skirmishes with French troops continued for hours, until officers from both armies mediated the end of the incident. Following these events, the French and the Ottomans made an agreement: Ottoman soldiers had to stay out of town and withdraw to their camps. They could enter the city only without their weapons.[30]

This first manifestation of violence can be analysed as being at the intersection of various levels (urban street fights and two armies in the middle of a fragile truce) and of various types of conflict (soldiers against soldiers, neighbourhood against occupiers, street provocations and international politics). But even after calm had returned to the neighbourhood, violence was not over: on 9 March 1800 (*17 ventôse an 8, Shawwal 12, 1214H*), French authorities demanded that Nasif Pasha execute the leaders of the fights. Their bodies were then publicly displayed in Ezbekiyye Square:

> Le général en chef ayant exigé justice de l'assassinat de deux grenadiers de la 175e demi-brigade, tués par des soldats de l'armée du grand vizir dans la journée du 12 ventôse en faisant patrouille dans le Kaire, cinq Osmanlis coupables de ce crime qui ont été arrêtés, viennent d'être étranglés aujourd'hui par ordre du pacha, et leur corps exposés sur la place Ezbekyeh, 5 autres ont eu la tête tranchée. [Because the commander-in-chief demanded justice for the killing of two grenadiers of the 175th half-brigade killed by soldiers of the Grand Vizier's army on patrol in Cairo on the 12th Ventôse, today, five Ottomans guilty of this crime who were arrested were just strangled by order of the Pasha and their bodies exposed on Ezbekiyye square and five others were beheaded.][31]

State violence, part of an agreement between the French and the Ottomans to save the truce, also had an urban dimension in the form of this public spectacle in the square: it was intended to impress both the population and Ottoman soldiers. As Nicolas Turk describes, the bodies of the Janissaries were displayed 'in front of the house of Mohammed Bey Alfi, residence of General Kléber', thus symbolizing the foreign grip on the city.[32] In this case, the urban space was not only the scene of the theatre of violence, but was also given a strong symbolic dimension.

The revolt itself began in the context of military clashes between the French and the Ottoman armies on the outskirts of Cairo, when tension arose after a disagreement about the modalities of the evacuation (and after secret manoeuvres by the British). Al-Jabarti explains that the crowd began to revolt at the sound of the first skirmishes and killed a few French soldiers, who were leaving town to rejoin their regiments on the outskirts.[33] But urban street factions and the Ottoman army rapidly converged to fight the French. It may be that the Ottoman army had been preparing for this situation for months.[34] The convergence was made possible by the involvement of the *naqib al-ashraf* whom the French made destitute: ʿUmar Makram. With the help of another noble figure, Sayyid Ahmad al-Mahruqi, he channelled the expression of popular violence and organized factions loyal to him: 'the Turks of Khan al-Khalili and the Maghribis', but also those whom al-Jabarti calls the 'common people of the city' (*ʿammat ahl al-balad*).[35] In this configuration, the revolt began with an entanglement of scales and social strata: the Ottoman army, the leader of the urban nobility, the chief of the anti-French faction, allied factions, and the population of a city loyal to its former leader. The most active part of the population was composed of gangs of young men, whom al-Jabarti describes as 'common people, rabble and mob' (*tawaʾif al-ʿamma wa-l-awbasha wa-l-hashara*).[36] The word *taʾifa*, used here to describe the gangs of young men, indicates that it was in no way an indistinct mob, but rather organized groups of young men with a clear social profile. It is the same word that is used for guilds and professional organizations. In normal times, such groups, which were part of the clientele of a faction, were canalized and their potential violence was controlled. But in this revolt, they were clearly called by the head of the faction to join the fight against the French in conjunction with the Ottoman army: their potential for street violence was used as a strategic instrument. They rapidly took control of the narrow streets of the city (*aziqqa*), not acting on the scale of the battlefield on the outskirts, but on the scale of the city itself and of its complex map. Mobilization occurred at the sound of the very distinctive shouting of members of the gangs.

On the next day, troops accompanied by the whole pro-Ottoman urban administration, until then in exile (*naqib al-ashraf, kethuda* and various notables), entered the city through the gates Bab al-Nasr and Bab al-Futuh, and took possession of the al-Jamaliyya neighbourhood, the stronghold of this coalition of anti-French factions.[37] Even in the middle of a battle involving powerful armies, symbolic dimensions remain important: this Ottoman return to the city was conducted according to the rules protecting the dignity of the urban administration. This also had a practical advantage for the Ottomans: inside the city, nothing was more efficient than the gangs of young men, who could harass French troops, and the support of the population of an allied quarter. This coalition of soldiers, notables and gang members advanced as far as the Dhu al-Faqar caravanserai (*wikala*).[38] At this point, a new type of urban violence exploded: sectarian violence against Christians. It began with the call by Nasif Pasha to kill Christians (*al-nasara*) and to start a holy war against them (*jahadu fihim*).[39] Was he thinking of the French occupiers or of the Christian inhabitants of the city? The fact is that, benefiting from the call's ambiguity, the gangs of young men interpreted this order as an authorization to kill Copts and Syrian Christians. This might be the first time in early modern history that the struggle against European occupiers made local Christians collateral victims, opening a new chapter in the typology of urban violence discussed in this essay. Urban authorities, who in normal times were responsible for civil peace in the city, by choosing to use violent gangs in the context of a war, took the risk of sparking sectarian violence, as did the Ottoman authorities in calling for *jihad*. Makram, a moral figure, who should have granted security for all civilian inhabitants of the city, made himself the accomplice to a massacre by choosing to use gangs against the French. Sectarian violence was also the vengeance of one faction against another, and even of one quarter against another: not only vengeance for recent events, but probably also the expression of old rivalries, sometimes dating back to the Middle Ages, which in normal times would be contained. The gangs looted Christian houses in the quarters of Bayn al-Surayn, Bab al-Shaʿriyya and al-Muski.[40] They killed men, women and children until the Christians organized the defence of their quarters. Muslims living in these quarters were not spared violence, a fact that indicates that the violence was also that of one quarter against another and not just of one religious community against another.

On the next night, the battle concentrated on Ezbekiyye Square, with a mix of battlefield-style fighting and urban factional fighting.[41] Ottoman troops were on one side, together with the gangs, and the French on the other around their headquarters in the al-Alfi house. The factions in revolt had fortified their neighbourhoods with barricades on the side of al-Jamaliyya. At this point the French enacted a new kind of violence: the bombarding of the civilian quarters in revolt with cannon and bombs, which pushed the Ottoman army and the factions to decide to retreat to avoid the destruction of the city. This battle is said to have resulted in the death of nine hundred civilians and four thousand soldiers.[42] But some of the insurgents refused to retreat, and persuaded many others to stay. They then went back to Ezbekiyye to confront the French in the context of the continuation of sectarian violence against Christians and this time also Jews, facilitated by the pretext of the ambiguous authorization to kill the French. The next few days witnessed the combination of the regular army on the outskirts and the factions in the barricaded half of the city. Ottoman troops, including Albanian regiments and Janissaries, mixed with gangs on Ezbekiyye. The whole urban economy of craftsmen and workers was mobilized to produce weapons. Each barricade was under the supervision of a notable (for example al-Alfi, whose house on ʿAbd al-Haqq Street had been seized by the French), accompanied by Ottoman and Mamluk soldiers. Most of the looting and uncontrolled violence stopped, except in the case of fighters whom al-Jabarti describes as not part of the urban social order: not only local Maghribis (a popular faction in Cairo that traditionally escaped the supervision of noble factions and might in a way be compared to a kind of plebeian faction), but also fighters who came from the Arabian Peninsula[43] and gathered with local Maghribis and a Maghribi leader from outside the city (*wa-iltafat ʿalayhi taʾifa min al-maghariba al-baladiyya wa-jamaʿa min al-hijaziyya*).[44] For al-Jabarti, this uncontrolled group was responsible for the kinds of violence that a notable of the city could only disapprove of: terror against civilians, searching and looting of houses with women stripped naked and probably raped. Al-Jabarti also describes with horror how a young girl was beheaded and her blonde hair defiled.

From a social point of view, we see here the frontier between the urban factional violence with its codes, even in times of war, and another kind of violence, one perpetrated by those whom most people perceived as fanatics. Part of the crowd followed them, however. Shaykh al-Bakri was the next target of this mob: his house was looted and the female members of his family taken prisoner with him. All were taken to al-Jamaliyya, the stronghold of the insurgents (and of the faction opposed to al-Bakri) and humiliated.[45] At this point, a process of social solidarity among notables occurred, and a mediation was conducted to protect al-Bakri from vengeance. He was hosted at a merchant's house and the women of his family, who had also been stripped naked, were given clothes.

This violence against a notable and then the mediation to save him are a reflection of both the weakness of the urban order in times of crisis and of its strength. Shaykh al-Bakri had first tried to calm things down. But his legitimacy was now close to zero: neither the crowd nor his fellow notables of other factions respected him any longer. He had lost all his social and political aura during the first revolt, in spite of his attempt to build a kind of consensus against adversity; and most Cairo factions and social groups rejected the policy of collaboration with the French he embodied. His own faction, weakened by these events, became the target of a very violent expression of the crowd's discontent. From his clients to his own family, his entourage was an object of contempt for every part of society. Stories about his morality emerged again, as well as a story about his daughter.

Such attacks are part of a social construction of opposition. In the codified context of public and private morality, the spreading of rumours about his sexual orientation or about the moral behaviour of his family was part of the destruction of his political legitimacy. It was also a kind of coded authorization of violence against him and his family, in spite of their belonging to the caste of nobles. According to the dominant codes among the crowd and the factions, he whose morality is publicly despised does not deserve the respect his class privilege would normally command. And in such cases, in the context of a revolt, the code is quite clear: violence against al-Bakri's house and his family, though breaking the taboo against violence against a notable, even of an adverse faction, had been made more legitimate by the allegations about his morality. This explains why a gang of popular young thugs looted al-Bakri's house and repeatedly raped his wife during the revolt.[46]

Violence came to the scale of the house and of intimacy. And on the map of the city, it came on this occasion to the very core of al-Bakri's identity and spatial stronghold. The al-Bakri family happened to be saved eventually by elements of rival factions. Thanks to the revolt, the intervention of legitimist pro-Ottoman nobles, who had taken over a number of neighbourhoods and had begun to restore the old regime, was accepted. Reinstating a mediation with the (temporarily) defeated faction was a way of affirming their social influence. To control the plebeian violent agitation, the street was the first element on the map to be the object of the newly established control. This was later extended to entire neighbourhoods. Al-Bakri and his family were saved and hidden. The social order could not have allowed the savage execution of a noble chief of a faction; noble men at the head of factions had earlier not hesitated to use violence and sexual assault by proxy.

Even if al-Jabarti admits it only with difficulty, many of the violent acts were perpetrated by people of the city, and not only by fanatics who had come from Arabia: they were either members of popular factions who did not respond to the notables or even members of traditional factions acting with the tacit consent of notables. Elements external to the city (a few Maghribi – difficult to differentiate from the traditionally stigmatized group of Cairo Maghribis – and Hijazi fighters) were few. During the battle, the French gathered in Coptic quarters and houses, a fact that further reinforced the sectarian divide by identifying the Copts with the occupiers.

The situation changed completely when Ottoman troops were defeated by the French outside Cairo and had to retreat to Syria. Inside the city, Ottoman troops tried to hide the news from the insurgents so that resistance would continue, but soon French troops barricaded in the city received strong reinforcements from outside. Both Bulaq and Cairo were encircled. Many Copts and Syriac Christians fled the city for fear of further violence. In the battle that followed, mostly around Ezbekiyye Square, the French used heavy artillery, destroying entire quarters, including al-Fawwala and Ruwayʾi.[47] Ezbekiyye Square, a zone whose beauty al-Jabarti praises, citing a poem by Shaykh al-ʿAttar ('In al-Azbakiya joys delighted me and times of marvellous company gave me pleasure'[48]), became a battlefield: 'calamitous events descended upon it.'[49] After ten days of heavy fighting and bombardment, a truce was negotiated at the centre of Ezbekiyye Square. Moderates among the shaykhs tried to resolve the revolt: Sharqawi, ʿArishi, Mahdi, Fayyumi and Sarsi negotiated with General Thomas Alexandre Dumas (1762–1806), the son of a French marquis and a West Indian slave (and the father of Alexandre Dumas, the famous writer). Dumas was acting for Kléber, who was still involved with the military aspects of the battle against the Ottomans.[50]

But once back on the side of the insurgents, the negotiators were beaten by their own people for having accepted a degrading truce. Al-Jabarti notes that the crowd of insurgents was incited to refuse the offer of a truce by the Maghribi from outside Cairo, who could afford to act like extremists as they had 'no house or family to protect'; in other words, they did not belong to the traditional category of urban notables in charge of urban affairs. Al-Jabarti also contests the hierarchical position that Maghribi leaders took, outside of the traditional framework of notability and nobility; for him, they were just 'imposters' and 'looters.'[51] Here al-Jabarti probably expresses a sentiment of contempt towards people who are not urban nobles of (more or less mythical) prophetic ascendance (*ashraf*), but rather people from another sociological milieu, probably artisans from lower guilds. The designation as Maghribi (from the Maghrib) is a way of establishing that these people were outside of the traditional category of local notables and nobles (and not part of a recent migration, since Maghribis are known to have been in Cairo for centuries). It has not been established whether external insurgents from the Maghrib were present in the city in addition to the old Cairo 'Maghribis'.

This episode is very telling: it is the moment in the revolt when both the French and the factions of pro-Ottoman notables lost control over social order in the city. It is no doubt the only moment during the *expédition d'Egypte* when the revolutionary French almost managed to export revolution to Egypt: in the paradoxical way of a truly popular revolt against themselves and against the Ottoman old regime at the same time – a Parisian-style revolution of artisans and workers! But, of course, it proved to be only an ephemeral expression with no other political conceptualization, as seen in the fear expressed by conservative al-Jabarti in his chronicle. The figure of the Maghribi leader was the sign of a threat to the dominant social order to which both pro- and anti-French factions belonged. Once the offer of truce was rejected, the French attacked on 6 April (*Shawwal 22*) and a fierce repression began, lasting more than ten days with renewed bombardment of civilian quarters and fierce street fighting. The repression was terrible, with many episodes of violence used either as punishment or as a means of terrorizing the population.

At the end of the revolt, the French reinstated the power of the notables. But the whole group was obliged to pay high taxes as punishment for their inability to control the crowd, and their social status was lastingly damaged, as was the social connivance between notables (*a'yan*) of various factions, whose rivalries had helped the occupiers to broaden their grip on the city and the general population (*'amma*), that is, the popular element.

After Menou, Hutchinson and Yusuf Pasha signed the evacuation treaty in June 1801,[52] the Ottoman restoration focused both on the Mamluk question and on the power of local notables, including those installed by the French. Livingston's study illustrates how the latter group managed to retain a certain influence in the restored old regime system.[53] In the context of a reinforcement of British influence on local politics, Makram returned from exile and recovered his position as *naqib al-ashraf*. Al-Bakri, whose daughter was executed, was expelled from the city and lost his position as chief of the al-Bakri clan.[54]

Conclusion

This episode of the second Cairo revolt against the French has been seen here as an occasion to reflect on questions of spatiality and scale in the phenomena of urban violence. What the Cairo events illustrate is the entanglement of scales, but also the complex relationship between popular political violence and the violence of repression. Violence has many forms; here we have proposed a typology. There was the violence of occupation and repression, when terror was used as a tool of governance to submit local society to a new order. There was violence against the occupation troops and in general against the symbols of foreign occupation. There was also the violence of opposition factions against collaborationist factions, their representatives and their neighbourhoods, and the violence of popular factions or gangs outside of this scheme, or in a biased relationship with it, as well as episodes of sectarian violence. And, seen from another level, there were a number of micro-events of violence between single individuals in the context of the general turmoil.

From an anthropological point of view, different kinds of violence can also be identified, for example institutional, popular collective against soldiers, popular collective between factions, but also vengeance against individuals, either representatives of a power or a faction or members of their families, including women. And there is the extreme violence that goes against all codes but does not always come from outside society, even if it is sometimes embodied by external elements – for example, in the case of Cairo, by Hijazi fighters (there is also the recourse in narratives of violence to such external figures in order to distance it from local society). The French bombardment of civilian quarters can also be classified as an example of extreme violence that goes against all codes.

From a spatial perspective, violence during this revolt happened at various scales and in a variety of places: military battles outside of the city, street riots inside the various neighbourhoods, violence against buildings including houses, and violence inside houses. The city itself also became a battlefield, its fate linked to events on other battlefields. One of the main areas of conflict was Ezbekiyye Square, a space bordered by the prestige houses of many notables and dedicated in normal times to leisure; for example, each year, with the arrival of the high waters, it became the site of a water festival.[55] What happened in this square is a good summary of all these various types of urban violence and can explain much about the entanglement of space and scale in the course of violence events. The map in figure 1.3 is an attempt to combine both perspectives: it shows the different places of contention during the riots, the different targets and types of violence, with a concentration on small spaces of contention pertaining to various scales.

What happened in Cairo in these early years of the nineteenth century, and a new era in the history of the Middle East, is presented here as an occasion to reflect on the categories of urban violence. It has echoes both in other events in this same city of Cairo[56] and in other cities of the

46 Nora Lafi

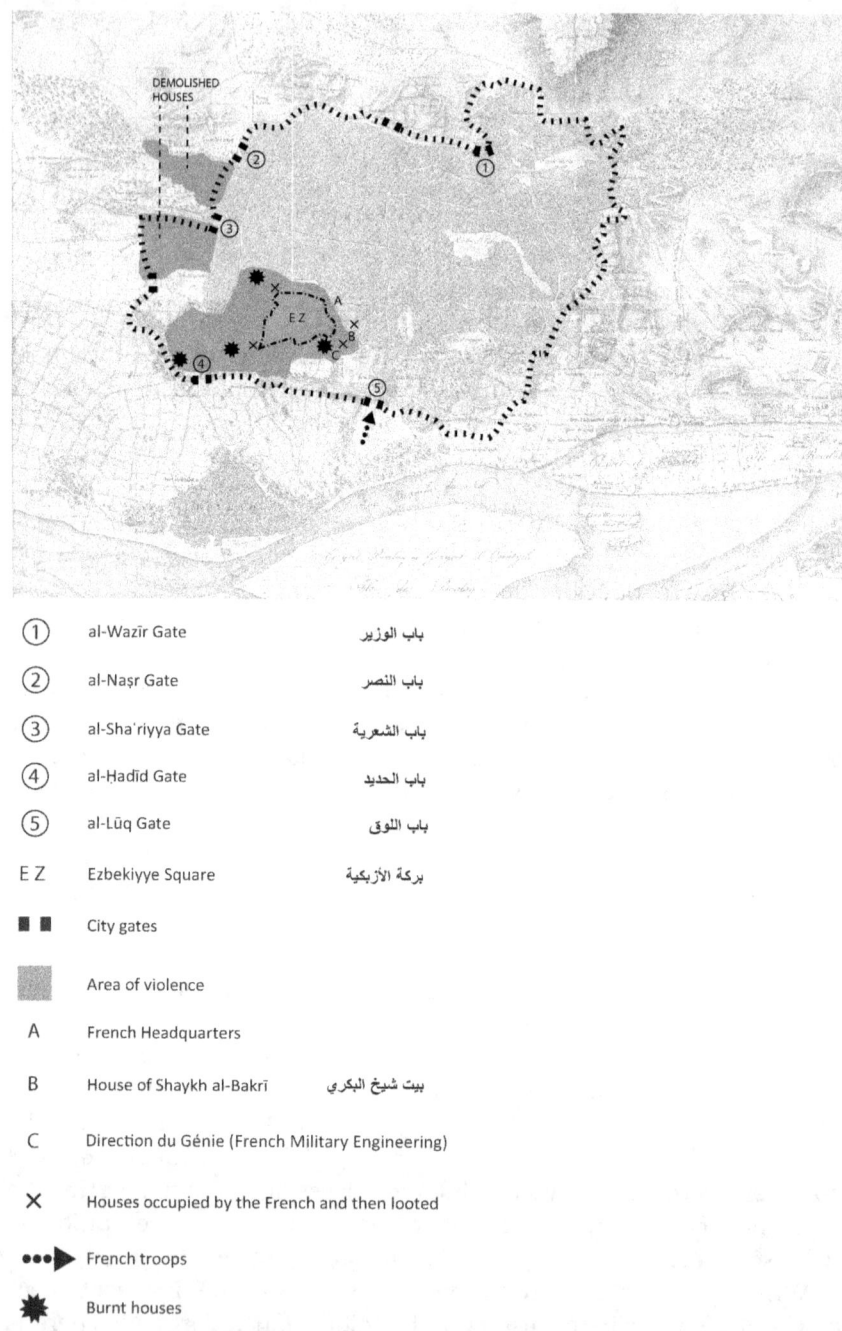

①	al-Wazīr Gate	باب الوزير
②	al-Naṣr Gate	باب النصر
③	al-Shaʿriyya Gate	باب الشعرية
④	al-Ḥadīd Gate	باب الحديد
⑤	al-Lūq Gate	باب اللوق
E Z	Ezbekiyye Square	بركة الأزبكية
■ ■	City gates	
▓	Area of violence	
A	French Headquarters	
B	House of Shaykh al-Bakrī	بيت شيخ البكري
C	Direction du Génie (French Military Engineering)	
X	Houses occupied by the French and then looted	
●●●▶	French troops	
✹	Burnt houses	

Figure 1.3. Mapping Violence in Cairo, 1800. Drawn with the help of Melody Mosavat.

Middle East, where the nineteenth century was marked by a series of revolts; to understand them, one has to take into account the various dimensions of which Cairo is an example. What happened in Cairo is also an invitation to reflect from a theoretical point of view on the nature of urban violence. The Cairo revolt confirms intuitions that violence comes from within society, which in 'normal' times is controlled but which in times of trouble is inserted into stakes in which scales are entangled. The Cairo case also invites us to refine our existing conceptions of what we might call the geographies of contention in Middle Eastern cities at the end of the Ottoman era and the beginning of the colonial one.[57]

Violence, indeed, is not only a factual element, but also a defining feature of changes in society and the sign of a challenge to existing equilibriums. The conditions for its sparking are to be found both in the organization of local societies, which has to be understood in the light of historical anthropology, and in the confrontation with new impulses and stakes. The urban map of violence not only tells us much about factual events, but also gives an insight into the very nature of urban societies and into the nature of the challenges confronted in times of change. What the Cairo case also indicates is that an interpretation that analyses violence only as present inside society, kept under a lid and then freed in times of trouble in accordance with a mere mechanical dichotomy would not be satisfactory: what historians and social scientists have to analyse are precisely the complex relationships between different types of violence, different stakes at various levels and the urban space. From this perspective, Cairo in 1800 provides a founding example.

Notes

1. This research is part of the joint ZMO–SOAS programme 'Urban Violence in the Middle East between Empire and Nation State', financed by the German DFG and the British AHRB.
2. For a view on this question, see A. Winton. 2004. 'Urban Violence: A Guide to the Literature', *Environment & Urbanization* 16(2), 165–84. See also G. Ajimer and J. Abbink (eds). 2000. *Meanings of Violence: A Cross-Cultural Perspective*, Oxford: Berg.
3. C. Tilly. 2003. *The Politics of Collective Violence*, Cambridge: Cambridge University Press. See also C. Tilly and S. Tarrow. 2007. *Contentious Politics*, Boulder, CO: Paradigm. C. Tilly began his study on urban violence with research on nineteenth-century France: A.Q. Lodhi and C. Tilly. 1973. 'Urbanization, Crime and Collective Violence in 19th-Century France', *American Journal of Sociology* 79(2), 296–318.
4. On this context: J. Cole. 2008. *Napoleon's Egypt: Invading the Middle East*, New York: Palgrave.

5. The present study is based mostly on dossiers found in the National Archives of Egypt (NAE) (NAE, Dar al-Kutub, al-Hamla al-Faransiyya, Nr. 11, March 1800, Correspondence between Kléber and Mustafa Reys Effendy and letter by French general François Etienne de Damas [1764–1828] to the Grand Vizir), in the archives of the French Army in Vincennes (SHAT) and in the central archives of the Ottoman Empire in Istanbul (BOA) (BOA, A. DVN.SKT. Boxes 2572 to 2589, as well as on the reading of chronicles by al-Jabarti and Nicolas Turk and of the correspondence of various actors in the events. In Istanbul, all petitions of the year 1214H were read, but only one is relevant to the situation in Cairo: the call for help sent by a soldier.
6. On this subject, see N. Lafi. 2011. *Esprit Civique et Organisation Citadine dans l'Empire Ottoman*, Aix-en-Provence: Université de Provence.
7. N. Turk. 1950. *Chronique d'Egypte (1798–1804)*, ed. and trans. G. Wiet, Cairo: Imprimerie de l'Institut Francais d'Archéologie Orientale, 205 (161 in the Arabic original 'Jamahir wa ʿUmalin'). See also al-Jabarti. 1879–80. ʿAjaʾib al-Athar fi ʾl-Tarajim wa-l-Akhbar, vol. 4, Cairo: Bulaq (republished 1997, Cairo: Madbuli), 89: 'wa-kharaja ʿiddat min ʿasakirihim yakhlaʾuna wa-yaqlaʾuna abwab al-darb wa-l-ʿaṭf wa-l-harat'. For a comparative perspective on both chronicles, see ʿA. ʿUmar. 1978. *ʿAbd al-Rahman al-Jabarti wa Nicolas Turk: Dirasa Muqarana*, Beirut: al-Jamiʿat al-Arabiyya.
8. Al-Jabarti, ʿAjaʾib al-Athar fi ʾl-Tarajim wa-l-Akhbar, 140.
9. On this episode, see BOA, C..AS..106 4777 1212 Z 16, 1 June 1798. On the previous attempts of the Ottoman central government to stop the French fleet in the Mediterranean with the help of Algerian corsairs, see BOA C..AS..192 8276 1212 Z 29 (14 June 1798).
10. On these events: al-Jabarti, ʿAjaʾib al-Athar fi ʾl-Tarajim wa-l-Akhbar, 83: 'Wa-amma ʿUmmar Afendi naqib al-ashraf fa innahu lam yatamin, wa-lam yahdar…'. See also J. Livingston. 1994. 'Shaykh Bakri and Bonaparte', *Studia Islamica* 80, 125–43; and M. Ramadan. 1986. *Dawr al-Azbar fi ʾl-Hayyat al-Misriyya Ibbana ʾl-Hamla al-Faransiyya*, Cairo: s. ed.
11. Al-Jabarti, ʿAjaʾib al-Athar fi l-Tarajim wa-ʾl-Akhbar, 72.
12. Livingston, 'Shaykh Bakri and Bonaparte'.
13. A matter that Kléber himself admitted about the example of Rosette: J.-B. Kléber. 1988. *Kléber en Egypte (1798–1800)*, vol. 1, Cairo: Imprimerie de l'Institut Francais d'Archéologie Orientale, 171.
14. On these events: G. Baer. 2009. 'Popular Revolt in Ottoman Cairo', *Der Islam* 54(2), 213–42.
15. Livingston, 'Shaykh Bakri and Bonaparte', note 9a.
16. On this event: N.I. Nasser. 2004. *Al-Rafd wa-l-Ihtijaj fi ʾl-Mujtamaʾ al-Masri fi ʾl-ʿAsr al-ʿUthmani*, Cairo: Cairo University Press.
17. Al-Jabarti, ʿAjaʾib al-Athar fi ʾl-Tarajim wa-l-Akhbar.
18. Turc, *Chronique d'Egypte (1798–1804)*, 41 (28 in the Arabic version 'Jamahir waʿUmalin').
19. R. André. 1968. 'Quartiers et Mouvements Populaires au Caire', in P.M. Holt (ed.), *Political and Social Change in Modern Egypt*, London: Oxford University Press, 104–16.

20. SHAT, Extrait du rapport officiel du général en chef Kléber, Carte du Caire LII-128-0001-H.
21. al-Jabarti, ʿAjaʾib al-Athar fi ʾl-Tarajim wa-l-Akhbar. See also Livingston, 'Shaykh Bakri and Bonaparte', 131. On the secret plans of the Foreign Office: G. Haddad. 1970. 'A Project for the Independence of Egypt', *Journal of the Oriental Society* 90(2), 169–83.
22. On the urban plebeian hypothesis, see C. Cahen. 1958, 1959. 'Mouvements Populaires et Autonomisme Urbain dans l'Asie Musulmane du Moyen Age', *Arabica* 5(3), 225–50; 6(1), 25–56; 6(3), 233–65.
23. Livingston, 'Shaykh Bakri and Bonaparte', 131.
24. Al-Jabarti, ʿAjaʾib al-Athar fi ʾl-Tarajim wa-l-Akhbar.
25. Livingston, 'Shaykh Bakri and Bonaparte', 135.
26. SHAT, Extrait du rapport officiel du général en chef Kléber, Carte du Caire LII-128-0001-H.
27. The French used the incident as an excuse to delay their evacuation: NAE, Dar al-Kutub, al-Hamla al-Faransiyya, Nr. 11, March 1800, Correspondance between Kléber and Mustafa 'Reys Effendy and letter by French General François Etienne de Damas (1764–1828) to the Grand Vizir: 'J'ai l'honneur de prévenir Votre Excellence que les troubles momentanés, qui ont été occasionnés dans la ville du Kaire par des soldats échappés de l'armée ottomane… ont mis le général Kléber dans l'impossibilité absolue d'évacuer le Kaire le 45e jour après la ratification du traité correspondant au 23 Ventôse ou 18 du mois de Chawwal.'
28. Al-Jabarti, ʿAjaʾib al-Athar fi ʾl-Tarajim wa-l-Akhbar, 321.
29. Turk, *Chronique d'Egypte (1798–1804),* 77 in the Arabic version 'Jamahir wa ʿUmalin'.
30. Al-Jabarti, ʿAjaʾib al-Athar fi ʾl-Tarajim wa-l-Akhbar, 140 and NAE, Dar al-Kutub, Al-Hamla al-Fransiyya, No.11, March 1800. See also J.F.L.C.C. de Damas d'Antigny. [1799]. *Rapport fait au Gouvernement Français des Evénements qui se sont passés en Egypte depuis la Conclusion du Traité d'el-Aʿrych jusquʾà la fin de Prairial An 8,* Cairo: Imprimerie Nationale.
31. NAE, File 5001-000 276, Dar al-Kutub, al-Hamla al-Faransiyya, Nr. 31, March 1800, Rapport du général en chef Kléber au ministre de la guerre Alexandre Berthier.
32. Turk, *Chronique d'Egypte (1798–1804),* 96.
33. Al-Jabarti, ʿAjaʾib al-Athar fi ʾl-Tarajim wa-l-Akhbar, 324.
34. On this point: BOA, C..AS..110 4946 1214 N 20, 15 February 1800. One month before the revolt, the Ottoman central government gave the order to mobilize as many men as possible in Cairo to fight the French. Men from Anatolia were sent to Cairo.
35. Al-Jabarti, ʿAjaʾib al-Athar fi ʾl-Tarajim wa-l-Akhbar.
36. Ibid.
37. SHAT, Extrait du rapport officiel du général en chef Kléber, Carte du Caire LII-128-0001-H. Nasif Pasha and the legitimist urban administration were accompanied by 10,000 Ottoman soldiers, 2,000 Mamluks, 8,000 armed inhabitants of neighbouring villages and what Kléber describes as a 'populace'.

38. Al-Jabarti, *'Aja'ib al-Athar fi 'l-Tarajim wa-'l-Akhbar*, 325.
39. Ibid.
40. Ibid.
41. Ibid., 326.
42. NAE, Dar al-Kutub, al-Hamla al-Faransiyya, Nr. 11, March 1800.
43. Ottoman sources show how the central government in Istanbul tried to use the possible existence of a French project to conquer Mecca as a tool for mobilization in the name of Islam. But it is not clear whether such fighters answered such a call. BOA, C..AS.. 713550 1214 L 29, 26 March 1800. The chronicle *Nusuş Yamaniyya 'an al-Hamla al-Faransiyya 'ala Mişr* (al-Sayyid Mustafa Salem (ed.). 1989, 140–142) also invokes rumours of an attack against Mecca and calls for mobilization against such an attack in the name of Islam and for the sending of men to Cairo to fight the French. Already in 1799, the Vizier Mustafa Pasha had placed preparations for an attack against the French under the auspices of a conflict of Muslims against miscreants (*kuffar*). BOA, C..AS..783665 1214 Ra 29, 31 August 1799.
44. Al-Jabarti, *'Aja'ib al-Athar fi 'l-Tarajim wa-'l-Akhbar*, 330.
45. Ibid.
46. Ibid.
47. NAE, Dar al-Kutub, al-Hamla al-Faransiyya, Nr. 11, March 1800. Report by Damas.
48. T. Philip and M. Perlmann (trans.). 1994. *'Abd al-Rahman al-Jabarti's History of Egypt*, vol. 3, Stuttgart: Steiner, 150.
49. Al-Jabarti, *'Aja'ib al-athar fi al-tarajim wa-l-akhbar*, 338–39.
50. Livingston, 'Shaykh Bakri and Bonaparte', 139.
51. Al-Jabarti, *'Aja'ib al-Athar fi 'l-Tarajim wa-l-Akhbar*, 340.
52. On the negotiations that led to this treaty: BOA, HAT, Files 240 to 257. See also for the month of October BOA, C..ML.. 44 2030 1216 C 02, 10 October 1801.
53. Livingston, 'Shaykh Bakri and Bonaparte', 142.
54. Al-Jabarti, *'Aja'ib al-Athar fi 'l-Tarajim wa-l-Akhbar*, 663.
55. Une Société des Géographes (ed.). 1825. *Dictionnaire Géographique Universel*, vol. 2, Paris: Kilian, 403–4: 'Le Caire n'est pas sur le Nil même, mais à 400 toises de la rive droite de ce fleuve. Avant d'arriver à cette ville, on rencontre les petites villes de Boulaq et du Vieux-Caire, qui lui servent de port ... La plus grande est la place Ezbekyeh. Pour s'en faire une idée, il faut la comparer à la place Louis XV à Paris, sa superficie est égale à 66 arpens de Paris, à peu près celle de l'intérieur du Champs de Mars. Au mois de septembre, quand la crue du Nil est au maximum, elle est remplie de plusieurs pieds d'eau et ce vaste bassin est couvert de barques, qui sont illuminées la nuit et donnent à ce lieu un aspect très pittoresque. Le sol, qui se couvre de verdure pendant l'hiver est sec et poudreux au printemps. La place est bordée par le quartier des Coptes, l'ancien palais d'Elfybey, et les maisons des cheikhs les plus riches.'
56. See for example M. Badrawi. 2000. *Political Violence in Egypt (1910–1925): Secret Societies, Plots and Assassinations*, Richmond: Curzon; and W.J. Ber-

ridge. 2011. 'Object Lessons in Violence: The Rationalities and Irrationalities of Urban Struggle during the Egyptian Revolution of 1919', *Journal of Colonialism and Colonial History* 12(3). See also the events of the 2011 revolution.
57. On this concept and its relation to the work of C. Tilly, see: D. Martin and B. Miller. 2003. 'Space and Contentious Politics', *Mobilization* 8(2), 143–56.

✢· Chapter 2 ·✢

A Capital Challenge
Managing Violence and Disorders in Late Ottoman Istanbul

NOÉMI LÉVY-AKSU

My chapter will address the question of violence in the Ottoman capital at the end of the nineteenth century, focusing on the perception and management of criminality and public disorders by the Ottoman state and some local actors. The reign of Abdülhamid II (1876–1909) remains infamous for its struggle against political opponents, widespread censorship and the omnipresence of spies. I argue that it was also a time that witnessed new steps in the rationalization of the approach to security issues, a process that started with the suppression of the Janissary corps and led to the constitution of police forces in charge of maintaining order in the Ottoman cities. The increasing interest in urban violence concerned not only the state: despite the censorship, the press of the time offered an extraordinary sample of everyday violence in the capital, displaying murders, quarrels and various aggressions with information on their actors and settings, and often adding moral comments.

This double process made urban violence more visible, more public. The object of knowledge useful for the state in governing, it aroused mixed feelings of fascination and repulsion in the newspapers, which were one of the rare spaces where it was possible to deal with and comment on everyday life in the city. These two approaches shared a common appreciation of the main risks to security in the city: they stigmatized the different forms of marginality, and drew a profile of the 'standard' actor of violence that included social and moral dimensions, such as low social status, loose family bonds and deviant behaviours.

What mattered here was less the degree of violence than its actual or potential subversive dimension for the political, social and/or moral order. Paradoxically, the publicity given to violence enhanced its potential subversiveness and had the power to amplify the political, social and spatial effect of local incidents, a fact that could have an impact both on the occurrence and spread of urban violence and on its management by the state. This was especially the case for the forms of violence that bore a collective dimension, such as intercommunal violence and workers' aggressions against employers, two cases that I will briefly study here. Beyond their singularity, those kinds of events were analysed and managed through a pattern that reflected the political and social agenda of the different actors: stigmatization and criminalization of the marginal and lower-class categories, alliance between the state and the notables to restore order, communication by the state and the media to minimize the scale of the events and to praise the role of the state and the elite. Needless to say, this virtuous circle was far from reflecting the complexity of the issue of violence in the capital. I will explore here some of the political and social implications that hid behind the apparent objectivity displayed by the state documentation and the emollient accounts of the media. After investigating how urban violence was constructed as a public issue at the turn of the century, I will examine the implications of this process for the characteristics and management of urban violence through two case studies: a case of intercommunal violence in Haydarpaşa in 1885 and the recurrent social conflict that set the porters and the French port company in opposition to each other.

Violence as a Public Issue

In this part, I will examine how both the state and the media constructed public order as an object of policy and discourse. I argue that, during the Hamidian reign and at the beginning of the Young Turk period, there was an attempt to objectify the concept of public order. Formerly defined in relation to religious norms or specific disorders, public order and its various forms or disruption began to be studied with rational methods such as statistics, reports, and comparison with other countries. This new approach was central to the elaboration of state policy.

Of course, this attempt at objectivization did not lead to objectivity: it was overdetermined by the social characteristics and political intentions of its actors. Public order in the capital was indeed an important item in the politics of legitimization of power that was central to the Hamidian period. At the same time, security and urban violence had an important role in the affirmation of a critical discourse on state and society in the press and some segments of society. In these two senses, they became public issues.

Public Order and Violence: The State's New Approach

From the point of view of the Ottoman state, this process was characterized by an increasing rationalization of the management of urban violence and disorders. Even though the various aspects of this rationalization were never related to a comprehensive project, they modified thoroughly the perception and definition of urban violence at that time.

The main aspect of this concern of the state with a more efficient approach to public order was the reform of the police organization, which took place at the beginning of the reign of Abdülhamid II. The process that led to the creation of modern police forces in the empire started with the abolition of the Janissaries in 1826.[1] As the main armed force in the empire, the Janissaries were in charge of maintaining order in both urban and rural areas. In the Ottoman capital, they were divided into a multiplicity of forces, according to their spatial and functional attributes. Due to their numbers and their integration in economic and social life, they had become a threat to the regime and were the protagonists of several revolts against the sultan's authority in the eighteenth and early nineteenth centuries, hence their bloody dissolution by Mahmud II. To fill the void left by their suppression, the *Polis Nizamnamesi* (Police Regulation), issued in 1845, enacted the creation of police forces. The process of the creation of modern police forces in the Ottoman Empire is beyond the scope of this chapter; let it merely be mentioned here that the Hamidian reign constituted a turning point in the organization of these forces.[2] The creation of the Ministry of Police (*Zaptiye Nezareti*) in 1879 accompanied an effort to increase the number and efficiency of the police during the following decades. As the political and economic centre of the empire, the capital was a priority, but the reforms concerned the whole country.

To establish comprehensive control over space and individuals, the power used several tools. The sultan was personally involved in the process, to such an extent that the obsession of Abdülhamid II with his own security and with the surveillance of his subjects became the most (in-)famous characteristic of his reign. The constitution of an extensive network of spies organized by and accountable to the Palace is one of the topoi of the memoirs, travel accounts and historical studies of the period. Though often described as a symbol or a symptom of the sultan's paranoia, this use of spies should be considered within the broader framework of a new state approach to the security issues, which redefined the scope and aims of state control. Among the other aspects of that policy, the multiplication of police stations (*karakol*) in the capital and the provincial cities increased state presence and made possible a better knowledge and surveillance of the urban space. As Jens Hanssen convincingly demonstrated for Beirut, police stations were unevenly distributed in the cities; they were established in accordance with the ethno-religious and economic characteristics of the districts and their potential for violence. Used as a preventive and dissuasive tool against potential disorders, that network of police stations also made possible a more rapid intervention in case of troubles. Although the lack of relevant sources does not allow us to estimate the real impact of this spatial control on crime and disorder, the police stations undoubtedly played an essential role in familiarizing urban people with the new police forces and increasing the state's ability to patrol the urban setting.[3]

Closely connected to the multiplication of police stations, and another dimension of this state concern with public order, was the use of local actors to provide information, settle conflicts or frighten and punish undesirable people. The instructions published in 1896 on the missions of the police, gendarmery and army in the capital pointed out the necessity of collaboration between local actors and police.[4] For instance, the night watchmen appointed and paid by a neighbourhood's inhabitants were to gather information about suspicious people and to assist the police in case of disruption of order. The police use of ruffians, called *kabadayı*, was another of these interactions with local actors. Yedi Sekiz Hasan Paşa, the much-feared police chief of Beşiktaş, the district of the Yıldız Imperial Palace, was thus known to be at the head of one of the most influent *kabadayı* gangs of the time.[5] As with irregular troops in the army, these ruffians extended the sphere of state control and palliated at least to some extent the lack of means often mentioned by the sources. However, they were also associated with arbitrary means, violence and depredation, privatizing the settlement of conflict for their own interest and prestige. Therefore, if the strategy of utilization of intermediaries by the regime of Abdülhamid II can be considered the most pragmatic way to extend the scope of its control under the conditions of the time, it did not result in state monopolization of control and violence. After the Young Turk Revolution, the new authorities would address the status and role of these local collaborators vis-à-vis the state in a perceptibly different way, with an emphasis on the state monopoly over security matters and a strategy of suppression or direct incorporation of intermediaries.

Parallel to these developments 'in the field', public order and disorders were the objects of a new state discourse, and standardization of police reports was one aspect of this new approach. The Tanzimat period not only transformed state organization, it also had an impact on written practices, attested by diverse prescriptions for the adoption of a clear and plain style.⁶ In the case of the Ministry of Police, this concern emerges clearly when we look at the thousands of reports conserved in the Ottoman archives. Whereas the archives of the local police stations have disappeared, the available documents are the correspondence between the central police stations of the capital, the Ministry of Police and the Imperial Palace of Yıldız. Remarkably synthetic, the reports offered only a short summary of the facts, describing their most important characteristics: in general a brief description of what happened (who, when, where) together with an account of the police intervention and/or what should be done. Direct speech and the first person were almost never used to report the words of the actors or witnesses of the facts, nor was there mention of the names of the policemen who wrote the report or managed the case. On the contrary, impersonal phrases such as 'it must' or 'it is necessary' were widespread ways to formulate the measures recommended by the police forces. To put it in a nutshell, those reports focused on the description of their object, made as clear and concise as possible, apparently leaving aside all marks of subjectivity.⁷

Quite frustratingly for a social analysis of violence, those reports indicate a high level of centralization in the management of public order. The Ministry of Police and the Palace were informed about a multiplicity of small local, insignificant incidents, unlikely to degenerate into major disorders or to threaten state security. Even the absence of troubles could be the subject of a report, as is attested by the hundreds of reports with a single sentence stating that order reigned in the city.⁸ While most studies on the Hamidan regime point out the regime's obsession with the surveillance of the elite and political opponents, a look at the archives suggests that this was only one aspect of police activity at that time: police were involved in social control in its broadest sense, and the authorities seemed eager to be informed about all aspects of everyday life in the capital.

The same concern can be observed in the development of statistics on urban crime and disorders at the end of the nineteenth century. As for the standardization of state documentation, the importance of statistics and other measurement tools was a general trend in the Tanzimat period. First applied to demography and the economy, the Ministry of Police experimented with the new tools in the 1890s.⁹ In 1891, a six-page register reported and quantified several aspects of police and justice activity in the Ottoman capital for the previous months.¹⁰ The first table listed the cases tried in the Istanbul courts during that period, with the kind of crime, its penalty, as well as the gender, nationality and religion of the criminals. Similar documents can be found for the following years, but the absence of regularity and the variations in the categories used make it difficult to draw any conclusions on the actual level of violence in the capital.

Things changed with the Young Turk Revolution. The reform of the police institution took almost a year and resulted in the dissolution of the Ministry of Police, replaced by the General Directorate of Security (*Emniyet-i Umumiye Müdüriyeti*) under the authority of the Ministry of Home Affairs in July 1909. However, even before this reform and only a few months after the Unionists came to power, statistics began to be used in a much more systematic way to apprehend and manage urban violence in the capital. Every two weeks, reports were issued, quantifying murders (*katl*), battery and injuries (*darp ve cerh*) and thefts (*sirkat*) in the capital.[11] Monthly and yearly statistics were also available for the first years of the second constitutional period. Among the offences against persons, besides murders and injury, indecent acts (*cebren fi'l-i seni'*) and violations of honour (*hetk-i irz*, i.e. sexual aggression), appeared frequently, whereas robbery (*sirkat-i adiye ou hirsizlik*), arson (*kasten ifa'-a harik*) and forgery (*sahtekarcilik*) were often mentioned as offences against property. Various disorders were also registered, such as noise, gambling, vagrancy and begging. The categories used to qualify the different violent acts were sometimes drawn from the Ottoman penal code of 1858, but they remained fluid and variable, showing evidence of the police's empirical approach, shaped by fieldwork rather than legal texts.[12]

Neither under the Hamidian regime nor during the Young Turk period did these statistics reach a level of regularity enabling a quantitative and qualitative analysis of violent acts in the Ottoman capital, but they testified of the new approach to this phenomenon. The capital was an exceptional setting, but to a lesser extent we can observe the same process in the provincial cities. While the police forces had only limited resources in terms of knowledge, personnel and funds, collecting and centralizing data on the various kinds of violent acts and deviant behaviours seem to have been a priority for the Ottoman authorities. As Cengiz Kırlı observed for the reign of Mahmud II, the aim was not always repression:[13] to put it in Foucauldian terms, knowledge was a tool of government and qualifying/quantifying/archiving criminal acts and offences was one of the ways the state strengthened its control on society. Beyond their singularity and often their anecdotic character, the thousands of cases registered every year by the Ministry of Police and the Palace made sense within the framework of this project.

Looking at Violence through the Press: A New Publicity for Violent Acts

The state was not the only actor to adopt a new perspective on public order and crime at the turn of the century. During the same decades, the local newspapers gave these issues increasing publicity. A survey of several newspapers published in Istanbul in French (*Stamboul*) and Ottoman Turkish (*Ikdam* and *Tarik*) during the reign of Abdülhamid II gives us insight into the way the press dealt with various incidents and troubles that occurred in the city. These newspapers opened their columns to short articles giving a sample of everyday violence in the capital. Written with an apparent objectivity, these pieces of news reflected at the same time the concern of the social and intellectual elite about urban transformations and the supposedly increasing urban violence.

Interestingly enough, censorship, omnipresent during the reign of Abdülhamid II, did not seem to apply to these pieces of news, although their accumulation gave quite a dark picture of the insecurity in the Ottoman capital. Why was the Ottoman power so tolerant of this publicity given to urban violence? First, these articles were far from being subversive: while displaying the facts, they denounced the transgression and emphasized the return to order that followed. In this sense, they brought readers face to face with everyday life and invited them to condemn the deviant behaviours described.[14] Besides, a lot of news concluded with thanks to the police or a polite invitation to be vigilant, concentrating criticism on the perpetrators of violence or on non-state actors of order like municipal agents or night watchmen. Therefore, these pieces of news offered a space of editorial freedom in which it was possible to give some publicity to various aspects of urban life.

The facts described in the newspapers were highly heterogeneous and fragmentary, but taken as a whole they gave a quite coherent picture of the temporal, spatial and social dimensions of urban violence in the capital. The temporal factor appeared at several levels. First, there were some connections between urban violence and the political and religious calendar: religious celebrations like Easter and Ramadan, and political tensions and wars were contexts in which specific acts of violence, like intercommunal violence, were most likely to occur.[15] The overrepresentation of the night was another kind of temporal factor. Night appeared as the time of breaking the order – all the more dangerous because street lighting was insufficient and the police forces scarcer by night. A favoured time for thieves and murderers, night was also linked to the various manifestations of urban marginality, such as prostitution and drunkenness, which were often denounced as key factors in urban violence.

This temporal dimension was closely linked to a spatial one. Most of the news focused on the central Galata-Pera districts of the city, which concentrated several factors of risk, such as ethno-religious diversity, a significant proportion of foreigners, places of entertainment, bordellos and taverns. As for the overrepresentation of the night, it is difficult to know the extent to which this tropism reflected an exceptionally high rate of violence or the writers' fascination with and/or repulsion from these districts. One may note that they contrast with the statistics previously mentioned, according to which the historical peninsula featured a higher rate of crime than Galata-Pera. However, as it is, this overrepresentation drew a map of violence on which marginality did not coincide with the margins of the city but with one of its centres, unlike what could be observed in several great cities of the time, for instance the Parisian suburbs (*faubourgs*) and London's East End. The fact that the most conspicuous violent acts did not take place in the periphery made them more visible – and intolerable – for the 'honest' dwellers of the city, notables and economic and/or intellectual elite who frequented these districts as inhabitants or consumers of their commercial and cultural facilities. This proximity contributed to creating both a familiarity with violence and a feeling of discontent, which became obvious after the Young Turk Revolution when critical voices were able to express themselves in the newspapers, the streets and the parliament. Insecurity in the capital then emerged as a major political issue.

During the Hamidian time, criticism remained based on a social ground, with a stigmatization of the perpetrators of violent acts that contrasted the honest citizens with the members of the urban lower class. The latter included not only the individuals who lived at the margins of society (beggars, vagrants, prostitutes, etc.), but also the urban working class, who played an increasing role in the economic and social life of the capital. The news and chronicles stigmatized the supposed moral depravation of these categories, quite apart from the acts of violence they were involved in. The young bachelors (*bekar*) were especially targeted, since youth and lack of family bonds appeared as a specific threat to the moral and social order.[16] Celibacy was associated with some professional categories, such as the firefighters (*tulumbaci*), the boatmen (*kayıkcı*) and the porters (*hammal*), to constitute the profile of the 'usual suspects' in the city.

At a time when censorship was at its peak, these kinds of news constituted one of the few windows the media could open onto real life.

Without presuming their reliability, those pieces of news contributed to transforming urban violence into a public issue. The state not only tolerated this trend but also encouraged it with the Ministry of Justice's publication of the 'Journal of the Courts' (*Ceride-i Mehakim*, 1873–1901, and *Ceride-i Mehakim-i Adliye* from 1901 on). The journal published the copies of the verdicts of the empire's Nizamiye courts, with an emphasis on the capital and on cases of murder and injury.[17] Taking justice outside of the law court, that journal illustrated the idea that crimes not only concerned their perpetrators and victims but the whole society, and that the state was ensuring the maintenance and/or restoration of order. From this point of view, displaying control over violence took its place within the policy of legitimization of power.[18]

The liberation of the press was one of the first and most celebrated changes that occurred after the Young Turk Revolution in 1908. Although the nature of the violent acts described in the news published during the following months did not differ in a significant way from that under the 'old regime', the style of the language and the attitude towards the facts changed radically. Violence in the capital was described as close to anarchy, and the police were blamed in harsh terms for their corruption and inefficiency.[19] Armed gangs terrifying the people, as well as prisoners released from jail with the general amnesty of summer 1908 who had soon returned to their criminal activities, were the main protagonists of the violent acts mentioned.[20]

While before the revolution, the narratives of whatever cases of violence reported were always depicted as devoid of any political dimension and were limited to the stigmatization of uneducated and destitute individuals, violence in the aftermath of the Young Turk Revolution was most often analysed through a political prism. This politicization took several forms, in accordance with the political affiliations of the newspapers or the journalists: among the supporters of the Young Turks, perpetrators of violent acts were suspected of having been instrumentalized by provocateurs and reactionary forces, whereas critical voices accused the state of provocation. On 6 April 1909, Hasan Fehmi, chief editor of the oppositional newspaper *Serbesti*, was assassinated, a crime that was never solved but which many observers attributed to the Unionists. Following the military suppression of an attempted countercoup in Istanbul (known as *31 Mart Vakası*), the 25 April proclamation of a state of emergency made it possible to ban oppositional newspapers. These two developments were clear signals that the state acknowledged the political and potentially subversive power of the press and would try to suppress it by legalized means of coercion and arbitrary violence.

Dealing with Violence in the Capital: Two Case Studies

The first part of this chapter dealt with the transformations in the state and media approaches to public order and violence. In this part, I would like to go a little further, using two case studies to illustrate how these new policies on and perceptions of security issues had an impact on the management of violent acts and sometimes even on their occurrence. The first case is one of intercommunal violence and the second is related to a social conflict in the ports of the capital.

The first case occurred in 1885 in Haydarpaşa, a district on the Asian side of Istanbul. It started when a cross, soiled with mud, was found in front of the shop of a Greek grocer. Immediately, some Greek inhabitants of the neighbourhood gathered and demanded that the perpetrators of this blasphemous act, whom they believed belonged to the Jewish community, be arrested without delay. Police entered the synagogue at the time of the prayer and asked four Jewish notables to find and hand over two Jewish suspects. Meanwhile, a Greek crowd had begun to attack the houses of Jews in the neighbourhood. Despite the intervention of the army, the troubles then spread to other neighbourhoods in the city, like Tatavla and Hasköy on the European side, two districts hosting important Greek and Jewish communities. Order finally returned three days later, when two gendarmes were found guilty of the blasphemous act and the police arrested a number of rioters.

This case illustrates several dimensions mentioned before. Occurring around the Jewish Pesach and Greek Easter, it was one of the many incidents related to these festivals, traditionally considered an exacerbating factor for intercommunal tensions.[21] The reaction of the Ottoman authorities was almost immediate, testifying to the attention given to collective violence, especially when it involved non-Muslim subjects. First to intervene, the police were unable to stop the Greek mob and so had to ask the army to assist. The troops occupied the neighbourhood and, according to *Stamboul* newspaper, Şevket Paşa, the head of the Selimiye barracks, participated personally in the operations 'night and day' during the following days.[22] Focusing on the military intervention, the same newspaper's account of the events is emblematic of the compromise between displaying reality and avoiding censorship. Whereas the facts were all but a success from the point of view of public order (several days of riots in different parts of the city), one of the articles ended with emollient praise of Şefket Paşa, stating that 'all the inhabitants of Kadiköy unanimously praise Şevket Paşa ... always the first to intervene in case of fire [or] bloody quarrels in order to restore order'.

Besides their rhetorical tricks to avoid censorship, the articles on these troubles used the traditional social dichotomy to describe and analyse this outburst of violence: the actors were stigmatized as a destitute, uneducated and fanatical mob, whereas the good role was given to the notables. The efforts of the notables from the different communities were presented as decisive for the restoration of order. For instance, the Greek newspaper of the Patriarchate, *Faros tou Bosforou*, wrote, 'MM. Hazzopoulo, Yacoumi, Aron de Léon and Apik effendi did their best to calm down the mob, saying that the author of the insult was already in the hands of justice'.[23] A slightly different list of names appears in the *Stamboul*, which paid homage to the ones 'who prevented things from becoming even more serious': 'MM. Avédis Harenz, Gulbenkoghlou, Apik effendi Oundjian, who distributed bread to the poor Jews; MM. Hazzopoulo, Yacomi calfa and Yanco, who made great efforts to bring the two parts together'.[24] With these names, the notables from different communities appeared as unanimously mobilized against violence, using their traditional ways of influence: charity on the one hand, exhortation on the other hand. This was not only a communal issue, as the presence of Armenians among the intervening notables illustrates. Public order was a major concern for the local notables, who strengthened their legitimacy vis-à-vis their community and the Ottoman authorities with their mediation. Whereas the police reports almost never mentioned the role of the notables, the newspapers emphasized it and offered these actors publicity beyond the limits of their district.

The way this outburst of violence was settled shows the limits of the transformations that reforms adopted under the reign of Abdülhamid II brought to policing. The police forces were unable to solve the case on their own and only the intervention of the army managed to suppress the riot. Besides, the state still appeared to depend on non-state actors such as the local elite when incidents took on a collective aspect and involved several communities. The comparison with a quite similar case that occurred in 1874, before Abdülhamid II's accession to power and the creation of the Ministry of Police in 1879, highlights the continuities and changes in the management of such cases. On 28 June 1874, a Greek child disappeared in the neighbourhood of Balat, on the Golden Horn. A few days later, his corpse was found floating in the water in the same district. A part of the local Greek community then accused the Jews of having perpetrated a ritual murder, and riots between Greeks and Jews lasted until mid July. As in 1885, since the police forces were unable to settle the conflict, military forces were sent to the place. Community notables also condemned the violence and participated in pacifying the crowds, as did the religious leaders. For instance, the *Neologos*, a Greek newspaper published in Istanbul, mentioned several meetings between the Chief Rabbi and the Greek Patriarch, and reproduced a letter from the Greek Patriarch to his community which stressed the harmony that ought to reign between the different communities, appealing both to their quality as Christians and to their duty as Ottoman subjects.[25]

In both 1874 and 1885, the exact influence of the newspapers on the propagation of violence and its settlement is difficult to appreciate, but the impact of the media is not in doubt. Even though the proportion of readers was low, especially among the lower class that was held responsible for the violence, newspapers changed the temporal and spatial scale of the propagation of news and rumour within the city and beyond it. The authorities were well aware of this power of the press, and trials against newspapers accused of provocation and encouragement of violence were not the exception, especially for the newspapers published by the non-Muslim communities. In 1874, the redactor of the Greek newspaper *Typos* was tried, accused of stirring the Greek mob against the Jews by describing the mutilated corpse of the child in such a way that it seemed to support the theory of a ritual murder. He was sentenced to six months in jail and a fine, but he appealed against this judgement. Interestingly enough, together with other local newspapers that had condemned the riots and lauded efforts of the state, notables and religious leaders to settle the conflict, the *Neologos* vehemently took the side of the redactor of the *Typos* on the grounds of his sincerity and against the penal responsibility of the press.[26] During the reign of Abdülhamid II, censorship and the fear of penalty weakened the provocative role of the newspapers and made it almost impossible for community-run newspapers to voice critical interpretations of the facts. The various newspapers printed in the capital produced similar narratives of the incidents, echoing the official version. However, even deprived of any critical perspective, the diffusion of information per se was likely to play a role in the spread of troubles such as intercommunal riots.

The second case I would like to mention briefly is one of violence occurring in the framework of social conflicts during the Hamidian times. The end of the nineteenth century witnessed increasing foreign capital penetration into the empire, which boosted the development of industry and great companies. As a result, the new urban proletariat began to play a growing role in the social and economic life of Istanbul, including the field of urban violence. Besides their overrepresentation in everyday crimes and offences, the members of the working class were involved in social conflicts that often led to violence against property and/or employers. The conflict between the workers of the port and the Société des quais de Constantinople was emblematic of the tensions and violence triggered by the new economic configuration. The French company was granted a concession to modernize Istanbul's port in 1890, but until the end of the Hamidian reign, it had to face the hostility of the local porters, whose activity was threatened by the technological innovations. Many state documents commented on the conflict; for example in 1895 an imperial order (*irade*) stated the importance of taking measures 'concerning the persistent conflict between the workers and the Société des quais' (*mavnaci esnafı ile rihtim sirketi beyninde tahaddus eden ihtilafın hakkinda*) 'in order to prevent troubles from occurring' (*bir guna uygunsuzluk zuhuruna asla meydan verilmemesi*).[27]

The actors in these protests were the *hammal* (carriers) previously mentioned for their overrepresentation in violent cases reported by newspapers and state documentation.[28] To a certain extent, the conflict involving the port company perpetuated the traditional struggle that set different groups of porters in conflict for the control of space in the capital. Most of the porters were affiliated with specific teams based on spatial or ethno-religious criteria. These teams attempted to monopolize portage in a neighbourhood, district or specific economic sector, but police reports seem to indicate that incidents and strife frequently occurred between them; for example, in January 1898, about ten Kurdish porters fought against a team of Muslim and Christian firefighters and porters over the right to carry some goods to a bakery in Makriköy (nowadays Bakırköy, on the Marmara shore).[29] This struggle for turf led some teams or neighbourhoods to ask for police protection from the aggressive incursions of other teams into what they considered to be their legitimate scope of activity. For instance, in August 1890, four neighbourhoods located in the district of Tophane submitted a petition to the police authorities to be granted the right to form their own team of firefighters and porters against the hegemonic ambition of the neighbouring team of Galatasaray in their district.[30] Even when they were not involved in these kinds of conflicts, the porters had the aforementioned profile of the 'usual suspects' for the authorities. Bachelors and migrants were numerous among them, and the collective dimension of their activities appeared as a potential threat to public order.

The conflict with the port company can be analysed in the framework of this struggle for the control of space. What was at stake was the economic control of the port. The Société des quais wanted to control all the activities of the port – loading and unloading goods and carrying them to their recipients in the capital – whereas the porters stood against that monopoly.[31] However, in several respects, this conflict differed from the traditional rivalries between the teams of porters in the city. As a large foreign company, the Société des quais could rely on substantial financial means and diplomatic support, and could apply pressure to the Ottoman state to settle the conflict in its favour. Besides, like other foreign companies in the empire, it had been granted the right by the Ottoman state to employ private agents to ensure the security of its staff and goods. Despite this inequality of forces, the porters were able to organize actions such as breaking machines and verbal and physical threats against the workers and employers of the company.[32] For instance, in June 1907, the director of the Société des quais complained to the Ministry of Police after thirteen porters stopped working and tried to prevent other porters from continuing their activities. Three of them were also accused of making death threats to the representative of the company.[33]

The Société des quais, the state and the newspapers dealt with these kinds of conflicts as a mere issue of public order, denying their economic and political dimensions. The authors were disqualified as violent troublemakers and the only solution proposed was police intervention to restore order. However, the recurrence of incidents and the company's complaints about the police's lax attitude towards the actors in the troubles seemed to indicate that the Ottoman authorities' management of the issue had a political agenda. Everyday violence perpetrated against the foreign companies compelled them to ask for state protection when their private security agents (*kolcu*) were insufficient to control the situation. Through this security issue, the Ottoman state could restore some balance in its relationship with those companies and the foreign states that supported them. From this point of view, the eradication of these kinds of incidents was obviously not a priority for the authorities. Therefore it is not so surprising that, in his account of the 1907 incident mentioned above, the director of the Société des quais complained that the verbal and physical violence of the *hammal* had taken place in the presence of a police officer who contented himself with observing the facts, without intervening.[34]

As Donald Quataert has suggested, one can go one step further and see these porters and similar actors of the urban proletariat as a potential ally of the state, which was able to instrumentalize them for its dirty work in the capital.[35] The most striking example that Quataert gives is the key role played by Muslim, mostly Kurdish, *hammal* in the Armenian pogroms orchestrated by the Ottoman state in Istanbul in 1896.[36] Although there is little doubt that the state instrumentalized porters in the case discussed above, evidence is lacking to maintain that the Ottoman state was behind the porters' recurrent attacks on the port company in the capital. To say the least, this argument and our two case studies point to the necessity to analyse public order and disorders as complex configurations involving a multiplicity of state and non-state actors, as well as various personal and political agendas.

Conclusion

In this chapter I have tried to highlight some aspects of the perception and management of urban violence in Istanbul during the Hamidian reign. I have argued that, together with state modernization and social and economic transformations, urban violence was at the core of two mutually linked processes: the state's attempts to evaluate the forms and extent of urban violence and growing publicity in the new media. These transformations had an impact on the representation of violence, its management and its scale. Especially in the capital, urban violence became a public issue that different actors could use to enhance their legitimacy or for political ends. This political dimension of urban violence became much more obvious after the Young Turk Revolution in various forms: political debates on insecurity, riots and political assassinations.

The limits of the sources make it difficult to appreciate the real extent of urban violence in the capital or the efficiency of its control by the state during the Hamidian reign. Whereas the newspapers showed a certain fascination with sensational cases of murders and deviant behaviours in the modern central districts, the power holders were obviously more concerned with social control in its broadest sense, namely surveillance of the whole urban society and repression of behaviours that constituted a danger for the political, social and moral order. For the authorities, crime took a lower priority than collective disorders involving actual or potential violence. The repertoire of state policy towards these kinds of troubles included a wide range of strategies: parallel to prevention and legal means of coercion, some of the cases mentioned in this chapter point out the absence of repression of violence or its encouragement, not to mention the direct use of violence. From this point of view, under the reign of Abdülhamid II, police missions were clearly designed to serve the interests of the regime rather than to protect property and people – a characteristic that the political ruptures introduced by the Young Turk Revolution and later by the proclamation of the republic would little affect.

Notes

1. Several works published in Turkey in the 1940s gave detailed accounts of the various institutional steps of this process. See, for example, H. Alyot.

1947. *Türkiye'de Zabıta*. Ankara: Kanaat Basımevi. For a more recent and critical evaluation of the process, see F. Ergut. 2004. *Modern Devlet ve Polis, Osmanlı'dan Cumhuriyet'e Toplumsal Denetimin Diyalektiği*. Istanbul: Iletişim. For a brief survey in English, see Glen W. Swanson. 1972. 'The Ottoman Police', *Journal of Contemporary History* 7(1/2), 243–60.

2. For a more detailed account of the transformations in the police forces during Abdülhamid II's reign, see N. Lévy-Aksu. 2008. 'Une Institution en Formation: la Police Ottomane à l'Epoque d'Abdülhamid II', *European Journal of Turkish Studies*, 8.
3. J. Hanssen. 2005. *Fin de Siècle Beirut: The Making of an Ottoman Provincial Capital*. Oxford: Oxford University Press, 207–9.
4. 'Dersaadet ve bilad-i selasede asayiş vazifesiyle mükellef olan nizamiye ve jandarma asakir-i Şahanesiyle polis memurlarinin suret-i hareketlerine dair talimat' (1896), see O.N. Ergin. 1995. *Mecelle-i Umûr-ı Belediyye*, vol. 1, Istanbul: Büyükşehir Belediyesi Yayınları, 114–16.
5. Born in 1883 in Istanbul, Ziya Şakir gave a detailed – though somewhat fictionalized – account of these collusions between the police and ruffians. See Z. Şakır. 1943. *Yarım asır evvel bizi idare edenler*, vol. 2. Istanbul: Anadolu Türk Kitap Deposu.
6. M. Aymes. 2010. *'Un Grand Progrès - sur le Papier.' Histoire Provinciale des Réformes Ottomanes à Chypre au XIXe Siècle*. Paris and Leuven: Peeters Publishers.
7. The increasing concern with the professionalization and formation of the police during the Young Turk period led to a further standardization of these reports. Textbooks used in the newly created police schools included some chapters on writing police reports, where general recommendations were illustrated with samples of model reports. See, for example, the chapter entitled *Organization of Police Reports and Samples (Zabt varakalarinin tanzimi ve numuneleri)* in H. Niyazi. (1329) 1913. *Polis Dersleri*. Dersaadet, 63–54.
8. The expression *asayiş ber-kemal* ('order reigns' or 'all is well'), which can be found in many of these reports, became one of the symbols of Abdülhamid II's regime. Both his admirers and detractors still widely use it today to praise the ability of the sultan to maintain order or to denounce the set language and censorship of the time.
9. Z. Toprak. 2000. 'Osmanlı Devleti'nde Sayısallaşma ya da Çagdaş İstatistiğin Doğuşu', in Ş. Pamuk and H. İnalcık (eds), *Osmanlı Devleti'nde Bilgi ve İstatistik*. Ankara: Başbakanlık Devlet İstatistik Enstitüsü, 95–112.
10. BOA, Y.MTV 50/1, 04.L.1308 (H) [12 May 1891].
11. BOA, ZB 601/86, 1 Tesrin-i sani 1324, 14 November 1908; BOA, ZB 601/91, 5 Tesrin-i sani 1324 [18 November 1908].
12. On pragmatism as an intrinsic characteristic of the police forces, and on the specific approach to the law it induced, see P. Napoli. 2003. *Naissance de la Police Moderne. Pouvoir, Norme, Société*. Paris: La Découverte.
13. C. Kırlı. 2000. *The Struggle over Space: Coffeehouses of Ottoman Istanbul, 1780–1845*. Ph.D. dissertation. Binghampton: State University of New York.

14. I owe my reflections on this kind of news to Anne-Claude Ambroise-Rendu's work on the 'faits divers' in Third Republic French newspapers. A.-C. Ambroise-Rendu. 2004. *Petits Récits des Désordres Ordinaires. Les Faits Divers dans la Presse Française des Débuts de la Troisième République à la Grande Guerre*. Paris: Editions Seli Arslan.
15. On how public order in the capital was affected during Ramadan and Easter, see N. Lévy-Aksu. 2013. 'Troubles Fêtes: Les Perceptions Policières de Pâques et du Ramadan à Istanbul au Tournant des XIXe et XXe siècles', in N. Clayer and E. Kaynar (eds), *Penser, Agir et Vivre dans l'Empire Ottoman*. Leuven: Peeters, 321–38.
16. According to the 1907 census, bachelors constituted 21 per cent of Istanbul households and the average age of marriage for men was thirty. These figures include only the permanent dwellers of the city, and the migrants should also be taken into account to appreciate the extent of the phenomenon. C. Behar and A. Duben. 1991. *Istanbul Households: Marriage, Family and Fertility, 1880–1940*. Cambridge: Cambridge University Press, 57–58.
17. For an extensive account of the transformation in the judiciary institution during Abdülhamid II's reign and the function of the new Nizamiye courts, see A. Rubin. 2011. *Ottoman Nizamiye Court, Law and Modernity*. New York: Palgrave Macmillan.
18. S. Deringil. 1998. *The Well-Protected Domains, Ideology and the Legitimation of Power in the Ottoman Empire, 1876–1909*. London and New York: I.B. Tauris.
19. For examples of these harsh criticisms of the police, see *Stamboul*, 24 and 26 October 1908.
20. See, for example, *Sabah*, 28 Cemaziyelahir 1326 (H), 28 July 1908 and *Stamboul*, 31 July 1908.
21. See, for example, an anti-Judaic pamphlet written by some Greeks in Balat in 1881 (BOA, Y. PRK. ZB. 1/82, 1298.B.7 (H), [4 June1881] and the case of blood libel in Izmir in 1901. E. Benbassa. 1986. '1901'de İzmir'de Cereyan Etmiş bir Kan İftirası Vak'ası', *Tarih ve Toplum* 30, 44–50.
22. *Stamboul*, 21 April 1885.
23. *Faros tou Bosforou*, 20 April 1885.
24. *Stamboul*, 21 April 1885.
25. *Neologos*, 13 July 1874.
26. *Neologos*, 18 July 1874. See also *La Turquie*, 18 July 1874.
27. BOA, İ.HUS, 21.Ra.1313 (H) [1 September 1895].
28. Many pieces of news in the various newspapers mentioned quarrels involving porters and resulting in injuries or even the deaths of some protagonists. See, for example, *Stamboul*, 19 May 1900, reporting a quarrel between two rival groups of porters in Galata, in which three of the porters were wounded.
29. BOA, Y.PRK.BŞK 49/66, 2 Kanunsani 1312 [5 January 1898]. Many volunteer firefighters were recruited among porters, and the teams of firefighters and porters often overlapped.

30. BOA, Y.PRK.ZB 5/118, 4 Agustos 1306 [16 August 1890].
31. D. Quataert. 1983. *Social Disintegration and Popular Resistance in the Ottoman Empire, 1881–1908.* New York: New York University Press, 95–120.
32. BOA, Y.PRK.ŞH 3/65, 5 Subat 1306 [17 February 1891]; BOA, ZB 485/59, 11 Agustos 1324 [24 August 1908].
33. BOA, ZB 46/23, 20.Ca.1325 (H) [1July 1907].
34. BOA, ZB 46/23, 20.Ca.1325 (H) [1July 1907].
35. Quataert, *Social Disintegration and Popular Resistance,* 170–75.
36. Florian Riedler's contribution to this volume provides a detailed analysis of this pogrom.

⁕ Chapter 3 ⁕

Gendered Obscenity

Women's Tongues, Men's Phalluses and the State's Fist in the Making of Urban Norm in Interwar Egypt

HANAN HAMMAD

With the permission of the landlady, Zakiyya ʿAli Muhammad ʿAsi, a poor unemployed man started to install a kiosk to sell groceries in the open space adjacent to the landlady's house in the city of al-Mahalla al-Kubra in 1945. The project seemed to advance well to secure a job and a source of income for the man, except that the female vegetable vendor Zakiyya al-Safti decided that the project would hinder and compete with her business. Al-Safti, her daughter and her son tried forcefully to stop the man. The noisy quarrel brought the landlady to her balcony to ask them to stop and let the poor man make a living. ʿAsi, who was affluent and respected in the community and whose name was adorned with the title *Hajja*, made it clear that it was her property and she gave her blessing to the kiosk project. Al-Safti slandered the landlady publicly telling her: '[you are] a whore, prostitute, daughter of a dog, you and your daughter are fucked, you are the wife of a pimp, come down here and I will satisfy myself beating you up' and 'who could take my place? [you] *labwa* [lioness, a metaphor in Arabic for a sexually aggressive woman], the fucked one who fucks people one after another for one piaster or one-and-a-half, you're making yourself *hajja* [a female Muslim who performed pilgrimage to Mecca and Medina], while you went to Medina to fuck'. Zakiyya also slandered the policeman who tried to intervene, and he eventually took her to the police station. At that point, she had already established a thick record of reported fights against porters, policemen, customers and fellow vendors. At the court, Zakiyya faced harsh punishment of one-and-a-half months in jail with hard labour and a 5 EGP fine. In addition, her two children were fined 5 EGP each and the three of them had to pay 15 EGP damages to the landlady. In his justification of the harsh punishment, the judge pointed to Zakiyya's record of quarrelling, and described her as *imra'a suqiyya*.[1] *Imra'a suqiyya* literally means a common marketplace woman, but its connotation is an obscene riff-raff woman who has a bad temper and who habitually employs dirty language. What Zakiyya had done throughout her professional life, as was reported in fifteen misdemeanour cases in the court records between 1929 and 1945, was defend her right to the urban space as a place to live and work. Her sharp tongue, rich swearing lexicon, loud voice and courage to fight against her contenders and state agents were her main equipment to assure her right to the city. Zakiyya was not alone; many men and women were involved in quarrels that consisted mostly of exchanging verbal threats and oral abuse to secure their right to live and work in the city.[2]

Literature on urban violence in the Middle East has focused on incidents of grand-scale violence among men as critical expressions of ethnic, political and social conflicts. In these exceptional events, women are either ignored or regarded as victims. Meanwhile, the masculine gender identity of the acting parties has often been overlooked in favour of underpinning the socio-economic and political impulses. This chapter employs incidents of minor urban violence – that is, casual confrontations in which a few individuals exchanged verbal and/or minor physical abuse – to examine the gendered and classed construction of obscenity in interwar Egypt. What I term throughout the chapter as 'ordinary' urban violence means verbal quarrels, loud arguments, swearing, expletives, oral threats and sexually vulgar body gestures and expressions that marked daily interaction in urban neighbourhoods, workplaces, marketplaces, cafes, and entertainment hangouts. Although they may have appeared aggressive and could have caused emotional pain or damage to reputations, these casual confrontations were not fatal and did not cause serious physical injuries. These clashes did not display the deliberate use of arms, very often broke out spontaneously and few individuals were involved. The recurrence of spontaneous verbal and minor physical confrontations among the urbanites, and between them and state agents, made this type of urban violence an ordinary routine. 'Ordinary' urban violence did not provide hallmark events; nonetheless, it could signify anxiety over social reconfiguration, social incoherence, deterioration of life quality and a state–society struggle to establish urban 'normativity'.

Analysing how male and female urbanites employed profane language and gestures in their daily encounters and how these practices were represented in the legal discourses during the period of rapid urbanization and industrialization, I argue that obscenity was constructed through the struggle among urban populations, and between them and the state, over the urban space. Obscenity as a legal construction and a social category in the moments of 'ordinary' violence is no less important than grand-scale riots as a class and gender performance. Profanity as uttered and performed in these encounters provides an important text of the social construction of class, gender and sexuality in modern Egypt. It captures the tropes employed by lower classes to carve out their space while struggling against the state's attempts to refashion the fast-growing cities based on middle-class moral values. Profanity and obscenity during these 'ordinary' encounters carried different meanings in relation to class and gender, and were employed by state functionaries to construct the cultural backwardness of the urbanite poor and the working classes. In its quest to control public order in the ever-expanding urban spaces in the first half of twentieth-century Egypt, the state criminalized offensive language and sexual bodily gestures that were common in these casual quarrels, and labelled them a violation of public decency and the 'norm'. What social groups and the state labelled 'obscene' and a 'violation of public morality' illuminates important aspects of the social transformation associated with rapid urbanization and industrialization.

Rapid Urbanization, Dense Urbanity

In the first half of the twentieth century, Egyptian towns witnessed unprecedented population growth and rapid urbanization. This was an acceleration of a trend of migration from the countryside into the cities that had started in the mid nineteenth century, in addition to natural population growth. The 1907 census shows that 238,637 out of 654,470 people, representing one-third of the population of Cairo, were born in other parts of the country.[3] With the industrialization drive during the interwar period, Egyptian towns experienced rapid expansion and intensive population growth associated with the establishment of large modern factories. The population of the town of al-Mahalla al-Kubra, whose records provide most of the evidence for this study, increased from 44,000 people in 1927 to more than 115,000 in 1947. This population increase was a direct result of the establishment of the Misr Spinning and Weaving Company (MSWC) in 1927. Owned by Bank Misr, MSWC became the largest Egyptian-owned textile factory in colonial Egypt, and its workforce steadily increased from 2,000 in 1930 to 27,000 in 1945. Urban spaces not only became a breeding ground for labour strikes and political protests, but also for all sorts of violent confrontations, both collective and individual, signifying social tension, class conflict and the continuing encroachment of the state upon society. Rapid socio-economic reconfiguration and the loss of urban social coherence were expressed in confrontations among male and female co-workers, neighbours, residents and state agents. Verbal abuse and minor physical violence on a daily basis was not unusual in the ordinary interaction in urban spaces. Until 1930, the misdemeanour court cases from the entire centre of al-Mahalla al-Kubra (*markaz*), which included the town and many dependent villages, numbered an average of only four hundred cases a year. Beginning in 1935, when the records of misdemeanour cases tried in dependent villages were kept in separate files from those tried inside the town, the number of misdemeanour cases reported from inside the town alone reached an average of two thousand cases annually.

With increasing population density, urban expansion, rising costs of living and the failure of public services to meet rapid population growth, it became harder for the urban population, the lower classes in particular, to make ends meet and protect their privacy. Women faced increasing hardship in performing their daily chores. Female housemates and neighbours had to negotiate among themselves on a daily basis their shares of limited space and the limited capacity of urban services. As a scholar on working-class women in Cairo observed, these women were so crafty with their limited sources that they were able to play with an egg and a stone.[4] Meanwhile, public disputes and feuds very often broke out among them over shares of resources, which in a marginal economy can be anything from money to personal contacts.[5] This intense process generated disagreements, arguments and fights around the clock. For example, bringing water from public fountains to homes and disposing of wastewater in houses that lacked a fresh water supply and a drainage system were primarily female-only duties in working-class slums. Very often, women threw used water into the alleyways, rather than carrying it to the public gutter. Usually, there was an explicit agreement on the premises regarding where and when each family could throw its used water. Throwing water onto dusty streets can make roads very slippery and unpleasant smelling, particularly in winter. Disagreements on space and the timing of throwing water were a perfect source for daily disputes among female neighbours.[6] State agents had the right to interfere to prevent residents from throwing dirty water in alleyways, which often led to confrontation between those state agents and residents.[7] State agents also increasingly interfered to stop men from bathing in canals and public fountains, seeing in this practice a violation of public order.[8] Men who could not afford public bath fees took advantage of these open sources of running water because it saved them the trouble of bringing fresh water home and of getting rid of used water. The state's policies to increase its grip and impose urban control inevitably triggered popular opposition and resistance. Most popular resistance to growing state power did not take the form of mass rebellion, but rather of individual protest against or evasion of official policies and attacks on officials who represented the government.[9]

Houses in which an entire family lived in one room and shared the sole bathroom and the interior courtyard with many other families became common. Housemates and neighbours had to negotiate their shares of limited space and the limited capacity of urban services among themselves on a daily basis so that they could get by and make ends meet. Anxiety over density and lack of privacy made managing shared spaces problematic. There were as many reasons for the deterioration of relations among housemates as for mutual accommodation and support. Lack of privacy in these shared houses generated violent confrontations among housemates and neighbours. Husbands got into fistfights with male housemates who they thought were watching them in intimate situations with their wives.[10] Husbands also fought with female housemates for interfering with their relationships with their wives.[11] Women fought with male housemates when the latter came to the house with male friends without giving enough warning of the presence of strange men.[12] Routine encounters between housemates, such as negotiating what time to close the exit door, could turn into violent confrontations.[13] The high demand for housing due to the large number of rural immigrants encouraged some landlords and landladies to evict their old tenants or pressure them to pay higher rent. Disagreements between landlords and landladies and their tenants sometimes developed into violent quarrels.[14] There were also fights over rent and overdue charges.[15] Conflicts over the proportion of urban space that should be used to conduct business generated violent confrontation among vendors and between vendors and state agents.[16]

The Precious Text of Profanity

The words that never circulated in print but were used in fights among men and women in urban neighbourhoods can be shocking when heard or read in the public domain, such as in court records. The Egyptian dialect has an extraordinarily abundant vocabulary of obscenity, but in both colonial and post-colonial Egypt, publishing swear words and performing profane gestures in the mass media was completely forbidden and subject to censorship. Language had to conform to what was considered public decency. Vocabulary used by the working classes in the streets was not used in literature or 'respected' performance art. The rise and development of the mass media since the late nineteenth century can be read as a history of censoring the verbal and body languages of ordinary life in the Egyptian urban realm. The state increasingly placed itself as a guardian of public morality to make sure that no public performance violated public order and morality, and according to the Law of Theatre in 1911, police had the power to shut down any theatre that did not comply with this rule.[17] Building on the 1883 Legal Code, Article 155 of the Native Penal Code in 1904 made violating public morality (*hurmat al-adab wa-husn al-akhlaq*) by the press or other means punishable by up to one year in jail or a fine of 50 EGP.[18] This became the basis of all legal amendments throughout the first half of the twentieth century, most notably the 1937 Penal Code. Egyptian intellectuals censored the Egyptian colloquial language and excluded words and expressions that the educated stratum deemed inappropriate. For example, Ahmad Taymur Pasha's pioneer work to document the Egyptian colloquial language excluded all maxims that referred to sexual organs.[19]

Words and gestures that were constructed as a taboo in print culture and other forms of mass media were thus pushed out of the sight of the educated classes. Yet, they were never out of earshot in the ordinary urban scene. Men and women in their daily interaction utilized the rich Egyptian lexicon of coarse language and expressions to convey every form of offensiveness and vulgar humour about sexual matters in explicit detail. As in many other cultures, swearing is fascinating in its protean diversity and poetic creativity, while being simultaneously shocking in its ugliness and cruelty.[20] Fortunately, court records, particularly records concerning cases of obscenity and offending pubic morality, document some of this language that the print culture never cared about or was unable or unwilling to document. Although misdemeanour court records tended to narrate 'ordinary' violence in the urban space in brief and formatted formula that fulfilled the state's need for documentation and ignored the voice of lower-class defendants, these records preserved the profanity that was deemed obscene. It quoted people's coarse language as it was uttered during confrontations, even when state bureaucrats rephrased people's testimonies in standard Arabic. Misdemeanour cases were mostly incidents of ordinary violence among individuals and groups that included verbal abuse and minor injuries. These cases were narratives through which individuals and the state constructed obscenity and what was meant to be the social norm in the urban space. With a strong concern for social control and urban order, the state stigmatized and criminalized lower-class language and body expression under the rubric of obscenity and violation of public decency. On the other hand, lower-class individuals manipulated the state's power and utilized the legal system to assure their rights to urban space.

In 'ordinary' confrontations, taboos around sex, genitals, religion and excretion were spilled out into public and private domains. Words and phrases like 'fuck', 'whore', 'deflowered', 'pimp', 'faggot', 'adulterous', 'child of adulterers', 'bastard', 'damn your religion', 'damn your father/mother' and 'I'll poke your eyes' were used equally by men and women. Profanity was used publicly and heard across urban spaces, and was by no means restricted to sex workers or inhabitants of the licensed prostitution quarters.[21] Court records on which this study is based show that swearing was commonly uttered in neighbourhoods inhabited by *ahrar*, meaning people who were not involved in the sex trade. Phrases accusing the addressee of practising prostitution, having illicit sex or losing their sexual honour were commonly used among *ahrar* family members, neighbours and strangers, as well as against state agents trying to enforce public order and control.[22]

Expletive phrases and profanities were formulated in swearing, cursing and verbal threats. Men and women used offensive language and gestures centred on sex and intimate parts of the body to humiliate their opponents. Women evoked taboos about sex and the female body as much as men did. Women uttered words and performed gestures pointing at male and female genitals to show their toughness and underscore their will and ability to fight shamelessly. Profanity in 'ordinary' confrontations was one of these practices that destabilized the female–male binary, to use Judith Butler's term.[23] As in the case of the vegetable vendor Zakiyya al-Safti, women mastering the ability to craft sensational sexual claims took a big risk to take the other side in a public battle. During a police investigation, Ahmad ʿAli Rashwan and his wife testified that their 26-year-old neighbour Nabawiyya Muhammad Masʿud practised illicit prostitution. Due to lack of evidence, Nabawiyya was set free without facing any charges. Once she left the police station, she went along with her mother and sister to Ahmad's house. Standing outside the house, the three women cursed him and his wife viciously and loudly.[24] The three women screamed at the couple calling them 'whores and sons of bitches'. They told the wife: 'we went to the [police] station and came back honourable, not like you. My son was fucking you downstairs while he [your husband] was upstairs. He [your husband] makes his friends fuck you'. This shockingly offensive verbal attack was not rare in such confrontation. The violation of sexual taboos for the sake of humiliating a neighbour was a revenge tactic employed equally by men and women against male and female opponents.

Women's Tongues and Men's Phalluses

Women did not hesitate to use provocative or indecent language and gestures in public; and when they used it against state agents, the latter would report and take action against hostile and insulting behaviour. A scholar of the history of women in modern Egypt argues that, given Egyptian women's established reputation for public taunting, verbal abuses against soldiers or representatives of the government were peculiar to females resisting the growing state power.[25] As far as records reveal, men and women equally performed gestures that conveyed offensive sexual meanings such as the middle-finger gesture and waving fists and arms, gestures that are called *tadri'* in Egyptian colloquial Arabic. Women tended to be verbally offensive against men and women, as well as violently stripping other women of their clothes and beating them on their genitals. Exposing one's genitals in the face of state agents was an exclusively male practice. When a policeman tried to stop the 20-year-old Zaki al-Bastawisi al-Atrush from bathing in the Bahr al-Ma'ash canal, al-Atrush exposed his phallus and said, 'Take this, I'll terminate your life'.[26] This was an episode in the efforts of the state to control the urban space and public hygiene while people were struggling to deal with poverty and lack of resources. Seeking an unprecedented role in controlling the urban space and regulating public morality, the state outlawed bathing in public under the rubric of protecting public morality against any action that might violate public decency (*yakhdish al-haya' al-'amm*) in villages and cities.[27] Article 338 of the Native Penal Code (*Qanun al-'Uqubat al-Ahli*) of 1904 forbade being naked in public roads and bathing in public places in cities and villages in a manner that violated decency and made it punishable by a fine of up to 1 EGP or up to one week in jail. Thus, the convenient way for poor males to cleanse their bodies was incorporated in the state's construction of obscenity. For the urban poor whose homes lacked running water and sewage systems, this regulation did not make much sense and needed to be challenged, which al-Atrush did. In addition to violating public decency and bathing in public, al-Atrush was convicted of insulting a state agent while on duty.

Both men and women deliberately used nudity to sexually humiliate female opponents. The divorced mother Sabha Gad al-Haqq tried to talk to her son when she accidentally saw him helping his father selling *falafel* and other street food. The 50-year-old ex-husband had not allowed the mother to see their son and was angered when she approached their food stand in the street. Due to Sabha's known record of illegal prostitution, the husband's current wife and a neighbouring coffeehouse waiter (*qahwagi*) helped push her violently away. The three of them attacked Sabha, tore her clothes off to the point that she became naked in the public street and they beat her on the genitals.[28] The court considered this assault to be sexual abuse and a violation of a sense of decorum (*hatk 'ird* and *khadsh haya'*). The court made it clear that sexual abuse was not restricted to sexual intercourse and consequently could be committed by a female against another woman.

There is not a single reported case in which a woman stripped herself naked in public during a confrontation, whereas men frequently resorted to revealing their genitals to insult their male and female opponents. Tensions leading to these 'sexually violent' confrontations were not unusual among urbanites. For example, a grudge had built up between a 19-year-old weaver Ibrahim Ramadan al-Samahi and his neighbour Muhammad Matar in Abu al-'Abbas Street. To express his anger, al-Samahi exposed his genitals in front of Matar's maid when he was on the rooftop of his house. Two neighbours, a man and a woman, corroborated the maid's testimony, claiming they had witnessed the incident; however, both witnesses were known to be seeking to get al-Samahi out of his house so that they could rent it. Interestingly, because of these circumstances and the known grudge among these neighbours, the court doubted that al-Samahi had committed the shameful action, and consequently the defendant was acquitted.[29] As far as legal documents reveal, men exposing their phalluses in the faces of other men were less often reported, which might indicate that it took place less frequently or that it was more tolerated and people did not find it worth reporting.

Judging Obscenity, Obscene Justice

Starting with the Native Penal Code (*Qanun al-'Uqubat al-Ahli*) in 1883 and 1904, the state introduced a wide range of laws with the purpose of controlling what was called *haya' 'amm* (public decency) and *husn al-adab al-'amma* (good public morality). Without specifying what public decency and morality meant, these laws allowed state agents to send individuals to court to face penalties of up to one year in jail or a fine of up to 50 EGP for a wide range of daily practices. Legal knowledge and the ways it was produced and practised since the late nineteenth century increasingly became a bureaucratic exercise of interpretation, one that created different ways of thinking about the judicial process and about gender itself.[30] The penal code introduced 'shameful action' (*fi'l fadih*) as a crime of violation of decency in public. In a gendered approach to morality, Article 241 punished those who committed shameful action in private (*wa-law fi ghayr 'alaniyya*) if the victim was a woman.[31] In another gendered aspect of the law, the state treated the action of exposing one's genitals in public differently depending on the gender of the victim. If a man exposed his penis in the face of another man, the defendant would be charged only with *fi'l fadih*. If he did so in the face of a woman, he would also be convicted of violation of female decorum (*khadsh haya' untha*).

The state was entitled to review the popular lexicon and oversee how people spoke and acted in public. Parts of the popular thesaurus became not only a social taboo, but also an outlawed and punishable crime. Certain words, expressions, gestures and body language became illegal in public and/or even in private. The 1904 Penal Code made cursing somebody a misdemeanour punishable by up to one week in jail or a pecuniary fine. The same punishment was applicable for quarrelling and launching attacks that caused minor harm but no injury, even if the attack did not include battery.[32] This was in addition to the 1883 Code that defined libel and slander as attributing a fault (*'ayb*), disgracing a person's moral standing (*i'tibar*) or accusing a person of violating laws or the norm (*namus*), and made them punishable with up to three months in jail or a 20 EGP fine. Falsely accusing someone of committing a crime was punishable with up to six months in jail if the defamation had caused disrespect in the family and community. In practice, when people from the lower classes slandered each other with accusations of practising prostitution, the court dismissed libel and slander claims.

The employment of offensive language in 'ordinary' urban violence was certainly not new, but the increase in reporting it to the court raises an interesting question and is worth an explanation. It could simply reflect the population increase. Yet, court records reveal that most cases of obscenity in interwar Egypt took place in lower-class neighbourhoods and working-class slums. Most disputing parties shared lower-class status, and all defendants were lower class. Victims seeking redress for torts were mostly women. Very often, casual disputes developed into fights in public and provided male and female neighbours with entertainment in streets, alleyways and through windows and balconies. Watching these fights provided anecdotes for chats and gossips. A great number of these 'ordinary' fights went undocumented because nobody got hurt, or the confrontation took place in the absence of state agents, or no party sought the involvement of the state. Some cases accidentally attracted the attention of state agents, leading the latter to interfere and document them, particularly when these casual ordinary fights got very loud and attracted spectators, sparking a melee. Occasionally, confrontations accidentally developed into excessive violence, and one or more parties would have to be hospitalized. This increased the chances that the incident would be reported.[33] The state apparatus that connected hospital reports with police reports increased the likelihood that these incidents would be reported, even if victims did not wish to use the power of the state or press a charge. Once the state became involved, the fighting parties lost control over the legal procedures, even if they chose to reconcile. In many incidents, one party or another took advantage of the laws and the state's power and reported the incident to fight defamation and curses. Through this process, what seemed to be powerless lower-class people participated in defining morality, obscenity and what violated their sense of shame and shyness (*haya*ʾ). In the periods of rapid urbanization and rural migration into towns, urbanites looked down on the newcomers and took pride in being natives (*awlad al-balad*) who enjoyed deep roots in urban space and traditions. Incoherence and a lack of understanding of mutual traditions between urbanites and rural migrants sometimes triggered alarming violence. While socio-cultural prejudice led to violent confrontations among neighbours, they lacked the organic mechanism to solve their disputes amicably. They hence invited the state's intervention and utilized the legal system against their opponents to mediate their conflicts and regulate people's morality and behaviours.

Through these three-party struggles, the urban 'norm' was redefined, and gender and class differences were signified. Hamida Ahmad Ibrahim and her daughter sued their neighbour Muhammad Hassan al-Rashidi in the working-class slum of ʿIzbat al-Delta for revealing and waving his phallus in their faces. Both women considered this a shameful action and a violation of their shyness (*fiʿl fadih khadasha hayaʾhuma*).[34] During an 'ordinary' confrontation, al-Rashidi evoked the women's origin in the nearby town of Samanud in a derogatory fashion. He said, '[you are] whores from Samanud (*sharamit Samanudiyya*), you and your daughter go out to be fucked'. The two women were no more restrained in utilizing offensive language centred on the sexual life of al-Rashidi and his family. Noticeably, women used their sharp tongues, but the man used both his tongue and phallus. At the court, al-Rashidi was convicted of libel and slander (*sabb wa-qadhf*) and of committing a shameful action. He was punished with a suspended sentence of one week in simple jail, a 20-piaster fine for the first violation and a 30-piaster fine for the second. However, the civic lawsuit in which the two women were seeking redress for a tort was more interesting. The judge rejected the mother's claim and made the defendant pay only 50 piasters damages to the daughter. The judge punished al-Rashidi for his offence against the state and the society, not against the direct female victims. The ruling included an important remark on the legal construction of obscenity. The judge concluded that the financial compensation should not exceed the harm caused by the violation; and the harm (*taʿrid*) done by al-Rashidi to the two women depended on the environment in which all the parties lived. Witnesses testified that the mother had provoked the defendant and initiated cursing him in front of his house. According to the judge, what al-Rashidi had said was common language among this (lower) class, and a sexual curse was not taken literally in this environment. The judge thus established, on behalf of the state, the gendered and classed construction of obscenity.

This was a legal pattern and a common practice. The concern of state officials was not so much with social morality per se but with deviations from appropriate and permissible legal behaviour. Changing social and economic realities led male administrators and bureaucratic intermediaries to invoke the discretionary power of the state in order to regulate the public behaviour of its subjects.[35] Court cases show that the penal legislation and the bureaucratic interpretation created different ways of thinking about the judicial process and gender. The woman Fatima Muhammad ʿIsa filed a tort case against her female housemate Yasmin Farag al-Miligi in ʿIzbat Abu Ghasha, asking 5 EGP damages because Yasmin had said to her on the public street on 24 August 1941, '[You are the] daughter of a dog, see who took you in the car and fucked you for four days after you had a fight with your husband and he made you leave the house; all housemates have fucked you'. The judge said, 'the court sees that the environment in which the defendant and the victim live is used to cursing with extremely obscene words that are not meant for their actual meaning; these words are widely used among them'.[36] Thus, the court decided that the requested damages sum was exaggerated. The verdict was to make the defendant pay 1 EGP damages and the lenient penalty of a 50-piaster fine and the expenses of the tort case.

Gendered-Classed Trails

The legal interpretation by judges recognized the expressive power in the language of the lower classes, but often rejected the tort claims in defamation cases. Male interpreters of the law regarded expressions like 'whore', 'prostitute' and 'fucked' as commonplace phrases among this class (*ʿamma*) when they were uttered by or against lower-class women. Judges treated these phrases as curses, not as serious accusations of practising prostitution that could be proved or denied. While acknowledging the expressive power of the language of the lower classes and how it was used and what it meant, legal interpretation stigmatized the lower classes in general as uneducated, crude, offensive, rude and impolite. More importantly, male judges were deliberately denying the victims' right to gain pecuniary compensation for their grief. Theoretically, obscenity laws derive their content from a consideration of community morals and values. The perceptions and reactions of members of the community are essential in determining the outcome of an obscenity case. Yet, community morals and the criminal code frequently differ. Relevant community standards are local, not national, and what locals meant remained ambiguous.[37] There was no verdict on any obscenity case in which the court required any empirical evidence of community standards.

In the official construction of the moral order, the lower class's language was judged to be obscene, and to use its vocabulary was an offence against the state and its middle-class bureaucrats and judges, but was not always considered offensive to lower-class victims. Meanwhile, the state's construction of obscenity usually assumed that upper-class women never got involved in offensive violence. When two women from the notable Samra family hit their maid, causing her miscarriage, the court dismissed the testimony of the maid and the medical report supporting her. The judge stated, 'The politeness and natural shyness of women in this class would not allow them to attack the maid.'[38]

Verdicts in libel and slander cases were judgment on the morality and the public behaviour of lower classes. The state became more concerned about public order. From the middle-class standpoint, exchanging obscene language and publicly committing shameful actions among the lower classes was a manifestation of their collective backwardness and obscenity. In the first half of the twentieth century, the ignorance and lack of civilization of the common people became dominant discourses among the educated public. Judges' rulings against female vendors and their labelling of working-class women as vulgar riff-raff women (*suqiyya*) resonated with the prevailing discourses of the educated Egyptians. The educated classes often invoked images of rural decay and criminality. Their goal was twofold: to employ their education and progressiveness as political capital, and to suggest the immediate need for social reform projects.[39] Such projects were intended to guide the urban and rural working classes towards the adoption of 'reformed' norms of behaviour and social and cultural practices that were deemed more in line with the modern world. Representations of uncivilized peasants and poor urbanites served to rationalize the expertise of social scientists and reformers and to underscore the civility of the urban educated middle class (*effendiyya*).⁴⁰ These legal and intellectual discourses criminalized language and behaviours that did not conform to the 'normative' educated middle class, a phenomenon witnessed across the Middle East and beyond since the late nineteenth century.⁴¹

State bureaucrats and bureaucratic procedures played a major role in constructing obscenity through erratic rather than consistent legal practices. Wahib Yusuf ʿAbdullah sued the car salesman Tawfiq Abu Samra and his worker Ibrahim Handusa because both men hit him and told him in a loud voice in the public street, '[You are] a son of dog, a son of a whore (*sharmuta*), damn your father and brother, you are all sons of dogs, pimps (*maʾrrasin*)'.⁴² Witnesses supported this account. He accused them of violating his sexual honour (*khawd fi ʾl-ʿird*) and asked for 5 EGP in damages. The state officials who documented the case described what the businessman and his worker said as 'words that violate the norm (*namus*)'. The term *namus* sounded very archaic, and it is unimaginable that common people ever used it in their narrative. Yet, the judge dismissed the accusation because what was said was widely used among the public or, as he put it, 'words run on the tongues of common people that were not meant to defame sexual honour'. The court made each defendant pay only 50-piasters damages to the victim, only 10 per cent of what he had asked for.

The court took a different stand when two women employed almost the same phrases to slander a man. In documenting the accusation of violation of the norm, the court scribe employed the same archaic term, *namus*, which provides little information. The court harshly sentenced the 50-year-old married woman Ammuna Muhammad Khatir to two weeks in jail, a 2 EGP fine and 3 EGP in damages to the male neighbour ʿAbd al-Ghani ʿAli Yusuf, whom she had publicly called 'whore, faggot, son of dog, no manners'.⁴³ Yusuf and Khatir were neighbours and had exchanged the verbal abuse when Yusuf asked Khatir and a second woman, who was acquitted, to remove some wood they had placed in front of his house. Because the neighbours were able to reconcile, the appeals court suspended the jail sentence. Once the state got involved in regulating ordinary encounters among neighbours, it monitored the neighbouring dynamic in order to construct gender and moral regimes in the urban space. The unusually harsh sentence could have been an attempt to maintain male superiority in the gender regime, in which women must not show toughness in dealing with men who are equal to them in socio-economic status. The court was lenient with the tailor ʿAbd al-Hamid Gumʿa, who had slandered a woman named Dawlat Muhammad Abu ʾl-Khay in the street, calling her 'daughter of dog, whore, you are fucked and your mother go fuck'.⁴⁴ The court sentenced the defendant to fifteen days in jail with labour, or a 1 EGP fine. In the tort case, the court made the man pay the female victim only 3 EGP, while the victim had asked for 10 EGP.

The social construction of honour was centred on sex and women's sexuality. Women's honour, virginity and chastity occupied high and important positions in the culture. The female body as a form of capital for the family honour and the vulnerability of women's reputations explain why more women than men were keen to report verbal defamation assaults against them. Legal records show that the state officials' concern was not so much with sexual morality per se, but with violations of honour. Sexual honour stood for a set of gender norms that provided the logic for unequal power relations in both private and public life.[45] Virginity was emphasized and cherished as a social ideal across classes. Unmarried females who were assumed to be virgin with no previous sexual experience were considered more vulnerable to obscene language and gestures, particularly slanders concerning their sexual honour and exposure to male genitals. Calling a woman who had never been married 'deflowered' and accusing a woman of having had sexual intercourse and losing her virginity prior to marriage was one of the worst forms of defamation, even when it was uttered privately.[46] The court was more sensitive about the defamation of virgins than of married women. In the case above of the fight between the mother and daughter and their male neighbour, the judge awarded the daughter damages because she was a virgin, which made her exposure to al-Rashidi's penis and his calling her a whore more distressing and a more sensitive offence than doing so against the mother. Defaming the sexual honour of a married woman was no less important a matter and was taken seriously by both victims and the state. An on-duty policeman reported that he witnessed the railway inspector Ibrahim Badawi calling his married neighbour in public 'prostitute daughter of a dog'. It turned out that the neighbour had refused to provide Badawi with a sexual favour and he had told her stepson, 'Do not leave the house, your stepmother wants you to leave so that she can bring another man to fuck her in the house, you know she is a fucked woman and her demeanour is like adulterous prostitutes (*fawahis*)'.[47] Badawi was sentenced to one week in jail and the defamed woman won the tort case. The court made Badawi pay her 2 EGP in damages and cover her legal expenses.

In tort cases, the lower classes contributed to the social construction of gender and sexuality as reflected in the way they composed their profane curses and reported their grief to the state. It was not unusual during 'ordinary' confrontations among neighbours to mock women who sought to highlight their feminine beauty and sexual attractiveness and who violated the modest dress code, which was not standardized by any means. Bahiyya Ahmad al-Hamaqi and her husband Muhammad Ahmad al-ʿAttar slandered their neighbour al-Sayyid Shihata on the public street calling him 'a son of dog, rotten pimp, your wife wears white and red [make up] and goes out to be fucked in the street, you are a husband of a prostitute'.[48] The couple was fined 2 EGP in the tort case and had to pay 3 EGP in damages to the victim, in addition to covering the legal fees for the case. The community and the court praised those who refrained from physical assault on women. A fight broke out over the rent between the landlord ʿAbd al-Galil ʿAshur and his wife, on one side, and their tenants and housemates Rashida Muhammad ʿAli and her husband, on the other. Rashida refused to pay overdue payments and insisted on dropping four months rent. The loud fight attracted many neighbours, who testified that Rashida physically attacked the landlord although the latter refrained from assaulting her. The landlord sued the couple, asking for 10 EGP in damages for publicly insulting him. In a countersuit, Rashida accused the landlord of hitting her and causing her to lose her child, a claim that the court dismissed entirely, despite the medical report proving the miscarriage. The landlord won the sympathy of the neighbours and the judge because during the confrontation he repeatedly told Rashida: 'I'm not going to hit you because you are a woman'.[49] The judge speculated that Rashida had a miscarriage because of her excessive physical effort during the fight. The landlord was acquitted, while Rashida and her husband had to pay 5 EGP in damages for slandering the landlord. Yet, both Rashida and the landlord were convicted of quarrelling and exchanging indecent curses. They were fined 2 EGP each, which the appeals court reduced to only 1 EGP each. This case shows that in the legal construction of obscenity, profane language and gestures were an offence against the society, which actually meant an offence against middle-class sensibility. Perpetrators were punished not because of the pain they caused to opponent victims, but because they offended middle-class morality.

Conclusion

It cannot be assumed that there was a standardized meaning for every verbal and gesture expression in Egypt in the first half of the twentieth century. Much of the meaning depended upon context, and upon the shared values and intuitions of the speaker and the addressee. In the decade of rapid urbanization and population growth, the tension between ordinary practices of the inarticulate urban population and the increasing state power led to the construction of obscenity as a social and legal category. The legal and bureaucratic apparatus increasingly stigmatized and criminalized lower-class foul language and gestures under the rubric of protecting public morality. Lower-class men and women were not breaking any language rules, but were using their language, their 'norm'; it is a norm perfectly in keeping with their social network structure. The lower classes did not employ offensive sexual language or sexual gestures in public to challenge the state or middle-class codes of language and behaviour; they were actively establishing that norm and selectively utilizing the state's power for their interest, a process that discursively drew gender and class boundaries. When people sued each other for shameful action (*fiʿl fadih*), the violation of sense of shyness and shame (*khadsh hayaʾ*) and the defamation of sexual honour (*taʿn fi ʾl-ʿird*), they took advantage of the state's laws to establish their own construction of gendered obscenity. Social incoherency and anxiety might have deactivated or inhibited the efficacy of communal mechanisms to contain conflicts, such as the mediation of neighbours and relatives, rather than bring them to the attention of the state. The values of tolerance and forgiveness were replaced by the state's power and intervention. People were also becoming more aware of the state's role in restructuring the society, and cherished the possibility of empowering themselves by means of the state's law and power, a trend that could be traced back to the nineteenth century.[50] While troubled with social incoherence and anxiety over public order, the state employed incidences of 'ordinary' violence to control the lower classes and to impose middle-class morality as the urban norm.

Notes

1. Magistrates Court of al-Mahalla 1945, file 7792, case 924. Hereafter, these records will be quoted in the following format: Magistrates 1945/7792/924.
2. Among many other examples, a 25-year-old female vendor Aziza Wahbat al-Qadi was convicted twice of slandering police officers during their work in keeping public order. In her second offence, she was harshly punished with three months in jail with labour: Tanta Appeal Court 1947/7550/3359. There was also the case of a female fish vendor, Badiʿa Murgan, who was accused of publicly insulting the principality's inspector while he was on duty. Magistrates 1936/6766/502.
3. Ministry of Finance of Egypt, Statistical Department. 1909. *Population Censuses Conducted in Egypt 1907*, Cairo: Government Press.
4. E.A. Early. 1993. *Baladi Women of Cairo: Playing with an Egg and a Stone*, Boulder, CO: Lynne Rienner Publishers.
5. Early, *Baladi Women of Cairo*, 151.

6. Magistrates 1945/7791/490 and Magistrates 1939/6779/321.
7. Magistrates 1936/6766/502 and Magistrates 1939/6781/2914.
8. Magistrates 1939/6781/2914.
9. J. Tucker. 1985. *Women in Nineteenth-Century Egypt*, Cambridge: Cambridge University Press, 143.
10. Magistrates 1938/6776/2088 and 2080.
11. Magistrates 1938/6775/1424.
12. Magistrates 1938/6776/2355.
13. Magistrates 1943/6864/2139 and Magistrates 1945/7791.
14. Magistrates 1938/6775 and Magistrates 1945/7791/268.
15. Magistrates 1945/7793/1904.
16. Magistrates 1929/3961/2403 and Magistrates 1936/6766/502.
17. 'al-Ahkam al-Qanuniyya Lat'ihat at-Tiyatrat', *al-Waqaʾiʿ al-Misriyya*, 17 July 1911.
18. K. al-Misri (compiler). 1931. *Qanun al-ʿUqubat al-Ahli Mudhayyal bi-Ahkam al-Mahakim al-Ahliyya li-Ghatyat 1930*, Cairo: al-Maktabat al-Tujariyyat al-Kubra, 77.
19. A. Taymur Pasha (ed.). 1956. *al-Amthal al-ʿAmmyya Mashruha wa-Murataba ʿala 'l-Harf al-Awwal min al-Mathal*, 2nd edn, Cairo: Matabiʿ Dar al-Kitab al-ʿArabi.
20. G. Hughes. 1991. *Swearing: A Social History of Foul Language, Oaths and Profanity in English*, Oxford: Blackwell, 3, 11.
21. For 'ordinary' confrontations in prostitution quarters, see H. Hammad. 2011. 'Between Egyptian "National Purity" and Local Flexibility: Prostitution in al-Mahalla al-Kubra in the First Half of the Twentieth Century', *Journal of Social History* 44(3), 751–83.
22. For examples of defaming sexual honour between children and parents during 'ordinary' fights, see Magistrates 1939/6779/505 and Magistrates 1939/6779/1052.
23. Judith Butler. 1999. *Gender Trouble: Feminism and the Subversion of Identity*, New York: Routledge.
24. Magistrates 1937/6773/2896.
25. Tucker, *Women in Nineteenth-Century Egypt*, 146.
26. Magistrates 1939/6781/2914.
27. Al-Misri, *Qanun al-ʿUqubat al-Ahli*, 155–56.
28. Magistrates 1944/6917/505.
29. Magistrates 1943/6864/2528.
30. M.M. Ruiz. 2005. 'Virginity Violated: Sexual Assault and Respectability in Mid- to Late-Nineteenth-Century Egypt', *Comparative Studies of South Asia, Africa and the Middle East* 25(1), 214–27.
31. Al-Misri, *Qanun al-ʿUqubat al-Ahli*, 110.
32. Al-Misri, *Qanun al-ʿUqubat al-Ahli*, 160.
33. Magistrates 1945/7791/490 and Magistrates 1939/6779/321.
34. Magistrates 1937/6770/492.
35. Ruiz, 'Virginity Violated'.
36. Magistrates 1941/6789/418.

37. D. Linz, E. Donnerstein, B.J. Shafer, K.C. Land, P.L. McCall and A.C. Graesser. 1995. 'Discrepancies between the Legal Code and Community Standards for Sex and Violence: An Empirical Challenge to Traditional Assumptions in Obscenity Law', *Law & Society Review* 29(1), 127–68.
38. Magistrates 1944/6918/1150.
39. M. Gasper. 2009. *The Power of Representation: Publics, Peasants, and Islam in Egypt*, Stanford: Stanford University Press; and L. Ryzova. 2009. 'Efendification: The Rise of Middle Class Culture in Modern Egypt', Oxford: Ph.D. dissertation, University of Oxford.
40. O. El Shakry. 2008. 'Peasants, Crime, and Tea in Interwar Egypt', *ISIM Review* 21(Spring), 44–45.
41. For the case of Anatolia, see the contribution by N. Lévy-Aksu in this volume. Russia is a good example of similar phenomena outside the Middle East: see S.A. Smith. 1998. 'The Social Meanings of Swearing: Workers and Bad Language in Late Imperial and Early Soviet Russia', *Past & Present* 160(1), 167–202.
42. Magistrates 1938/6776/1372.
43. Magistrates 1938/6776/1379.
44. Magistrates 1945/7791/1786.
45. Ruiz, 'Virginity Violated'.
46. Magistrates 1941/6788/232.
47. Magistrates 1944/6917/841.
48. Magistrates 1940/6861/2322.
49. Magistrates 1945/7793/1904.
50. K. Fahmy. 1999. 'The Anatomy of Justice: Forensic Medicine and Criminal Law in Nineteenth-Century Egypt', *Islamic Law and Society* 6(2), 224–71.

Part II

Symbolic Politics of Violence

※ Chapter 4 ※

Urban Violence, the Muharram Processions and the Transformation of Iranian Urban Society
The Case of Dezful

REZA MASOUDI NEJAD

The social history of Iranian cities has involved discussions of escalating urban violence during religious rituals; however, this study aims to unfold a more complex relationship between religious rituals and urban violence during the modern transformation in Iran. This discussion focuses on Muharram processions in the city of Dezful, a medium-sized city in the south-west of the country in Khuzestan. After providing a brief background on Muharram commemoration, the discussion explains how the Muharram processions historically channelled social tension and violence in Dezful, based on Heydari and Neʿmati divisions.

Iranian urban society experienced a major transformation when the Pahlavi State initiated the modernization project in the 1920s. Although the transformation of urban society was driven by the modernization project, it was not determined by the project. The shape of cities was deterministically transformed and engineered; however, the traditional urban society went through a more complex transformational process. The second section of this chapter explores the intense period of social transformation by addressing the Muharram rituals in Dezful. The discussion focuses on the violent period of social transformation, a passage towards integrating the Heydari and Neʿmati parts which took place in the early 1950s when the Muharram processions were rearranged in the city. The last section describes the new arrangement of processions in Dezful and articulates its social connotations. The discussions in the last two sections explain the role of Muharram rituals in ending the violent period and ritualizing the establishment of a new social organization.

This study is based on historical texts and more than forty semi-structured interviews held during 2005 and 2006. This chapter, however, refers to only a limited number of the interviews directly. The majority of interviewees who mentioned the traditional rituals before the 1950s spoke based on their experiences. Interviewees also narrated the oral history of the city and the Muharram rituals in Dezful. The aggregation of interviews depicts the landscape of the city during the last century, helping to provide an analytical reading of urban transformation and violence through the medium of the Muharram rituals.

Muharram Rituals and Traditional Iranian Urban Society

Every year, Shiʿa Muslims observe Ashura day, the 10th of Muharram,[1] as the day of the martyrdom of Husayn ibn ʿAli, the grandson of the prophet and his few companions in the late seventh century. The remembrance is held over fifty days; it begins on the first of Muharram and lasts until forty days after Ashura day, known as the day of *Arbaʿin*.[2] However, the commemoration is mainly held during the first ten days of Muharram and is particularly intensified from the 7th to the 10th of Muharram.

Shiʿa Muslims have developed various rituals throughout history to commemorate Ashura. The rituals are categorized in different ways, for example Nakash[3] categorizes the rituals into five major groups:[4] (1) the memorial service session, or *majlis*, (2) the pilgrimage to Hussain's tomb, (3) the public procession, (4) the representation of the tragedy in the form of plays, and (5) flagellation. Calmard[5] explains that the rituals originated mostly in their Arab environment in Iraq and then were highly developed in Iran, mainly during the Safavid era in the sixteenth to eighteenth centuries. In fact 'the greatest impetus for the development of the Ashura celebration as a popular religious and artistic phenomenon came with the rise of the Safavid.'[6] Calmard notes that by the time of Shah ʿAbbas I, 1587–1629, ceremonies in the month of Muharram had become a civic-religious festival in Iran and the core of socio-religious life.

The Buyid dynasty initiated the public procession as a Shiʿi ritual to commemorate Ashura in Baghdad in the tenth century.[7] During the Safavid era, the procession was developed into a complex symbolic funeral that comprised numerous sub-rituals and rites. The procession generally involved carrying symbolic coffins and bodily expressing grief over the tragedy of Ashura. Tavernier's testimony[8] about the Muharram festival in Isfahan in the seventeenth century indicates that the procession on Ashura day was an elaborate ritual and the core of the festival. The historical records of the Safavid era by Tavernier and other observers (including Chardin, Antonio de Gouvea and Della Valle)[9] show that the processions were not solely a religious practice, but also a social manifestation that reflected a concrete social reality and the tensions within Iranian urban society. According to the historical accounts, the Heydari–Neʿmati division in urban society was particularly articulated through the Muharram processions during the Safavid era.

The Heydari–Neʿmati division began with the establishment of two major Sufi schools in the fourteenth century; one school was led by Mir Heydar Tuni (d. 1427), who was a Shiʿa, and the other school was headed by Shah Neʿmatollah Vali (d. 1431), who was a Sunni.[10] Mirjafari argues that the dispute between the two schools arose particularly in Tabriz, where both Sufi orders had gained followers. The division between the Shiʿa and Sunni orders led to a political dispute when the Aq-Qoyunlu dynasty took power in some parts of Iran and supported the Neʿmatis during the second half of the fifteenth century. By the rise of the Safavids, who proclaimed Shiʿa as the state religion in the early sixteenth century, the Sunni leaders had lost their power. Under the Safavids, Iranians mostly became Shiʿa; moreover, successors of Shah Neʿmatollah Vali, who had a good relationship with the Safavids, converted to Shiʿa Islam. In such a context, Heydari–Neʿmati was no longer a religious division, but now a social division.[11]

An Italian traveller who visited Tabriz, the early Safavid capital, reported the Heydari–Neʿmati division as a social constitution during the Safavid era as early as 1571.[12] Chardin,[13] who visited the capital city of Isfahan in the 1670s, describes the city as divided into Jubareh-Neʿmatollahi in the west and Dardasht-Heydari in the east. Chardin explains that the tension between the two parts increased during Muharram.

The Heydari–Neʿmati division was well established as the social structure of Iranian cities during the Qajar era because of the traditional local ruling system, which was tied to urban landlordism. All Iranian cities, even medium-sized and small cities, were usually governed based on several boroughs run by landlord families that teamed up as Heydari and Neʿmati. Lambton[14] explains that the landowning classes, including landlords and landholders, were the most powerful element in Iranian society during the Qajar era (1781–1925). Traditionally, holding or owning land was not a right, but a privilege granted by the shah (king). 'Although lands could be sold, inherited and bestowed upon others, the security of property only came from the shah's recognition of somebody's claim to a piece of land.'[15] In such a context, there was always competition between local governors and influential figures to receive the privilege of owning or holding lands as the source of power. Landlord families also disputed over sources of water. In this context, Perry[16] describes the Heydari and Neʿmati as two 'moieties' (halves) that were like two parties in a democratic system and that competed with each other for greater power. This competition divided the city boroughs into two equal parts, Heydari and Neʿmati moieties. The competition between local ruling families who were the main patrons and sponsors of the commemoration of Ashura was reflected in the Muharram rituals.

The social implication of the Muharram processions was the main subject in the narrations of interviewees who described the ritual in Dezful during the late Qajar and the early Pahlavi eras (1920s to 1930s). The interviewees explained that the processions ran throughout the commemoration period, but were mostly carried out between the 7th and 10th of Muharram and on the day of *Arbaʾin* (the 20th of Safar). The processions have always been organized by *hayʾats* (unions) – also known as *dastehs* (groups) – that are fundamentally associated with *mahallat* (quarters). The unions carried the processions towards the homes of landlords who were the main patrons of the rituals, under whose influence the unions stood. This was a symbolic visitation; the unions showed their affiliation with the landlords who symbolically gave donations to the unions on these occasions. The quarters also carried processions towards neighbouring quarters with which they held social intimacy. Obviously, the main procession was (and is) on the day of Ashura, which was a symbolic funeral procession to a cemetery. The processions generally involved the carrying of various symbolic coffins and flags; participants in the procession commonly perform chest-beating (*sineh-zani*) to express their grief over the tragedy of Ashura.

Mahalleh, or quarter, can be defined as the settlement of an independent social group that is socially and spatially bounded. The traditional quarter has its own public places such as a mosque, shops, public bath and school. However, such an idealistic definition does not reflect the reality. Throughout my fieldwork in seven historic cities I came across many old quarters that do not have most of these community places. The procession appears to be a ritual by which a quarter practises its social solidarity, distinguishing itself from others, as each quarter organizes its own Muharram procession independently. In other words, the procession manifests the idea of the quarter. For example, the small quarter of Fuladiyun in Dezful does not have its own shopping place; nevertheless, it is identified as a quarter by having its own *hayʾat* and procession (based

Figure 4.1. A public procession at a cemetery in Dezful on the day of Ashura. The photograph is dated 1931. From the collection of the Saba Photo Studio, Dezful; copyright unknown.

on interviews in 2005 with Mr Hantush and Mr Karami in Dezful). To find out to which quarter a neighbourhood belongs, it is enough to see which *hay'at* the habitants of the neighbourhood join for the procession. For instance, I asked H.M. Amir-Gholami whether his neighbourhood was traditionally a part of the Siahpushan Quarter. Describing the ritual before the modern transformation, Mr Amir-Gholami (born 1921) said: 'We did not run our procession with Siahpushan Quarter; we had our own *hay'at* and procession in Kornasiyun' (February 2006, Dezful). This statement simply explains that he was in a neighbourhood affiliated with the Kornasiyun Quarter, which has a separate social identity from the Siahpushan Quarter.

As described, in this context the procession appears as the means by which people practise their social solidarity, affiliation and intimacy. Notably, the solidarity of neighbourhoods as a quarter was not a static relationship and could change for socio-economic reasons; such a change would be directly reflected in the Muharram processions. For example, Haj Eydi Masoudi (b. 1926) mentioned:

> We were [living] in the quarter of Luriyun and the quarters around were Sobbiyun, Kenar-e Ab [riverside], Gavmayshiyun, Sarmidun and

Sarmidun-e kochok [the small Sarmidun]. Each of them was really a limited [small] quarter. However, all of these quarters were integrated later in about the 1950s as Motahede-ye Hoseyni [United Hoseyni]. This integration was represented mainly in the procession. (September 2005, Dezful)

The procession routes were a spatial medium to practise urban social organization, and thus addressed the fact that Iranian city quarters were historically divided between Heydari and Neʿmati. During the late Qajar era (the early twentieth century), Dezful was internally governed based on six boroughs, including Siahposhan, Heydar-khuneh, Mahalleh-ye Masjed, Qaleh and eastern and western Sahrabedar (figure 4.2). The first two boroughs were bonded as Heydari and local governors of other boroughs were allied as Neʿmati. Dezful was not alone in this; for example the city of Ardabil, in the north-west of the country, historically had six major *mahalleh*s, grouped into three Heydari and three Neʿmati. In this context, the processions were carried through each part of the city separately. This reflects the fact that Iranian urban society was not traditionally an integrated social system; rather it was structured in two parts.

Some of the boroughs in Dezful, such as Siahpushan, include only one quarter; however a borough like Masjed comprises several quarters. As already mentioned, I use 'quarter' to refer to a community that is socially and spatially concreted. However, here, 'borough' refers to an area of the city that was under one local governor. The borough can be considered the smallest polity in the traditional Iranian city. It is the equivalent of the parish, the smallest unit of local government in traditional English cities. Therefore quarter has a social connotation whereas borough is a political unit. Although I use two different English terms, quarter and borough, both are called *mahalleh* in Farsi. In fact, throughout more than forty interviews in Dezful, interviewees used *mahalleh* with four different meanings: they used it as 'the place', usually the centre of a quarter; it can also mean 'neighbourhood'; additionally, it refers to the larger area in the city that can be called a 'borough'; nevertheless, it mainly refers to 'quarter', which is usually bigger than a neighbourhood and smaller than a borough.

The processions of each quarter were run within the area (Heydari/Neʿmati) that the quarter was associated with. Nevertheless, tension and violence between quarters have always occurred at the rituals. Fights would break out whenever the processions crossed at a junction or over who has priority to pass along a thoroughfare. Interviewees commonly blamed local governors (landlords) for the violence in Dezful during Muharram. They mostly commented that landlord families took Mu-

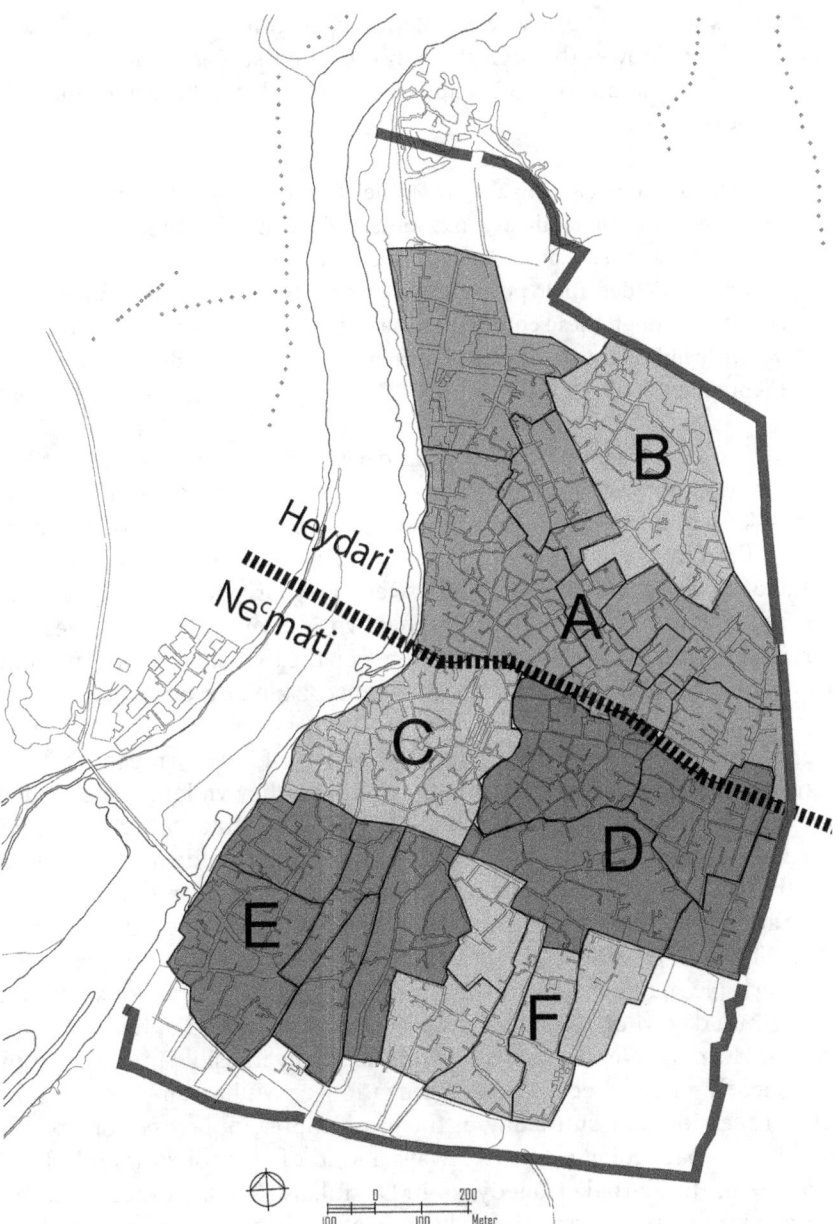

Figure 4.2. The traditional boroughs and the Heydari–Neʿmati division in Dezful (1920s): (A) Heydar-Khuneh, (B) Siahpushan, (C) Qaleeh, (D) Mahalleh-ye Masjed, (E) western Sahrabedar and (F) eastern Sahrabedar. The borders between quarters are highlighted. The map is constructed based on information aggregated from interviews.

harram as an opportunity to challenge each other and to wield their socio-political power through the hands of their subjects and gangs. For example, E. Masoudi (b. 1926) spoke of the violence between quarters in the Heydari area:

> Each landlord had a gang and when they had a dispute [over an estate or a source of water], their gangs fomented a conflict between people with some simple excuse during Ashura ceremonies. It was the way that they wielded their power through society and controlled urban society. Through these conflicts in the Ashura ritual, people broke the ʿalam [symbolic flag] of other quarters and tore their drums apart. (September 2005, Dezful)

The tension between quarters within each part (Heydari or Neʿmati) of the city was not usually too serious. However the crossing of the Heydari–Neʿmati border by a procession was seen as an attack or humiliation; it therefore caused serious violence. The oral history of Iranian cities is full of stories about the conflict between Heydari and Neʿmati quarters during Muharram. Throughout my fieldwork in other Iranian cities, interviewees spoke of serious tension between the two moieties in cities like Hamadan, Ardabil and Bushehr. Mr Ahmad-zadeh described the crossing of the Heydari–Neʿmati border by a procession in Dezful: 'Carrying a procession by a *hayʾat* through the other part of the city meant that the *hayʾat* was going to make trouble for them. So they violently challenged the *hayʾat* of strangers' (September 2005, Tehran). In another interview, Mr Habashi (b. 1928), from a Neʿmati quarter, narrated: 'My father told me that we went to Heydar-Khuneh to run a procession and they strewed dust and poured hot water from the roofs on us ... it was back in the pre-Reza Shah era [1925–41]' (September 2005, Dezful). The crossing of the Heydari–Neʿmati border was usually done by minor processions, but not on Ashura day when the major processions were carried out.

The Heydari–Neʿmati division was physically invisible in the city, but was clearly manifested in the organization of Muharram processions. The procession on Ashura day, as the most important procession, exhibited this in particular, and was always a kind of symbolic funeral of the martyrs of the Karbala tragedy; so in Dezful, as in many other cities, all processions were directed towards a cemetery. However, the processions of the Heydari and Neʿmati quarters proceeded to different cemeteries. Heydari quarters ran their Ashura procession to a cemetery associated with and named after the shrine of Rud-band in the north of the city. The processions in the Neʿmati part, however, centred on the Bul-Ala shrine and cemetery[17] in the south-east part of the city (figure 4.3).

Transformation of Iranian Urban Society 99

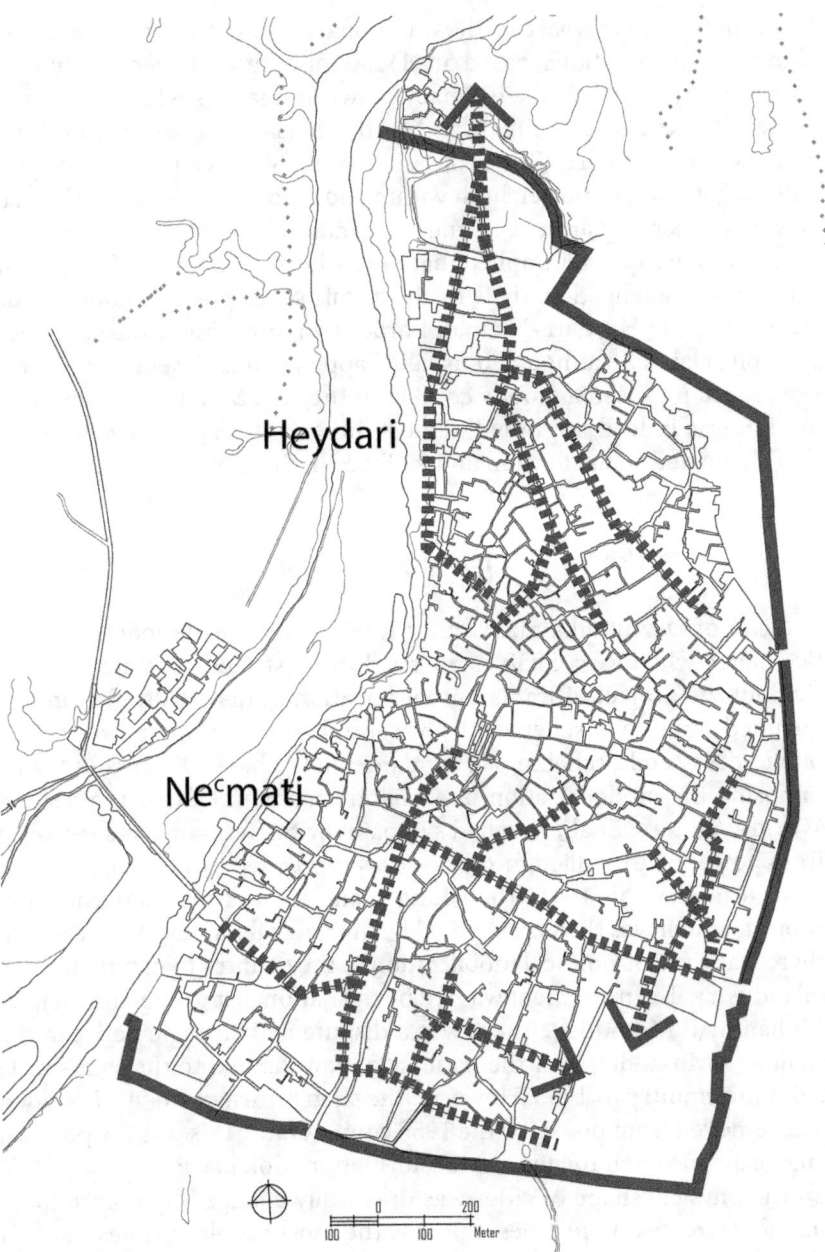

Figure 4.3. The traditional division of the Ashura procession and the major procession routes in Dezful.

These discussions reveal that the traditional processions were a manifestation of social relations, based on (1) the solidarity between neighbourhoods as a quarter, (2) the intimacy between quarters within each part of the city, Heydari or Neʿmati, and (3) the division of quarters into Heydari and Neʿmati parts. The processions were always a part of the symbolic negotiation of power, both within and across the Heydari–Neʿmati border. As each quarter was under a landlord family, challenging the procession of a quarter implied that the authority of that landlord family was being challenged by their rivals. In this socio-political context, the crossing of the Heydari–Neʿmati border by a procession was a serious symbolic claim. So although it usually happened during a minor procession, it often caused a bloody conflict in the city. Muharram commemoration was indeed not only the most important religious event, but it also channeled social tension and violence in the city.

The Violent Passage of Urban Society

The city of Dezful, like many other Iranian cities, experienced a drastic change when Reza Shah established the first modern state and carried out the project of Iranian modernization in the 1920s. The project included numerous schemes, from centralizing political power to the public dress code scheme. He fundamentally changed the country by imposing the modernization in a military manner. During the Second World War, Reza Shah, who had sympathy with Germany, was removed from power by the Allied forces and was succeeded by his son, Mohammad Reza Shah, in 1941. The young shah followed the modernization project, which was then accelerated by the new oil money. After the war, there was a major political mobilization in the country to nationalize the oil industry. The movement was led by the nationalist prime minister, Dr Mohammad Mosaddeq. There was a dispute and struggle between the shah and Mosaddeq over the nationalization that led to the shah's exile from the country in 1953. However, the shah returned when Mosaddeq was removed from power by the 1953 coup d'état.[18] This was the political landscape in which the urban transformation took place.

The physical shape of cities was drastically changed by superimposing new streets on old cities; this was the most visible manifestation of the new modern state. The urban shape was directly engineered and restructured, however the traditional urban society was not changed by plan, but transmuted through a complex process over time. The urban society, based on Heydari and Neʿmati moieties, was transformed into an integrated social system. The new social constitution in Dezful was recognized in the early 1950s and signified by rearrangement of the Muharram procession routes. The new spatial orchestration of processions aimed at representing the end of social division and commemorating the integrity of all quarters. This transformation was not a smooth process, but occurred through a violent transitional period during the late 1940s and early 1950s, so most of the interviewees were able to describe this period based on their personal experiences.

A social movement against landlords arose during the late 1940s and early 1950s in Dezful. The movement sought to transform the traditional social order, since urban society was no longer under the control of landlords. Interviewees explained that Reza Shah aimed at centralizing the political system and abolished the local ruling system associated with landlord families. When the Allied forces removed Reza Shah from power in 1941, the Allied troops, which had a military base in Dezful, also diminished the landlords' influence in the city.

Mr A. Shiravi (b. 1926) explained that the modern state offered a new alternative for landlords at political and financial levels. Politically, the modern institutions governed the city; from a financial perspective, the new state became the major employer in the city. Shiravi noted, 'large numbers of projects were carried out by the state, such as construction of roads, silos and military bases; all of these needed workers' (February 2006, Dezful). He explained that it was an entirely new landscape in the urban economy, especially for working-class people.

Reza Shah's reign was ended by the invasion of Iran by the Allied troops that had a military base in Dezful; they became a new employer in the city, at least for a while. Mr Ahmad-zadeh talked about the effect of the Allied troops in Dezful:

> The Allied troops in 1941 were one of the first things that changed the traditional city; people were working for them and used their facilities to make better conditions for the city. People became familiar with other cultures because of the Allied troops ... including Indians, Russians and Americans. Moreover, the Allies became an employer in the city, which decreased the landlords' domination. (September 2005, Tehran)

In this context, people sought to transform the traditional social order in Dezful. In contrast with the modernization as an imposed process, this was a bottom-up movement. Unsurprisingly, people started challenging the power of landlords during Muharram rituals. For example, H.E. Masoudi (b. 1926) narrated an event during the 1940s about carrying the *nakhl* of their quarter. A *nakhl* is a wooden structure that symbolizes the coffin of Husayn in Karbala, which is carried through the processions. He narrated:

> Sheykh-Reza's *nakhl* belonged to [the *hay'at* of] Sarmidun ... When I was young and about 17–18 years old, we [some young friends and I] were opposed to carrying the *nakhl* when the landlord's son was sitting on it, because he was humiliating people when they were carrying the *nakhl*; so we pulled him down and demolished this custom and later a young clergyman sat there and read the holy Quran when people were carrying the *nakhl*. (September 2005, Dezful)

It is worth noting that the Muharram rituals were one medium by which the landlord families wielded their authority over quarters. For example, interviewees mentioned that no *nakhl* or *'alam* (symbolic flag) would be taken into the processions without the permission of the quarter's landlord. The Muharram rituals thus became an opportunity to challenge landlord authority in the city.

The movement against landlords in Dezful escalated when Dr Mosaddeq became prime minister and carried out the first land reform in Iran (1952),[19] and nationalized the oil industry. Mr Arab (interviewed in September 2005, Dezful) explained that during that time a large number of political parties were established in Dezful. However, the new political parties were initiated and functioned based mainly on local issues and concerns. The Labour Party (*Hezb-e Zahmatkeshan*) led the movement against landlords in Dezful. Mr Ahmad-zadeh stated, 'people were looking for someone to lead them against landlords, to end the feudal system in the city ... people did not care about the national policy of the [Labour] party, their favour was to challenge landlords in quarters' (September 2005, Tehran). Mr Arab made a rather interesting statement about the political parties in the city in this period:

> Political parties were established in Dezful like other cities, but they followed local issues and did not care about real political aims of the parties. Dr Gosheh-Gir led *Hezb-e Zahmatkeshan* [Labour Party] in western Sahrabedar [in Dezful]; and our quarter [eastern Sahrabedar] established *Jebhe-ye Melli* [National Front]; these two parties were in fact on the same political side, but in the city they opposed each other; people just followed landlords or local leaders [of the Labour Party]. (September 2005, Dezful)

As Mr Arab stated, at a national level the two parties were allied and supported the nationalization of the oil industry, which was mainly led by Mosaddeq, the leader of the *Jebhey-e Melli* (National Front).[20] However, in Dezful the two parties opposed each other, as they followed local issues. The interesting point is that only a few interviewees in Dezful were aware of the role of the National Front in Dezful. Although the National Front and Labour Party led the urban tension in Dezful, the situation is better illustrated as it is narrated in the oral history of the city, in which people usually talk about 'the Party of Landlords' and 'Labour Party'.

In this situation, the city was mainly divided into quarters that supported or challenged the landlords (*khans*). As Mr S.T. Ashrafi-zadeh (interviewed in February 2006, Dezful) stated, the city was divided between the khans' party and the Labour Party. Ashrafi-zadeh (b. 1932) narrated that those who supported the landlords were called *Hetun*, which means 'liars' in local slang. In response, those who supported the Labour Party were called *Baqun*, after the name of Dr Bagha'i, the leader of the Labour Party. *Baqun* means 'frogs' in the local dialect of Dezful. Ashrafi-zadeh explained that when Mosaddeq took power, tension escalated in the city. The movement against landlords turned into an ugly and bloody conflict between quarters in 1953, when Mohammad Reza Shah was exiled during the nationalization of the oil industry.

All quarters in the borough of eastern Sahrabedar, in the Neʿmati part, supported the landlords; other quarters challenged landlords. The main reason that eastern Sahrabedar supported the landlords was that the Qutb family had a well-established socio-economic power base in this borough. This family was the most influential landlord family at the time in the city. Interviewees mostly narrated the situation based on the division of the city into Sahrabedar (eastern and western) and other quarters. However, the borough of western Sahrabedar did not actually support the landlords. Interestingly, many interviewees from Heydari quarters even simplified the story as the conflict between Heydari and Neʿmati in Dezful (figure 4.2).

The early 1950s have a negative image because of the bloody violence between quarters in Dezful. However, this period is also seen as a transitional period in which urban society attempted to abolish the traditional domination by landlords. Mr Ahmad-zadeh said:

> Because of the movement between 1950 and 1953, people joined together to challenge landlords; so many local disagreements and conflicts were conciliated. [Traditionally] the conflict between quarters was serious, [so] that some of the quarters were walled and people did not pass through other quarters. They were just passing on the main city road; if they passed on a local road, they were in trouble. (September 2005, Tehran)

He also stated:

> Although the Land Reform [of the 1960s] released villages from landlord authority in Iran, in Dezful they had already lost their power between 1950 and 1953 ... they have never recovered their power ... after 1953, they have not been influential in the city anymore. In other words, the landlords' power was demolished in Dezful one decade sooner than in the other parts of Iran. (September 2005, Tehran)

Interviewees have narrated the ending of the violence in the 1950s in different stories and accounts; however all the stories have pointed out that the violence ended during Muharram. For example, one of the stories narrates that the *hayʾat* of Qupi Agha-Hoseyni in the Heydari part, led by Ayatollah Faregh, a well-respected clergyman, visited an evening service session in the quarter of Shahrokn al-Din in the Neʿmati part. The quarter of Shahrokn al-Din was the residence of the Qutb family. In exchange, the *hayʾat* of Shahrokn al-Din visited the Heydari part the day after. These visitations during Muharram ended the violence and tension between quarters. The next year, the heads of the *hayʾats* of all quarters decided to celebrate the reconciliation and friendship between quarters by symbolically exchanging visits throughout the Muharram processions.

The Rite of Urban Passage

The abolishing of traditional landlord domination implied the end of the Heydari–Neʿmati division in the city. The Muharram rituals still represented social realities; so new procession schedules and routes were initiated in Dezful, aimed at signifying the end of violence and traditional division in the city. Although the 1950s violence was not actually between Heydari and Neʿmati quarters, for people the end of the landlord era inevitably meant the end of urban division and the integration of all quarters of the city.

The Muharram procession routes were re-organized to celebrate the integration and intimacy between Heydari and Neʿmati quarters in the early 1950s. The processions were reorganized based on three episodes or sessions (figure 4.4). The first session is the afternoon of the 9th of Muharram (the day of Tasuʿa), when all Neʿmati quarters run their processions through the Heydari part of the city. The second episode is the morning of the day of Ashura, when all city quarters carry out the Ashura procession together to the cemetery and shrine of Rud-band in the north of the city (figure 4.5). The second episode symbolically represents the new integrity of all quarters. Finally, Heydari quarters carry out their processions through the Neʿmati part on the afternoon of Ashura day.

The establishment of the new processions has three significant implications. The first is related to the ritualization of the integration of the Heydari and Neʿmati quarters. Borrowing Van Gennep's idea,[21] the process of transformation of urban society can be explained as follows. The traditional urban society in Dezful was exposed to modernization during the 1930s and 1940s. It was then in a liminal stage during the late 1940s and early 1950s, when the traditional social organization was in transition during a violent period. Finally, urban society established new social relationships through the post-liminal, or incorporation, stage by the early 1950s, when the new procession schedule was established. This process from the traditional urban society to the integrated or transformed urban society can be described as a process from structure to anti-structure and back to structure, in Turner's terms (1969)[22].

In fact, the changing of the spatial organization of processions is a rite itself. I would like to call it 'the rite of urban passage' by which not only the violence stopped, but also urban society ritually established new social relationships. According to the idea proposed by van Gennep and Turner, the commemoration of Ashura is a cyclical ritual that is carried out in a liminal status, which is a reversible state, every year. However, what is called the 'rite of urban passage', here, is a post-liminal rite by which society transits from one state to another irreversibly. The rite of urban passage ritually ends violence and signifies that the traditionally divided urban society has transitioned into an integrated society.

The second implication is that the new processions represent the integration of the social moieties. This is particularly exhibited by the procession on the morning of the day of Ashura, which is staged by all quarters together. The new procession format is based on the same general logic as the traditional procession: both arranged in order to practise social organization. The traditional processions were a vehicle to practise the Heydari–Neʿmati division; however, the transformed ritual is constituted to practise social integration.

The third implication involves processions on Tasuʿa afternoon and Ashura afternoon. All Neʿmati quarters carry their procession throughout the territory of the Heydaris on Tasuʿa; then Heydari quarters ritualistically visit the Neʿmati part of the city on Ashura afternoon. These two sessions symbolically represent that the city is no longer divided into two territories. However, as each of these sessions is dedicated to only one of the moieties, the schedule also implies and preserves the idea

106 Reza Masoudi Nejad

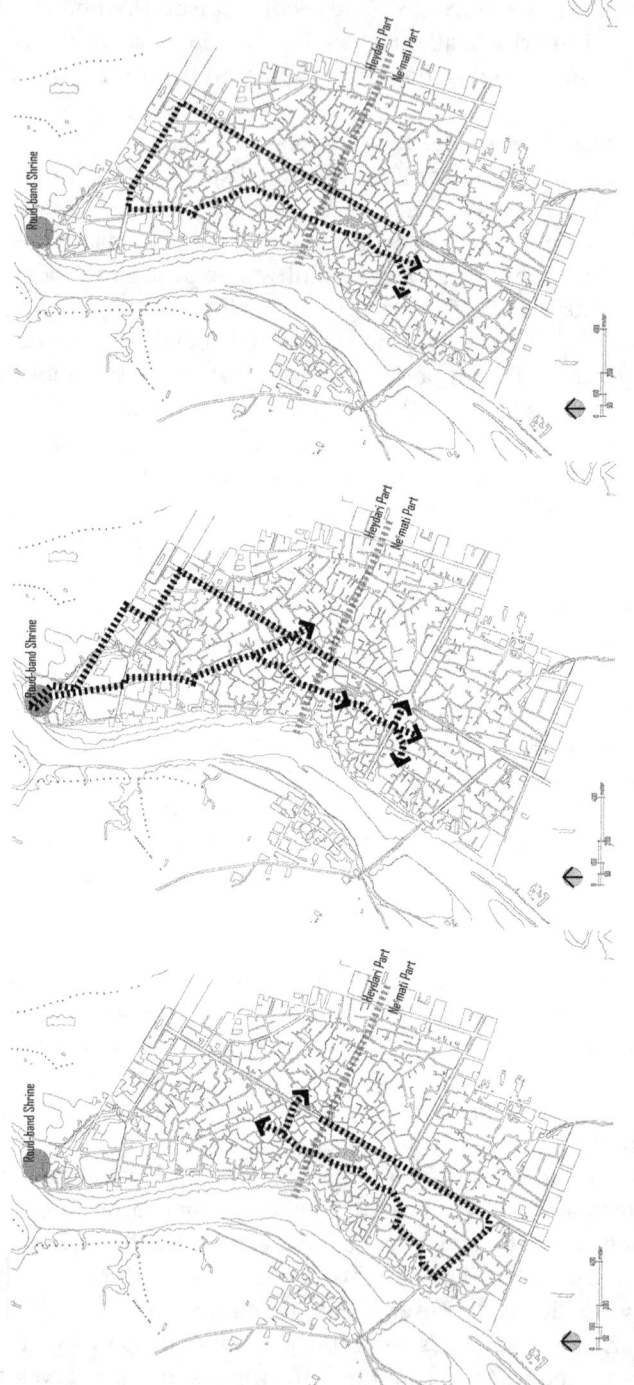

Figure 4.4. The main routes of processions in Dezful since the 1950s: the procession of Tasuʿa afternoon (left), Ashura morning (middle) and Ashura afternoon (right).

Figure 4.5. The procession of Ashura morning, when all city quarters run their processions to Rud-band Shrine. Dezful, 2006.

of division. On the one hand, the processions are scheduled to practise social integrity, but on the other, they maintain the idea of traditional division.

After more than half a century, the Muharram processions are still organized based on the 1950s schedule. Although many people nowadays know nothing about the traditional division, the ritual schedule acknowledges the loyalty of their quarter to Heydari or Neʿmati moieties, as the Neʿmati quarters run their processions on the afternoon of Tasuʿa and the Heydari quarters on the afternoon of Ashura. Consequently, large numbers of new *hayʾat*s based on modern residential areas stage their processions following a schedule that is organized according to the identification of quarters as Heydari or Neʿmati. The hypothetical border between the Heydari and Neʿmati quarters is thus extended through the modern city to divide all new *hayʾat*s as Heydari or Neʿmati (figure 4.6). However, some of the new *hayʾat*s are categorized by their founder's social affiliation with an old Heydari or Neʿmati quarter. This means that the new procession schedule transmits the idea of traditional division of quarters into both the present and the future.

On the one hand, the Muharram rituals channel and stimulate tension among different segments of society, but on the other hand the rituals also appear as a mechanism to control violence and urban unrest. The reorganized processions are aimed at practising the modern reality of urban society in Dezful; however, the orchestration of processions simultaneously keeps alive the idea of traditional urban division. The processions manifest a discursive relationship not only between past

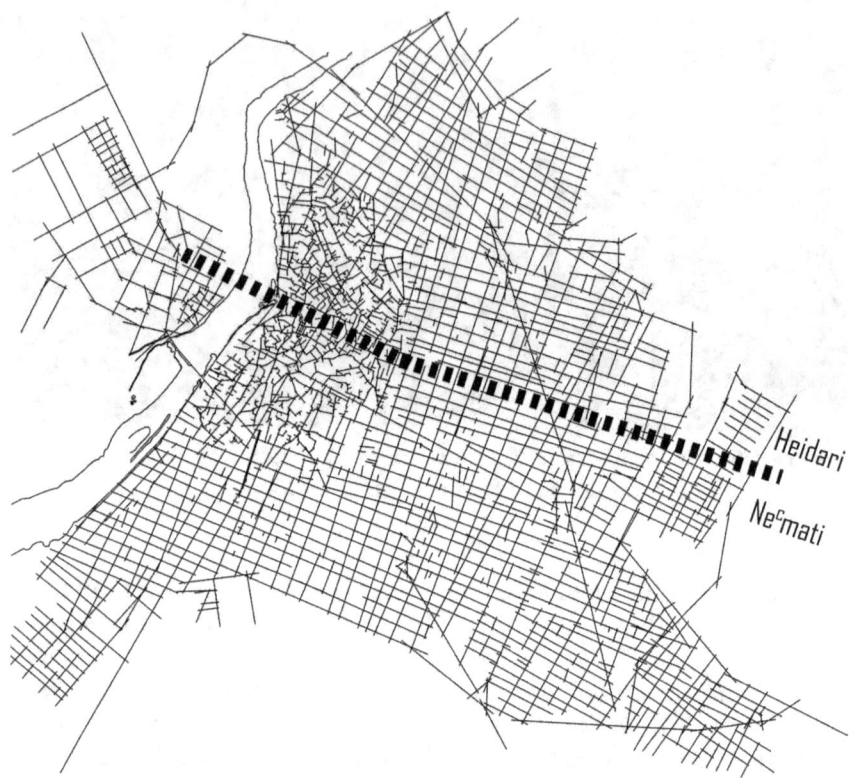

Figure 4.6. Extending the border between Heydari and Ne'mati quarters through the modern city. Dezful, 1990s.

and present, but also between violence and peace; these do not address dichotomist statuses, but are intrinsically entwined as part of a process.

Notes

1. Muharram is the first month in the Islamic lunar calendar.
2. *Arba'in* is an Arabic term, meaning 40th; it is the 20th of Safar, the second month of the Islamic calendar.
3. Y. Nakash. 1993. 'An Attempt to Trace the Origin of the Rituals of 'Ashura", *Die Welt des Islams* 33(2), 163.
4. Also see C.E. Bosworth, C. Hillenbrand and L.P. Elwell-Sutton (eds). 1983. *Qajar Iran: Political, Social and Cultural Change, 1800–1925.* Edinburgh: Edinburgh University Press; J. Calmard. 1996. 'The Consolidation of Safavid Shi'ism: Folklore and Popular Religion', in C. Melville (ed.), *Safavid Persia: The History and Politics of an Islamic Society,* London: I.B. Tauris,

139–90; A.J. Hussain. 2005. 'The Mourning of History and the History of Mourning: The Evolution of Ritual Commemoration of the Battle of Karbala', *Comparative Studies of South Asia, Africa and the Middle East* 25(1), 78–88.
5. Calmard, 'The Consolidation of Safavid Shi'ism'.
6. M. Ayoub. 1987. 'Ashura', in E. Yarshater (ed.), *Encyclopaedia Iranica, Vol. II*, London and Boston: Routledge & K. Paul, 875.
7. A. Faqihi. 1978. *Al-e Buyeh Va Awzaʿ-e Zaman-e Ishan: Ba Nimudar-e az Zendegi-ye Mardom dar an ʿasr* [Buyids and the Condition of Their Era], Tehran: Entesharat-e Saba; M.M. Mazzaoui. 1979. 'Shiʿism and Ashura in South Lebanon', in P. Chelkowski (ed.), *Taʾziyeh, Ritual and Drama in Iran*, New York: New York University Press, 228–37.
8. J.B.Tavernier. 1684. *Collections of Travels Through Turkey into Persia, and the East-Indies, Giving an Account of the Present State of Those Countries: Being the Travels of Monsieur Tavernier, Bernier, and Other Great Men: Adorned with Many Copper Plates*, London: Moses Pitt, 161. Tavernier's travelogue was published in Persian in 1957. The oldest English copy that I have examined was published during 1684–1688; it is kept in the SOAS library archive.
9. In French, see: J. Chardin. 1671. *Le Couronnement De Soleïmaan Troisième Roy de Perse, et ce qui s'est Passé de plus Memorable dans les Deux Premières Années de son Regne*, Paris: Barbin – with a translation in Farsi: J. Chardin. 1993. *Safarnameh-ye Shardan: Matn-e Kamel*, Tehran: Tus. For the narrations of A. de Gouvea and Della Valle in English, see B. Rahimi. 2004. *Between Carnival and Mourning: The Muharram Rituals and the Emergence of the Early Modern Iranian Public Sphere in the Safavi Period, 1590–1641 C.E.*, Florence: European University Institute, 177–81; and in Farsi, see N. Falsafi. 1985. *Zendegani-ye Shah ʿAbbas Avval*, Tehran: ʿIlmi, 584–87 and 848–54.
10. J.R. Perry. 1999. 'Toward a Theory of Iranian Urban Moieties: The Haydariyyah and Niʿmatiyyah Revisited', *Iranian Studies* 32(1), 51–70; W.M. Floor. 1987. *Justarhaʾi az Tarikh-e Ejtemaʿi-ye Iran dar ʿAsr-e Qajar* [The Inquests of Social History of Iran in Qajar Era], trans. Abu 'l-Qasim Sirri, Tehran: Tus; and H. Mirjafari. 1984. 'Heydari va Neʿmati', *Ayandeh* (9), 741–54.
11. See H. Mirjafari. 1979. 'The Haydari–Niʿmati Conflicts in Iran', trans. John R. Perry, *Iranian Studies* (12), 141; Mirjafari, 'Heydari va Neʿmati', 746.
12. G. Barbaro et al. 2010. 'Narrative Most Noble Vincentio d'Alessandri', in *Travels to Tana and Persia, and A Narrative of Italian Travels in Persia in the 15th and 16th Centuries*, Cambridge: Cambridge University Press, 224.
13. Chardin, *Le Couronnement de Soleïmaan Troisième Roy de Perse*.
14. A. K. S. Lambton. 1953. *Landlord and Peasant in Persia: A Study of Land Tenure and Land Revenue Administration*, London, New York, Toronto: Oxford University Press.
15. W.M. Floor. 1998. *A Fiscal History of Iran in the Safavid and Qajar Periods, 1500–1925*, New York: Bibliotheca Persica Press, 125.

16. Perry, 'Toward a Theory of Iranian Urban Moieties'.
17. Bul-ᶜAla is the local pronunciation of Abu-ᶜAla.
18. See A. Banani and E. Abrahamian (eds). 1978. *State and Society in Iran*, Chestnut Hill, MA: Society for Iranian Studies; H. Katouzian. 2003. *Iranian History and Politics: The Dialectic of State and Society*, London: Routledge Curzon; S.M. Cronin (ed.). 2003. *The Making of Modern Iran: State and Society under Riza Shah (1921–1941)*, New York and London: Routledge Curzon.
19. As a social-nationalist leader, Mosaddeq had issued a Land Reform Act in August 1952; this was one of the first land reforms in the Middle East. The act forced landlords to turn over 20 per cent of the land revenue to their tenants. For more, see, I. Pappé. 2005. *The Modern Middle East*, London: Routledge; F.E. Moghadam. 1996. *From Land Reform to Revolution: The Political Economy of Agricultural Development in Iran 1962–1979*, London: I.B. Tauris.
20. Although the two parties were allied during the nationalization of the oil industry, disagreements later arose between them at the national level.
21. A. van Gennep. 1960. *The Rites of Passage*, London: Routledge & K. Paul.
22. Turner, V. 1969. *The Ritual Process: Structure and Anti-Structure*. London: Routledge & K. Paul.

❧· Chapter 5 ·❧

Symbolic Politics and Urban Violence in Late Ottoman Jeddah

ULRIKE FREITAG

This chapter focuses on one well-studied incident of urban violence, the attack on and the public and very cruel killing of twenty-two people in Jeddah in 1858. The event gained international prominence not only because it occurred in a major Red Sea port, Jeddah, but also because it was directed against the representatives of Western powers. Among the victims were the British vice-consul, the French consul with his wife and a good number of the resident Christian community of Turkish and Russian nationality.[1] In consequence, when the Ottoman authorities seemed slow to react, the British proceeded to shell the town, inflicting severe punishment upon the people of Jeddah and causing a number of fatalities. This was followed by several rounds of investigations and the eventual arrest, execution and exile of some of the instigators and perpetrators of the initial attack.

The contemporary Western sources called this episode variously a 'massacre', 'revolt', or 'uprising', and contemporary and later Arabic ones called it '*fitna*', '*ghazu*' or '*tadakhkhul*'. These terms refer to varying sequels of events before and after the actual attack on the foreigners. William Ochsenwald and recently Philippe Pétriat have studied the events in great detail.[2] While Ochsenwald's study is the first scholarly discussion of the Jeddah massacre, Pétriat is mainly interested in the role of the Hadhrami merchants who were singled out by the European powers as the main culprits. He argues that they were part of an urban merchant class whose interests collided with the competing merchant interests of Europeans and their protégés. Thus, he moves the argument away from religious fanaticism to one about changing international economic and political relations.

The dimension which this chapter proposes to add to this literature is the consideration of the spaces in which the violence took place and a discussion of the various uses made of these spaces by the different actors involved. I will not discuss the question of the legitimacy or lack thereof of the different types of violence exercised by those involved, who included urban notables, an urban crowd, representatives of different levels within the Ottoman administration in the Hijaz and Istanbul, the captain of a British man-of-war, and the British and French governments – this list reflects the very different scales on which one can consider the events. Rather, I foreground the spatial aspects of this violence within the city of Jeddah, as far as this can be ascertained from the (mainly foreign) sources. The findings will be set in the context of other uses of urban space in Jeddah, as well as that of a number of other violent incidents within Jeddah. I will also consider the different moral frameworks in which the relevant actions were grounded or with which they were justified.

Mid-Nineteenth-Century Jeddah: A Small Port City in a Changing Environment

Situated in the Ottoman province of the Hijaz, Jeddah was a smallish city of some fifteen to twenty thousand inhabitants.[3] It derived its importance from its dual function as, firstly, the port of Mecca and thus the port where most Muslim pilgrims disembarked during their journey to the holy cities of Islam, and secondly as a port in the Red Sea trade. For much of the seventeenth and eighteenth centuries, Jeddah had been a statutory entrepôt in the trade between the Indian Ocean and Egypt.[4] It only slowly lost this function in the first half of the nineteenth century. As long as sailing was the only means of transport, trade and pilgrimage followed distinct seasonal patterns, which often enough forced pilgrims and merchants to spend quite some time in the Hijaz.[5]

After steamships were introduced in the Red Sea in 1837, Jeddah became a coaling station in 1860. Steamships operated independently of the monsoon and, after 1869, the opening of the Suez Canal invigorated trade and thus prompted a commercial expansion which came to an end only in the 1880s.[6] It seems that the commercial expansion of the early and mid nineteenth century prompted a great number of merchants to establish themselves in Jeddah. This might have been eased by a certain change in the elites: sources report the exodus of many of the city's merchants after the first Wahhabi raids on the Hijaz, which never entered but often threatened and repeatedly besieged the city between 1803 and

1813, and the upheavals linked to the Egyptian expedition to the Hijaz.[7] Although details are difficult to establish due to the absence of records, the leading Maghrebinian merchants, for example, who are regularly mentioned in early travel reports as being almost as wealthy as their Indian and Egyptian colleagues, fade into oblivion, whereas the presence of Indian, Persian and Hadhrami merchants seems to have become more prominent around the middle of the nineteenth century.[8] Examples of families whose rise or arrival can be linked to the first part of the nineteenth century are Ba 'Ishn (Hadhramawt), Zahid and 'Ali Rida (Persia).[9] At the same time, it is reported that the Indian merchant Faraj Yusr, who was among the intended victims of the 1858 attacks, was for some period the *shaykh al-tujjar* and the largest lender to the Ottoman authorities, who, without his financial support, would have lost control of parts of the Hijaz.[10]

Jeddah, which the Ottomans had recovered from Muhammad 'Ali of Egypt in 1840, served until the 1860s as the official seat of the Ottoman governor of the province of the Hijaz (until 1864 called *Habeş eyalet* because of the inclusion of coastal regions of Eritrea and Ethiopia). This province included the holy cities of Mecca and Medina. Since the eighteenth century, the governors (*walis*) had their seat in Jeddah until it was officially moved to Mecca in the latter part of the nineteenth century. However, the governors often moved between Jeddah and Mecca, not least to keep an eye on their local rivals, the Sharifs of Mecca.[11] These claimed descent from the Prophet and had ruled the Hijaz for centuries under various overlords. They continued to hold some degree of power under the Ottomans under a tenuous and frequently contested agreement about sharing revenue (notably the Jeddah customs) and power. While it is not clear when exactly the seat of the *wali* was officially moved from Jeddah to Mecca, *walis* tended to spend more time in Mecca during times of tension in order to control the Sharifs.[12] On the local level, a *qa'immaqam* or local governor represented the governor at the level of the next lower unit, the *sanjaq*, which was not limited to the city but included some adjacent villages. Ottoman power in Jeddah was mostly embodied by a small garrison (more troops were stationed in Mecca and Medina) and a basic administration comprising a director of finance and customs as well as a number of officials, such as the judge and the *muhtasib* (described in the European sources mostly as chief of police), who was second in command after the *qa'immaqam*.[13]

The local population was organised in guilds, the most powerful of which was presumably that of the merchants. Their head makes an appearance as the shaykh of the merchants in the events of 1858. Each quarter had its own representative. Although details remain hazy and names cannot easily be reconstructed for this period, it seems that the Ottoman authorities were already convening local councils from time to time in the 1840s (i.e. before the official implementation of the first round of provincial reforms) if they felt the need to consult on particular issues.

The Mid Nineteenth Century: A Period of Rapid Change

Why was there tension in the 1850s, and what was changing, in addition to the aforementioned economic patterns and the (partial?) turnover in the elite? Clearly, the Ottoman reassertion of control and early attempts at centralization altered the balance of power between the Sharifs and the *wali*s, so that after an initial honeymoon, relations quickly deteriorated and resulted in mutual incriminations at the seat of imperial power in Istanbul. The problems were at times linked to rivalry over resources and issues of security, but also to modifications to the political system, such as the introduction of advisory councils in local government.[14]

Another major issue, however, was the coinciding of European commercial and imperial expansion. Since the French armies under Napoleon Bonaparte had occupied Egypt (1798–1801) and then Muhammad ʿAli had established himself in Egypt and begun to expand beyond its borders, Britain had become nervous about its commercial interests in the area. More importantly, it feared for the safety of its shipping between the Gulf, Arabia and India. This explains to a large degree the first military and, from 1820, increasingly political intervention in the Gulf, as well as the occupation of Aden in 1839.[15] It is also the probable reason for the transformation of the existing agency of the East India Company in Jeddah, probably held by a British Oriental subject (a 'native' in EIC parlance), into a vice-consulate, and the appointment of a British, rather than the previous 'native' (i.e. Iraqi-Armenian) vice-consul in 1838. A year later, the French in their turn established a consulate in Jeddah.[16] The consuls, who under the capitulations exercised fairly far-reaching authority over those under their 'protection', soon began to clash with the Ottoman authorities over these capitulatory rights.

Due to its function as a port city, and as a main port for pilgrims who often stayed for long periods or settled in Jeddah (as well as, preferably, in Mecca or Medina), the city of Jeddah can be considered to have been a distinctly cosmopolitan town. Although only a few Christians resided there permanently, while Jews and Banyans seem to have made temporary visits, the presence of strangers in the city was not, in itself, a bone of contention, even if they did not profess the Muslim faith.[17]

Thus, merchants from the Ottoman realms, the areas bordering the Red Sea and the western Indian Ocean all congregated in Jeddah. However, in comparative terms, the absence of an established Christian community gives the violence of 1858 a somewhat different flavour from the contemporaneous clashes in Syria, as the link between Christians and imperial powers was far more evident in Jeddah than in the other cities of the Ottoman Empire.

The presence of the consuls crystallized a number of issues which caused tensions, both at the political level between the foreign powers (notably Britain) and the Ottoman Empire or its subjects, and at the local level between local merchants and their foreign competitors. The first general issue was the application of the capitulations and of the Anglo-Ottoman trade convention of 1838, which not only liberalized trade (thus breaking certain monopolies established under Muhammad ʿAli) but also imposed unfavourable customs dues. Given that, in this period, the consuls themselves often engaged in trade and were asked by foreign traders to support their claims, this proved to be an almost continuous bone of contention. Such disputes involved merchants of different origins who often were traders and held official functions at the same time.[18] A case in point on the Ottoman side is ʿAbdallah Agha, an Egyptian who repeatedly managed to get himself appointed to the position of *muhtasib*. He is reported to have exploited his position to levy taxes on Indian shopkeepers, who then asked for help from the British consul, who, in turn, was also active as a merchant, a practice which only began tapering off after 1858. This meshing and exploitation of functions resulted in some serious mutual misgivings, intrigues, attempts to effect dismissal, and even attempted and successful murder.[19]

The question of who was eligible to claim foreign protection against Ottoman officials or Ottoman protection from foreign demands was a second thorny issue at the very heart of the 1858 violence, as will be shown below. That foreign, or rather foreign-protected, merchants who flocked to Jeddah in the nineteenth century were considered an economic threat – in addition to the political difficulty of accepting foreign protection for residents of the empire – is clear, for example, from the conflict between the Greek merchant firm Toma (or Thoma) Sava & Co. and local merchants who organized a boycott of this firm.[20]

Such economic tension was not entirely new. In 1727, a group of English traders belonging to the East India Company had been murdered at their dinner table during a stopover in Jeddah. While the case warrants further investigation, there also seems to have been an underlying issue of competition, possibly between a Gujarati merchant and the English merchants. In addition, and as in the 1858 events, the Ottoman authorities felt slighted and the violence was, again, committed by what both the Ottoman commander and English observers alike described as a 'mob'.[21]

Thirdly, European powers, notably Britain, had pressured the Ottoman Empire into attempting to prohibit the slave trade, which caused major resentment in the Hijaz. Many slaves were imported through Jeddah or via the caravan trade and marketed, mainly in Jeddah and Mecca. Thus, since spring 1855, the issue of a possible prohibition of slavery was hotly debated among merchants and served as a rallying call for the Sharif against the Ottomans.[22]

When, in October 1855, an Ottoman officer arrived to investigate the situation and ordered an announcement prohibiting slave trade, a revolt broke out in Mecca. A few days later, an abortive attempt was made in Jeddah to tear down the flags of the foreign consulates and to murder all persons under foreign protection.[23] This was followed by an attempt on the British consul's life in June 1856 in the midst of reports of continued unrest across the region due to the slavery controversy.[24] In January and February 1857, a sultanic *ferman* informed the *walis* of Tripoli, Egypt and Baghdad about the prohibition of trade in African slaves. While other provinces were instructed likewise in due course, the Hijaz was exempted.[25] In May 1858, the authorities were pondering how they might be able to achieve greater acceptance of an eventual prohibition of this trade. They devised the plan to dramatically increase the taxes levied on imported slaves from 12 per cent to 25 per cent of their sales value in order to discourage the trade. The outcome of this initiative is not known but the slave trade in the Hijaz continued, albeit under growing restrictions and pressure.[26]

The Evolving Urban Space of Jeddah

In the years preceding the violence of 1858, it was not only the political environment of the Hijaz that had changed beyond recognition. The city of Jeddah itself was undergoing a process of urban change, although this is only rudimentarily documented. Carsten Niebuhr, who visited Jeddah in November 1762 in the course of his journey to the Yemen, left a fairly detailed plan of the walled city, commenting on the dilapidated state of its wall.

The map he published indicates the major installations which he and his companions noted, in particular the wall and major gates.[27] Among the other buildings marked are the residence of the governor (no. 1) and the customs house (no. 11). Both the plan and the written description make it clear that the houses on the seafront were large structures built of coral stone. He describes a number of them, including the one he

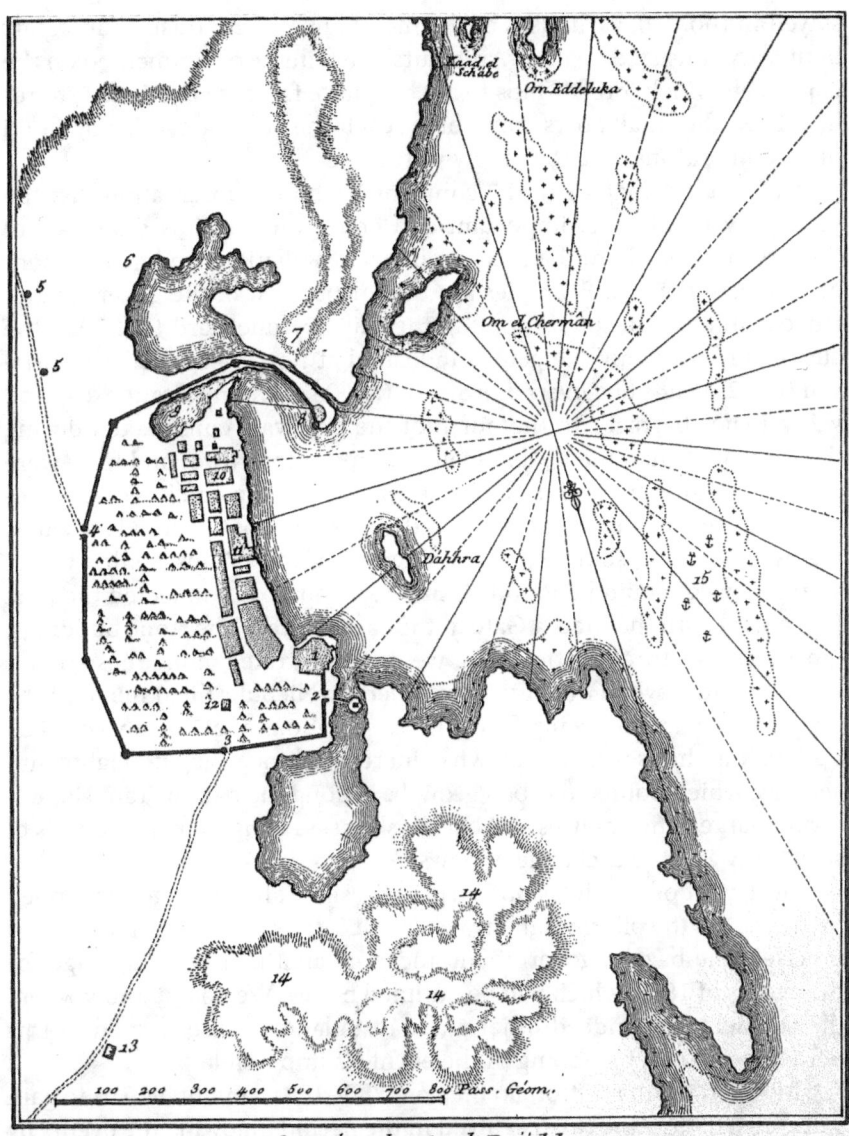

Figure 5.1. Carsten Niebuhr, sketch of the city of Jeddah.

Legend:
1. The house of the Pasha
2. Bab al-Sharif
3. Bab al-Jadid
4. Bab Mecca
5. Watchtowers
6. Sea-salt collection point
7. Christian cemetery
8. Destroyed tower
9. So-called Port of the Galleys
10. Niebuhr's house
11. Customs House
12. House of the Chief of Police
13. Eve's Tomb
14. Hills of coral rock and shells
15. Anchorage of ships of India and Suez

stayed in (no. 10), as 'houses of the merchants'. In contrast, a large part of the city consisted of 'poor Arab huts'. Niebuhr also commented on the coral reefs which forced ships to anchor quite far from the actual shoreline. Even the small boats could only reach the actual port during flood in certain seasons, due to the low water level.[28]

An Ottoman map of 1851[29] confirms Niebuhr's observation that the seafront was the most important and hence most solidly built part of the city. This is where the major military installations and government offices were housed. Examples are the former seat of the governor and current military hospital (no. 32), the military dockyard (no. 30a), the customs house (only the gate is indicated at no. 28), an artillery garrison (no. 23) and the governor's diwan (no. 24). An important exception was a major barracks to the north of the city wall, constructed during the time of Muhammad ʿAli. Smaller ammunition stores and forts were situated at different points along the walls, securing quick access to defences if needed. Tamisier describes the extension of the grand bazaar as following a north–south extension lined with small shops, behind which storage spaces could be found.[30] Another main axis connected the port in the west with the Mecca Gate in the eastern wall. The stone buildings, mostly two or three stories high, were concentrated along these major thoroughfares, while the huts mentioned by Niebuhr filled much of the remaining space. It seems from the descriptions that the space taken up by stone houses had somewhat increased since the late eighteenth century, which points to urban growth.[31] Along the bazaar, Tamisier describes large coffee houses and barber shops, serving as major centres of sociability and the exchange of news.[32]

This layout of the city is not surprising, since almost all goods arrived by sea, as did the pilgrims and travellers. It is thus also natural that it was precisely the bazaar, government and port area that was the stage for the events of 1858, which will be outlined below. We do not know where the consulates or indeed other trade installations were located in this period, so an exact mapping of the events is impossible.

However, another Ottoman map of 1880–1881[33] might help us to gain some idea of how the town evolved in the period following the events by depicting a number of new features, such as the land gained by building a new sea wall in 1879. On this newly gained land, the quarantine installation (no. 20), a new 'petrol store' (no. 19), a space for prayer (no. 22) and a 'municipal coffee house' (no. 23) were to be found, together with, most importantly, new landing facilities for boats. The customs house (no. 24) and postal store (or post office, no. 17) were now immediately adjacent to large enclosures or courtyards (*hawsh*, pl. *ahwash*), as they are translated today.

Symbolic Politics and Urban Violence   119

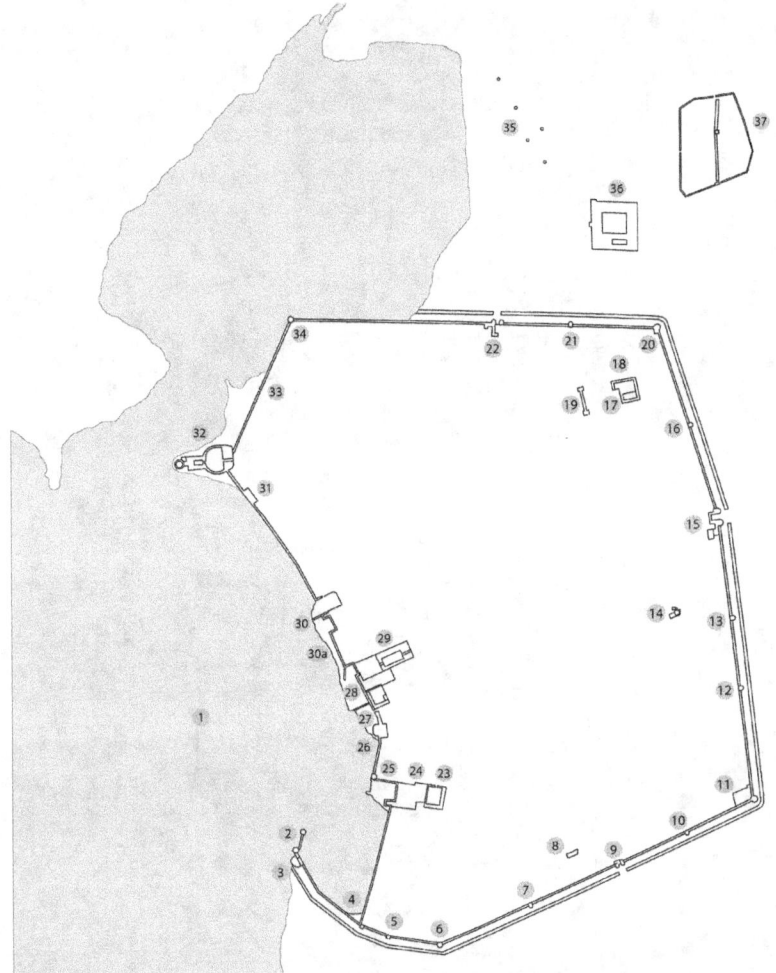

Figure 5.2. Map of Jeddah, 1851, drawn after an Ottoman map of 1851 by Melody Mosavat.

Legend:
1. Red Sea
2–7, 10–14, 16, 20–21, 34. Towers lining the city wall
8. Fort of the Sharif
9. Gate of the Sharif
15. Mecca Gate
17. Gate
18. Ammunition store
19. Guard of ammunition store
22. Medina and New Gate
23. Barracks of the Artillery
24. Diwan of the Governor of Jeddah
25. The Minister's Gate
26. Derelict fort
27. Grainstore Gate
28. Customs Gate
29. Derelict building
30. Maghrebinian Gate
30a. Dockyard
31. Fort
32. Military hospital
33. Gate of the Martyrs and Secret Gate
35. Windmills
36. Barracks
37. Tomb of Eve

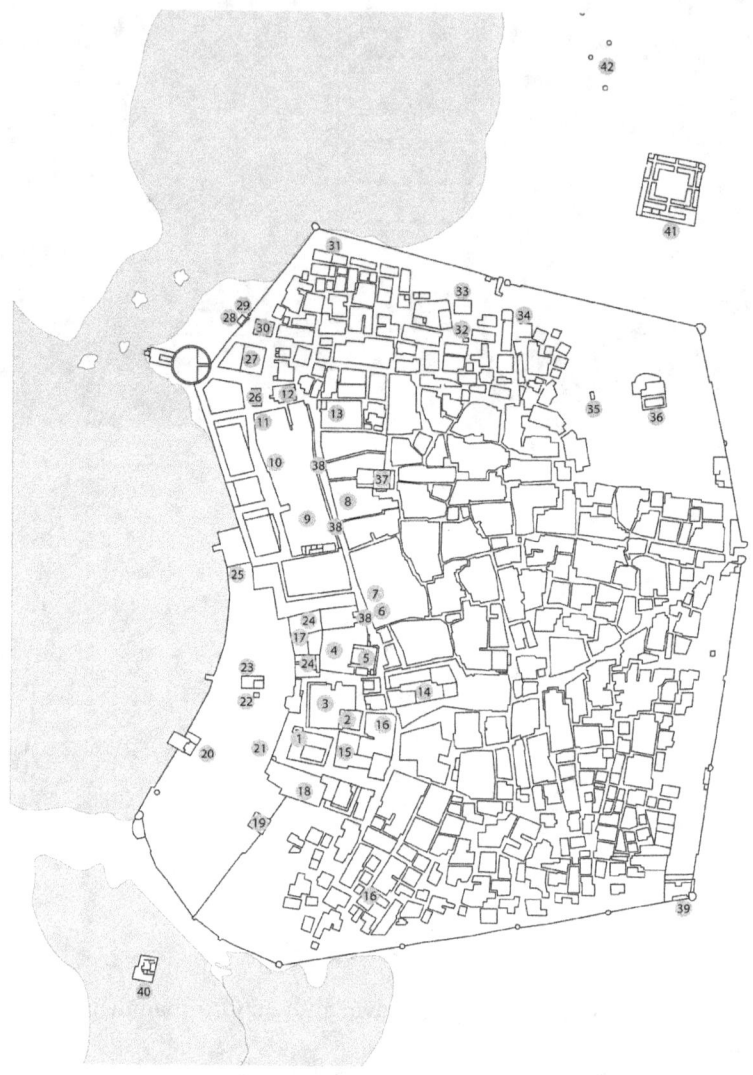

Figure 5.3. Map of Jeddah, 1880/81, drawn after an Ottoman map of 1880/81 by Melody Mosavat.

Legend:
1–4, 6–9, 13, 15–16, 18, 37. Warehouses and caravanserais
5. ʿAkkash Mosque
10. Rubat of the Sada
11. Rubat Ba Dib
12. Mosque of Bakir Pasha
14. Provincial grainstore
17. Postal store
19. Petrol store
20. Quarantine
21. Police station
22, 32. Prayer rooms
23. Municipal coffee house
24. Customs
25. Maghrebinian Gate
26. Rüşdiyye School
27. Sayyid Saqqaf Effendi Musa
28. Graveyard of the Martyrs
29. Gate of the Forty
30. Ba 'Ishn
31. French Consulate
33. English Consulate
34. Government House
35. Police station
36. Cemetery
38. Market
39. Hospital
40. Tomb of Shaykh Abu 'l-ʿUyun
41. Barracks
42. Derelict windmills

If one assumes that not the entire urban fabric changed overnight, it seems plausible that in the 1850s quite a few of the *ahwash* marked on the plan for 1880 might have already existed (nos. 1–4, 6–9, 15–16, 37). But what were these *ahwash*? Wellsted, who visited Jeddah in 1831, describes what he terms spacious caravanserais with large squares, 'lofty arched passages, affording a cool retreat to the numerous merchants who, with their merchandise, take up their quarters there'.[34] These were at the centre of commerce in the city, as they served to store goods. While some only seem to have consisted of an enclosure, buildings lined others on one or more sides. Some of these were inhabited permanently by the city's merchants; others offered rented accommodation on the upper floors and are given different names by various travellers, probably on the basis of terms familiar elsewhere, such as caravanserai, khan and wikala.[35] Arabic documents from the first half of the nineteenth and the early twentieth centuries, by contrast, tend to use only the aforementioned term *hawsh*. A *hawsh* could serve shops as storage.[36] It could also contain small separate units (ʿ*uzla*, pl. ʿ*uzal*) for rent. The ʿ*uzal* were often used by merchants spending only part of the year in Jeddah, although waqf documents and later reports indicate that some of these spaces were also rented out on a more permanent basis.[37] Burckhardt describes some well-built public khans in the town, with good accommodation, where the foreign merchants resided during their short stay here. In these khans were large open squares with arched passages, which afforded a cool shade to the merchants for the greater part of the day.[38]

The account of one of the people fleeing from the attack of 1858 gives an impression of how the spatial arrangement along the shore might have been, and confirms that at least one of the places targeted by the attackers was also located in the central area: the aforementioned Toma Sava & Co. was located between the ʿAkkash mosque and the customs house. It seems to have consisted of a large courtyard with a door towards the road, and a building of probably two floors (presumably facing the sea), as well as possibly a smaller building inside the courtyard that housed the offices of the firm. The roof seems to have been connected to the (lower) roof of an adjacent house and to have bordered on the courtyard of the customs house, which in turn had a door opening towards the sea. This allowed a number of people congregated at Toma Sava & Co. on the afternoon of the attack to flee via the courtyard of the customs house and hence to the waterfront and a British ship anchored in Jeddah harbour.[39]

Behind this line of *ahwash* and merchant houses was the main market street, discernible on Niebuhr's map and on the plan of 1880/81 (no. 38). It was lined with buildings serving as stores, offices and merchant houses. Tamisier describes two small passages, probably running parallel to this main market, where cloth and tobacco were sold, and where tailors, coppersmiths and blacksmiths maintained workshops. He also mentions areas with restaurants and coffee houses frequented by locals and strangers.[40]

The Violent Outbreak of 1858

In June 1858, a conflict arose which crystallized the already existing conflicts between merchants from Jeddah and elsewhere, which, as discussed above, were exacerbated by foreign diplomatic intervention and Ottoman authorities who tried to straddle the middle ground between considerations of international diplomacy and imperial and local interests.[41] It involved Salih Jawhar, a trader of Indian origin who had a dispute with the former co-owner of a merchant ship, Hasan b. Ibrahim Jawhar. Salih Jawhar appealed to the Ottoman governor to change the flag of his vessel from the British to the Ottoman one. A merchant council endorsed this act. Hasan Jawhar then approached another Indian merchant, the aforementioned Faraj Yusr, who was standing in for the British vice-consul for a few days during the latter's absence. Hasan Jawhar asked Faraj Yusr to demand from Salih Jawhar certain business accounts; but Salih Jawhar, who was not on friendly terms with Faraj Yusr, refused to comply.

At this point, Acting British Vice-Consul Page returned and felt he had to act, possibly without being aware of all the details. He decided that the vessel in question should be seized under British law which forbade the changing of the flag.[42] Page resorted to the help of Captain Pullen, the commanding officer of a British warship that was anchored off Jeddah, to survey a possible route for a telegraph cable. When the British party had boarded the merchant vessel, Page lowered the Ottoman flag and hoisted the British one. Allegedly, he or other British seamen then trampled on the Ottoman flag.[43] As this incident is not noted in any of the Western documents, and, perhaps more importantly, as there are no obvious eyewitnesses from the Arab or Ottoman side to confirm it, this might well only be a rumour.[44] In his discussion of racial violence, Glassman has emphasized the role of the deliberate spreading of inflammatory rumours in the run-up to violence, if – and this is a crucial point – the crowds were receptive to such rumours.[45]

When the Ottoman authorities noticed the change of flags, the *qaʾimmaqam*, Ibrahim Agha, assembled a group of notables. They consisted of the aforementioned ʿAbdallah Agha, of Shaykh Ba Ghaffar, a Hadhrami and Head of the Commercial Tribunal and the representative (shahbandar) of the merchants, ʿAbdallah Ba Harun, who was also Shaykh al-sada, and four more merchants, namely ʿUmar Ba Darb, Yusuf Ba Naja, Shaykh al-ʿAmudi and Selim Sultan (a former Greek slave) to deliberate further action. They held their meeting on the afternoon of 15 June in the customs house, which was situated in the central port area. Meanwhile, a crowd of armed townspeople, presumably mostly from among those working in the port and the bazaar which ran behind the first line of buildings, began to gather outside.[46]

The accounts vary on the exact course of further events. Reportedly, the *qaʾimmaqam*, upon leaving the meeting towards evening, prevented the angry crowd from heading towards the ship, but might have indicated the direction of the British consulate by waving his arms. As he apparently tried to stop the attacks first on the British and then the French consulate, this might well have been a misunderstanding. Another version has it that the instigator was ʿAbdallah Agha, with his aforementioned long history of conflict with the British consul, while still others implicated Salih Jawhar and a number of other merchants.[47] Given the preponderance of Hadhrami merchants in the meeting, it is perhaps not surprising that this group was also blamed for the massacre.[48] As for the crowd, it is possible that rumour could play upon a certain popular anti-Christian sentiment and popular anti-imperialism.[49]

At any rate, the British consulate, the exact location of which is uncertain, was the first to be attacked. The British consul was torn from his bed and, apparently still alive, thrown out of a window of his house. In the street, his body was ripped apart by the mob, which consisted mostly of artisans and port workers. The crowd, apparently led by two merchants, then turned against the French consulate (where the consul and his wife were killed) and the trading house of Toma Sava & Co. There, a large group of Christians and Muslims had gathered to greet Sava Moscudi who had just returned from a journey. The Muslims left when they saw the mob, while the Christians apparently did not understand the gravity of the situation until sympathetic Muslim colleagues warned them.[50] The house was raided and many of those present killed.[51] The consulates and the merchant house were also thoroughly pillaged. In spite of earlier incidences of violence against Western representatives, these events stand out as a series of particularly cruel and publicly visible acts.

While the mob attacking the Christians was large, a number of other people, among them many Ottoman officials (like the surgeon, the head of the artillery and the captain of the port) but also some locals, sheltered those fleeing from the violence.[52] Interestingly, Faraj Yusr, who was identified with a pro-British position, was saved by his neighbour, ʿAdallah Nasif, one of the main notables of Jeddah and the agent of the Sharif of

Mecca.⁵³ However, Nasif was amongst those suspected of complicity in the affair (albeit too old to have directly taken part). Besides feelings of humanity, a possible motif for Nasif's action could have been that Faraj Yusr was, after all, one of the most prominent merchants and notables of Jeddah, and as such was considered a local, in spite of his affiliation with the British consulate.⁵⁴

Why did no Ottoman forces intervene? There is little information on the police force, which in later years consisted of Egyptian troops.⁵⁵ It seems from the consular reports that the main force consisted of the small Ottoman garrison. This had been somewhat depleted to accompany the *wali* to Mecca for the pilgrimage, and its commander felt that he needed the remainder of the troops to guard the city against potential Bedouin attacks. He therefore did not send any soldiers to calm the situation.⁵⁶

Public Violence or Retributive Justice: Punishing the Perpetrators

Upon hearing of the events, the *wali* conferred with notables from Mecca, including some from Jeddah who were visiting Mecca. He then made his way to Jeddah with troops to restore order. Once news reached Cairo, and from there Constantinople and the European capitals, a diplomatic wrangle ensued between the European and Ottoman governments, and the Ottomans eventually agreed to send an officer from Constantinople to the site of the unrest. Meanwhile, Captain Pullen had received orders to enforce swift punishment of the culprits. Oblivious to the agreement between London and Constantinople on the further course of action, he attempted to order the *wali* to execute the culprits.⁵⁷ When the latter refused to act without prior consent from Constantinople, Pullen shelled Jeddah for three days. This was punctuated only by abortive negotiations. At least one family of five and two female slaves were killed, fairly heavy damage inflicted on the city and a number of boats in the harbour destroyed.⁵⁸

Besides feeling that he had to pressure the *wali*, there was a second reason why Pullen felt he had to act: this being the period of pilgrimage, many Indian and Algerian pilgrims had come to the Hijaz. While they were in Mecca during the time of shelling (and thus not likely to be harmed), they would nevertheless take home a clear message: '... and they can now tell in every remote corner of the Mahometan world how England and France avenge the murder of their Consuls and their other subjects.'⁵⁹ This concern, particularly about Indians, is not surprising given that Captain Pullen, in his first account of the revolt, reported on the rumour that an Indian shaykh from Delhi, having apparently come for the pilgrimage, had something to do with the affair.[60] After all, the Indian Mutiny had just been brought under control. Already two years earlier in the context of the Mecca revolt of 1855–56, the British had been worried about the transmission of anti-Christian sentiment from India to the Hijaz, notably through pilgrims and the prominent Indian exile of Indo-Hadhrami extraction, Sayyid Fadl. This individual was once again invoked in 1858 as trying to spread as much anti-British sentiment as possible, to the extent that the British Resident at Aden asked Captain Pullen for help in requesting the Ottoman authorities to hand over Sayyid Fadl or else move him to some remote corner of the Ottoman Empire.[61]

Finally, a truce was agreed upon and sixteen people were arrested, mostly commoners (a shoemaker, a mariner, a tobacco vendor, a ship pilot, etc.).[62] Once the Ottoman envoy from Constantinople arrived and authorised the execution of the culprits, Pullen sent an officer to determine the place of execution, which was carefully selected for its visibility by all potential future troublemakers: 'It was on a dry spit of coral reef, running out into the inner harbour, and so situated as to be visible both from the town and from the merchant-vessels'.[63] Of the sixteen people eventually arrested as the result of two rounds of local inquiry, eleven were executed on 5 August. The spectators were more or less limited to British sailors. The execution, described by a British report as 'a sickening and appalling scene of butchery', was also witnessed by merchant vessels, which had been 'called together by order of Captain Pullen, whose motive in so doing was that this instance of retributive justice should be known in India'.[64] Thus, Pullen clearly not only wanted to impress on the local, but also on the imperial and international scale.

Although Pullen had officially declared that the foreign demands for compensation were thereby satisfied, he nevertheless convinced the British ambassador that the real culprits were still at large. Under pressure from the British and French governments, a joint commission consisting of a French, a British and an Ottoman official started another investigation. It concluded on 2 January 1859 that, while the executed may have been the perpetrators of violence, the real responsibility lay elsewhere, namely with the notables who had taken part in the meeting at the customs house.[65] Altogether, another thirteen individuals were indicted.[66] Eleven were imprisoned and/or exiled.[67] The two who were considered the ringleaders, Shaykh al-ʿAmudi and ʿAbdallah Agha, the *muhtasib*, were executed on 12 January 1859 in front of the customs house. The *wali* had been reticent about this execution (which, after all, included one of his own officials), as he feared that it might increase public anger rather than solve any of the problems, thus inadvertently reflecting on the precariousness of Ottoman rule.⁶⁸ When the European representatives rejected this argument, he tried to at least convince the British and French to execute the two men at night outside the city.⁶⁹ Once again, the Europeans were adamant about the need for a public execution, which

> was an act of public justice, indispensable as an example, without which there would be no security for the lives of Christians in any port of the Red Sea. The immediate effect has been to inspire a salutary fear among the inhabitants of Jeddah. ... But at Mecca public prayers have, I understand, been offered up in favour of the criminals, who are no doubt considered martyrs by a conclave of Musulman fanatics gathered together in that so-called holy city.⁷⁰

On the same day, a public proclamation by the 'local government' was 'published in the quarters of Jeddah, and at the Mecca gate of the town' and sent to all cities in the Hijaz. It gave an official version of the events which avoided giving any reason for the uprising of 'the lower orders of the people' in Jeddah, which was 'most grave and contrary to law, and opposed to the will of the High Government of His Majesty and to the dictates of humanity'. 'Abdallah al-Muhtasib was therein charged with instructing al-ʿAmudi to mobilize the Hadhramis against the consuls and Christians. In contrast to this avoidance of a discussion of the events, the investigations and trial are described in quite some detail, clearly in order to justify the execution both in terms of Islamic law and sultanic prerogative, and in terms of deterring such acts in the future.⁷¹

Interestingly, this line of arguing has left a trace in the work of one of the Arab historians reporting what they saw as the 'great schism' (*fitna ʿazima*).⁷² al-Hadrawi, an Egyptian who had come to Mecca as a child and was twenty-two years old when the revolt broke out, left no doubt in his book on the 'Merits of Jeddah', written in 1863/64, that the attackers acted contrary to Islam's rulings on how to treat non-Muslims and those asking for protection, violating the 'conditions for those asking for protection, and of the *ahl al-dhimma* and those who had concluded contracts' (*yukhalifu din al-islam, wa-lam yadru ʿan shurut al-mustaʾminin wa-ahl al-dhimma wa-'l-muʿahidin fi dar al-islam*).⁷³ Incidentally, al-Hadrawi's argument closely resembles the Ottoman official statement, and thus reflects one particular Muslim perspective on the events. That this might have suited the Europeans well, who Dahlan says had even suggested the drafting of such a resolution to the *wali*, is another matter.⁷⁴

The Moral Framings of the Jeddah Violence

Clearly, both the Ottoman proclamation and its echo in al-Hadrawi's report of the events, cited above, appeal to a particular, religiously grounded morale. However, the crowd (and its leaders) clearly pursued a different logic, based on a different type of moral reasoning.[75] This was also rooted in Islam, but more in a general notion of its defence than in a particular legal tradition invoked by the Ottomans. Furthermore, it is interesting to note that religious officials and students seem to have played no significant role in the unfolding events, in contrast to events elsewhere in the Middle East.[76] While the Ottoman claim of instinctive local loyalty to the Ottoman flag as the main cause of the uprising might, as Pétriat put it, be subject to doubt, it nevertheless may well have served as a symbolic rallying point embodying a wider unease with developments.[77]

To some extent, this sentiment can be found in Dahlan's version of events, although it was written in the 1880s and thus might not reflect very precisely the feelings at the time in question. Nevertheless, it is worthwhile to briefly consider it: Dahlan relates the meeting of *wali* Namık Pasha with the Meccan notables. They suggested mobilizing local Bedouins in defence against the British bombardment or sabotaging and burning the British man-of-war. For fear of European aggression against other Muslim cities and the Ottoman Empire, the *wali* rejected this offer of help. Dahlan describes the joint Ottoman–European investigation of the incident as highly manipulative, and thus implicitly as void of the Islamic justification given in the Ottoman version of events, and the day of execution as a 'dreadful day on which the torment of all Muslims greatly intensified' (*wa-kana dhalika 'l-yawm yawman muhawwilan ishtadda fihi al-karb 'ala jami' al-muslimin*).[78] This event, Dahlan assures us, was 'one of the greatest calamities for the adherents of Islam'. As if he needs to further convince his readers, he adds another episode to relate the danger posed by Europeans: upon the arrival of the new Sharif 'Abdallah, the European representatives who had taken part in the inquiry went to greet him and demanded a visit to Mecca. The Sharif, who appears to have been Dahlan's direct source, is said to have realized that an islamically founded answer would not have deterred the Europeans. 'But', he reportedly told Dahlan, 'God inspired me with a convincing rational answer' (*fa-alhamani Allah lahum jawaban 'aqliyyan*), namely a description of the hardships of the journey to Mecca and the paucity of its sights.[79] Such a position might well reflect a popular anti-imperialism, in Dahlan's case clearly inspired by religion. It resembles the anti-European sentiment evident in the wave of more or less contemporaneous uprisings in the Middle East and India, quite independent of the question of a direct Indian influence on events in Jeddah, which the British had so clearly feared.[80]

The course of events that unfolded followed a certain logic, which incidentally shows that the parties involved initially deemed notions of justice based on the legitimacy of the Ottoman imperial institutions suitable to solve the problem at hand. Salih Jawhar resorted to an Ottoman court, which adjudicated in his favour. A consular court contested this ruling and forwarded its own to the *qa'immaqam* (here termed the vice-governor).[81] The latter again tried to play by the rules (and possibly for time) by 'requesting the matter of the Flag might be deferred, until he could hear from the Pasha [i.e. the *wali*] at Mecca'. However, the vice-consul forced a decision by ordering Captain Pullen to seize the vessel. Oblivious to the last meeting of Jeddawi notables after this decision which immediately preceded the violence, Pullen then attributes the spreading of this message – which from a local point of view constituted a violation of procedure – to an attempt 'to break down the English and French Consular flagstaffs', an endeavour which descended into the violence described above.[82] Indeed, the symbolic act of breaking flagstaffs, with which the attack on the British consulate reportedly started, was reiterated at the French consulate, albeit after the staff defending the consulate had been attacked.[83] The grounding of the violence in a particular moral order can be further supported by the aforementioned aid that a notable extended to Faraj Yusr, even though a number of other non-governmental individuals also intervened to help those who were being persecuted. Possibly they were driven by the Islamic norm of protecting *dhimmi*s (protected non-Muslims) and foreigners, evoked by the government declaration.

The following events, from Captain Pullen's attempts to compel the Ottoman authorities to set up an inquiry by shelling Jeddah, the deliberations of the various committees of investigation and the two rounds of executions each also followed their own ritualized logic referring to a particular moral imperative. Without recapitulating what has already been discussed in some detail, it is clear that the Ottomans, however uneasy they seem to have been with developments, could, to some extent successfully, invoke imperial notions of Islamic law and protection to legitimize their actions vis-à-vis the population. In contrast, the British and French felt that they had to carry out the just punishment of murderers, if necessary by brutal force, albeit only for the higher aim of instilling respect for their empires among Muslims of the Peninsula and beyond. Thus, for each of these parties, the violence of 1858 was the logical outcome of different processes of ritualized negotiations on an imperial scale which had broken down or in which one party was seen to have violated the rules.⁸⁴ One of the problems was their differing interpretations of what constituted the rules and, hence, legitimate action.

Needless to say that, while the Ottomans and the British each felt that they were acting within the law (or rather: different sets of laws, with the possible exception of Pullen's gunboat 'diplomacy') and thus using legitimate 'force', they considered the actions by the crowd to be lawless 'violence'. Obviously, 'Ottoman' means the announced official position, rather than all individual Ottoman actors. Thus, one would need to distinguish whether Ottoman individuals were acting more on an imperial scale (like the governor) or were entangled in local trade and politics. Thus, there is evidence for the active involvement or at least complicity of some low-level officials in the violence, most notably (but not exclusively) the *muhtasib*. They thus shared the perspective of local merchants on European encroachment as a danger to the empire and, more pertinently, to their own immediate economic interests.⁸⁵ Others who were probably posted to Jeddah for only a short term were among those who rescued victims of the original attack.

The Spatial Dimension of the Jeddah Violence

The practical and symbolic reasons for which all parties chose more or less the same space to engage in violence, namely the customs square and adjacent areas, are clear.⁸⁶ This was the area where the world of the city and the mostly Muslim outside world came into close contact, and in the 1830s Tamisier described it as the most remarkable of Jeddah's open squares.⁸⁷ If Jeddah was considered to be the door to Mecca (*bawabat Makka*), then the customs square was the physical location of this door, connecting sea and land, and the area through which everyone arriving or departing had to cross. It was visible to ships passing by and anchoring. The small boats landed there, bringing people ashore; and goods were stored in the warehouses there, some of them later sold in the adjacent souk. As mentioned earlier, it was also the area where the main political institutions of the Ottoman state were located, namely the seat of the governor, the customs house and possibly still some military forces. Furthermore, it was the space close to which the (Christian) foreigners had their trading houses and presumably also their consulates, in the immediate vicinity of those of the Ottomans, Indians, Hadhramis and other Arabs. Thus, it was a space in which political and commercial interests converged and clashed. And it was a space where labourers, artisans, slaves and notables interacted in their daily work in the harbour and the bazaar, and where restaurants and coffee houses for passers-by were located. In short, it was an ideal space for popular mobilization.[88]

It is thus not surprising that the square was also the regular scene of different types of gatherings and manifestations which aimed at or concerned a wider public and which were linked to the political, economic or social life of Jeddah. Thus, it was the place where delegations of the quarters and guilds greeted arriving officials with dances and shows of joy. From 1859 onwards, it became the location where the Egyptian *mahmal* arrived, once its transport changed from caravan to boat.[89] Early photographs by the Dutch Orientalist Christiaan Snouck Hurgronje show a chaotic embarkation, drawing curious crowds, followed by a ceremonial procession across the town, combining elements of a military parade with popular manifestations of joy.

It might be interesting to note that the earlier massacre of the mid-eighteenth century took place inside a house which was then destroyed and never rebuilt.[90] The 1856 attempt on the British consul's life also occurred inside his house. In contrast, the rioting of 1858 aimed initially at the publicly displayed symbols of foreign power – the flagstaffs and flags – as had been the case in the abortive unrest of 1855. This was a clear reaction to a similarly public and symbolic act, the change of the Ottoman flag on the disputed Indian vessel. Whether the murders of 1858 had been premeditated or not is difficult to establish, but the fact that the British consul was not murdered in his bed but thrown down onto the street below, where his body was mutilated, shows the attempt to display publicly the wrath of the perpetrators.

The year 1858 constitutes a turning point in the contestation over who could be tolerated in this public space of Jeddah's harbour and customs, and thus in the city. There were later instances of tension and disturbance in the city, and the Europeans clearly feared that the events of 1858 might be repeated. However, it seems that, after 1858, the Ottoman authorities effectively prevented such outbursts within the space of the city; the 1895 attack on the British vice-consul (and some of his colleagues) was staged during an evening stroll along the shore, well outside of the walled city. The demonstrative use of violence, exemplified in the shelling of the town and, probably to a lesser extent, by the public executions, continued to resonate in the memory of both Ottomans and the local population, as was indeed the intention of the British. Thus, modern historians of Jeddah all discuss the event, and in 2010 a novel entitled '*Fitnat Jidda*' was published in Beirut.[91]

The place where the violence had taken place was transformed in the context of the urban renewals started in 1879 by *wali* Nashid Pasha and the local *qa'immaqam* Nuri Pasha. They built a new sea wall, draining the land and thus extending the busy space between the sea and the town. The harbour area was laid out anew, making more room for the needs of customs and quarantine.[92] Thus, the politics of opening Jeddah further to the outside world, both economically and politically, which had been symbolically opposed in the 1858 uprising, continued. The very same space of the violence was now transformed to accommodate even more foreign goods and people, irrespective of their religious belonging, and it was no longer openly contested.

In the course of the urban reforms, the offices of the *wali* and of the British and French consulates were moved to the northern edge of the city. Where, earlier on, huts had separated the wall and gates from the built-up area, a new quarter with representative buildings was erected. Making use of the available space and the fresh breeze from the north, wealthy merchants built spacious houses of four or five floors, in which the foreign consuls rented their locations. Although the climate and prestige are not to be neglected, an interesting remark in a consular letter of 1879 indicates that security reasons may have figured as well. In the context of arguing for a new Christian cemetery, British Consul Zohrab writes that, in addition to a number of other reasons rendering it unsuitable, the location of the cemetery to the south of the walled city was no longer adequate, given that 'after the massacre of 1858 the Christians removed to the northern side of the town'.[93] This might have been deemed safer, given the presence of the large Ottoman barracks just outside the (northern) Medina gate. Concerns about safety also dominated the French consul's attempts to persuade the Foreign Ministry to purpose-build a house because most rented spaces were connected to neighbouring houses by terraces and thus could easily be entered through a number of passages.[94] Nevertheless, prestige, availability, structural safety after rainfalls and lease conditions seem to have been as much a concern with regard to the consulates' move.

By the end of the nineteenth century, the functions of the port, the political institutions and the foreign consulates had become disentangled to some extent. Thus, the decoration and illumination of the British consulate in 1902 – when the coronation of Edward VII was celebrated twice in Jeddah because news of the cancellation of the initial date due to Edward's illness had not reached the consulate in time – was a visible gesture, but in a less prominent place than it would have been in 1858.[95] This is not to say that the consulate could not have dared such a public display in its old location; but by 1902, the Ottoman Empire had a much firmer grip on the provinces it retained, the Hijaz being no exception, and it could thus guarantee the safety of the consuls, at least within the walls of the city.[96]

Notes

I would like to thank Nushin Atmaca for her incessant help in finding the relevant materials and for her comments, and Rasmus Elling, Nelida Fuccaro, Till Grallert, Nora Lafi, Fatemeh Masjedi, Ellinor Morack, Philippe Pétriat and Claudia Ghrawi for all their helpful suggestions.

1. A list of those killed can be found in PRO (Public Record Office), FO (Foreign Office) 881/848, List of Persons Murdered at Jeddah on the Night of 15 June 1858, encl. 3 in No. 88.
2. W. Ochsenwald. 1977. 'The Jidda Massacre', *Middle Eastern Studies* 13(3), 314–26; P. Pétriat. 2010. *Fitna Djeddah, les Hadramis dans l'Èmeute du 15 Juin 1858*, unpublished Mémoire de Master 2, Paris: Université Paris 1; idem. 2013. 'Notables et Rebelles, Les Grands Marchands Hadramis de Djedda au Milieu du XIXe Siècle', *Arabian Humanities* 1, retrieved 13 December 2013 from http://cy.revues.org/1923; idem. 2013. *Les Grandes Familles Marchandes Hadramies de Djedda, 1850–1950*, unpublished Ph.D. thesis, Paris: Université Paris 1, 113–71.
3. In the absence of statistical data, these figures are based on the estimates of the travellers C.-E.-X. Roche d'Héricourt. 1841. *Voyage sur la Côte Orientale de la Mer Rouge, dans le Pays d'Adel et le Royaume de Choa*, Paris: Bertrand, 18, and C. Didier. (1854) 1985. *Sojourn with the Grand Sharif of Makkah*, Cambridge: Oleander Press, 61, who visited Jeddah in 1841 and 1854 respectively.
4. For details, see M. Tuscherer. 2002. 'Trade and Port Cities in the Red Sea–Gulf of Aden Region in the Sixteenth and Seventeenth Century', in L. Fawaz and C. Bayly (eds), *Modernity and Culture: From the Mediterranean to the India Ocean*, New York: Columbia University Press, 28–45; and D. Kimche. 1972. 'The Opening of the Red Sea to European Ships in the Late Eighteenth Century', in *Middle Eastern Studies* 8(1) 63–71.
5. M. Tuscherer. 1993. 'Le Commerce en Mer Rouge Au Alentours de 1700: Flux, Espaces et Temps', in R. Gyselen (ed.), *Circulation des Monnaies, des Merchandises et des Biens*, vol. 5, Bures-sur-Yvette: Peeters Publishers, 175f.
6. A. Raymond. 2002. 'A Divided Sea', in L. Fawaz and C. Bayly (eds), *Modernity and Culture from the Mediterranean to the Indian Ocean*, New York: Columbia University Press, 46–57; C. Dubois. 2002. 'The Red Sea Ports during the Revolution in Transportation, 1800–1914', in L. Fawaz and C. Bayly (eds), *Modernity and Culture from the Mediterranean to the Indian Ocean*, New York: Columbia University Press, 58–74; W. Ochsenwald. 1982. 'The Commercial History of the Hijaz Vilayet, 1840–1908', *Arabian Studies* 6, 57–76. For trade in the late eighteenth century, see C. Niebuhr. 1774. *Reisebeschreibung nach Arabien und Anderen Umliegenden Ländern*, vol. 1, Copenhagen: Hofbuchdruckerei Nikolas Möller, 280–83. For reports on the state of affairs in the crucial period 1805–1840, see Ali Bey el-Abbasi. 1816. *The Travels of Ali Bey*, vol. 2, London: Longmans, 43; F. Mengin. 1823. *Histoire de l'Égypte sous le Gouvernement de Mohammed-Aly*

ou Récit des Événemens [sic] Politiques et Militaires qui Ont Eu Lieu depuis le Départ des Français jusqu'en 1823, vol. 2, Paris: A. Bertrand, 420–25; and J.R. Wellsted. (1837) 1978. Travels in Arabia, vol. 2, Graz: Akademische Druck- und Verlagsanstalt, 279. A good survey is contained in Pétriat, 'Les Grandes Familles Marchandes', 59–112.

7. For the political history, see A. Vassiliev. 1998. The History of Saudi Arabia, London: Saqi, 140–47.
8. G. Viscount Valentia. 1806. Voyages and Travels to India, Ceylon, the Red Sea, Abyssinia, and Egypt in the Years 1802, 1803, 1804, 1805, and 1806, vol. 3, London: 331–33; Ali Bey. The Travels of Ali Bey, 44; J.L. Burckhardt. 1829. Travels in Arabia, London: Henry Colbourn, 21f.; Mengin, Histoire de l'Égypte sous le Gouvernement de Mohammed-Aly, 420–25.
9. J.R.L. Carter. 1979. Leading Merchant Families of Saudi Arabia, London: Scorpion Publicatons, 49f., 160f.; M. Field, The Merchants: The Big Business Families of Saudi Arabia and the Gulf States, New York: The Overlook Press, 14–21.
10. PRO, FO 195/375, Page, Vice-Consul Jeddah to Ambassador, Constantinople, 13 Jan. 1857; for a rather imprecise biography, see M.ʿA. Maghrabi. 1994. Aʿlam Jidda, vol. 3, 2nd edn, Jeddah, p. 431–38.
11. There are various indications as to when the governors formally moved to Mecca. Thus, the successor of Namik Pasha, Ali (1859–1861/62), spent most of his time in Mecca. See W. Ochsenwald. 1984. Religion, Society, and the State in Arabia: The Hijaz under Ottoman Control, 1840–1908, Columbus: The Ohio State University Press, 149, 165, 168; cf. A.E. Osmanoğlu. 2004. Hicaz eyaletinin teşekkülü (1841–1864), MA thesis, Istanbul: Marmara University, 40. Sebile Yapici helped me to read the Turkish text.
12. Osmanoğlu, Hicaz eyaletinin teşekkülü, 40.
13. The information in Osmanoğlu, Hicaz eyaletinin teşekkülü, 34–46, on which the following is based, can be partly supplemented by A. Birken. 1976. Die Provinzen des Osmanischen Reichs, Wiesbaden: Reichert, 252, as well as by Ochsenwald, Religion, Society and the State in Arabia, 157.
14. For the political situation here and in the following, Ochsenwald, Religion, Society, and the State in Arabia, 136–51; Pétriat, Les Grandes Familles Marchands, 143–45.
15. On Britain's empire in the Gulf area, see J. Onley. 2007. The Arabian Frontier of the British Raj, Oxford: Oxford University Press, 29–38; on the occupation of Aden, see R.J. Gavin. 1975. Aden under British Rule, London: Hurst, 22–38. For a general political history of the Red Sea in the first half of the nineteenth century, see R.J. Daguenet. 1997. Histoire de la Mer Rouge de Lesseps à nos Jours, Paris and Montreal: L'Harmattan, 9–188.
16. For details, see U. Freitag. 2012. 'Helpless Representatives of the Great Powers? Western Consuls in Jeddah, 1830s to 1914', in Journal of Imperial and Commonwealth Studies 40(3), 357–81.
17. More systematically on this issue and on the chronology of the presence of non-Muslim residents, see U. Freitag. 2011. 'The City and the Stranger: Jed-

dah in the Nineteenth Century', in U. Freitag et al., *The City in the Ottoman Empire: Migration and the Making of Urban Modernity*, London and New York: Routledge, 218–27.

18. For example, Ministère des Affaires Etrangères (MAE), Centre des Archives Diplomatiques de Nantes (CADN), Ambassade de France à Constantinople, série D, correspondence consulaire: Djeddah 1, Consul of France, Djeddah, to Ambassador, Constantinople, 12 June 1842; and PRO, FO 195/375, Vice-Consul Cole to Foreign Office, 4 May 1854.
19. FO 195/175, Extract of despatch from Vice-Consul C. Cole at Jeddah, 11 Nov. 1853; Vice-Consul Page to Ambassador, Constantinople, 27 Oct. 1856; Vice-Consul Page to Ambassador, Constantinople, 13 Jan. 1857; MAE, CADN, 2MI3228, M. Sabatier, Jeddah to Ministry of Foreign Affairs, Paris, 29 Nov. 1858.
20. The affair is documented in FO 195/375 and discussed in some detail by Pétriat, 'Fitna Djeddah', 43–47.
21. Details of this affair can be found in IOR Orme Ms, vol. 5, fol. 103–46, cf. R. Barendse. 2009. *Arabian Seas 1700–1763*, vol. 1, Leiden and Boston: Brill, 213, but wrongly dating it to 1726. A. Das Gupta. 2001. 'The Maritime Merchant and Indian History', in A. Das Gupta, *The World of the Indian Merchant 1500–1800*, Delhi: Oxford University Press, 24, places the blame squarely on a certain Gujarati merchant named Ali Bey, without giving any evidence. The affair is alluded to in J. Bruce. 1790. *Travels to Discover the Source of the Nile, in the Years 1768,1769, 1770, 1771, 1772, and 1773*, vol. 1, Edinburgh: J. Ruthven, 274, dating it to the 1740s.
22. The instrumentalization of the slavery issue is explicitly suggested, for example in Vice-Consul Page, Jeddah, to Ambassador, Constantinople, 4 Aug. 1856, FO 195/375.
23. Vice-Consul Page, Jeddah, to Ambassador, Constantinople, 27 Oct. 1856, FO 195/375, Pétriat, 'Fitna Djeddah', 29–35; and E. Toledano. 1982. *The Ottoman Slave Trade and its Suppression: 1840–1890*, Princeton: Princeton University Press, 129–35.
24. Vice-Consul Page, Jeddah, to Ambassador, Constantinople, 9 June 1856, FO 195/375.
25. Toledano, *The Ottoman Slave Trade*, 135–38.
26. Başbakanlık Osmanlı Arşivi, A.MKT.UM 494/40.
27. For the map, see Niebuhr, *Reisebeschreibung nach Arabien und anderen umliegenden Ländern*, vol. 1, table LV p. 278. The plan reverses East and West, North and South.
28. C. Niebuhr. 1772. *Beschreibung von Arabien: Aus eigenen Beobachtungen und im Land selbst gesammelten Nachrichten*. Copenhagen and Leipzig: Möller für Breitkopf, 353, my translation.
29. BOA (Başbakanlık Osmanlı Arşivi), PLK 45.
30. A detailed description is contained in M. Tamisier. 1840. *Voyages en Arabie, Séjour dans le Hedjaz, Campagnes d'Assis*, vol. 1, Paris: Louis Deséssart, 80–85.

31. Tamisier, *Voyage en Arabie*, vol. 1, 87, 90f.
32. Ibid., 84f.
33. Drawn by Melody Mosavat on the basis of an Ottoman map dated 1880–81, a copy of which was given to me in Jeddah. While I have been unable to trace this map in the Ottoman archives, BOA I::DH..826 66580 of 17 Jan. 1881 mentions the preparation of a map after the length and width of each building had been measured. This was in the context of wide-ranging, mostly military, repair works that were initiated from 1879 onwards.
34. Wellsted, *Travels in Arabia*, 282.
35. The terminology is very imprecise; R.F. Burton. 1893. *Personal Narrative of a Pilgrimage to Al-Madinah & Meccah*, vol. 2, London: Tylston & Edwards, 269, mentions two large *wikala*s in 1853, Wellsted speaks of caravanserais, and Burckhardt uses the term *khan*.
36. An inheritance document dated 22 Aug. 1841 in the possession of Mazen al-Saqqaf, Jeddah, consulted in November 2012, and another one used by Pétriat, *Les Grandes Familles Marchandes*, 449–53, dated 31 Mar. 1932, mention only these two terms.
37. E. Rüppell. 1838. *Reise in Abyssinien*, vol. 1, Frankfurt: Siegmund Schmerber, 172. Although the inheritance documents cited by Pétriat, *Les Grandes Familles Marchandes*, 449–53 date from the twentieth century, they confirm the historical report.
38. Burckhardt, *Travels in Arabia*, 19; for a more recent description, see Wahib Kabili. 2004. *Al-Hirafiyun fi Madinat Jidda fi 'l-Qarn al-Rabi' 'Ashar al-Hijri*, 3rd edn, Jeddah, 108.
39. FO 195/579, Walner to Acting Consul, Cairo, 17 Aug. 1858, enclosure 1, deposition by Myrealiki A. d'Antonio and Company, p. 7f. and enclosure 4, deposition by Nicolaos Sabbide, 5f.
40. Tamisier, *Voyage en Arabie*, vol. 1, 82–84.
41. The following is based on FO 195/579, Pullen to Secretary of the Admiralty, 19 June 1858.
42. This course of events is presented in the 'Memo of Events preceding the Jiddah Massacre', sent by Captain Pullen, Suez, to Captain Frushard, Jeddah, on 24 Aug. 1858, FO 78/1402. The account by W. Ochsenwald, 'The Jidda Massacre of 1858', 317f., differs slightly, but he also gives the Ottoman version of events.
43. A.Z. Dahlan. 1887–88. *Khulasat al-Kalam fi Bayan Umara' al-Balad al-Haram*, Cairo: 321.
44. Pétriat, 'Fitna Djeddah', 59f.
45. J. Glassman. 2011. *War of Words, War of Stones: Racial Thought and Violence in Colonial Zanzibar*, Bloomington: Indiana University Press, 232f.
46. FO 195/579, Walner to Acting Consul, Cairo, 17 Aug. 1858, enclosure 1, deposition by Myrialaki d'Antonio, 3f.
47. FO 881/848, Acting Consul-General Green to Earl of Malmesbury, 6 July 1858, encl. 2, M. Emerat to Count Walewski, Alexandria, 9 July 1858, FO 78/1402, Extract from Commander Cruttenden, to Consul-General, Egypt,

Suez, Sept. 1858, ibid., Précis of Captain Pullen to Secretary of the Admiralty, 25 June 1858.
48. This issue is discussed in detail by Pétriat, 'Fitna Djeddah'.
49. On these matters, Freitag, 'Helpless Representatives of the Great Powers?', 361.
50. FO 195/579, Walne to Acting Consul, Cairo, 17 Aug. 1858, enclosure 1, deposition by Myrialaki d'Antonio, 6; MAE, CADN, MI 3228, Sabatier, Jeddah to Ministère des Affaires Étrangères, 3 Nov. 1858.
51. FO 195/579, Walner to Acting Consul, Cairo, 17 Aug. 1858, enclosure 4, deposition by Nicolaos Sabbide, p. 4, on the role of the *qa'immaqam*, Pétriat, 'Fitna Djeddah', 89f. For further events, FO 881/848, Emerat to Count Walewski, Alexandria, 9 July 1858, 26–29.
52. FO 78/1488, note by Consul Walne, Cairo to Foreign Secretary, 16 Mar. 1859.
53. Ochsenwald, 'The Jidda Massacre of 1858', 318.
54. On the accusations against Nasif, see Pétriat, 'Fitna Djeddah', 66f.
55. FO 685/1, Vice-Consul Stanley, Jeddah, to Colquhon, Consul-General, Cairo, 18 Sept. 1860.
56. Ochsenwald, *Religion, Society, and the State in Arabia*, 144.
57. Ochsenwald, 'The Jidda Massacre of 1858', 319.
58. FO 881/848, Vice-Consul Calvert to Acting Consul-General Green, 8 Aug. 1858, p. 94f. For Pullen's letters to *wali* Namık Pasha, see BOA, I_HR_00160, Pullen to *Qa'immaqam*, 23 July 1858, 28 July 1858, 5 Aug. 1858. I am grateful to Feras Krimsti for providing me with copies of these documents.
59. FO 881/848, Vice-Consul Calvert to Acting Consul-General Green, 8 Aug. 1858, p. 96.
60. FO 195/579, Pullen to Secretary, Admiralty, 25 June 1858.
61. FO 78/1488, Brigadier Coghlan, British Resident, Aden to Captain Pullen, 30 Oct. 1858.
62. Pétriat, 'Fitna Djeddah', 64.
63. FO 881/848, Vice-Consul Calvert to Acting Consul-General Green, 8 Aug. 1858, p. 96f.
64. Ibid., p. 97.
65. Ochsenwald, 'The Jiddah Massacre of 1858', 322, a copy of the report is contained in CADN, 2_MI_3228, Sabatier, Le Caire, to Minister of Foreign Affairs, 2 Jan. 1859.
66. On the quality of the indictments, see Pétriat, 'Fitna Djeddah', 69f.
67. CADN, 2_MI_3228, Sabatier, Le Caire, to Minister of Foreign Affairs, 12 Jan. 1859 with accompanying correspondence.
68. CADN, 2_MI_3228, Sabatier, Le Caire, to Minister of Foreign Affairs, 2 Jan. 1859, encl. 1, undated letter from Namiq Pasha.
69. Pétriat, 'Fitna Djeddah', 93, quoting at length from a letter from Sabatier to the Foreign Ministry of 2 Jan. 1859.
70. FO 78/1488, Walne, Jeddah to Earl of Malmesbury, Foreign Department, 19 Jan. 1859.

71. Enclosure in ibid.
72. A. b. M. al-Hadrawi. 2002. *Al-Jawahir al-Muʿadda fi fadaʾil Judda*, Cairo, 43.
73. Ibid., 44.
74. Dahlan, *Khulasat al-Kalam*, 323.
75. This perspective was inspired by E.P. Thompson's considerations on moral economy and the (rather loose) application of the concept to Middle Eastern riots by E. Burke III. 1986. 'Towards a History of Urban Collective Action in the Middle East: Continuities and Change 1750–1980', in K. Brown et al., *Urban Crises and Social Movements in the Middle East*, Paris: L'Harmattan, 42–56, notably 49. As the original concept is much more closely linked to food riots and thus squarely economic issues, I have, however, avoided the term 'moral economy'. See E.P. Thompson. 1971. 'The Moral Economy of the English Crowd in the Eighteenth Century', in *Past and Present* 50, 76–136.
76. Burke, 'Towards a History of Urban Collective Action', 45.
77. Pétriat, 'Fitna Djeddah', 59.
78. Dahlan, *Khulasat al-Kalam*, 322f., the quote is found on p. 323.
79. Ibid., 323.
80. Burke, 'Towards a History of Urban Collective Action', 49; for a comparative view on these uprisings, J. Cole. 1989. 'Of Crowds and Empires: Afro-Asian Riots and European Expansion, 1857–1882', *Comparative Studies in Society and History* 31, 106–33.
81. Pullen's report mentions that 'after due deliberation at the Consulate, the Vessel was adjudicated to be forfeited to the Crown'; in a French report, the 'Consulate' mutates into a 'tribunal Consulaire'. FO 78/1402, 'Memo of Events preceding the Jiddah Massacre', Captain Pullen, Suez to Capt. Frushard, Jeddah, on 24 Aug. 1858, FO 881/848, M. Emerat to Count Walewski, Alexandria, 9 July 1858.
82. FO 78/1402, 'Memo of Events preceding the Jiddah Massacre', Captain Pullen, Suez to Capt. Frushard, Jeddah, on 24 Aug. 1858.
83. FO 195/579, Walner to Acting Consul, Cairo, 17 Aug. 1858, enclosure 1, deposition by Myrealiki A. d'Antonio and Company, and FO 881/848, M. Emerat to Count Walewski, Alexandria, 9 July 1858.
84. On the ritualistic aspects of violence, see A. Blok. 2000. 'The Enigma of Senseless Violence', in G. Aijmer and J. Abbink (eds), *Meanings of Violence: A Cross-Cultural Perspective*, Oxford and New York: Berg, 23–38; for violence in consequence of broken negotiations, see Tilly, *The Politics of Collective Violence*, 16 and 194–220.
85. Pétriat, 'Fitna Djeddah', 122–28; on the problems of distinguishing between 'force' and 'violence', see Tilly, *The Politics of Collective Violence*, 26–31, 55–80.
86. In an interesting variation, Dahlan, in *Khulasat al-kalam*, who somehow merges the two waves of execution, mentions the customs office as the site of the execution of all but al-ʿAmudi and ʿAbdallah al-Muhtasib, who he says were executed in the bazaar.

87. Tamisier, *Voyage en Arabie*, vol. 1, 85.
88. One such coffee-house owner, a certain Ahmad Sabahy, rescued a number of Christians. FO 78/1488, Consul Walne, Cairo to Foreign Secretary, 16 March 1859, enclosure: 'List of persons who conducted themselves in a manner more or less praiseworthy ... on the 15th of June 1858 and following days'.
89. al-Hadrawi, al-Jawahir al-Muʿadda, 45.
90. Bruce, *Travels to Discover the Source of the Nile*, vol. 1, 274. He mentions that this massacre occurred some twenty-four years earlier. If this is linked to the date of the visit, this event would have occurred in 1745; if to the date of writing, sometime around 1762–64, see the biographical note in the abridged version, London 1835, xxiv.
91. Dahlan, *Khulasat al-Kalam*, 323; cf. M.M. al-ʿAlawi, *Fitnat Jidda: Riwaya*. Beirut 2010: al-Kaukab, for a survey of local historiography that is nevertheless informed to a large extent by British sources; Pétriat, 'Fitna Djeddah', 96–102.
92. Ochsenwald, *Religion, Society, and the State in Arabia*, 180; al-Hadrawi, al-Jawahir al-Muʿadda, 45f.
93. FO 195/1251, Consul Zohrab to the Marquis of Salisbury, 13 Nov. 1879.
94. On the French consular building and the damages inflicted by rains, see CADN, Const. Amb., série D, Djeddah, vol. 6, Letters by Consul Descouture to Ambassador, Constantinople, 7 Nov. and 4 Dec. 1895.
95. FO 195/2126, Dewey, Jeddah, to O'Connor, London, 24 June 1902 and 11 Aug. 1902.
96. That this was different for the countryside is evident from the Ottoman order that British subjects were not to leave Jeddah in the heat of summer for the surrounding villages, reported in FO 195/2061, Hussain to O'Connor, 18 Sept. 1899.

Part III

⸘ ◆ ⸘

Communal Violence and its Discontents

※ Chapter 6 ※

The 1850 Uprising in Aleppo
Reconsidering the Explanatory Power of Sectarian Argumentations

FERAS KRIMSTI

In the middle of the nineteenth century, several cities and regions in the Arab provinces of the Ottoman Empire, such as Mount Lebanon, Aleppo, Nablus, Jeddah and Damascus, witnessed episodes of urban violence. In current scholarship, these outbursts are singled out from the cities' wider histories of uprisings and clashes due to their apparent 'confessional' character. The 1850 uprising in Aleppo is one of these cases. It was triggered by the introduction of military recruitment and a new head tax by the Ottoman authorities. On 16 October 1850, hundreds of the city's inhabitants from the eastern suburbs, particularly the quarters Qarliq, Bab al-Nayrab and Banqusa, rioted. The protesters joined forces and marched to the palace of the *vali*, Mustafa Zarif Pasha, who refused to let them before him and later withdrew to the fortress al-Shaykh Yabraq. The insurgents then marched to the house of ʿAbdallah Babinsi, *mütesellim* of the city. ʿAbdallah Babinsi, however, publicly refused to lead their insurrection. In what followed, they first attacked houses inhabited by Christians. The next day, the insurgents launched an attack on the district of al-Saliba, where they began to pillage and plunder. Churches, private homes and shops were looted and burned down; Christians were attacked, injured and in some cases killed. Through negotiations, the noblemen of the city, led by ʿAbdallah Babinsi, succeeded in calming the rioters, who formulated demands and addressed them to the *vali*. The governor agreed to the demands at first. When, however, reinforcement arrived from Diyarbakır, he arrested ʿAbdallah Babinsi, and his troops launched an attack on Bab al-Nayrab, Banqusa and Qarliq. On 8 November, the rebels were defeated. The governor was deposed by the Ottoman authorities, the victims were compensated for the losses incurred, stolen goods had to be restored and the leaders of the insurrection were exiled. ʿAbdallah Bey was sent to Istanbul to be brought to trial, but he never arrived there alive.[1]

Moshe Maʿoz's monograph *Ottoman Reform in Syria and Palestine, 1840–1861*, attempted to interpret the events as a response to the Tanzimat reforms. This chapter of the political history of Aleppo, according to him, represents 'the process of transformation which the Tanzimat gave rise to in the Syrian town'.[2] He regards the 1850 events as part of a series of violent outbursts against Christians and Europeans in other cities in the Arab provinces of the Ottoman Empire. His argumentation, though well informed, often has an essentialist bias. The idea that there existed a primordial conflict between Christians and Muslims is the thread running through his argumentation – he considers the events of 1850 to have been an 'outburst of Muslim fanaticism'.[3] Masters summarizes the basic problem of this approach as follows: 'Maʿoz's interpretation seems to take Muslim hostility towards Christians as a societal constant in the relationship between the religious communities in the city, and this assumption is not justified by Aleppo's history'.[4] Primordial and essentialist reasoning is fortunately no longer predominant in Western historical research devoted to these events. A number of excellent articles and studies examine administrative, economic and other aspects of the 1850 uprising.[5] Still, the question of the explanatory power that can be attached to religion and sectarian conflict lingers in the background and poses problems. In recent studies of mid-nineteenth-century uprisings and bloodshed, the sectarian question is either omitted or the role attributed to it has shifted from a reason for conflict in and of itself to a political tool in the hands of European powers, their representatives in the Ottoman Empire and the minorities living there, especially Ottoman Christians. Makdisi terms it a 'culture of sectarianism'[6] that provided a religious and essentialist rhetoric that gave European powers the right to intervene in the internal affairs of the Ottoman Empire and allowed the Christians themselves to attract European protection and support.

This short chapter will undertake a micro-historical analysis of some aspects of the 1850 events. It is hoped that such an analysis provides a deeper understanding of the underlying processes that brought about the uprising, and that it can contribute to discarding more superficial assumptions about the nature of the events. Rather than premising primarily 'confessional tensions' as a definite cause of the uprising, this chapter attempts an unprepossessing investigation into the complex realities of those drawn into the events. For a nuanced picture of the events to emerge, first the language of contemporary reports identifying the rioters is examined. Afterwards, the spatial unfolding of the events will be analysed. It will thus be shown that although those attacked and those attacking were undoubtedly Christians and Muslims, respectively, they were inhabitants of a city living complex realities under particular historical circumstances. The notion of an attack on 'the Christian population' or 'the Christian quarter' has to be regarded with caution for its inability to picture these realities adequately.[7]

I will draw mainly on two reports, most probably by Christian eyewitnesses to the events, that are kept in the archive of the Greek Orthodox Patriarchate in Damascus.[8] The texts are two chronological accounts of the 1850 events in Aleppo. Since they are grouped together with other writings addressed to Dimitri Shahada[9] and his handwriting can be found on account no. 1, it is very probable that they were written for his attention. Other primary sources will also be referred to in passing.

The Events through Narration

Contemporaries to the events have referred to the rebels and the victims in different terms and have made use of very different language. In a letter, dated 19 October, Nathaniel William Werry (1782–1855), the English consul in Aleppo, informs Stratford Canning (1786–1880), the British ambassador to the Ottoman Empire, about the uprising in Aleppo in the following way:

> It is my painful duty to communicate to Y. E. that disturbances of a very serious and disgraceful nature have occurred in this City, arising I believe from the aversion of the Islam population here, and generally in this district against the Conscription, of which advantage has been taken by the population and their parizans here to vent their fanatical spirit against the Christian population of this City.[10]

Werry's choice of words is significant; he depicts two monolithic blocks, the 'Islam population' and the 'Christian population'. He does not stand alone with this view of the events. A contemporary Jewish writer in his private notebook also 'attributes the outbreak of the events to Muslim religious fanaticism sparked by provocative Christian behavior';[11] Harel, who has studied the source, stresses that it does not distinguish between different Muslim affiliations or Christian groups – the Jewish writer only speaks of 'Muslims against Christians'.[12] Even accounts by local Christians like those of the Maronite bishop Bulus Arutin (1788–1851) and the Syrian Catholic teacher Na''um Bakhkhash (d. 1875) draw a picture of 'Muslim' resentment against 'the Christians'.[13] Nevertheless, Arutin refers to the insurgents not only as 'the Muslims' (*al-islam*), but identifies them as coming from Bab al-Nayrab, Qarliq and Banqusa, and calls them 'masses of pillagers' (*jamahir al-nahibin*) or simply 'the people' (*al-qawm*) – without characterizing them by their religion. The victims of the events, on the contrary, are called 'the Christians' (*al-masihiyyun*, *al-nasara*). But in one place, they are explicitly referred to as 'the Christians living in al-Saliba' (*al-masihiyyun al-sakinun al-Saliba*).[14]

From the two Arabic reports by anonymous writers kept in the Greek Orthodox Patriarchate in Damascus, an even more complicated picture emerges. Account no. 1 distinguishes between different groups. The rebels very frequently appear simply as 'inhabitants' (*ahali*) of Qarliq, Banqusa and Bab al-Nayrab, and, in the beginning, their actions are described independently. They are once stated as being explicitly opposed to 'inhabitants of the city who wanted to keep the order' (*jamʿ ghafir min al-muhafizin min ahali 'l-balda lladhina bi-'l-itaʿa*). In other parts, the rebels are simply referred to with verbs in the third-person plural (*nahabu, ittajahu*, etc.) – without a particular noun, and without mention being made of any confessional, social, ethnic or economic background. Sometimes, they are called the 'masses' (*jamahir*). Interestingly, during the description of the rebels' fight with the Ottoman soldiers, they are again referred to as 'inhabitants of the city' (*ahali 'l-balda*), for example:

> Let us return to how the Christians (*al-masihiyyun*) had to suffer from Thursday morning till noon. Thanks to the special care and intercession of the day's patron saint ... they survived without any harm being done to them. If this war had lasted two or three more hours, much of their blood would have been spilled and if the inhabitants of the city (*ahali 'l-balda*) had won, none of them would have been allowed to live.[15]

Thus, those attacked during the uprising are called 'the Christian people' (*al-shaʿb al-masihi*) – interestingly, once in the immediate context of a mention of the 'Jewish-Israelite people' (*al-shaʿb al-israʾili al-yahudi*) and another time in an emotional exclamation: 'Woe to the Christian people [*al-shaʿb al-masihi*] – how much did they have to suffer in these awful days from terror and danger!' Importantly, one passage refers to the 'notables of al-Saliba' (*akabir al-Saliba*). References to the 'inhabitants' or the 'people' create a close link between the account and reports about earlier uprisings in the city of Aleppo, which had no confessional dimension at all. Contemporaries writing about such events frequently mention the 'inhabitants' or the 'people' as principal actors during episodes of urban contention. One example is a comment by Ulrich Japser

Seetzen, a traveller residing for some time in Aleppo at the beginning of the nineteenth century. In his reports, he calls the people revolting in Aleppo in 1804 '*wuláhd el béllad* or children of the town, as they are usually called here'.[16] It is surprising and at the same time telling that even a stranger with a limited knowledge of Arabic recalls the notion as idiomatic, and writes it down in his personal notes. By employing a very similar notion, account no. 1 also situates itself within this tradition of violence and reporting of violence.

Account no. 2 is already closer to Werry's rhetoric, as it starts as follows: 'On October 16, 1850 ... an uprising started, originally initiated by the Muslims (*islam*) of Qarliq, Banqusa and Bab al-Nayrab'. An antagonistic relationship between the city's 'Muslims' (*islam*) and 'Christians' (*nasara*) is thus depicted, but here and in other places more differentiated than in Werry's report; quarters are precisely given. The anonymous author underlines: 'No Muslim (*min al-islam*) – besides some rare cases – was there who did not commit these atrocities; not even ten per cent out of a hundred'. And he generalizes more: 'Muslims of all quarters gathered in huge numbers (*wa-tajamharat al-muslimin jamahir jamahir min sayr sawayih*)'. One section is particularly striking:

> Who can describe the humiliation of the Christians (*al-nasara*) ... in these days? They were constantly, day and night, afraid of the Muslims (*al-islam*) who menaced: 'On this day or in the next hour or on the next day we will cut you down with our sword and kill you'.

Despite this pronouncedly more 'sectarian' rhetoric, the unknown author sometimes comes close to the style of the author of account no. 1. He also refers to the rebels as 'inhabitants of the city' (using slightly different expressions: *ahali 'l-balad* and *ahl al-balad*) while describing their combat with the Ottoman soldiers: 'On the morning of Wednesday, the 6 November, the inhabitants of the quarters of Qarliq, Banqusa and Bab al-Nayrab (*ahali 'l-balad min sawayih Qarliq wa-Banqusa wa-Bab al-Nayrab*) returned to combat'.

At the other end of the spectre, very surprisingly, the Protestant missionary Ford even more radically states that the attack on the Christians was altogether unmotivated and the choice of victims almost accidental:

> For some time past nothing but an occasion has been wanted for an outbreak. Such an occasion was presented by the arrival of an order, addressed to the Pasha of the province, to raise a conscription of soldiers, by taking a certain number by lot from all who were of proper age and circumstances to enter the army. As might be supposed, this

> measure was very unwelcome to the Mohammedans ... [T]hey resolved to effect their object by a popular tumult. Having determined a blow, *it was of little consequence to them upon whom it should fall* [italics mine].[17]

In view of these diverging points of view, it also has to be asked to what degree the notion of a 'Christian population' is a meaningful entity in this particular historical context. Despite the general availability of a language of religious differentiation between Christians and Muslims, as was employed by *shariʻa* courts, for example, it has to be underlined that it was 'enmeshed in a range of competing discourses of obedience, allegiance, and loyalty inherent in local society'.[18] The Christians of Aleppo were anything but a unified whole that could be contrasted with the city's Muslims as another unified whole. The Christians were divided among themselves as adherents of different churches with different rites, liturgies and independent hierarchies: the Greek Orthodox (*rum*), the Armenian Christians (*arman*), the Jacobite Syrians (*suryan*) and the Maronite Christians.[19] The Greek Orthodox Christians of Aleppo were under the authority of the ecumenical Patriarch of Phanar; the Armenian Patriarch was responsible for all other Christians. Thus, the Christians of Aleppo were no self-evident unit – neither with respect to liturgy and rite nor in administrative matters. Furthermore, due to the activities of Latin missionaries[20] among the Christians of Aleppo in the second half of the seventeenth century, a movement towards communion with Rome began, which resulted in a fierce dispute.[21] The number of Catholics among the Christians of Aleppo grew steadily. The established churches, fearing for their future, frequently sent petitions to the Porte pleading for intervention.[22] This undermined whatever 'Christian solidarity' may have existed, even after the Ottoman Porte officially recognized the Uniate churches in 1839. Aversion, distrust and bitterness reigned.[23] The seemingly self-evident notion of 'the Christians' of Aleppo then becomes questionable – not even at an emotional level can we speak of a unified Christian community.

Furthermore, it has to be taken into consideration that not only the designation 'Christians' but also 'Muslims' is very vague. It has frequently been noted[24] that the rioters who attacked the Christian quarter mostly came from the eastern suburbs of the city, notably from the quarters Qarliq, Bab al-Nayrab and Banqusa. These quarters were inhabited by a very heterogeneous, mostly poor population with a rural background, among them many Kurds, Turkmen and other non-Arab and Bedouin elements who had migrated to the city.[25]

Sectarian Rhetoric or Hybrid Language

Bearing all this in mind, it still seems legitimate to ask how the rhetoric employed in the sources should be interpreted, if not in sectarian terms. Why should eyewitnesses, in particular, speak of an attack on the 'Christians' as a group by the 'Muslims' as a group if it was not the confessional motif in particular that led to the attack? Such a confessional dimension seems to have been felt, or at least articulated. Possibly, the reports and letters represent instances of a developing sectarian rhetoric as envisaged by Ussama Makdisi for nineteenth-century Lebanon. Makdisi understands sectarianism as a 'practice that developed out of, and must be understood in the context of, nineteenth-century Ottoman reform' and as 'a discourse that is scripted as the Other to various competing ... narratives of modernization'.[26] According to him, it refers to the 'deployment of religious heritage as a primary marker of modern political identity'.[27] Religion in the case of Aleppo, too, could have become 'the site of the colonial encounter in the Ottoman Empire in that European officials defined the parameters of reform through a modernization discourse couched in terms of a religious civilizational clash'.[28] Thus, no religious violence devoid of social and cultural meaning would at least be reflected in the writings examined above. Following Makdisi, one could argue that, instead of an upswell of latent primordial religious solidarities and hostilities, sectarianism was actively produced at that time, and thus reflections of its genesis can be traced in the writings examined above – very pronouncedly in Werry's consular correspondence.

On the other hand, it can also be argued that what *sounds* like sectarian rhetoric may not *be* sectarian by nature. Watenpaugh has drawn our attention to moments of hybridization reflected in the language of such writing.[29] He observes phenomena of hybridization in the expression of new ethnic ideas. The language used to refer to existing conceptions of difference can be grafted onto newly developing ideas of difference. In the case of mid-nineteenth-century Aleppo, the Christians distinguished themselves less by their religious 'otherness' – a century-old given that had rarely resulted in bloodshed – than by their economic 'otherness'. A language of religious differentiation being available, this language was possibly grafted onto this new 'otherness'. The Protestant missionary Ford wrote the following lines about the attack on the Christians, emphasizing the new 'Christian' attitude:

> The Christians in Aleppo, of all sects, number between fifteen and twenty thousand. They are more wealthy [sic], and more polished [sic]

in their manners, than their brethren in most eastern cities; and are correspondingly more proud and vain-glorious. They have been wont to consider themselves as the aristocracy of Syria … Their wealth, instead of being usefully employed, or even prudently concealed, has been ostentatiously displayed in splendid furniture and gorgeous dresses, as also in the costly decoration of their churches.[30]

The idea that the 1850 events were also economically conditioned has already been suggested by Masters who, basing himself on Wallerstein's world-system model, considers the events 'an aftershock of Syria's incorporation into the capitalist world system'.[31] He argues conclusively that the riots were a direct result of government demands (higher taxes and more manpower for the army), that those rioting – poor Muslims from the eastern suburbs – were under great strain from economic changes, famine and oppressive direct taxation, and finally that those who were attacked – mostly Catholics – had risen as a new entrepreneurial class.[32] Harel, however, has drawn our attention to the fact that an economic argumentation alone seems insufficient in view of the fact that the Jews also benefited from economic change. Nevertheless, they were not attacked in 1850.[33]

Many Christians distinguished themselves not only economically; the important point seems to be that, with the beginning of the Tanzimat reforms, they had recently begun to be perceived as being politically different, privileged. Moshe Ma'oz in particular – although adopting sectarian arguments – has interpreted the riots in the context of a reaction to the changes implemented during the Tanzimat period in urban politics.[34] The 1850 uprising took place in the era of the *Hatt-ı Şerif* of Gülhane, which was promulgated in 1839. The decree dealt with provincial administration, the welfare of Ottoman subjects and the status of non-Muslim citizens; security of life, honour, fortune, and a regular system of levying taxes were to be guaranteed for all Ottoman subjects.[35] It is important to underline that not only the equal status granted implicitly to non-Muslims, but also the introduction of direct taxation and conscription, as well as the restructuring of provincial administration were among the measures that deeply affected provincial politics and society.[36] The new perception of the Christians can thus be considered a result of a 'disturbance of the delicate socio-political balance … that regulated Aleppine society for many generations'.[37] Unlike Harel, who, despite this striking insight, like Ma'oz, does not eliminate the religiously coloured notions of 'offence', 'humiliation', 'disappointment' and 'hatred' from his argumentation, and even refers to 'religious fanaticism'[38] and dismisses economic motivations altogether, I would like to argue that, as a socio-political group, the Christians, and particularly the Catholics, benefited economically and politically from the opportunities created by the Tanzimat reforms more than other groups displaying this betterment. In the words of David, who avoids sectarian argumentations: 'The citizens of Aleppo rose against a set of measures taken by the state to redefine its relations with the population'.[39] Masters calls the result a political 'disjunction' of the Christians in a 'framework of social discontinuity'.[40] This caused socio-political tension in Aleppo, which did not decrease until after the eruption in 1850.

Neither of the reasons given above – economic betterment and socio-political shifts – can alone fully explain what happened in 1850; instead, the fact that they occurred together and that they were intricately entangled should be accepted as the major reason for the eruption of violence in Aleppo. To a certain degree, difference building up on the basis of these developments coincided with religious difference, but by no means fully. For this reason, most of the eyewitnesses' reports quoted above operate within the framework of a language of sectarian differentiation, some of them more, some less. But – through spatial reference and precisions, through reference to notions like *ahali 'l-balad* anchored in the city's history, and through economic observations added immediately – their identifications of actors all betray far more complex realities than solely a society marked by confession. These hints sometimes receive less interest than they deserve beside shockingly overt confessional attributions, which are, of course, in themselves, not untrue.

Now, a glimpse at the stage of the city during the uprising and the spatial patterns of the events seem to corroborate the hypothesis of a multi-causally determined breakdown.

The Events through Spatial Patterns

The idea that in 1850 an attack on the 'Christian quarter(s)' of Aleppo took place has been brought forward in various places. Frequently in this context, the toponym 'al-Judayda' is used interchangeably with 'al-Saliba',[41] although the two places can be clearly distinguished. While 'al-Judayda' covers the northern suburbs in general, 'al-Saliba' refers to a western *mahalla* in al-Judayda, architecturally strongly marked by the presence of five churches. Although it was part of al-Judayda, it was separated from it by some gates. While al-Saliba was an administrative unit, al-Judayda was not – rather the *mahallat* of which it consisted were administrative units. We have to distinguish between al-Judayda and al-Saliba with regard to the 1850 uprising, all the more because Arutin and the author of account no. 1 underline that the insurgents only attacked confessionally mixed quarters in al-Judayda – except al-Saliba – on the first day and al-Saliba, which was inhabited exclusively by Christians, on the second day. Taking these important distinctions into consideration, according to administrative districts as indicated by the Ottoman census of the year 1849[42] (serving as an indicator of its overall Christian population), the number of male Christians can be compared to the rioters' movements in the city. For the analysis of the rebels' way through the city, one has to rely mostly on the two reports from the Greek Orthodox Patriarchate in Damascus; other sources remain far more general about the spatial unfolding of the uprising. (For the resulting comparison, see table 6.1)

The census document provides detailed information about the Christian, Jewish[43] and Muslim inhabitants of Aleppo; only males were counted because they were liable to taxes and military duties. It allows for some very general observations on demographic patterns of concentration. For the northern suburbs, a number of 8,210 male Christians is indicated. They lived in 1,527 households (*khanas*). (For the sake of comparison: male Muslims in the northern suburbs totalled 2,352; the Muslim population there lived in 817 households.) For the rest of the city, the census document gives the number of 541 male Christians (335 *intra muros*, 118 in the eastern suburbs, 88 in the western suburbs) and 133 Christian households (95 *intra muros*, 16 in the eastern suburbs, 22 in the western suburbs).

The first important observation one can make is that in some of the places where riots and lootings took place, a large number of Christian inhabitants is attested – one can thus conclude that greater numbers of Christians were living in the places where the uprising took place. The Ottoman census of Aleppo, for example, gives 472 male Christians (or 148 houses inhabited by Christians) in al-Saliba, 789 Christians (or 90 houses) in Tumayat and 326 Christians (or 77 houses) in Zuqaq al-Arbaʿin. In contrast, there are numerous districts that were not affected by the events and where, as expected, we find very few Christians. An example is provided by al-Nuhiyya, where 6 Christian houses were located, with the Christian males there numbering only 29. However, the number of districts that were not attacked but for which relatively high numbers of male Christians are attested – and consequently presumably many Christian residents of both sexes and all age groups – is striking. Thus, in some quarters that were part of al-Judayda, we find large numbers of Christian inhabitants: in Qastal al-Harami, which was not affected by the uprising, male Christians totalled 699 and the Christian population lived in 146 houses. In al-Akrad 453 male Christians (80 Christian houses) were counted, and in al-Hazzaza even 794 male Christians (91 Christian houses). These places were not attacked. The same holds true for some rather remote western suburbs with small numbers of Christians. More surprisingly, some eastern quarters, where the insurgents came from (Tatarlar, Shakir Agha, al-Malandi and ad-Dallalin), even had a few Christian inhabitants – yet they were not attacked.[44] David, too, points out that there were many areas with a mixed population where no attacks took place, and he also hints at individual cases of neighbourly assistance, in which Christians were protected by their Muslim neighbours.[45] The parallel to the 1860 massacre of the Christians in Damascus is striking. Ten years after the uprising in Aleppo, in Damascus, the rioters did not attack those Christians living in the mixed quarter of Bab al-Musalla.[46] In view of these data, residential patterns and attacks, the notion of an attack on the 'Christian quarter(s)' of Aleppo loses much of its base. There were quarters inhabited by a greater or smaller number of Christians; some of them were attacked, some were not. The attacks were limited to several locations in the northern suburbs of the city.

Al-Saliba, which was inhabited by an overwhelming Christian majority and which came under attack, is a special case. But to what degree can it be considered a 'Christian quarter'? Tamdoğan-Abel points out that the notion of 'quarter' has different meanings: it can refer to a topographical or administrative division, a network of social bonds or an identitary reference point.[47] But the notion of 'quarter' is not only problematic for the multiplicity of meanings attached to it; it is also marked by its fluidity. According to Tamdoğan-Abel, a quarter is a 'configuration', 'et s'il y a configuration, il peut y en avoir plusieurs' ('and if there is configuration, there can be more than one').[48] The quarter, then, has to be considered as a network of overlapping nets of social relations; it is essentially dynamic. Conceiving a quarter only in terms of confession means falling back into Orientalist conceptions of the Islamic city, and leads to mentally constructing Aleppo as a city 'profoundly split between hostile communities ... a dislocated city, broken up into closed, inward-looking sectors.'[49] But al-Saliba was not closed, not inward looking and dislocated, not only characterized by its confession; instead it had an important socio-economic network. This becomes clear if, for example, one compares the map of Aleppo by Rousseau published in 1825 under the title 'Plan de la ville de Hhaleb et de ses environs dressé de 1811 à 1818 par la Société de géographie' with the first draft of the map drawn in 1811 by Vincent Germain, the son of a merchant from Aleppo.[50] The map itself, according to Raymond, differs little in the two versions, but the list of toponyms provided is considerably enlarged in the later version. With regard to al-Saliba, it is remarkable that artisanal

Table 6.1. Number of Christian and Muslim inhabitants in quarters with a Christian population.

Quarter	Number of male Christian inhabitants/ number of their households	Number of male Muslim inhabitants/ number of their households	Looting took place (yes/no)	Quarter	Number of male Christian inhabitants/ number of their households	Number of male Muslim inhabitants/ number of their households	Looting took place (yes/no)
NORTHERN SUBURBS							
al-Saliba	472/148	–	yes	al-Qawwas	132/29	69/21	no
at-Tumayat	789/90	–	yes	Marʿashli	173/36	62/19	no
al-Shamali	123/33	2/1	yes	Turbat al-Ghurabaʾ	220/44	8/2	yes
ʿAbdalhaiy	202/51	–	yes	al-Mugharbaliya	158/21	68/24	yes
al-ʿAtawi al-Kabir +al-Saghir	171/39 + 62/14	17/9 + 29/10	yes	al-Almaji	924/72	134/44	yes
al-Hazzaza	794/91	126/38	no	al-Sharʿasus	336/71	50/26	yes
al-Ghattas	32/6	–	no	Juqur Qastal	150/26	92/35	yes
Shakarji	45/7	–	location unclear	at-Tabbala	165/31	56/24	no
Abdarrahim	213/60	102/25	yes	al-Mawardi	60/14	91/31	yes
Zuqaq al-Arbaʿin	326/77	38/13	yes	Kharab Khan	62/18	131/54	yes

The 1850 Uprising in Aleppo 153

Bala Burghul	135/36	8/2	yes	Kujak Kallasa	94/16	14/7	no
Bait Muhibb	155/32	30/12	yes	Aghyur	570/112	419/135	no
al-Akrad	453/80	69/25	no	al-Nuhiyya	29/6	113/35	no
Jisr al-Kaʿka	174/57	23/16	no	ʿAntar	17/3	104/37	no
al-Basatina	139/32	173/61	yes	Zuqaq al-Qir	51/10	3/1	yes
Qastal al-Musht	85/19	92/28	no	Qastal al-Harami	699/146	229/82	no
EASTERN SUBURBS				QUARTERS INTRA MUROS			
Tatarlar	68/11	249/98	no	Bab Qinnasrin	2/1	419/169	no
Shakir Agha	12/2	160/74	no	Sahat Biza	22/6	527/210	no
al-Malandi	9/2	234/89	no	al-ʿAqaba	42/11	178/89	no
ad-Dallalin	29/1	464/173	no	Jubb Asadallah	128/37	301/146	no
WESTERN SUBURBS				Jallum al-Kubra	93/28	861/346	no
al-ʿAinaya	36/9	479/152	no	al-Bayada	3/1	572/268	no
al-Shammaʿin	43/9	145/56	no	Suwayqa ʿAli	16/4	191/82	no
al-Kattab	9/4	-	no	al-Bandara	3/1	157/26	no
				Bahsita	4/1	145/59	no
				al-Masabin	22/5	236/91	no

Note: The administrative districts touched / not touched by the uprising in 1850 are indicated. The data stem from BA, NFS.d.03726 (numbers of male Christian and Muslim inhabitants) and account nos 1 and 2 (identification of quarters looted).

activities receive a lot of space: factories of golden yarn, silk factories and dyeing factories appear in great number in the 1818 version of the map.[51]

The two reports from the archive of the Greek Orthodox Patriarchate in Damascus provide us with information about houses and workshops of the wealthy Christian merchants looted in 1850. Account no. 1 lists – along with the number of looted and damaged church buildings – 240 looted houses and 20 plundered shops in streets outside of al-Saliba, and 161 buildings inside al-Saliba. Account no. 2 also contains a detailed description:

> In the quarter of al-Saliba, 164 houses were looted,[52] and in most cases nothing but ruins and ashes remained. They stole diamonds, pearls, gold, silver, amber, cashmere, money, silk, tissue, clothes of value, furniture of high quality, fabrics, Kermes dye, embroidered garments, woven scarves, and so on and so forth. Most of the house owners were masters in weaving and embroidering, and everything that had to do with their work was in their houses, which were shops at the same time. Everything which was stolen or damaged, in al-Saliba alone, amounted to 24,000 *kese*.]

We cannot but conclude from the above observations that what occurred in 1850 did not unfold necessarily in an exclusively confessionally marked space. Rather, we must envision a targeting of some particular points of the city. Al-Saliba, which came under attack, was not only 'Christian' but was also an important economic and political hub.

But why then were churches one of the insurgents' main targets? It is undeniable that the Christian buildings were especially targeted for sacking. Chad Emmett thinks that the question where, how and why a place of worship is built or treated is in general indicative of interreligious attitudes. He establishes a typology of ten possible constellations and tries to demonstrate that a changing handling of architectural givens may hint at conflict or mutual understanding among inhabitants of different beliefs.[53] Although Emmett's hypothesis is not wrong, it is surely an oversimplification: a particular attitude does not necessarily lead to a certain spatial practice, and a spatial practice does not necessarily hint at a certain interreligious relationship. Social configurations of utmost complexity determine spatial practices – indexing them with the notions 'tolerance' and 'intolerance' seems to be misleading.

In Aleppo, the five churches of al-Saliba had existed since at least the sixteenth century. For centuries, church construction had been severely restricted, and permission had had to be granted by the sultan. The existing churches were therefore considered nearly inviolable. No records have come down to us that speak of earlier attacks on Christian church buildings during episodes of urban contention. Shortly before the Tanzimat reforms, the question of church construction and renovation was still a serious political issue.[54] Only ten years later, the situation was fundamentally different. During the Egyptian occupation, three new churches were simultaneously built in al-Saliba and even outside of it, in al-Shar'sus. The construction of the monumental Roman Catholic church al-Sayyida lasted more than ten years (1833–1843). Interestingly, for the period following the restoration of Ottoman rule in 1840 in Aleppo, incidents involving churches started to be recorded. Some Muslims seem to have entered the Syrian Catholic church, stealing a candleholder and beating a priest.[55] In 1848, Bakhkhash wrote in his diary that a *firman* by the sultan had been read aloud that allowed the Christians to restore and construct churches without asking for the authorities' permission.[56] In consequence, building activities intensified – in May 1849, all Christian communities conducted church construction works.[57] The inhabitants reacted; in June 1849, Muslim inhabitants and the *vali*, the *mufti* and the *kadı* stopped the works in al-Shar'asus.[58] Both sides sent petitions to Istanbul. Meanwhile, work went on in al-Saliba.[59] All this makes it clear that church buildings were a part of the city's space where political change that destabilized the 'old order' manifested itself drastically. Furthermore, churches were also symbols of a very earthly economic prosperity. Jean Marmarbaschi, the secretary of the Patriarch of Antioch, gives an idea of the wealth that was displayed in the Syrian church of Aleppo: 'Mgr Djarvé transporta donc à Alep tout ce que son église avait de plus cher et de plus précieux en ornements, vases sacrés, livres manuscrits, dont plusieurs remontaient jusqu'au sixième siècle de l'ère chrétienne' ('Mr Djarvé thus brought to Aleppo all the most expensive and most preciously ornamented things his church had, holy vessels, manuscripts, some of them going back to the sixth century of the Christian era').[60] The two accounts from the archive of the Greek Orthodox Patriarchate of Damascus also strengthen this impression. Silver, liturgical instruments, robes, coins, furniture and icons are mentioned among the things that had been stolen or destroyed.

The sacking of the churches – places of worship fundamentally important for the religious practice of the communities centred in al-Saliba – was a conscious act of desecration of the sacral. But it was more than that: shortly before the 1850 uprising in Aleppo, the role that churches played in the urban space had changed fundamentally; churches were now infused with a new economic and political symbolism. Al-Saliba was booming, and it had grown in political and economic importance far beyond the local sphere. It is interesting to note in this context that only a few years after the uprising, in 1859, the quarter al-Saliba appears as the setting of the novel *Way idhan lastu bi-ifranj* ['Whoops, this means I am not a European'], by the Lebanese intellectual Khalil al-Khuri, who ironically depicts the ongoing process of Westernization there.[61]

Conclusion

These insights remind us to be careful not to use simplistic or one-sided explanations to fill *lacunae* that arise from a still insufficient knowledge of the historical context and the manifold factors that play a role in sparking urban unrest. It cannot be doubted that, in 1850, those attacking were Muslims and those attacked were Christians. But they were more than that; they were inhabitants with economic interests and needs, they were political beings with their particular place and status in society. What also needs to be seen more clearly is that those drawn into the events were members of a society that underwent many profound changes in the mid nineteenth century.

This chapter is also a tribute to the microhistorical approach in historiography.[62] Whereas 'syntheses necessarily depict the historical landscape from afar'[63] through portrayal of large patterns, microhistory has the advantage of including 'the hypotheses, the doubts, the uncertainties'[64] in its narration. For this reason, Ginzburg advocates 'a constant back and forth between micro- and macrohistory, between close-ups and extreme long-shots, so as to continually thrust back into discussion the comprehensive vision of the historical process through apparent exceptions',[65] recognizing that 'reality is fundamentally discontinuous and heterogeneous'.[66] I suggest such a back and forth with regard to the 1850 events. Microhistorical analysis can help us to stay alert to both causalities and contingencies of the historical process without having to resort to sectarian argumentations.

From the above microhistorical observations of the 1850 events, it should be obvious that no such thing as an essentially antagonistic relationship between the city's Christian population and its Muslim majority existed – neither as a primordial factum nor had it yet become a political instrument. Certainly, the consular correspondence and local eyewitnesses employ a language that is in some cases reminiscent of later sectarian rhetoric. But it has also been shown that the Christian 'otherness' that was perceived may have been more economic and political than religious – or only outwardly religious; according to Masters, they had 'voluntarily chosen to dissociate themselves from the city's tradition of brokered politics'.[67] Nevertheless, it could be shown that a not-negligible number of Christians had been protected by their Muslim neighbours. The notion of a 'Christian quarter' also seems to be quite an ephemeral one, if one looks more closely at it. Although, of course, al-Saliba was well known as the 'Christian quarter' of the city, in everyday life and in administration a quarter is never a closed entity with only one characteristic, and it may well be that it was not primarily attacked due to its 'Christian character'. It was notably a place of economic importance and had even very recently become a place of political symbolism where the churches, as visual manifestations, came to represent the process by which the Tanzimat reforms were implemented.

A desirable perspective for further research would be to step back from the close-up, as suggested by Ginzburg, and consider the long shot. Then the 1850 uprising in Aleppo does not appear that historically unique anymore. If one looks more closely at the events, the reasons, the actors and their motives, the sequence of actions and their spatial unfolding, similarities to earlier uprisings and moments of urban unrest become visible. Although without any doubt the 1850 events represent an important break in Aleppo's urban history that marks a political, economic and civic turning point, they can also be read 'back' into a long history of 'street politics'.[68] Food shortages, the introduction of new taxes and extortions by *vali*s brought about many clashes in the streets of Aleppo, notably at the end of the eighteenth and the beginning of the nineteenth centuries. Repeatedly, Ottoman governors were chased away from the city.[69] In the years 1775, 1786 and 1804, for example, the inhabitants of Aleppo – the chronicles, mostly written by Christian authors, refer to them unanimously as *ahl al-balad* – besieged the *vali* in his seraglio and finally succeeded in forcing him out of the city. Then the people took control of the city until the next *vali* was sent from Istanbul a few weeks or months later. That these continuities indeed existed can be hypothesized on the basis of contemporary accounts. Their language provides a glimpse of a long tradition of narrating episodes of urban unrest, not necessarily with a confessional dimension. It is no coincidence that the reports about the 1850 events refer to the insurgents as *ahl al-balad*, as has been shown in the first part of this short study.

Earlier research on the 1850 events focused almost exclusively on patterns of change and radical discontinuities – and with good reason. However, possible continuities and moments of stabilization have received far less scholarly attention. A historiographical problem lies at the base of this picture: the 1850 events lie at a historiographical fissure. Bodman's well-known monograph on Aleppo's factional politics covers only the period until the 1820s; it thus stops short of the 1850 events. Work on the 1850 events, on the contrary, has tended to emphasize the singular character of the uprising in 1850, notably Maʿoz, who emphasizes its connection to the onset of the Tanzimat reforms, or has tended to connect it 'forward' in time, to events like the 1860 Damascus massacre.

To sum up, studying the language employed by eyewitnesses to describe the events while at the same time analysing the urban fabric and spatial patterns in detail leads one to the conclusion that the explanatory power of sectarian argumentations alone is rather limited. Instead, if one takes into consideration the complexity of the urban fabric, those attacking and those attacked emerge as economic and political actors of relevance in the city's history, with their very own and particular profiles. Microhistorical analysis allows us to learn more about these profiles, how diverse they are and how they changed – and thus also why one section of a society could turn so violently against another.

Notes

1. Summaries of the events can be found in: J.-C. David. 2008. 'Aleppo: From the Ottoman Metropolis to the Syrian City', in S.K. Jayyusi (ed.), *The City in the Islamic World*, 2 vols, Leiden: Brill, vol. 1, 348f.; B. Masters. 1990. 'The 1850 Events in Aleppo: An Aftershock of Syria's Incorporation into the Capitalist World System', *International Journal of Middle East Studies* 22, 5–9; B. Masters. 2001. *Christians and Jews in the Ottoman Arab World: The Roots of Sectarianism*, Cambridge: Cambridge University Press, 158–61; M. Maʿoz. 1968. *Ottoman Reform in Syria and Palestine, 1840–1861: The Impact of the Tanzimat on Politics and Society*, Oxford: Clarendon Press, 101–7.
2. Maʿoz, *Ottoman Reform*, 101.
3. Maʿoz, *Ottoman Reform*, 105; and M. Maʿoz. 1966. 'Syrian Urban Politics in the Tanzimat Period between 1840 and 1861', *Bulletin of the School of Oriental and African Studies* 29, 295.
4. Masters, 'The 1850 Events', 12.
5. See Masters, 'The 1850 Events'; Masters, *Christians and Jews*, 158–61; H. Kuroki. 1999. 'The 1850 Aleppo Disturbance Reconsidered', in Institut für Orientalistik (ed.), *Acta Viennensia Ottomanica. Akten des 13. CIEPO-Symposiums vom 21. bis 25. September 1998 in Wien*, Vienna: Selbstverlag des Instituts für Orientalistik, 221–33; and A. Vrolijk. 2002. 'No Conscripts for the *Nizâm*: The 1850 Events in Aleppo as Reflected in Documents from Syrian and Dutch Archives', *Journal of Turkish Studies* 26(2), 311–38.
6. See U. Makdisi. 2000. *The Culture of Sectarianism: Community, History, and Violence in Nineteenth-Century Ottoman Lebanon*, Berkeley: University of California Press. It should be underlined, however, that Makdisi deals exclusively with nineteenth-century Ottoman Lebanon and is careful not to include other cases of contention that seem similar at first glance,

for example the violence in Aleppo in 1850 and in Damascus in 1860. See explicitly ibid., 14. The question, however, of whether the 1850 events in Aleppo may be fruitfully explained with Makdisi's sectarianism paradigm still seems relevant.

7. The question of the Christian–Jewish / Muslim–Jewish relationship will not be further addressed in this chapter. For this subject, see especially Y. Harel. 1998. 'Jewish–Christian Relations in Aleppo as Background for the Jewish Response to the Events of October 1850', *International Journal of Middle East Studies* 30, 77–96.

8. The two reports are conserved in the section 'Damascus', *majmuʿa* 2, *raqm* 3 (*arshif* Dimitri Shahada). Account no. 1, entitled *Hawadith ma tawaqqaʿa min al-ghawayl bi-mahrusat Halab al-shahira fi l-yawm al-sadis ʿashar min shahr tishrin awwal gharbi sanat 1850* (The calamitous events which took place on 16 October 1850, according to the Gregorian calendar, in the protected town of Aleppo), is very detailed and the author speaks of 15 November as 'today'. Account no. 2, beginning with the words *Innahu fi 16 tishrin al-awwal sanat 1850...*, is probably written by a contemporary, but may also be a later copy. I will refer to these accounts henceforth as account nos 1 and 2. The two reports were edited and translated in F. Krimsti. 2014. *Die Unruhen in Aleppo. Gewalt im urbanen Raum.* Berlin: Klaus Schwarz, which is currently being revised for publication. I thank Dr Joseph Zaitun and Mrs Raja' Rajiha from the Greek Orthodox Patriarchate in Damascus for giving me access to the accounts.

9. Shahada was the representative of the Greek Orthodox Patriarchate in Constantinople. Little is known about him. He seems to have acted as an intermediary between the Greek Orthodox of Aleppo and Damascus and the Porte. In the aftermath of the 1850 events, he supervised the indemnification of the Christians.

10. Public Record Office, London, FO 195/302, Werry to Stratford Canning, 19 Oct. 1850. I thank Dr Johann Büssow of Eberhard Karls Universität Tübingen for kindly sharing scans of the consular correspondence concerning the 1850 events with me.

11. Harel, 'Jewish–Christian Relations', 79.

12. Ibid.

13. Cf. Masters, 'The 1850 Events', 9.

14. B. Qarʾali (ed.). 1933. *Ahamm hawadith Halab fi 'l-nisf al-awwal min al-qarn at-tasiʿ ʿashar*, Cairo: al-Matbaʿa al-Suriyya, 79–83 and passim.

15. A sentence added to the end of this report, then, must be a title added later by Dimitri Shahada, since it makes use of an entirely different rhetoric: 'The truthful news about the persecution of the Christians (*al-masihiyyun*) by the Muslims of Aleppo (*islam Halab*) in 1850'.

16. J. Zepter, C. Walbiner and M. Braune (eds). 2011. *Ulrich Jasper Seetzen. Tagebuch des Aufenthalts in Aleppo, 1803–1805*, Hildesheim, Zurich and New York: Olms, p. 134 ('wuláhd el béllad oder Stadtkinder, wie man [sie] hier gewöhnlich nennt'). See, very similar, ibid., 136.

17. K. Salibi and Y.K. Khoury (eds). 1995. *The Missionary Herald: Reports from Ottoman Syria, 1819–1870*, 5 vols, Amman: Royal Institute for Inter-Faith Studies, vol. 4 (1847–1860), 126.
18. Makdisi, *The Culture of Sectarianism*, 36. Speaking about Mount Lebanon, Makdisi thus brilliantly characterizes the role of a language of religious differentiation in a society whose social order was 'founded on the shared values and interests of a non-sectarian political elite'. This observation holds perfectly true for Aleppo as well.
19. For an excellent overview of the origins and early developments of the Eastern Church (or rather: 'churches') in Syria, see R.M. Haddad. 1970. *Syrian Christians in a Muslim Society: An Interpretation*, Princeton, NJ: Princeton University Press, 6–28. For the different Christian sects, cf. A. Raymond, 2002, 'An Expanding Community: The Christians of Aleppo in the Ottoman Era (16th–18th centuries)', in A. Raymond (ed.), *Arab Cities in the Ottoman Period: Cairo, Syria and the Maghreb*, Aldershot: Ashgate, 1; and B. Heyberger. 2003. 'Alep, capitale chrétienne (XVIIe–XIXe siècle)', in B. Heyberger (ed.), *Chrétiens du monde arabe. Un archipel en terre d'Islam*, Paris: Autrement, 55. See also Masters, *Christians and Jews*, 42–53, for an overview of the sectarian landscape of the Ottoman Arab lands.
20. Cf. Haddad, *Syrian Christians*, 17–24.
21. Cf. Raymond, 'Expanding Community', 1f. For a detailed overview of the uniate movement, see Haddad, *Syrian Christians*, 29–68.
22. See Raymond, 'Expanding Community', 10.
23. For example, hostility between the Melkite Catholics and the Orthodox reached a climax in 1848, when Sultan Abdülmecid recognized the Melkite Catholic rite as an official millet. The Melkite Catholic split caused serious trouble because the Orthodox Church lost a great number of believers, some of them from the city's elite. Cf. Haddad, *Syrian Christians*, 49ff. See also B. Masters. 2010. 'The Establishment of the Melkite Catholic *Millet* in 1848 and the Politics of Identity in Tanzimat Syria', in P. Sluglett and S. Weber (eds), *Syria and* Bilad al-Sham *under Ottoman Rule: Essays in Honour of Abdul-Karim Rafeq*, Leiden: Brill, 455–73, for an account of the long process leading to the creation of the Melkite Catholic millet.
24. See, for instance, Masters, 'The 1850 Events', 9f.
25. On the quarters under consideration and their ethnic, economic and social structures as well as habitat, see notably David, 'Aleppo', 338–42.
26. Makdisi, *The Culture of Sectarianism*, 6.
27. Ibid., 7.
28. Ibid., 10.
29. Cf. K.D. Watenpaugh. 2006. *Being Modern in the Middle East: Revolution, Nationalism, Colonialism, and the Arab Middle Class*, Princeton, NJ: Princeton University Press, 34.
30. Salibi and Khoury (eds), *The Missionary Herald*, 125.
31. See the subtitle of Master's article, 'The 1850 Events'.
32. Cf. in detail Masters, 'The 1850 Events', 12–17. Cf. also similar views in his

Christians and Jews, 130–68, notably 142f. It must be underlined, however, that Masters also devotes much space to the Tanzimat process in order to explain intercommunal dissonance, not only economic processes (ibid., 134–41).

33. Cf. Harel, 'Christian–Jewish Relations', 87, 91 and passim.
34. See Maʿoz, *Ottoman Reform*, 101–7.
35. Cf. ibid., 21f.
36. Cf. in detail ibid., 75–107 (chapters VI and VII).
37. Harel, 'Jewish–Christian Relations', 87.
38. Ibid., 91, 92.
39. David, 'Aleppo', 349.
40. Masters, 'The 1850 Events', 4, 5. David, 'Aleppo', 352, also suggests: 'Perhaps Muslims sought the wrong target when they attacked the Christians in 1850. They were attacking the symbol more than the reality; but the Christians, in explicitly rejecting certain tokens bound up with Ottoman principles and mechanisms for the co-habitation of communities, were one step ahead in the ongoing process of modernization'.
41. See the hybrid 'Salîba-Judayda' in Raymond, 'Expanding Community', 83.
42. BA, NFS.d.03726. For similar data, cf. H. Kuroki. 2003. 'Mobility of Non-Muslims in Mid-Nineteenth-Century Aleppo', in H. Kuroki (ed.), *The Influence of Human Mobility in Muslim Societies*, London: Routledge, 138–44, with a mapping of the number of *cizye* payers for the year 1849.
43. The situation of the Jewish population of Aleppo during the 1850 uprising is not in the focus of this short chapter and thus will not be further investigated. The census documents attest to a Jewish population in al-ʿAqaba, Jubb Asadallah, Jallum al-Kubra, ad-Dabbagha al-ʿAtiqa, al-Bandara, al-Masabin, Suwayqa ʿAli, Harat al-Yahud and, above all, in Bahsita, with a very notable Jewish population of 1,273 males and 229 Jewish houses. None of these quarters were attacked.
44. In a list comprising numbers of needy Roman Catholics in Aleppo that was written some time after the uprising, the Roman Catholic bishop Dimitriyus Antaki gives considerably higher numbers of Christians living in the eastern suburbs of the city – 250 male and female Roman Catholics alone (Archives of the Roman Catholic diocese, *siğğil* 5, ʿ*adad* 39). I thank Archimandrite Ignatius Dick for giving me access to the archives of the diocese.
45. Cf. J.-C. David. 1990. 'L'Espace des Chrétiens à Alep. Ségrégation et mixité, stratégies communautaires (1750–1850)', *Revue du monde musulman et de la Méditerranée* 55(1), 163. For the same observation, cf. Masters, 'The 1850 Events', 17.
46. See A.K. Rafeq. 1988. 'The Social and Economic Structure of Bab al-Musalla (al-Midan), Damascus, 1825–1875', in G.N. Atiyeh and I.M. Oweiss (eds), *Arab Civilization: Challenges and Responses. Studies in Honor of Constantine K. Zurayk*, New York: State University of New York Press, 299–307. Rafeq has studied the economic, ethnic and social fabric of its population and he has shown that despite different origins, activities and socio-economic

levels, a close pattern of integration can be identified. Joint ownership of houses and joint residence among these groups were not unusual.
47. Cf. I. Tamdoğan-Abel. 2004. 'Le Quartier (*mahalle*) de l'époque ottomane à la Turquie contemporaine', *Anatolia Moderna* 10, 123.
48. Tamdoğan-Abel, 'Le Quartier', 125.
49. A. Raymond. 2002. 'Islamic City, Arab City: Orientalist Myths and Recent Views', in A. Raymond (ed.), *Arab Cities in the Ottoman Period: Cairo, Syria and the Maghreb*, Aldershot: Ashgate, 5. He gives an overview of approaches to the 'Islamic' or 'Arab' city.
50. Cf. A. Raymond. 2010. 'Aux Origines du plan d'Alep par Rousseau: Le plan de Vincent Germain de 1811', in P. Sluglett and S. Weber (eds), *Syria and Bilad al-Sham under Ottoman Rule: Essays in Honour of Abdul-Karim Rafeq*, Leiden: Brill, 499–503.
51. Cf. Raymond, 'Aux Origines du Plan d'Alep', 509.
52. The fact that the report gives a higher number of looted Christian houses than actually existed in al-Saliba (according to the Ottoman census document) may be due to the fact that the entity counted differs in the two cases. In the Ottoman census, *khanas* are counted, whereas the Christian eyewitness departs from the house (*bayt*) as unit. It is also possible that the number of households grew within the year that elapsed between the census and the uprising.
53. Cf. C. Emmett. 2009. 'The Siting of Churches and Mosques as an Indicator of Christian–Muslim Relations', *Islam and Christian–Muslim Relations* 20(4), 452. For Emmett's typology, pp. 453–62.
54. David, in 'L'Espace des Chrétiens', 169, characterizes the Christians' overall impact on urban space before the Tanzimat reforms in the following way: 'Dans le cadre de la ville ottomane, avant les réformes du XIXe siècle, le pouvoir des chrétiens, fondé sur leur nombre et leur poids économique, ne s'exprime pas par une intervention directe sur l'organisation de leur espace urbain; c'est essentiellement un pouvoir défensif, qui vise à préserver un statut, un mode de vie, des biens' ('In the framework of the ottoman city, before the reforms of the nineteenth century, the power of the Christians, founded as it is in their number and economic weight, does not express itself as a direct intervention in the organization of urban space; it is essentially a defensive power aiming to guard a status, a way of life, property'). He too, then, considers the Tanzimat reforms a decisive turning point. In this sense, cf. David, 'Aleppo', 348.
55. Cf. Y. Qushaqji (ed.). 1985–1994. *Akhbar Halab kama katabaha Na'um Bakhkhash*, 4 vols, Aleppo: Matba'at al-Ihsan, vol. 1, 150f., 153.
56. Cf. Qushaqji (ed.), *Akhbar Halab*, vol. 2, 114.
57. Ibid., 135f.
58. Ibid., 142.
59. Ibid., 151.
60. J. Mamarbaschi. 1855. *Les Syriens catholiques et leur patriarche Mgr Ant. Samhiri*, Paris: Aux Bureaux de l'Univers, 5.

61. See Sh. Daghir (ed.). 2009. *Way idhan lastu bi-ifranj*, Beirut: Dār al-Fārābī.
62. For the origins and the beginnings of microhistorical research, which replaced the macroscopic and quantitative model dominating historiography between the mid-1950s and the mid-1970s, especially through the works of the *Annales* school, see in particular C. Ginzburg. 1993. 'Microhistory: Two or Three Things I Know about It', *Critical Inquiry* 20(1), 10–35. For a defence of the microhistorical approach to history in view of the postmodern challenge, see R.D. Brown. 2003. 'Microhistory and the Post-Modern Challenge', *Journal of the Early Republic* 23(1), 1–20.
63. Brown, 'Microhistory', 9.
64. Ginzburg, 'Microhistory', 24.
65. Ibid., 27.
66. Ibid.
67. Masters, 'The 1850 Events', 17.
68. The term 'street politics', first used by Asef Bayat in a study of the Iranian revolution, has already been employed by Büssow in a similar premodern context. See, therefore, J. Büssow. 2011. 'Street Politics in Damascus: Kinship and Other Social Categories as Bases of Political Action, 1830–1841', *History of the Family* 16, 108–25. The article deals with political change and popular contention in Damascus during the period 1830 to 1841, with a focus on kinship. See especially ibid., 109, on Asef Bayat; here also Büssow defines 'street politics' in a broad sense as 'all different forms of collective action by urban crowds that are political in the sense that they aim at articulating and defending the interests of a certain part of the local population'.
69. For a detailed overview of riots in the city of Aleppo before 1850, see H.L. Bodman. 1963. *Political Factions in Aleppo, 1760–1826*, Chapel Hill: University of North Carolina Press, chapter V.

❖ Chapter 7 ❖

The City as a Stage for a Violent Spectacle
The Massacres of Armenians in Istanbul in 1895–96

FLORIAN RIEDLER

The cases of extreme public violence that occurred in Istanbul between autumn 1895 and summer 1896 were extraordinary and in a way unprecedented. Up to six thousand inhabitants of the city, the overwhelming majority of them Armenians, were killed, many of them in plain daylight on the streets; an unknown number were wounded, shops were looted and houses and khans were destroyed. To find a comparable case of public scenes of violence in Ottoman Istanbul with as many victims, one has to go back at least to 1826, when loyal troops suppressed the city's Janissaries.

Although unprecedented, the violence did not surprise or seem 'senseless' to most contemporaries, though many were shocked by it. They were able to read the political messages that various actors expressed in various violent acts for different audiences.

This chapter explores the role of the city by viewing violence as a form of political communication. First, there is the question of how Istanbul became the site of violence on such an unprecedented scale. The events took place in the wider context of the persecution of the Armenian communities in Eastern and South-Eastern Anatolia. Thus, the centres of this persecution were located thousands of miles away in an environment very different from *fin de siècle* Istanbul, a modern and well-connected capital, which the government had eyed suspiciously and controlled obsessively since the Janissary uprising mentioned above. In the first part of this chapter I explain the interplay between the general context of violence and the events on the urban scale in Istanbul. I suggest that

Istanbul's role was that of a stage on which the political messages conveyed by violence could reach a maximum audience.

This stage character of Istanbul was particularly important to the Armenian nationalist groups who used the city to voice their demands in opposition to the Ottoman government. Two events organized by these groups, the demonstration at the Sublime Porte and the attack on the Ottoman Bank, stand out in this regard; the second section of this chapter will analyse them. The attackers of the Ottoman Bank in particular used the peculiar nature of Istanbul in their planning and choice of target.

If Istanbul was a stage for the different parties in the political conflict, it was far from a neutral stage. In the third section, I would like to develop a more nuanced picture of different effects and interdependencies of violence in an urban context such as Istanbul by way of a spatial analysis. This can help us to look beyond large and encompassing categories of actors such as 'Armenian' or 'Muslim' constructed by their political opponents and taken up by many contemporary observers. The aim of this chapter is to challenge the exclusively ethnic interpretation of violence suggested by such categories. Examining events on a finer scale can also reveal how the city itself, its social and material structures as expressed in different quarters, and even its buildings, can be regarded as actors that affected violence.[1]

The Context: Persecution of the Ottoman Armenians, 1894–96

The persecution that the Armenian communities of Eastern and South-Eastern Anatolia had to suffer during the 1890s was informed by the long-standing issue of how different groups should live together in this region. The role of the Armenian population was not the only issue at stake; the question also involved the relation between central state and local power holders, between peasants, tribes and townspeople, and between Sunni and non-Sunni Muslims. It had very practical consequences as well, such as who should be obliged to pay taxes and who would collect them, who could bear arms, and who could own land.[2]

The Ottoman historical experience in the war of 1877/78 gave this issue a political dimension, especially regarding the Armenians, who formed a sizeable minority in Eastern Anatolia. The key question was whether the policy of reforms that granted the sultan's non-Muslim subjects a degree of political participation was also to be pursued vis-à-vis the Armenian community, or if this would lead to secession and the expulsion of Muslims, as had been the case in the Balkans. This and the issue of foreign intervention invested the question with a more than purely local significance.

The persecution of Armenians lumped together these complicated and intertwined political and social questions. As many as one hundred thousand were killed in massacres in towns and villages in Eastern and South-Eastern Anatolia between 1894 and 1896. The main perpetrators of violence were Muslim inhabitants of the same cities, and armed bands that plundered the countryside. In some cases, regular military forces and Kurdish militia also took part in the massacres. On the opposite side there were a small number of armed Armenian guerrilla fighters who organized local resistance and sporadically attacked Ottoman forces.

When speaking of violence on such a scale, and with the Armenian genocide of 1915 that affected the same regions and communities in the background, it is impossible not to touch on the question of responsibility for the massacres and especially the responsibility of the Ottoman state. A number of pro-Turkish historians exaggerate the role of Armenian guerrillas and the intervention of the European powers in support of the Armenians, seemingly to excuse the state's excessive use of force. These historians understand violence as the side effect of a popular uprising against the threat of Armenian secessionism.[3] In contrast, a pro-Armenian historiography is convinced of the state's deep involvement in events. V.N. Dadrian in particular singles out the Ottoman sultan and state as the planners and perpetrators of a 'proto-genocidal' policy;[4] in analysing the psychological world of the Ottoman elite and the sultan, R. Melson speaks of a policy of 'massacre as restoration'[5] to subdue the culturally and economically very successful Armenian community.

However, other scholars are more cautious about an overall and direct responsibility of the sultan and state.[6] J. Verheij challenges what he calls the 'organization thesis', which claims that the state had a direct hand in organizing the massacres in toto. Instead, he breaks down the persecutions of 1894–96 into a sequence of events that in his opinion demonstrates an escalation of violence. According to this analysis, different actors were involved at different stages. Of these, the sultan and the Ottoman government were only two. Sometimes the state's involvement was direct, but many times it was indirect, creating psychological conditions that catalysed the massacres.[7]

Such a breaking up and sequencing of events is also useful in understanding how Istanbul got involved in the chain of events. The persecutions started in 1894 when the Ottoman army together with Kurdish militia brutally suppressed a minor tax revolt of Armenian peasants in Sasun, a remote area in the mountains of Eastern Anatolia. A handful of Armenian revolutionaries helped the peasants to organize resistance, which in turn triggered the state's stern reaction to what it believed to be a nationalist uprising. The attempt to cover up the massacre led to protests on an international scale and increased the pressure on the sultan from the European powers to adopt a reform plan for the eastern provinces of the empire.

At the beginning of October 1895 was the first wave of violence in Istanbul; it followed a demonstration organized by the Armenian revolutionary group Hunchak at the Sublime Porte. This demonstration was suppressed by the police and was followed by more attacks on Armenians in the capital. At the same time, the sultan had to accept the reform plan proposed by the Great Powers, which raised tensions in the provinces concerned.

The five months of autumn and winter 1895–96 saw the second, most violent phase of persecutions that produced the main body of victims. The Armenian communities in many Eastern and South-Eastern Anatolian cities and towns – like Trabzon, Erzincan, Bitlis, Erzurum, Diyarbakır, Malatya, Harput, Sivas, Maraş, Kayseri and Urfa – were massacred and their property looted. On top of these well-documented cases, an unknown number of Armenian villages in the wider region were plundered. In summer 1896, a third phase started with an outbreak of violence in Van, which was the only Armenian centre that had thus far been spared. There was heavy fighting between Armenian revolutionaries and the Ottoman army, in the course of which Ottoman artillery fire destroyed the Armenian quarter of the city. At the end of August 1896, as a reaction to this defeat, the Federation of Armenian Revolutionaries, or 'Dashnak', attacked the Ottoman Bank in Istanbul and took its staff hostage. The attack was followed by a general massacre in the Ottoman capital, in which thousands of Armenians lost their lives. Afterwards there were two smaller pogroms in two Anatolian cities before the violent persecutions came to an end.

The importance of events in Istanbul derived mainly from the city's symbolic position as the capital and seat of the sultan as well as from the real connections and communications between capital and provinces. The government took extremely seriously any immediate political action of nationalist Armenian groups. But also the cultural and economic progress of the Armenian community, which many Muslims saw as a threat to the traditional order of society, was visible in Istanbul as under a magnifying glass. In the following section I will analyse the symbolic political dimension of urban violence in Istanbul with reference to the struggle between the Armenian nationalist groups and the Ottoman state.

Political Violence and Urban Terrorism

The initial event that opened the cycle of violence in Istanbul was the demonstration on 1 October 1895 at the Sublime Porte, the official seat of the grand vizier, to protest against the suppression of Armenians in Eastern Anatolia in general and against the massacre in Sasun in particular. The demonstration was organized by two Armenian nationalist and revolutionary groups, Armenakan and Hunchak, both of which had been founded along with many other similar groups in the 1880s. In contrast to the liberal Armenian reform movement that had been developing in the Ottoman Empire since the 1840s, these groups promoted armed struggle to win political and social rights for the Armenian community. Hunchak in particular was influenced by socialist and revolutionary ideals that Armenian students had brought back from Russia. According to their programme, the ultimate goal was a socialist Armenia; their main work consisted of propaganda and training guerrilla fighters.[8]

As was obvious from the choice of site, the main addressee of this protest was the Ottoman government. Istanbul was not new to gatherings of big crowds voicing their political grievances. This had happened, for example, during the Crimean War in 1853 and before the deposition of Sultan Abdülaziz in 1876. Then, the politically active parts of the population, like madrassa students (*softa*), soldiers and craftsmen, took to the streets and occupied large open spaces within the city like the Hippodrome, which for centuries had been the traditional place for such political rallies because of its proximity to the palace of Topkapı. The new palace complex along the Bosphorus, to which the sultans had moved in the 1850s, remained off limits for such popular demonstrations. Only in extraordinary circumstances like the war of 1878 did refugees manage to stage a protest in this area.

What was unheard of in the 1895 demonstration at the Porte was that it was the non-Muslims who claimed a political role in such a public manner. Although the two to four thousand Armenian protesters pretended to be delivering a petition to the government, this could hardly veil the extraordinary nature of this political action. According to all reports, nobody was surprised that the initially peaceful demonstration turned violent, with police and protesters exchanging first insults and then bullets.[9]

The second, less obvious addressee of the protesters' political message was the Armenian establishment in the capital. The demonstration's starting point was the cathedral of the Armenian patriarchate in the quarter of Kum Kapı, half an hour's walk from the Porte downhill towards the shores of the Marmara Sea. The revolutionary organizers tried to blackmail the patriarch and the church congregation into taking part in their public demonstration. Twenty women from the provinces begged the patriarch to lead the protest march, which he immediately refused to do on the grounds that such an action would be illegal, adding that his way of helping the Armenian community was much more effective. He was shouted down with slogans like 'Liberty or death!', and the crowd began to march towards the Porte without him. The Hunchaks had used the same tactics before: in July 1890 some activists had provoked the patriarch inside the cathedral and had started a shoot-out with incoming police. Apparently it had been their intention to march together to the palace to deliver a petition to the sultan concerning Armenian suffering in Anatolia.[10]

In sum, revolutionary groups tried to exploit the social and regional rifts within the Istanbul Armenian community. The Istanbul poor were often identical to the labour migrants from Eastern Anatolia working and living in wretched conditions in the capital. It is said that Hunchak had a growing following from among such workers and that they composed the majority of the protesters. In contrast, the Armenian bourgeoisie of the capital was generally not in favour of revolutionary action, but supported evolutionary politics of reform. Overall, the relation between the Istanbul community and the Armenians in Anatolia had been a constantly recurring topic since the second half of the nineteenth century.[11]

Compared with the demonstration at the Porte, the attack on the Ottoman Bank that took place approximately one year later had a very different character. The attack did not try to impress with the numbers of participants, but by its coup-like character. It was executed by a small group of armed members of the Federation of Armenian Revolutionaries, the previously mentioned Dashnak. This group had been founded in 1890 in Tiflis with the objective of freeing Ottoman Armenia. At first, it was a confederation of smaller revolutionary groups, for a short time also including Hunchak, before it gradually transformed into a revolutionary party with cells all over the Ottoman Empire, the Caucasus and Europe. Propaganda, guerrilla activity in Eastern Anatolia, and arms smuggling across the Russian–Ottoman border were its main activities.[12]

In this regard, the attack on the Ottoman Bank was atypical, but in a very innovative manner it used the environment of the big city for what may be the first example of 'political terrorism' in Istanbul, as one historian of the party claimed.[13] Indeed some features of the attack on the Ottoman Bank resemble the traits of modern urban terrorism. For example, much of Dashnak's success in organizing violent political action in Istanbul depended on its ability to blend into the city. To avoid attracting attention, the activists disguised themselves either as Europeans or, on the opposite side of the social spectrum that the city had to offer, as Armenian porters.[14]

On 26 August 1896, a commando of twenty-six armed Dashnak activists entered the bank. Only a handful of them were party members, two of them students brought in from Europe especially for the coup; the majority had been recruited among the Armenian migrant workers in Istanbul. In the initial scuffle on entering the bank, two watchmen and one of the attackers' leaders were killed before the group managed to barricade the building. In the following hours they were able to repel all attempts by soldiers and a mob to storm the building, killing many of them with guns and homemade bombs.[15]

As an institution, the Ottoman Bank, which effectively functioned as the country's central bank, was a strategic target to a certain degree. By blowing up the building as they threatened to do, Dashnak could have caused real damage to Ottoman finances. The management of the bank was apparently very nervous about these prospects and so had been working on emergency plans.[16]

However, more important was the bank's symbolic and psychological value as a target. With the attack on the building situated in Galata and parallel attacks in different parts of the city, Dashnak wanted to demonstrate to the Ottoman government its ability to strike at any point in the empire, even in the capital. In his memoirs, the leader of the attackers, Armen Garo, gave further reasons for the group's tactics:

> [S]hould the undertaking succeed as we hoped, Constantinople would be occupied by European armed forces and the Armenian Cause would be resolved as desired ... After all, had not the great European powers warned the sultan only last May that the next time there were any disturbances in Constantinople they would land the armed forces of their twelve warships to restore order? With this in mind, we had chosen the occupation of the Bank [sic] Ottoman as a means to compel the ambassadors to execute their threat. We well knew that the bank, though in name Ottoman, was in reality a European establishment. Besides, should we succeed in holding as hostages the 150 European officers of the bank, the ambassadors' intervention would be immediate.[17]

In a conversation with a bank clerk, Garo reiterated this reasoning and added that, from a mid-term perspective, the damage to Istanbul's security and urban economy also aimed to radicalize the Armenian working class of the city and make them susceptible to Dashnak's radical political message.[18]

In fact, the European states intervened immediately on behalf of the clerks taken hostage in the bank; its vice-director who had been able to flee and the Russian dragoman negotiated a peaceful end to the occupation after only fourteen hours. The entire Dashnak commando was allowed to leave the bank and was transferred to a French ship bound for Marseille.

As was to be expected, Dashnak's demands as formulated in a declaration sent to the European embassies beforehand, and reiterated in the negotiations for ending the occupation of the bank, were not nearly fulfilled. The European powers did not land troops to stop the massacre of the Istanbul Armenians that had started once the news of the attack on the bank and other targets in the city had become public. In the following section I will describe this massacre in greater detail, as it reveals yet another facet of urban violence.

To a certain degree, contemporaries had expected a massacre. On the one hand, these expectations had been raised by the clashes between Muslims and Armenians after the demonstration at the Porte that had already claimed up to seven hundred victims among Istanbul Armenians. On the other hand, the news of the persecution in Anatolia had made the Christian population of Istanbul, in particular, uneasy, and in December had produced a panic in Pera. However, the rumour that a general massacre of Christians had started had proved unfounded at that time.[19]

The Massacres of August 1896

Many European eyewitnesses described the scenes of massacre that they were confronted with in the thirty-six hours after the attack on the Ottoman Bank.[20] These sources pointed to Muslims from Istanbul's lower classes as the main perpetrators of violence. Sometimes these were further specified as being Kurds and Laz, probably on account of their dress. To these lower-class perpetrators, the eyewitnesses also added madrassa students, who were clearly recognizable by the turbans they were wearing. It was occasionally claimed that outsiders like Kurdish militia also entered the city on the day of the massacres.

These perpetrators were organized in 'gangs' or 'mobs' that, as many observers claimed, appeared all over the city within an hour or two of the attack on the Ottoman Bank. They started hunting down Armenians on the streets, breaking into shops and khans to kill anyone hiding there. The attackers' weapons of choice were sticks or cudgels, sometimes fitted with nails or bits of metal at their ends, with which they would beat their victims to death.

Reading these eyewitness reports closely reveals a great deal of racial and religious stereotyping. Moreover, many European observers, such as diplomats, journalists and merchants residing in Istanbul, seem to have reproduced the discourse of 'dangerous classes' that associated violence in the city with the working poor. In Europe, middle-class writers used such incriminations, especially when workers appeared in public as a crowd.[21]

However, despite these shortcomings it is hard to reject these observations out of hand, because they are the only detailed descriptions we have. In fact, official Ottoman documentation gives only a very patchy and vague impression of the events. An example is a document the Ministry of War issued on 28 August on how to restore order in the city. It acknowledged the existence of gangs armed with sticks (*ahaliden yekdiğerine silahla veya sopa ile ta'arruz edenler*), but only very vaguely and in a general manner, without saying anything about their composition.[22]

As for the question of political responsibility, all contemporary European observers, including the diplomatic missions, were convinced that the Ottoman authorities were deeply involved in the massacres. They based this opinion on the observation that for two days police and soldiers did nothing to stop the massacres – sometimes even took part in them – and only on the evening of Thursday 27 August did they begin to collect the weapons from the gangs roaming the streets. Some contemporaries went further and accused the government and the sultan personally of planning and executing the massacres. From the uniform look of the cudgels, they inferred that they must have been produced in advance; and at least two observers claimed to have seen them being distributed at police stations. Although the term had not been coined yet, in their eyes the events amounted to 'state terror'.[23]

It is virtually impossible to say anything certain about how the massacres were planned (if they were planned at all), because there exists no documentation that could clear up this question. Different degrees of the state's involvement are conceivable. For example, on the one hand, the fact that the police did not on the whole intervene could point to direct orders by the authorities to let the massacres happen. On the other hand, we could also see this as part of a tacit understanding of what the favoured outcome of the situation would be. However, it is impossible to conceive that the police were too weak or too overwhelmed by what was happening, which was the official Ottoman line of defence.[24] Probably the Ottoman capital was never better policed than under Sultan Abdülhamid, who was suspicious of everybody and had installed an extended spy network to monitor the city.[25]

Like the perpetrators of violence, their victims too remain largely anonymous and their numbers uncertain. An official Ottoman report admits to as many as one thousand dead Armenians; European sources set the numbers much higher and go up to eight thousand Armenian victims out of a population of around two hundred thousand Armenians living in Istanbul. The fact that bodies were collected and thrown into the sea or delivered to the churches to be interred quickly made any serious statistics impossible.[26]

Regarding the identity of the victims, the British ambassador, like other contemporary observers, made the following observation: 'As far as it is known, the dead are almost exclusively Armenians of the lower classes, who came to Constantinople in great numbers ... to gain a living as porters, dock labourers, caretakers in offices etc.'[27] I will examine this statement further in the following by focusing on the places of urban violence. A spatial analysis can differentiate the first impression of indiscriminate violence and random killings on the streets and partly retrieve the victims from their anonymity by discovering their specific social identity.

Incidents were reported from a wide variety of places in the greater region of Istanbul, from as far as the villages on the Bosporus, Kadıköy and Kartal on the Asiatic side and the Princes' Islands.[28] In central Istanbul, the immediate places of massacres were those in the vicinity of the Ottoman Bank in Galata and other places where the Dashnak commandos struck – for example in Samatya, where they occupied an Armenian school. The reports also mentioned quarters like Balat, Salma Tomruk and Fener that were the homes of smaller Armenian communities. Places along the Golden Horn such as Hasköy, with its main Armenian quarter Haliçoğlu and Kasımpaşa, which were frequently cited as centres of massacres, constitute another interesting case. They had already been centres of persecutions in October 1895 after the demonstration at the Sublime Porte.[29] Together with the murders committed by the armed gangs, there was serious pillaging in which the Jewish population of these quarters along the Golden Horn apparently took part. Here there seems to have been a social competition between different local communities of newly arrived poor immigrants to Istanbul that underlay the Armenian–Ottoman political conflict.[30]

Observing violence on a yet finer scale, the immediate hiding places of Armenians who were not able or could not afford to flee the city came under attack. Houses of wealthy Armenians all over the city were pillaged. In some cases, such as in Hasköy and Kartal, Armenians took refuge in their churches, where they remained relatively save from their attackers. Apparently no church was sacked during the massacres, including the seat of the Armenian patriarchate at Kum Kapı. An American missionary explained this with political reasons: apparently the Ottoman government had recently installed the acting patriarch against opposition from within the Armenian community; consequently, the authorities did not want to undermine their candidate.[31]

Khans were another example of a typical hiding place for Armenians that, in contrast to churches, frequently became sites of violence. Khans were multifunctional buildings constituting the city's economic backbone by serving as warehouses, shops and workers' residences; they were located mainly in the business areas of Galata and on Istanbul's historical peninsula. For many Armenian migrant workers they were workplaces as well as homes in the city. Moreover, many khans had Armenian proprietors or managers (*odabaşı*). After the demonstration of 1895, several khans had already come under attack and their Armenian inhabitants had been killed.[32] These scenes were repeated in August 1896 on a much larger scale. The British consul general visited one ransacked khan in Istanbul, and left the following description:

> As in most cases, the mob attacked the iron doors with a battering ram, and the unfortunate Armenians, seeing their last hour approaching, began firing out of [the] window in sheer desperation. The soldiers thereupon joined in, returning the fire ... The pillage and slaughter in this house seemed at first sight to have been most thorough. There was not a door, chair, table, or drawer left intact; papers, broken glass, samples of goods strewed the floors, soaked in blood. The whole way down the staircase one could see the marks where the battered bodies had been dragged down; and a small room just under the roof, where, apparently the final stand had been made, was a gruesome sight. On the roof also there were pools of blood.[33]

We get an additional impression of how important khans were as sites of violence from the hearings of the special court that the Ottoman government created to deal with the events. In twelve cases, groups of Armenian workers who had barricaded themselves in twelve different khans had been arrested and stood accused of crimes such as resisting the police, firing guns, and throwing bombs from the windows of these khans.[34]

The protocols of these hearings, which were witnessed by the dragomans of the British embassy, give an impression of the Ottoman justice system's very selective and politically charged treatment of the events and its attempts to turn around the roles of victim and perpetrator. While Armenians on the slightest suspicion and on the most dubious evidence were sentenced to death, prison or exile of several years, the few Muslims under trial were usually sentenced to prison terms of a couple of months for being in possession of plundered goods.[35]

Most importantly, in some of the cases the trials reveal how apolitical motives informed violence. In two cases in which Armenian workers were accused of seditious behaviour, they were identified by their Muslim colleagues. In turn, the accused claimed that this testimony was false and that the accusers owed them money and wages and thus wanted to get rid of their obligations.[36]

These are just the more harmless of a host of accounts of Muslim and Armenian workmates pitted against each other. In the disturbances after the demonstration at the Sublime Porte there had already been recurrent stories of confrontations, in some cases deadly, between Muslim or Kurdish workers and their Armenian colleagues, for example at the Pera gas works and at the docks of Galata.[37] In August 1896, an American missionary claimed that the Kurdish porters at Istanbul railway station and at the customs house had killed their Armenian colleagues, 'in order to diminish competition in the profession'.[38]

To end on a more optimistic note, the city's social structure produced not only competition between individuals in the same social position and from a similar background of migration, but also cases of solidarity. The same missionary quoted above remarked that some 'Turks' reacted humanely and hid their Armenian neighbours. Solidarity on the basis of class was also possible, as the example of one Mustafa Ağa shows. The broom maker, who had his workshop on a central square in Beşiktaş, protected an Armenian family of labour migrants from Anatolia by stopping a gang of attackers in front of the bakery where the Armenians worked. He was protecting not only people with whom he shared the same working environment; Mustafa and his Armenian neighbours were all from similar regional contexts in Eastern Anatolia, which is why they called each other countrymen (*hemşeri*).[39]

Conclusion

In this chapter I have tried to examine how the complex political conflict including different parties described in shorthand as the 'persecution of Armenians' was inserted into the urban environment of Istanbul and how it played out under local conditions. The main parties to this conflict were the Ottoman state and its representatives, like government officials, soldiers and police, Armenian nationalists from different revolutionary groups, and local Muslim and Armenian inhabitants of the capital who were the main perpetrators and victims, respectively, of the violence and massacres.

In their assessment, all parties to the conflict glossed over internal differences and tried to construct large categories to mobilize support for their policies. For the Ottoman government, all Armenians were portrayed as anarchists threatening the legitimate order, whereas the Armenian revolutionaries constructed an Armenian nation that was unjustly oppressed by the Muslims, and thus they had no choice but to take up arms. In the actual environment of the city, however, other differentiations can be observed that the city itself brought into the conflict.

As the most pertinent factor, I stressed social distinctions that, however, were enmeshed in regional as well as ethnic and religious categories. Due to the specific social structure of Istanbul's Armenian community, it was mainly the poorer migrant workers who were attacked and killed. They were the easiest targets, because they lived in collective habitations in the dense business quarters of the capital or in the immigrant districts along the Golden Horn. Unlike wealthier Armenians, they had no means to relocate from the city to the countryside beforehand or to simply jump on a ship and escape to Alexandria, Athens, Varna or Marseille, as many rich Armenians did on the day the massacres started.

In many ways, these migrant workers were at the centre of events. First, they formed a link between the different locations of the conflict, between Eastern Anatolia and Istanbul. Because their families and home communities were affected by the persecutions there, Armenian nationalist groups had some success in mobilizing them. However, the degree of this mobilization is not easy to ascertain. By the same token, the government suspected them of harbouring and supporting terrorists. Thus they became the principal victims of the administrative persecution that commenced immediately after the massacres, as the authorities tried to cleanse the city of unwanted migrants and send them home to their provinces of origin.[40]

Notes

1. For a similar approach, cf. C. Humphrey. 2012. 'Odessa: Pogroms in a Cosmopolitan City', in C. Humphrey and V. Skvirskaja (eds), *Post-Cosmopolitan Cities*, New York: Berghahn Books, 17–64.
2. H.-L. Kieser. 2000. *Der Verpasste Friede: Mission, Ethnie und Staat in den Ostprovinzen der Türkei 1839–1938*, Zurich: Chronos, 113–33.
3. On the Turkish historiography, cf. J. Verheij. 1999. 'Die Armenischen Massaker von 1894–1896. Anatomie und Hintergründe einer Krise', in H.-L. Kieser (ed.), *Die Armenische Frage und die Schweiz (1896–1923)*, Zurich: Chronos, 91–93.
4. V.N. Dadrian. 1995. *The History of the Armenian Genocide: Ethnic Conflict from the Balkans to Anatolia to the Caucasus*, Providence, RI and Oxford: Berghahn Books, 111.
5. R. Melson. 1982. 'A Theoretical Inquiry into the Armenian Massacres of 1894–1896', *Comparative Studies in Society and History* 24(3), 495.

6. E.g. G. Lewy. 2005. *The Armenian Massacres in Ottoman Turkey: A Disputed Genocide*, Salt Lake City: University of Utah Press, 20–29; Verheij, 'Die Armenischen Massaker'.
7. Verheij, 'Die Armenischen Massaker', 100–105.
8. H. Dasnabedian. 1988. *Histoire de la Fédération Révolutionaire Arménienne Dachnaktsoutioun, 1890–1924*, Milan: Oemme, 11–28; S. Atamian. 1955. *The Armenian Community: The Historical Development of a Social and Ideological Conflict*, New York: Philosophical Library, 94–97.
9. Dadrian, *Armenian Genocide*, 119–21; *The Times* 3 Oct. 1895, p. 5; Currie to Salisbury, Therapia, 3 Oct. 1895, in *House of Commons Parliamentary Papers* (HCPP) 1896, vol. 95, no. C 7927, 30–32.
10. *The Times*, 29 July 1890, p. 5; and 30 July 1890, p. 5.
11. O. Kılıçdağı. 2010. 'The Armenian Community of Constantinople in the Late Ottoman Empire', in R.G. Hovannisian and S. Payaslian (eds), *Armenian Constantinople*, Costa Mesa: Mazda, 229–42.
12. A. Ter Minassian. 1996. 'Nationalism and Socialism in the Armenian Revolutionary Movement (1887–1912)', in R.G. Suny (ed.), *Transcaucasia, Nationalism and Social Change: Essays in the History of Armenia, Azerbaijan and Georgia. Revised Edition*, Ann Arbor: University of Michigan Press, 151–60; Dasnabedian, *Dachnaktsoutioun*, 29–36.
13. Dasnabedian, *Dachnaktsoutioun*, 47.
14. S. Vratzian (ed.). 1990. *Bank Ottoman: Memoirs of Armen Garo*, Detroit: Topouzian, 91, 102 and 106; for a discussion of the concept of urban terror, cf. H.V. Savitch. 2005. 'An Anatomy of Urban Terror: Lessons from Jerusalem and Elsewhere', *Urban Studies* 42(3), 361–95.
15. However, the number of 'Turks' killed, 370, may be an exaggeration; cf. Vratzian, *Bank Ottoman*, 96–139; Dadrian, *Armenian Genocide*, 138–42.
16. E. Eldem. 2007. '26 Ağustos 1896 "Banka Vakası" ve 1896 "Ermeni Olayları"', *Tarih ve Toplum Yeni Yaklaşımlar* 5, 122.
17. Vratzian, *Bank Ottoman*, 104.
18. Cf. Eldem, 'Banka Vakası', 120, referring to a conversation between Armen Garo and Gustav Wülfing; the same motives stated are by Baker in enclosure 4 of Herbert to Salisbury, Therapia, 27 Aug. 1896, in HCPP 1897, C 8303, 17.
19. L. Rambert. 1926. *Notes et Impressions de Turquie. L'Empire Ottoman sous Abdul-Hamid II, 1895–1905*, Geneva: Atar, 10 (20 Dec. 1895).
20. Cf. HCPP 1897, C 8303, *Correspondence Respecting Disturbances at Constantinople, August 1896*; Dadrian, *Armenian Genocide*, 144–45; for German diplomatic reports, cf. N. Saupp. 1989. *Das Deutsche Reich und die Armenische Frage 1878–1914*, Ph.D. dissertation. Cologne: University of Cologne, 89–110.
21. J. Scheu. 2011. 'Dangerous Classes: Tracing Back an Epistemological Fear', *Distinktion: Scandinavian Journal of Social Theory* 12(2), 115–34.
22. 'Taraf-ı Ali-i Ser'askeriden ba-Tezkire Irsal Olunan Ta'limiat Süretidir, 16 Ağustos 1312', in Hüseyin Nâzım Paşa. 1993. *Ermeni Olayları Tarihi*, Ankara: T.C. Başbakanlık Devlet Arşivleri Genel Müdürlüğü, vol. II, 342.

23. Rambert, *Notes et Impressions*, 18; W. Giesl. 1927. *Zwei Jahrzehnte im Nahen Orient*, Berlin: Verlag für Kulturpolitik, 117.
24. Tevfik Pasha to the Representatives of the Great Powers, Sublime Porte, 9 Sept. 1896, enclosure 1 in Currie to Salisbury, Therapia, 17 Sept. 1896, in HCPP 1897, C 8303, 49–50.
25. Eldem, 'Banka Vakası', 143–45; N. Lévy-Aksu. 2008. 'Yakından Korunan Düzen: Abdülhamid Devrinden İkinci Meşrutiyet Dönemine Bekçi Örneği', in N. Lévy and A. Toumarkine (eds), *Osmanlı'da Asayiş, Suç ve Ceza. 18.–20. Yüzyıllar*, Istanbul: Tarih Vakfı.
26. Eldem, 'Banka Vakası', 138.
27. Herbert to Salisbury, Therapia, 3 Sept. 1896, in HCPP 1897, C 8303, 33.
28. Herbert to Salisbury, Therapia, 31 Aug. 1896, in HCPP 1897, C 8303, 27; BOA, A.MKT.MHM 627-48 (21 Ra 1314); A.MKT.MHM 627-39 (18 Ra 1314), Sadaret to Seraskeriye and Zabtiye.
29. *The Times* 4 Oct. 1895, p. 3; and 5 Oct. 1895, p. 5.
30. Herbert to Salisbury, Therapia, 3 Sept. 1896, in HCPP 1897, C 8303, 33.
31. H.O. Dwight to Rev. Judson Smith, Constantinople, 31 Aug. 1896, ABCFM, Reel 609, 914.
32. Currie to Salisbury, Constantinople, 2 Oct. 1895, in HCPP 1896, C 7927, 22.
33. Report by Mr Max Müller, Enclosure to Herbert to Salisbury, Therapia, 3 Sept. 1896, in HCPP 1897, C 8303, 32. Müller's visit was to Küçük Oğlu Khan.
34. These were at the Vitalis Khan, Haraççi Khan at Mısır Çarşısı, Hacı Elia Khan, Findiklian Khan, Celal Bey Khan besides Vandi(?) Medrese, Cammondo Khan (in Stambul?), Khaviar Khan (Galata), Izmirli Oğlu Khan, Alexiadi Khan, Noradungian Khan (opposite Voivoda guard house), Khalil Pasha Khan (Galata) and Lorando Khan. Most of these structures are no longer identifiable.
35. Cf. FO 195-1928, Dewy to Block, Constantinople, 26 reports between 14 Sept. and 16 Nov. 1896, as well as table by Dewy, enclosure in Currie to Salisbury, Therapia, 29 Sept. 1896, in HCPP 1897, C 8305/8395, 67.
36. FO 195-1928, Dewy to Black, Constantinople, 14 and 21 Sept. 1896.
37. *The Times* 7 Oct. 1895, p. 5; and 8 Oct. 1895, p. 3, 7.
38. H.O. Dwight to Rev. Judson Smith, Constantinople, 31 Aug. 1896, ABCFM, Reel 609, 914.
39. H. Mıntzuri. 1993. *İstanbul Anıları, 1897–1940*, Istanbul: Tarih Vakfı, 7.
40. Cf. F. Riedler. 2011. 'Armenian Labour Migration to Istanbul and the Migration Crisis of the 1890s', in U. Freitag, M. Fuhrmann, N. Lafi and F. Riedler (eds), *The City in the Ottoman Empire: Migration and the Making of Urban Modernity*, London: Routledge, 160–76.

⁕· Chapter 8 ·⁕

Transforming the Holy City
From Communal Clashes to Urban Violence, the Nebi Musa Riots in 1920

ROBERTO MAZZA

Led by General Allenby, British troops entered Jerusalem in December 1917, ending Ottoman rule and opening a new and crucial era in the history of Jerusalem and Palestine. The history of Jerusalem has traditionally been depicted as the quintessential history of conflict and strife, of ethnic and communal tensions and of incompatible national narratives and visions. The transition from Ottoman to British rule marked a dramatic and radical change in the history of the city, often described as the beginning of a period of great transformation. Looking at the riots that took place in the city in April 1920, this chapter will explore the emergence of structured urban violence in Jerusalem and the ways it superseded communal violence. The context is provided by the political framework set by the British with the Balfour Declaration, the large-scale arrival of Zionists in Palestine and the reshaping of the urban fabric of Jerusalem.[1]

This chapter will first discuss some general definitions of communal and structured violence. These two types of violence are not necessarily distinct categories, but define different ways of understanding violence and its use. I will advance the idea that violence during the Nebi Musa riots became in some way elaborated and was no longer spontaneous. Arab political leaders used the Nebi Musa celebrations as an ideal time to test the degree of Arab resentment and to test violence as a political tool. Without suggesting a radical breakaway from the communal nature of early episodes of violence that occurred in Jerusalem, the rioting was no longer the spontaneous reaction of a population fearful of losing their land. This transformation is apparent when comparing the Nebi Musa riots with earlier violent events such as the intra-communal incidents between Christians in 1901 and the 1911 affair over the archaeological excavations close to the Haram al-Sharif.[2] Secondly, this chapter will provide a general background on the British Military Administration and the politicization of emerging nationalist movements in Palestine. It will argue that the transition from communal violence to structured violence was the result of the combination of a variety of factors: the arrival of the British, the establishment of the Zionist Commission and the spread of Palestinian nationalism. A separate section will show how the changes in the urban landscape, implemented by the British governor Ronald Storrs, played a major role in renegotiating the urban space of Jerusalem and in the radicalization of local politics through policies of confessionalization and segregation that eventually created the framework for the development of structured urban violence.

An account of the Nebi Musa riots, discussed in the last part of this chapter, will illustrate the shift from communal to structured violence with a focus on the importance of the new political conditions engendered by British rule.

Definitions

In late Ottoman Jerusalem, violence was common, but not in an organized form, and its expression was milder than in other areas of the Ottoman Empire. As we delve into a brief definition of key terms such as violence, communalism and urban violence, it is arguable that violence is generally associated with the destruction of life, the material world and meaning.[3] One point should be clarified in relation to the concept of violence: particularly to the Western mind, and without being too simplistic, 'violence' strongly connotes behaviour that in some sense is illegitimate or unacceptable.[4] However, I would argue that violence in Jerusalem was not an arbitrary expression of uncontrollable anger. It was rather used as a means of socio-political advancement; judgement on violent behaviour is therefore irrelevant in the development of this chapter.

As for 'communalism', defined as the competition between groups within the same political system based on ethnic, linguistic, racial or religious identities, it is important to stress that although Jerusalem at the beginning of the twentieth century was a city divided along religious lines, it was not a confessionalized city. Urban space was not entirely divided in accordance with religion, and shared spaces were a common feature of late Ottoman Jerusalem, as a variety of sources suggest.[5] Whereas the years between 1856 and 1860 were characterized by a complete rift between Muslims and Christians throughout much of Syria and Palestine (as a result of the promulgation of the 1856 Hatt-ı Hűmayun, which promised full equality regardless of religion for the citizens of the Ottoman Empire), Jerusalem proved to be a significant exception until the arrival of the British in 1917.[6] No major disturbances, whether organized or spontaneous, occurred in Jerusalem in the second part of the nineteenth century.[7] With the exception of the 1911 Haram al-Sharif incident over the alleged Christian violation of the shrine following archaeological excavations, the most common outbreaks of violence occurred mainly among Christians themselves over the control of holy places.[8] A good example is an incident involving Greek Orthodox and Franciscans on 4 November 1901, when, following a quarrel between a number of monks, the two communities became fully involved. Two dozen people were killed and many others were injured.[9]

Violent episodes involving individual members of different communities were indeed frequent in Jerusalem, but it seems that a number of factors prevented the outbreak of major communal violence. Looking at the socio-political configuration of Jerusalem, it is possible to say that the presence of a high-ranking Ottoman governor answering directly to Istanbul, and of foreigners and foreign consuls – a modernization process initiated by the Ottomans that marked the shift of the Jerusalemites from subjects to citizens – as well as the political organization of urban politics around a few notable families, all worked towards the prevention of communal violence and in a sense towards the partial integration of local communities.[10] Overall, conflicts or potential clashes were partly mediated through the socio-political structure of the city and partly controlled by the Ottoman establishment and the threat of foreign intervention. To this extent, communal violence in Jerusalem was clearly far from being organized, but at the same time it was not exclusively the outcome of irrational behaviour; it was more the tipping point of strained relations between communities.

The last term that needs to be clarified is 'structured violence', defined as the performance of violence following a script and rituals within a recognized arena, and I would suggest it represents the bridge between communalism and fully organized violence.[11] Structured violence, as developed in Jerusalem, displayed political aims propagated by the rhetoric of political empowerment and led by self-appointed leaders whose purpose was to set the stage for a large, organized political struggle. As argued earlier, the historical shift that occurred after the arrival of the British in 1917 led to coordinated efforts by both Zionists and Arabs to destroy one or more parties involved in the dispute. Evidence suggests that the organization of group mobilization in violent events became very visible in the spring of 1920. Without suggesting a full prearranged set of measures to adopt at a certain time in a certain place, the shift from communalism to structured violence occurred at the exact moment when inflicting damage on an enemy became in some way calculated, as we will see later through the discussion of the riots.

The British in Jerusalem

In December 1917, the focal point of the transition from Ottoman to British rule of Jerusalem was the military occupation of the city by British troops. The conquest of Jerusalem and Palestine proved to be a difficult task; the British attempted to take Gaza twice and only when General Allenby was offered the command of the Egyptian Expeditionary Force did things change. In April 1917, the Palestine campaign entered a new phase, which led eventually to the capture of Jerusalem.[12] A heated debate broke out in London over the occupation of Jerusalem; three weeks before the actual occupation, the War Office eventually formalized the main policies to be adopted.[13] This note already makes it clear that the British had scanty knowledge of the mechanisms regulating the urban life of Jerusalem. Internal security was to be the primary task of the new occupying force; non-Muslims would not be permitted to pass the cordon established around the Mosque of Omar.[14]

On 7 December, despite the cold and heavy rain, everything on the British side was ready for the assault on Jerusalem, which was surrounded. On the following day, the Ottomans began to withdraw from the city; the Ottoman governor and the German and Austrian consuls fled during the night.[15] No fight took place inside the city, and by 9 December Jerusalem was free of Ottoman and German troops. The occupation of the city then became a powerful political tool to be exploited. General Allenby made his formal entry into Jerusalem on 11 December, following plans that had been carefully devised by Mark Sykes. Allenby entered the city through the Jaffa Gate on foot, followed by a procession of British military officials and two small Italian and French contingents. He then read the proclamation of martial law and promised religious freedom. Jerusalemites were generally happy, if not about the arrival of the British then indeed about the end of the war.[16] However, this reality would soon change as local residents realized that the new rulers were to 'muddy the clear waters' of intercommunal relations.[17]

With Allenby's entrance into the city, military rule was officially established. The first governor of Jerusalem, General Bill Borton, set up the administration following the principle of the status quo ante bellum, which regulated the military administration of occupied territories.[18] The governorship of Borton lasted a few weeks, and Ronald Storrs, former oriental secretary in Cairo, was appointed in early 1918 as the new governor of Jerusalem.[19] Although specific plans had yet to be drawn up by the military administration and the Foreign Office in London, this appointment proved to be crucial in the social, political, religious, economic, urban and architectural development of the city. I will later argue that the British, mainly through Ronald Storrs, also contributed to the creation of the conditions that allowed violence to become a common political tool.

The first task of Storrs and the military administration was to cope with the general lack of food, medicine and fuel; in other words, they had to cater to the needs of the army and most importantly to those of the civilian population. Slowly, commerce, trade, bureaucracy, schools and legal courts were also re-established. The military was not supposed to deal with political issues, but in the end, despite decisions made in London, the military had to deal with local politics, as it was charged with enforcing the status quo. The Zionist Commission, representing the Zionist Organization and in charge of the application of the Balfour Declaration and the emergence of Christian–Muslim associations as part of the developing Palestinian national movement, reshuffled and redesigned the role of the military rule. I would argue that what was supposed to be temporary lasted for several years, as the future of Jerusalem and Palestine had yet to be decided.

In this context, the British relied in local matters on local notables de facto perpetuating the same 'politics of notables' implemented by the Ottomans. Early in 1918, Ronald Storrs appointed the most prominent member of the Husayni family, Musa Kazim, Mayor of Jerusalem. He was a political activist who, once in charge of the mayoral office, was initially tactful in his opposition to the British and Zionism; however, as we shall see later, he was dismissed after he played a major role in the Nebi Musa riots.[20] The leaders of local notable families were not only able to maintain their power once the British arrived, they increased it while becoming the leaders of the anti-Zionist movement that in this particular period took the form of the Christian–Muslim Associations.[21]

The arrival of the British, the establishment of the Zionist Commission, the spread of Palestinian nationalism and the politicization of the local elites were all signs that a paradigm shift was ready to take place, one that included violence as a political tool available to the parties involved. The British and the introduction of organized violence redefined urban space, too. Jerusalem was turned from a space for the development of citizenship into a sacred place.

Planning Jerusalem

The renegotiation of the urban space of Jerusalem, which then led to the radicalization of local politics and the introduction of structured violence, occurred mainly through the British governor Ronald Storrs and the civic advisor Charles Ashbee.[22] Both employed urban planning in an effort to control newly acquired territory and to satisfy personal desires. Ronald Storrs trained in classical studies at Pembroke College, Cambridge, also studied languages and was quite fluent in Arabic, knowledge that he used to be appointed to the Egyptian Civil Service and then to become oriental secretary to the British Agency in Cairo.[23] Full of himself, and imbued with never-ending self-esteem, Storrs, while appointed civil governor of Jerusalem in 1920, claimed to rule Jerusalem district like his 'predecessor' Pontius Pilate.[24] He imagined himself as an all-powerful governor in charge of every aspect of urban development, life and governance. Storrs believed that his tastes and ideas about urban space would have a benevolent impact on Jerusalemites. He unequivocally intertwined imperial interests with his personal views in his style of government. Aesthetics, a very high civic and religious sense, and a feeling that the communities of the city should be involved, all led Storrs towards the creation of the Pro-Jerusalem Society in 1918. The society was composed of the mayor of Jerusalem, the consular corps, the heads of the Christian denominations and other leading members of the British, Arab and Jewish communities. According to its statute, the main purpose of the Pro-Jerusalem Society was the preservation and advancement of the interests of Jerusalem: the provision and maintenance of parks, gardens and open spaces and the establishment of libraries, museums, music centres and theatres.[25] With an emphasis on preserving religious antiquities, the society promoted the communitarian notion that Jerusalem was a city of three faiths, rather than a space for equal citizenship. The very logo of the society was a religious symbol representing the Cross, the Star of David and the Crescent Moon.

The members of the society gathered on a regular basis between 1918 and 1924; however, it is clear that Storrs and Ashbee played the leading role.[26] Some of the most dramatic reforms implemented by the British under the aegis of Storrs were the renaming of the streets, as studied by Yair Wallach, and the confessionalization of the quarters in the Old City.[27] Wallach has noted that two-thirds of the names for the new city commemorated prophets, saints, scholars and kings; one third of the names were biblical; and the rest included names of crusader kings, Christian emperors, Muslim sultans and one Arab medieval scholar. Only one woman was commemorated – the crusader Queen

Melissanda. The names chosen made the streets of 'new' Jerusalem look ancient. Jerusalemites were reminded on every corner that they were walking the biblical city of the prophets, Jesus and Saint Paul. Names were not linked to British history, because Storrs chose to link street names to the history of Jerusalem, perhaps in an attempt to achieve some sort of sectarian harmony. This historical pathos was a new feature in Jerusalem and contrasted with the late Ottoman geographical division of the city. Jerusalemites called streets by various names that emphasized local characteristics, buildings or local residents. Storrs was radically changing this tradition and, in a manner of speaking, was dressing Jerusalem in biblical clothes. Not surprisingly, Ronald Storrs projected his own British and Victorian ideals in order to preserve the 'celestial' character of the city. He prohibited commercial advertisement close to the Old City, and brothels were forbidden within the walls; the sale and consumption of alcohol was regulated.[28] Religion as a marker of national identity was artificially enhanced and became the principle the British used to divide the Old City and to issue identity cards and passports. Whereas the urban space under the Ottomans was divided according to a mixed class–religion character, under the British the city became largely divided according to religious identities. The segregation model that developed upon the arrival of the British reduced social interaction and contributed to creating the idea of an inevitable conflict between communities.

The street names chosen were clearly linked with the history of Jerusalem, but none of them really symbolized the unity of the city; on the contrary, they suggested a clear religious cleavage of the city and failed to promote a sense of unity based on common citizenship – something the Ottomans had, to an extent, been able to promote in the last decade of their rule. Late Ottoman urban planning was driven by discourses of modernity through public works such as transportation, electric lighting and civic buildings – like the clock tower that for two decades dominated the skyline of Jerusalem before Storrs had it demolished for being ugly and not in line with the ancient walls.[29]

The British, through the agency of Ronald Storrs, set in motion a social and spatial process that aimed at the division and homogenization of the Old City and the city outside the walls according to religion; it may be defined as confessionalization or segregation. The British, whether consciously or not, contributed to the development of exclusive and 'asyncretic' religious identities, which made religion a key feature of Palestinian nationalism and favoured Zionism as an example of full secular nationalism. Salim Tamari has noted that this proved to be a retrogression from the Ottoman system.[30] Social interaction between communities was very common and not at all an empty cohabitation; it was based more on neighbourhood coexistence, as proved by the diaries and memoirs of local residents like Wasif Jawhariyya, Isman Turjman and Gad Frumkin and also of Western residents.[31] Jawhariyya noted in his memoirs, 'During the Ottoman rule we, the sons of Jerusalem of our different denominations, lived like a family, with no difference between a Muslim and a Christian'.[32] British policies, such as the aforementioned confessionalization of the Old City, which eventually ended with the division of the Old City into four communities – along with street naming, the demolition of the Ottoman clock tower, the regulation of buildings (colour and shape of the stones), the regulation of businesses inside/outside the Old City and the regulation of public transportation – catalysed the shift from communalism characterized by shared spaces to nationalism based on ethnic and religious identity characterized by the absence of shared space. However, it would not be fair to attribute to the British alone the structural changes that occurred in the city. Nationalism as an ideology, already fostered by the Ottomans, played a major role; the war and British support for Zionism through the Balfour Declaration also proved to be a strong impetus to nationalist mobilization. Then, quoting Tamari, 'all of a sudden, a Jew [including any local Jew] in Arab Palestinian eyes became the European, the intruder from a different ethnic community which was contesting ownership of the land' in Jerusalem and in Palestine.[33] The shift was indeed gradual and cumulative through the 1920s; however, I would argue that the Nebi Musa riots were the first major sign of a changing pattern that introduced violence as a political tool, and the first test of national struggle.

The Riots

Surprisingly, the Nebi Musa riots have not attracted much academic attention. Historians have regarded these events as being of secondary importance, mostly overshadowed by clashes between Arabs and Zionists like the Wailing Wall riots of 1929, or the revolts from 1936 to 1939. I suspect this lack of attention is due to the very fact that the British defined them as 'riots', a definition that involved a political judgement. Often, authorities label as riots events that are considered detrimental to public order and driven by supposedly 'irrational' mobs.[34] While riots are generally associated with spontaneous eruptions of violence, this is not always the case. Often, riots are meticulously planned and collectively executed actions of contention, as was indeed the case in the Nebi Musa riots.[35] I believe many scholars in search of the origin of the Arab–Israeli conflict have simply overlooked this event, labelling it as an example of communal violence. However, this was not the case at the end of the First World War. I would argue that at this stage the dispute was far from being a 'simple' communal issue, as it was clearly over projects, ideas and perceived threats that crossed the boundaries of communalism. The escalation from communal hostility to structured and politicized violence was becoming visible but not at all inevitable. However, I would argue, the presence of a less than coherent and consistent third party – the British – contributed to the polarization of the developing conflict between emerging national-political movements. British policies also redesigned the borders of Jerusalemite society and space, with short-term plans such as forbidding Muslims to enter the Church of the Holy Sepulchre and with long-term projects like the implementation of the Balfour Declaration. I would suggest that foreign intervention through occupation and the implementation of policies, or the threat thereof, is key to understanding the outbreak of the riots and more general conflicts in the city.

Nebi Musa was an Islamic religious festival that included processions from different towns around Jerusalem leading into the city; Muslims celebrated the prophet Moses during the same period as the Christian Orthodox Easter and the Jewish Passover. The central celebration was the long pilgrimage from the traditional burial site of Moses, near Jericho, along the road to Jerusalem.[36] The celebrations had the power to create a bond between people from various parts of Palestine who gathered in a single place for the festival. Indeed, in 1920, the leaders of the Arab political parties and associations exploited the excitement and enthusiasm aroused by the festival to make sure their voices were heard by both the Zionists and the British. On the other hand, Zionists, particularly those led by the revisionist Vladimir Jabotinsky, who proposed a more aggressive approach towards local Arabs, worked to heat up the atmosphere, already far from idyllic.

To show how a degree of structured violence was introduced and how the paradigm shift mentioned earlier took place, let us focus on the events that occurred at the beginning of April 1920. On Friday, 2 April, the first ceremony of the Nebi Musa festival passed without incident, and it seems that the small police force dealing with the procession was successful. Sunday, 4 April, was the day of the main pilgrimage from the shrine of the prophet Moses near Jericho to Jerusalem. Ordinarily, the route followed by pilgrims upon their arrival in Jerusalem included a walk along Jaffa Road. They then entered the Old City through Damascus Gate and from there reached the Haram al-Sharif. On this day, the procession stopped outside the Old City on Jaffa Road, just opposite the

Jaffa Gate. Notables and religious leaders, including a very heated group coming from Hebron carrying the Hebron banner, then started to deliver inflammatory political speeches, contrary to the usual protocol.[37] The choice of Jaffa Gate, I would argue, was not accidental. The gate represented one of the most important access points in the city, was not affiliated with any religious groups and was a symbol of modernity, as it was the seat of the Ottoman clock tower built in 1907 and later demolished by the British. Aref al-Aref, the editor of the popular nationalist newspaper *al-Suriyya al-Janubiyya* (The Southern Syria), published since 1919, declared, 'If we don't use force against the Jews, we will never be rid of them'. In response, the crowd chanted *Nashrab dam al-yahud* (We will drink the blood of the Jews). Khalil Baydas, also known as *Ra'id al-qissa al-filastiniyya* (the pioneer of Palestinian history), concluded his speech by saying, 'My voice is weakening with emotion, but my national heart will never weaken'. From a balcony, Musa Kazim al-Husayni, the mayor of Jerusalem, also spoke. After his speech, the crowd roared, 'Palestine is our land, the Jews are our dogs!' Pictures of Faysal were also displayed, and he was acclaimed as King of Syria and Palestine. A young al-Hajj Amin cried aloud: 'O Arabs! This is your King!'[38] This rhetoric polarized the situation, opening more avenues for open violent conflict and, as Charles Tilly stated, 'widening the political and social space between claimants'.[39]

While the first half of the procession was passing through the Jaffa Gate, the riot began between Christaki's pharmacy and the Credit Lyonnais. Available sources do not clarify the exact trigger, and it is arguable that more than one event functioned as a catalyst.[40] In the vicinity of the Arab rally, some Zionists were listening to the speeches. It is likely some belonged to the self-defence force organized by Vladimir Jabotinsky, by this time already enlisting six hundred troops performing military drills on a daily basis.[41] Already in early March, Jabotinsky was working to inflame the atmosphere, and he began to publicly predict a pogrom. Some evidence suggests that these Jewish spectators were quite provocative. Allegedly, a Jew pushed an Arab carrying a nationalist flag, and he tried to spit on the banner and on the Arab crowd.[42] According to testimony gathered by the French consul, some young Jews standing near Jaffa Gate attacked some Arabs after the speech delivered by Muhammed Darwish of the Arab Club (one of the Christian–Muslim associations).[43] All of these reports suggest only Jewish provocation; however, it is possible, though unreported, that Arab activities also triggered the riots.

Shops inside the Old City were looted after they had been the targets of a volley of stones, and spectators close to the New Grand Hotel were beaten with rocks. The crowd then moved down towards the centre of the Old City, where some Jewish shops were looted and several Jews were assaulted. Some of the Jews involved carried weapons, as in the case of two who fired from a house overlooking the procession route. Both were shot by the British-Indian police deployed by Ronald Storrs. The incident started at 10.00 A.M. and was practically over by midday. The night was quiet, and the pilgrims from Hebron, who were confined for the night in the police barracks, were taken to the Haram al-Sharif and from there escorted to St Stephen's Gate on their way to Nebi Musa. Disorder, however, broke out again early in the morning and lasted until 3.00 P.M., when martial law was declared following some cases of violent assault and looting. The following day, looting and violence continued, albeit on a smaller scale, although two cases of rape against Jewish girls were reported close to the Arab market near New Street; the police shot into an Arab mob to reach the house where the rape allegedly occurred. Although martial law was declared, looting was still carried out; in fact, it seems the police were not able to cope with the intricacy of the streets of the Old City – a labyrinth. By Friday, 9 April, the situation had slowly been brought under control, and only occasional incidents were still being reported. The reported casualties amounted to 251, of whom nine Jews and twenty-two Arabs were critically wounded. Five Jews and four Muslims had been killed; 211 Jews were reported wounded, as opposed to twenty-one Muslims and three Christians. Seven British soldiers were also injured; however, it appears that the police were never the target of the attackers, whether Arabs or Jews.[44]

Storrs seems to have ignored early warnings of impending troubles issued in the reports available in late April and in the Commission of Inquiry established by high commissioner of Egypt and commander-in-chief, Allenby. Zionists accused the local police force of being inadequate and mainly Arab in character. On Friday 2 April, the day before the outbreak, the ceremony had passed without incident; this led Storrs to think or at least to claim that the small, local police force could cope with the main procession. After the first day of riots, Storrs decided to withdraw the main bulk of the troops from the Old City, in order to enable business to proceed as usual. Storrs believed that showing normality restored could prevent the outbreak of further violence.[45] In brief, the military apparatus allowed the demonstrations to take place, and it adopted a 'wait and see' policy. Only when incidents became evident and events unstoppable did the military intervene to stop the violence.[46]

The riots had a visible impact on Jerusalem. The stage was now set for an open tripartite political battle among British, Arabs and Zionists; yet, this does not mean that escalation in the degree of hostility between these actors was inevitable. The British saw the riots as an expression of political and racial tensions, and did not consider these events an organized attempt to introduce violence as a political language in Jerusalem and Palestine. However, in my view, communal clashes were now superseded by structured violence, or at least by the threat of it. As performers of violence, both sides, Arabs and Zionists, realized that in this new context tactical pre-emption was vital, yet not to be deployed immediately because of the presence of the British, and in the case of the Zionists because of their demographic disadvantage. The riots were a bitter clash. They were politically motivated, but were not yet evidence of an open conflict. In other words, in April 1920, local values and alliances were renegotiated but not radicalized.[47] The confessionalization of space implemented by British policies played an important part in fostering the emergence of organized violence. From a space for the development of citizenship, Jerusalem had been transformed into a sacred space.

Conclusion

This chapter has shown how and why structured violence emerged in Jerusalem during the transitional era from Ottoman to British rule. The Nebi Musa riots that broke out in April 1920 epitomized a major change in urban and national politics, and were instrumental to the introduction of organized violence as a means of reaching political goals. Relationships between Zionists and Arabs were not inherently violent; in fact, violence was still an option rather than the normality. With the creation of political organizations on both sides – the Zionists with the Zionist Commission, later to become the Jewish Agency, and the formation of Muslim–Christian associations and later Arab societies – and the absence of political institutions, violence became a tool for political communication. This chapter has tried to answer an important question about the nature of this violence. Did the Nebi Musa riots introduce violence as a means to an end, or rather as an end in itself? The latter would certainly be a frightening conclusion. As shown, the introduction of violence in a more organized and sophisticated way was the outcome of a variety of factors: the British creation of a fertile framework; and a choice, certainly not well pondered in the long term, by the Zionist and Arab organizations.

This chapter has also highlighted how the urban policies implemented by the British contributed to a shift in the local urban alliances and in the relationship between communal identities and space. In the late Ottoman era, relations between communities were marked by a degree of coexistence that included shared religious and civic spaces. The Nebi

Musa riots marked the end of this state of affairs, opening a new chapter in the history of Jerusalem and of Palestine. For those who depict the Palestinian–Israeli conflict as something that goes back to time immemorial and regard violence as something naturally implanted in both communities, the study of the Nebi Musa riots shows the exact opposite. Collective organized violence was relatively unknown and little experimented with in Jerusalem; relationships between communities, though not always idyllic, were not continuously strained, and it is only with the introduction of political discourses over land control that relations between communities, gradually in time and radically in nature, changed. These riots were a first step in this direction.

Notes

1. I have already discussed these riots elsewhere, as I was originally interested in looking at this particular event in relation to the British administration, and have argued that the Nebi Musa Riots determined a major shift in the character of British rule, not only in Jerusalem but more broadly in Palestine. R. Mazza. 2009. *Jerusalem from the Ottomans to the British*, London: I.B. Tauris, 165–78; see also A. Jacobson. 2011. *From Empire to Empire: Jerusalem between Ottoman and British Rule*, Syracuse, NY: Syracuse University Press.
2. L. Fishman. 2005. 'The 1911 Haram-al-Sharif Incident: Palestinian Notables versus the Ottoman Administration', *Journal of Palestine Studies* 34(3), 6–22; D. Fabrizio. 2006. *Fascino d'Oriente*, Genoa: Marietti.
3. F. Coronil and J. Skurski. 2006. 'Introduction: States of Violence and the Violence of States', in F. Coronil and J. Skurski (eds), *States of Violence*, Ann Arbor: The University of Michigan Press, 5.
4. D. Riches, 1986. 'The Phenomenon of Violence', in D. Riches (ed.), *The Anthropology of Violence*, Oxford: Basil Blackwell, 1.
5. On communalism, see M.J. Wyszomirski. 1975. 'Communal Violence: The Armenians and the Copts as Case Studies', *World Politics* 27(3), 430–55.
6. On equality, see R. Davison. 1954. 'Turkish Attitudes Concerning Christian–Muslim Equality in the Nineteenth Century', *The American Historical Review* 59(4), 844–64.
7. D. Kushner. 1984. 'Intercommunal Strife in Palestine during the Late Ottoman Period', *Asian and African Studies* 18, 201.
8. For details on the Haram al-Sharif incident, see Fishman, 'The 1911 Haram-al-Sharif Incident'.
9. For details on the incidents that occurred on 4 November 1901, see Fabrizio, *Fascino d'Oriente*, 158–98.
10. Kushner, 'Intercommunal Strife in Palestine', 201–3.
11. C. Tilly. 2003. *The Politics of Collective Violence*, Cambridge: Cambridge University Press, 14.

12. A.P. Wavell. 1946. *Allenby: Soldier and Statesman*, London: George G. Harrap, 14.
13. The National Archives (TNA): Public Record Office (PRO) FO 371/3061, War Office to Headquarters Cairo, London, 21 Nov. 1917.
14. TNA: PRO FO 371/3061 War Office to Headquarters Cairo, London, 21 Nov. 1917. 'Prime Minister wishes to make first announcement of occupation of Jerusalem in House of Commons in following terms. (1) Manner in which you were received by the population, (2) That you entered Holy City on foot ... (5) That Mosque of Omar and area around it has been placed under exclusive Moslem control'.
15. C. Falls (ed.). 1930. *Military Operations Egypt & Palestine*, London: HMSO, 234–35; R. Mazza (ed.). 2011. *Jerusalem in World War One*, London: I.B. Tauris, 183–85.
16. On the British conquest of Jerusalem, see Mazza, *Jerusalem from the Ottomans to the British*, 111–46; Jacobson. *From Empire to Empire*, 117–47.
17. S. Tamari (ed.). 2000. 'My Last Days as an Ottoman Subject', *Jerusalem Quarterly* 9, 34.
18. N. Bentwich. 1923. *England in Palestine*, London: Kegan Paul, 20; B. Wasserstein. 1991. *The British in Palestine*, Oxford: Blackwell, 20; TNA: PRO FO 371/3384 Allenby to War Office, 23 Oct. 1918, 'Turkish system of government will be continued and the existing machinery utilised'.
19. For details on Storrs, see Mazza, *Jerusalem from the Ottomans to the British*, 158–63.
20. See Y. Porath. 1974. *The Emergence of the Palestinian-Arab National Movement 1918–1929*, London: Frank Cass.
21. Christian–Muslim associations began to be formed in several locations in Palestine early in 1918 with the purpose of fighting Zionism, but also to counter the British argument that Arabs in Palestine were divided along religious lines. See Mazza, *Jerusalem from the Ottomans to the British*, 68–73; Jacobson, *From Empire to Empire*, 148–59; L. Robson. 2011. *Colonialism and Christianity in Mandate Palestine*, Austin: University of Texas Press, 16–43.
22. On Ashbee, see C.R. Ashbee 1923. *A Palestine Notebook 1919–1923*, London: William Heinemann.
23. Details on Storrs can be found in R. Storrs. 1937. *The Memoirs of Sir Ronald Storrs*, New York: G.P. Putnam's Sons; A.J. Sherman. 1997. *Mandate Days*, Slovenia: Thames and Hudson; G.S. Georghallides. 1985. *Cyprus and the Governorship of Sir Ronald Storrs*, Nicosia: Cyprus Research Centre; Mazza, *From the Ottomans to the British*, 158–63.
24. Pembroke College, The Papers of Sir Ronald Storrs, Reel 10, Box III, *Evening News*, 21 Dec. 1920.
25. C.R. Ashbee (ed.). 1921. *Jerusalem 1918–1920, Being the Records of the Pro-Jerusalem Council during the Period of the British Military Administration*, London: John Murray, vii.

26. B. Hyaman. 1994. 'British Planners in Palestine 1918–1936', Ph.D. dissertation, London: London School of Economics, 362.
27. Y. Wallach. 2006. 'The 1920s Street-Naming Campaign and the British Reshaping of Jerusalem', presented at the Second World Congress for Middle Eastern Studies (WOCMES-2), Amman; see also Y. Wallach. 2008. 'Reading in Conflict: Public Text in Modern Jerusalem', Ph.D. dissertation, London: Birkbeck College.
28. *The Palestine News*, no. 5, 1 Aug. 1918; France, Ministry of Foreign Affairs (MAE), 'Maison Publiques', Series B Carton 113, Avis no. 43, Nantes.
29. Y. Avcı. 2011. 'Jerusalem and Jaffa in the Late Ottoman Period: The Concession Hunting Struggle for Public Works Projects', in Y. Ben-Bassat and E. Ginio (eds), *Late Ottoman Palestine*, London: I.B. Tauris, 81–102.
30. S. Tamari. 2006. 'City of Riffraff: Crowds, Public Space, and New Urban Sensibilities in War-Time Jerusalem 1917–1921', in P. Misselwitz and T. Rieniets (eds), *City of Collision: Jerusalem and the Principles of Conflict Urbanism*, Boston: Birkhäuser, 306.
31. W. Jawhariyya. 2004. *Al-Quds al Intidabiyya fi 'l Mudhakarat al-Jawhariyya*, S. Tamari and I. Nassar (eds), Beirut: Mu'assasat al-Dirasat al-Filastiniyya; S. Tamari. 2011. *A Soldier's Diary and the Erasure of Palestine's Ottoman Past*, Berkeley: University of California Press; Mazza, *Jerusalem in World War One*; G. Frumkin. 1954. *Derekh Shofet bi-Yerushalayim*, Tel Aviv: Dvir; B.V. Spafford. 1977. *Our Jerusalem*, New York: Arno Press.
32. Tamari, 'My Last Days as an Ottoman Subject', 34.
33. M. Benvenisti and S. Tamari. 2006. 'Jerusalem, between Urban Area and Partition', in P. Misselwitz and T. Rieniets (eds), *City of Collision: Jerusalem and the Principles of Conflict Urbanism*, Boston: Birkhäuser, 35.
34. Tilly, *The Politics of Collective Violence*, 18.
35. P.A. Gossman. 1999. *Riots and Victims*, Boulder, CO: Westview Press, 8–13.
36. Details on the festival can be found in Eddie Halabi. 2007. 'The Transformation of the Prophet Moses Festival in Jerusalem, 1917–1937: From Local and Islamic to Modern and Nationalist Celebrations', Ph.D. dissertation, Toronto: University of Toronto.
37. On the group from Hebron, see Henry Laurens. 1999. *La Question de Palestine*, Paris: Fayard, vol. 1, 508; TNA: PRO FO 371/5114 Arab Muslim–Christian Society to the Military Governor, Jerusalem, April 1920; TNA: PRO WO 32/9614, Report of the Court of Enquiry into the Riots in Jerusalem during Last April, Jerusalem, April 1920.
38. B. Morris. 2001. *Righteous Victims*, New York: Vintage Books, 95; T. Segev. 2001. *One Palestine Complete*, New York: Henry Holt, 128; TNA: PRO WO 32/9614, Report of the Court of Enquiry into the Riots in Jerusalem during Last April, Jerusalem, April 1920; Porath, *Emergence of the Palestinian-Arab National Movement*, 96–100; I. Pappé. 2010. *The Rise and Fall of a Palestinian Dynasty*, Berkeley: University of California Press, 197.
39. Tilly, *The Politics of Collective Violence*, 21.

40. TNA: PRO WO 32/9614, Report of the Court of Enquiry into the Riots in Jerusalem during Last April, Jerusalem, April 1920.
41. Wasserstein, *The British in Palestine*, 63. Laurens states that Jabotinsky's force was composed of two hundred men: Laurens. *La Question de Palestine*, 509.
42. M.F. Abcarius. 1946. *Palestine through the Fog of Propaganda*, London: Hutchinson & Co., 67; TNA: PRO WO 32/9614, Report of the Court of Enquiry into the Riots in Jerusalem during Last April, Jerusalem, April 1920.
43. French Ministry of Foreign Affairs (MAE). 1920. *French Consult to General Gouraud, Jerusalem, 8 April 1920*, Series B Carton 94, Nantes.
44. TNA: PRO WO 32/9614, Report of the Court of Enquiry into the Riots in Jerusalem during Last April, Jerusalem, April 1920.
45. TNA: PRO WO 32/9614, Report of the Court of Enquiry into the Riots in Jerusalem during Last April, Jerusalem, April 1920: 'Colonel Storrs inclines to consider the actual danger at the Nebi Musa festival itself was greater in the preceding year. The majority of witnesses are not of his opinion'.
46. For a deeper analysis of the riots in relation to the British Military Administration, see Mazza, *From the Ottomans to the British*, 165–78.
47. On local alliances, see Jacobson, *From Empire to Empire*; see also M. Campos. 2011. *Ottoman Brothers: Muslims, Christians and Jews in Early Twentieth-Century Palestine*, Stanford, CA: Stanford University Press.

Part IV

Oil Cities

Spatiality and Violence

❧· Chapter 9 ·❦

On Lines and Fences

Labour, Community and Violence in an Oil City

RASMUS CHRISTIAN ELLING

In December 1942, unrest broke out in Abadan, arguably Iran's first modern industrial city and home to the world's biggest oil refinery. Two scuffles in the bazaar provoked Iranians from the Ahmadabad neighbourhood to attack Indian labourers in the 'Indian Lines' of the Bahmashir[1] neighbourhood. Although not as bloody or widespread as more well-studied occurrences of unrest in Abadan, I will argue that this 'Bahmashir Incident' is an important case that can aid in understanding the interconnectedness of oil, space and violence.

This chapter has two aims. The first is to fill a gap in the existing literature on Abadan and the oil-producing province of Khuzestan in south-west Iran. This literature tends to focus on the struggles of the native Iranian labour movement against the Anglo-Persian, later Anglo-Iranian, Oil Company (A.I.O.C., henceforth 'the Company'), and specifically on the great oil strikes of 1929 and 1946, and the oil nationalization movement of 1951.[2] In this literature, one crucial element is normally either only mentioned in passing or simply neglected: imported Indian labour. Using material from, among other places, the underexplored British Petroleum Company archives, I will investigate the context of the Bahmashir Incident synchronically and the history of a particular community (the Indians) diachronically.

These investigations reveal an alternative labour history of Abadan, which, I will argue, can complement and challenge the existing literature.[3] Key Iranian leftist and nationalist accounts of Abadan's history tend to cast all violence in the binary terms of a struggle between 'the oppressor' (the British) and 'the oppressed' (the native Iranians). This chapter will instead propose that since Abadan had multiple subaltern agencies, urban violence operated on several levels. The presence of Indians in Abadan's labour hierarchy and social fabric challenges the idea of Abadan as a 'dual city'[4] and complicates simplistic interpretations of urban violence.

Secondly, by disentangling the web of interests spun between the Company, the British military and the diplomatic machinery, this chapter will nuance the notion, so often reiterated uncritically in Middle East studies, of 'The British' as a single, cohesive actor. The Company drew on the colonial legacy of British imperialism, was protected by the British military and was influenced by its major shareholder, the British government; yet, the Company was nonetheless an autonomous entity with a distinct mode of operation. In order to 'see like an oil company,'[5] this chapter uses the Bahmashir Incident to examine how the Second World War affected the Company in Abadan on the eve of victorious nationalist movements and the dissolution of the British Empire – events that eventually drove companies born in colonial settings into the present globalized world of neo-liberal corporate capitalism.

To achieve these two aims, I situate the Bahmashir Incident simultaneously within various scales or 'spaces'. On the macro-scale, nineteenth- and twentieth-century trade globalization had brought venture capitalism to new heights, rapidly enriching and empowering corporations that were brought to life in a favourable colonial setting to extract resources from the Third World. New patterns in energy politics gave immense importance to oil in places like Iran and to enterprises such as the Company.

On the mid-scale, most of the Company's activities were harboured within the Iranian province of Khuzestan. In this remote south-western corner of Iran, I will argue, the Company created a 'space of exception':[6] the area known in official correspondence simply as 'The Concession', which also refers to the contract with the Iranian state under which the Company operated. Here, the Company had negotiated and imposed its presence as an extraterritorial entity since 1908, operating within an existing nation state that was never formally colonized but was clearly under strong foreign influence. Within the Concession, the Company maintained vital interconnections between the rural and tribal hinterland of 'the Fields', where oil was extracted, and the modern refinery city of Abadan, from where it was exported.

Finally, on the micro-level, the Bahmashir Incident can be used to study the construction and contestation of urban space in Abadan. Kaveh Ehsani and Mark Crinson[7] pioneered the study of Abadan's spatial politics, and it is with inspiration from their fascinating works that the present study focuses on one community and one event in the belief that the micro-scale of urban violence can be understood only within the macro-scale of power politics.

This belief, in turn, mirrors another: that violence should be recognized as a fundamental aspect of everyday politics – not because human beings are innately violent, but because the very social processes and political structures that shape modernity were and are, more often than not, moulded and sustained by violence and coercion.[8] This is especially true for processes and structures that bring about rapacious frontier capitalist enterprises such as an oil industry.[9]

Abrupt, enclaval industrialization and mass labour migrations under the Company caused fundamental societal changes in Khuzestan. When oil was struck in Masjed-e Soleyman in 1908, the Company initially recruited unskilled labour among the local inhabitants in the Concession, including Lor, Bakhtiyari and Arab tribesmen, while Europeans handled engineering tasks requiring technical skills. However, with the oil industry's phenomenal expansion and insatiable appetite for labour, migrant workers flooded the region. In particular, the Company recruited labour from India and Ottoman Iraq, and then people from other parts of Khuzestan, from Iranian cities such as Tehran and Tabriz, as well as from Palestine and Europe. By the 1940s, local Khuzestanis made up only 40 per cent of the Company workforce.[10]

As early as 1910, however, worried British diplomats had presciently called for hiring, as far as possible, Iranian rather than Indian and Ottoman labour.[11] Indeed, the question of foreign labour soon became a key issue of contention between the Company and Iran – especially after the ascendancy of the assertive Reza Shah in 1925 and the concomitant wave of nationalist sentiment in the Iranian public. The Company claimed, in the beginning of operations with good reason, that it was impossible to find suitable replacements locally or in other parts of Iran. Company archives, however, also imply that recruitment was based on the Orientalist belief that particular ethnic groups were inherently predisposed to certain types of work. By institutionalizing a labour hierarchy shaped by these essentialist stereotypes, the Company believed it could optimize productivity and oil output.

This belief is echoed all the way up to 1982: in the British Petroleum company's official history, R.W. Ferrier argues that among Iranians, 'there was little understanding of the discipline and expertise required for complex industrial operation and little opportunity to attain the necessary technical proficiency'.[12] A more truthful analysis would rather propose that the Company, particularly in the first two decades of operation, systematically denied Iranians this opportunity, and that the Company's treatment of Iranians was in many ways racist.[13]

It was thus Iranians who comprised the general bulk of labour at the bottom of the hierarchy, toiling in the oppressive heat and dangerous conditions of the Fields and the refinery. For mid-level positions, the Company mainly recruited Indians, while for junior managerial and bureaucratic positions it relied on what Ferrier calls 'more capable workers' from among Iranian and Iraqi Christians (Armenians and Chaldeans) and Jews.[14] In short, the British and other white Europeans were at the top of the hierarchy, followed by non-Muslim minorities and Indians, and, at the bottom, Muslim Iranians – which included a diverse mass with numerous internal ethno-linguistic divisions.[15]

Coolie Lines: Khuzestan's Indian Labour History

In the first phase of labour migration between 1908 and 1920, Indians were brought to Khuzestan to work as skilled and unskilled labour in the Fields and as clerks and menial servants of the British in the rapidly growing cities of Abadan, Masjed-e Soleyman, Ahwaz and Khorramshahr. In 1910 in Khuzestan there were 158 Indians out of a total Company workforce of 1,706. This number doubled in three years; and by 1916, Indians made up nearly half of the workforce in Abadan, thus outnumbering Iranians. During the First World War, when oil from Abadan's refinery became crucial in propelling Britain's Royal Navy towards victory, the Government of India suspended a 1910 Emigration Act to further facilitate the flow of labour from India to Khuzestan.

In the second phase of labour migration, which commenced after the Government of India tightened its labour laws in 1920, Indian recruitment shifted to the middle ranks of the workforce. Instead of in the Fields, Indians now worked mostly in the offices, stores and homes of Company management, where they were engaged as salaried semi-skilled and skilled artisans, foremen, clerks, drivers, cooks and servants. There were 3,816 Indians in Abadan in 1922, when they made up one-third of the total workforce in Khuzestan as a whole, and their numbers peaked at 4,890 in 1925.[16] As Reidar Visser notices, the Indian community was now 'strong enough to make the celebration of Ramakrishna's birthday a major local event'.[17]

To manage the diverse population it had brought together, the Company relied on colonial methods from the British experience in India. Indeed, many of the British men who built and managed the oil industry had previously served in India. Charles Greenway, the managing director in Abadan from 1910 to 1919, had worked for a trading company in India; James M. Wilson, the key planner of the 1930s expansion of

Abadan city, had assisted Lutyen, the architect of New Delhi; and numerous other Company officers had served in the British India military. As Michael Dobe has noted, these links to India, especially trade, are 'crucial to an understanding of [the Company] within the regional and global contexts of the British Empire'.[18] The colonial context was echoed, Crinson adds, in the prevalence of the 'language of Anglo-India: there were memsahibs and sahibs, tiffin and chota-hazry, godowns, ayahs, and punkahs'.[19]

The British managers also brought with them specific ethnic preferences in personnel employment: Sikhs from the Punjab and Gujaratis were preferred for technical jobs and security; Chittagonians for harbour engineering and naval transport; Goans worked as cooks and servants; and Madrasis as clerks. In general, Indians performed the role of managerial middlemen between the British bosses and the mass of Iranian labour. As such, they were crucial to the day-to-day operation of the oil complex and an integral part of the social hierarchy in Company Abadan.

In the early days of Company operations, the Indians suffered with all other labourers under harsh, unsanitary conditions in the 'Coolie Lines': basic tents and mud huts – the type of dwellings ubiquitous in colonial industrial enterprises across the world that hired Indian migrant labour. For many Indians, especially the low castes impoverished in their homeland, a life as a 'coolie in the lines' was the promise of some sort of roof over one's head and the prospect of remittances for the family at home. 'Coolie', as *The Hobson-Jobson* glossary explains, referred broadly to a 'hired labourer, or burden-carrier', but as a particular *nomen gentile*, it originally signified something very close to 'slave'.[20] Indeed, pre-1920 labour indenture systems have been compared to slavery,[21] and recent scholarship has proposed a concept of 'Coolitude' to understand the historical plight of those indentured overseas.[22] Scattered evidence suggests that Indians were not always better off in early Company Abadan than the 'coolies' toiling in the tropical plantations of the Fijis and Guyana.

In 1920, the Government of India, under increasing pressure from disgruntled migrant workers abroad and brewing nationalist discontent at home, contacted the Company to address 'complaints of alleged ill-treatment' of Indian employees in Khuzestan. The Government stated that 'Indian feelings run high' on matters of labour emigration and, since there was no longer any wartime necessity, the Company's recruitment of large numbers of unskilled labour for Iran was in fact illegal.[23] This was one of many signs of tension and disagreement in the triangular power relation of the Company, the British government in London and the Government of India, with the latter regularly expressing concern about issues related to British-Indian subjects in Persia.

The first labour unrest in Khuzestan occurred in 1914, but it was in fact Indians who organized the first mass strike. In December 1920, some three thousand Indian employees demanded higher wages, a reduction in work hours, additional pay for overtime work, an improvement of living conditions and 'an end to vilification and molestation of workers by staff members'.[24] Since many strikers were from the Punjab, their protests were probably influenced by the 1919 massacre in Amritsar.[25] The following day, Iranian labourers followed suit and stopped work. Even though the Company agreed to an 80 per cent increase in wages and promised improvements, the discontent continued. The Indians had thus helped to introduce a new kind of political agency, as Stephanie Cronin points out,[26] setting in motion a long history of industrial action in Iran.

In 1922, former employees complained in the *Bombay Chronicle* about the inhumane conditions under which workers had been shipped to Khuzestan, and under which they then had to work and live. One of these employees, A.T. Mudliar, described life as a subaltern in Abadan as follows:

> The treatment meeted [sic] out to the Indian workmen is on the whole very bad and quite unbecoming. This maltreatment of setting up class hatred even in a foreign land is unbearable. No notice is taken of complaints of infringement of social privileges in a public space. Even complaints of assaults are allowed to pass over, so much so, even if the worst were to happen, it will not see the light of day.[27]

These statements prompted an official British inquiry, which simply rejected all charges of ill treatment. The British consul at Ahwaz even interviewed Mudliar about his writings in the *Chronicle*. When asked what he had meant by 'class hatred', Mudliar replied that it was a reference to both 'the stirring up of strife between different classes of Indians' and the 'racial prejudice exhibited by Europeans in their treatment of Indians'.[28] The official inquiry, however, concluded that the Indians were in fact treated much better than other employees, and enjoyed excellent accommodation and access to medical services.[29]

Also in 1922, Company-paid Arab tribes and the British-Indian regiment stationed in Basra attacked striking workers in Abadan who had demanded a doubling of wages. This strike saw Indians and Iranians united in action, but Sikh Indians bore the brunt of repression: two thousand were dismissed and expelled in the clampdown.[30] At a general meeting in London, Company representatives had to excuse delays in refinery extensions by reference to troubles created by 'seditionist agents'.[31] There was again unrest when, in 1924, an Indian mechanic organized a workmen's union and a general strike in Masjed-e Soleyman north of Abadan.[32] Once again, the Company responded with deportations of Sikhs. While Iranians filled the ranks of low-level occupations left by the rebellious Sikhs, Indian labour retained mid-level occupations and positions.

As Dobe concludes, the combined pressure of recurrent Indian-led protests, Tehran's increasingly vocal demands and Iranian public opinion forced the Company into gradually adopting a 'Persianization' recruitment policy. The old labour recruitment system in India was abolished in 1926, and a training programme introduced to prepare Iranian replacements for the Indian specialized labour – even for cooks.[33] However, in reality, the Company still found it very difficult or undesirable to replace the Indians. Well into the 1930s and 1940s, it was still Indian engineers who trained and directed Iranian artisans. Even though Iran again complained over the use of Indian labour in 1933, the Company started new recruitments in the Punjab in 1934.[34]

Violence in the Lines: Order and Disorder

The working conditions in Khuzestan were harsh, with long summers dominated by extreme heat and tasks that entailed significant risks and dangers. Work hours were long, breaks few and holidays very rare. Wages were low and employment subject to fluctuating Company demand. The labourers had very few avenues for expressing discontent and, as scholars such as Cronin have documented, the 'intimidation of the workforce in the interest of political and industrial discipline was notorious'.[35]

In the absence of an Iranian state apparatus and official law enforcement, the Company relied in the early days of Khuzestan operations on various legally dubious security measures. These included the Company's own police force and militias, networks of informants and the use of tribal Arab mercenaries as storm troopers in the event of labour unrest. The range of coercive measures and the scope of political interferences in Khuzestani bureaucracy is testimony to the breadth and profundity of Company power in Iranian affairs. However, this local exercise of power rested on an ambiguous legitimacy. As far back as 1924, diplomats had warned of the 'difficulties arising from [the] anomaly of [the] company's police in Persia'.[36] The ambiguity also included the security questions connected with the Indian presence.

While there are popular narratives of positive interaction between Indians and Iranians in Abadan, there is also scattered evidence of a long history of intercommunal tension and violence. Some of the tension ostensibly stemmed from different cultural values between locals and imported labour. As early as 1914, the Arab Sheikh of Mohammerah complained to the British consul at Bushehr about the behaviour of Indian workers. A Company officer responded that 'a really efficient police force' was needed to deal with problems such as drinking and gambling among the Indians.[37] Indeed, the Company was concerned that among its many temporary Indian labourers there could be 'a good many fugitives from justice and other bad characters' – particularly among 'the Pathans'.[38] The Company pressured the Government of India to share the expenses of maintaining in Abadan an Indian police force that could also 'quell disturbances', which indicated that concerns were not limited to petty crime.[39] Conversely, the Company was also concerned with protecting Indians, as British subjects, against the violence of Arab tribal guards.

In 1915, a row occurred between 'Hindoos and Mohamedans over a water-tap at one of the mud lines' that resulted in a general melee, with several injured on both sides.[40] While the mention in Company reports of religious denominations rather than nationality indicates a sectarian aspect, the incident seemed rooted in a much more mundane issue of water access. Similarly, in 1925, the director at Abadan wrote that due to the political climate and 'our peculiar circumstances in Persia', it would be unwise to lay down 'a hard and fast rule between Indians and Persians' on how to divide privileges such as access to housing among the labourers. In other words, the Company was aware of the tensions created by its social engineering.

Indians, in particular Hindus, were undoubtedly subject to prejudices. Ferrier relates that the 'Indians were frequently restless and suffered from some cultural claustrophobia in an alien and not always sympathetic environment.'[41] Latent racism in the Iranian nationalist and leftist movements also extended to attacks on Indians in conjunction with anti-Company agitation. In one notable example quoted by several scholars, a 1929 *shabname* (underground pamphlet) lamented that the Iranians, as 'glorious and noble sons of Darius', were ruled over by 'the half-burnt people from the Equator'.[42] Yet it also seems that the cultural dimensions of the Indian–Iranian tensions in Abadan were, if not a product of, then at least compounded by the social inequality in the Company labour hierarchy.

The relatively more privileged position of some Indian employees created much discontent among the Iranians. A 1927 article in the Persian-language newspaper *Habl-ol-matin* lamented that at the hospital in Abadan, Iranians had to 'stand around like the Persian Jews of old until such time as all of the Indians, Iraqis and the Jews have been attended to'.[43] As an article quoted by Kaveh Bayat from a 1928 issue of the *Shafaq-e sorkh* newspaper shows, Iranians believed that Indians were hired, despite being more costly, only to prevent Iranians from climbing the labour hierarchy and organizing to demand their rights.[44] Indeed, the British routinely placed Indians, Jews and Christians in the role of *sarkar* (foreman) to control the Iranian, Muslim workforce, and this domination often took the form of violence. As a key labour activist, Yusef Eftekhari recalls:

> Tormenting, molesting and beating the workers had become the regular business of the British and their subordinates ... It happened often that the British would kill a worker with beatings and kicks, and unfortunately they were never arrested by judicial authorities. In the factories of the oil company, beatings and insults were such a regular occurrence that even the Armenians and Indians favoured by 'the masters' [the British] would severely beat and injure the [Iranian] workers.[45]

Despite the fact that the Company had historically not treated Indians much better than Iranian labour, there were few if any indications of solidarity between the two groups beyond the early strikes. On the contrary, the general Iranian perception of Indians seems to have been that they were lackeys of British imperialism and symbols of Company injustice. This negative image of Indians was exacerbated by the occasional presence on Iranian soil of Indian troops in British service.[46]

When Reza Shah consolidated Iranian state rule in Khuzestan after 1925, the Company could no longer rely on autonomous tribal leaders to enforce its rule locally. Instead of merely buying off local strongmen, it now had to engage in an exceedingly complex game of meddling in Iranian administrative affairs while lobbying for British interventions on its behalf. In the Concession, the Company utilized a broad range of coercive mechanisms to secure oil output. Nominally legal measures included the use of the Iranian police, gendarmerie, military and juridical authorities to maintain order. The Company constantly expressed concern with the safety of its assets and personnel, and dissatisfaction with the skills and integrity of Iranian police. A relentless scuffle took place between the Company and the Iranian state, with the former demanding more and better policing and the latter seeking to relegate such expenses to the Company. This scuffle particularly intensified when the

Concession was rocked by labour unrest in the 1920s and again in the 1940s. During these crises, Iranian nationalists would criticize the ways the Company operated in Khuzestan as a space of exception to Iranian law and sovereignty.

The ethnic lines along which labour was hierarchized in this quasi-colonial space of exception generated discontent, which sometimes boiled over into violence. In March 1928, a rumour that ten thousand Iranians were to be fired and replaced by Indians sparked riots and attacks on Company buildings.[47] During the momentous 1929 strike in Abadan, Indian drivers were pulled out of cars carrying British Company officers. From the late 1920s, the increasingly anti-British Persian press reminded readers of British favouritism towards Indians, and in 1932, the Iranian government quoted this favouritism as one of the reasons for the cancellation of the original D'Arcy Concession.[48]

In other words, a growing Iranian nationalist movement interpreted the Company's social control and the movement of Indian labour to Khuzestan as an extension of British imperialism. At the time of the Bahmashir Incident in December 1942, there were 1,716 Indians out of a total workforce of 44,292.[49] The important difference was that, by then, Indians had generally moved to a higher-paid category in the labour hierarchy. This elevation was reflected in the shift in Company vernacular about Abadan's physical space, from 'the Coolie Lines' and 'mud lines' to 'the Indian Lines'.

Drawing the Lines: Spatial Politics of Coercion

The horrible living conditions of most oil workers in the early days of the Concession are a well-known topic.[50] Indeed, the Company's unwillingness or inability to provide adequate housing for the rapidly growing population was a constant theme in Company–State relations. All urban planning in Abadan had the aim of facilitating the sole purpose of the city: oil refinement and export. These sensitive industrial processes required that particular security measures were embedded into the fabric of the city. As colonial experience from India had taught the planners, a constantly growing, heterogeneous and restive population was a key challenge to running an efficient business operation. To meet this challenge, the Company pursued a strategy of spatial coercion, which generated tensions and violence – including the Indian-Iranian animosity that resulted in the Bahmashir Incident.

Before the expansion of Abadan in the 1930s, there was, on the one hand, the Company-built 'bungalow area', and on the other, Abadan

Town. The latter, in the words of Crinson, 'was not the Abadan [that the British] knew but an overcrowded insalubrious area, the supplier of non-European labour, the ubiquitous "native city" of colonial imagination'.[51] Indeed, as Visser points out, Company planning was mostly focused on insulating the European-inhabited area from the real and imagined germs of the natives.[52]

New workers swarmed in, but Abadan city, located on a small island squeezed in between two rivers, was inhibited from expanding. This geographic confinement generated, to the Company's concern, a tinderbox threat of social disorder. Urban planners recommended building a number of small, separate townships that, in the words of the architect, would be 'more easily and efficiently controlled'.[53] As Ehsani points out, the new plans for Abadan were marked by a 'glaring contradiction' between 'formal' and 'informal' space: in the blueprints, 'all unpredictable and spontaneous elements had been eliminated', and 'all details of collective as well as private life in the new urban space had been subjected to conscious planning and design'.[54]

Most importantly, the space was divided according to rank in the labour hierarchy: residential spaces were assigned to particular ethnic and social groups, and even the public spaces within and between the neighbourhoods were often segregated.[55] There were, for example, separate drinking fountains for Iranians and non-Iranians, and the Company made sure that British employees did not have to share the library or hospital with the Indians.[56]

The refinery itself, as both Crinson and Ehsani point out, acted as a formidable metal barrier in the centre of Abadan Island. In its protective shadow, the British staff lived in the top-class Braim neighbourhood with its spacious villas, neatly manicured lawns, clean streets, and full infrastructure of modern amenities and entertainment, including billiard clubs, boat races, cricket matches, flower shows and cinemas. From this comfortable distance, the British could nurture what Ferrier calls an 'enclave mentality',[57] fraternizing with non-British only if necessary.

At the other socio-geographic extreme was Ahmadabad, which was legally outside Company-owned land but of great importance, since 60 per cent of its inhabitants were Company employees.[58] Ahmadabad was originally built by Abadan municipality and later turned into what Ehsani calls a 'workers' squatter neighborhood': it was marked by 'a "native" architecture, bazaars, "informal" residential and commercial neighborhoods, illegal hovels and shanties, and especially forbidden places housing brothels, drug sellers, and smugglers, who made the most of the city's location on the border'.[59] In the 1940s, most of Ahmadabad had paved roads and electricity, but drinking water was found only in public fountains, the sewage system was primitive, there were no parks or recreational facilities and the neighbourhood was infamous for diseases.[60]

However, there was, as already indicated, a third layer in between the two extremes of Braim and Ahmadabad: the Indian Lines in the Bahmashir neighbourhood, squeezed in between the refinery and Ahmadabad, consisting of lines of barrack-like huts – small, but equipped with certain modern amenities. While this Company-built neighbourhood was nowhere near as posh or clean as Braim, in the 1940s it was still a far cry from the squalor of Ahmadabad. The Indian Lines had surfaced roads, electricity, piped drinking water and a sewage system. The Indians had an exclusive Artisans' Club, sports facilities and access to a nearby park. As compensation claims from the Bahmashir Incident tell us, some Indians even retained Iranian servants.

The military-colonial etymology of 'the Indian Lines', I propose, had the psychological effect on Abadan's British community of a defence line cordoning off the ever-increasing pressure of the Iranian masses in Ahmadabad and the shanty towns. More broadly, the Indian presence provided a sense of protection and familiarity to the British in Abadan: the servants catering their familiar food; the loyal regiment ready to be mobilized for their defence; the drivers navigating them through the 'native' areas; and, indeed, the very spatial unit of the Lines itself to separate white/British Abadan from 'dark'/non-British Abadan by a human-geographic layer of 'semi-British'. All these were reassuring, convenient aspects in a daily life that many of the British in 1940s Abadan must have felt was increasingly threatened by disorder, violence, anti-colonial nationalism and war.

Since the colonial legacy of social coercion was manifested physically in Abadan's urban space, disruption of order in this space was a sign of resistance. As Gail Ching-Liang Low points out in her deconstruction of Kipling's *The City of Dreadful Night*, the quintessential Anglo-Indian town – and, I will argue, thus also Abadan – was based on a topos of linearity and geometry:

> These geometric lines are not only literal descriptions of the physical settlement patterns of the European community, but are also vivid testimonies to the culture's persistent interest in demarcation, naming and segregation. The obsession with walls, detachment and spaces-in-between signals a fear, an imagined pressure from the native quarters, whose bodily secretions and metaphorical productivity threaten to run riot and spill over established boundaries. Lines of demarcation were also lines of defence.[61]

Whereas in the early days of oil extraction, Khuzestan was considered a 'lawless', isolated frontier, 1940s Abadan was a complex multicultural centre harbouring a diverse population, dissident movements and urban angst. By the time of the Second World War and the 1941 British–Soviet invasion of Iran, the socially engineered modus vivendi in Abadan, which rested on the Company's spatial coercion, was challenged from multiple angles – and the Indians soon became targets.

Crossing the Lines: The Bahmashir Incident

On 19 December 1942, two separate episodes of violence led to the Bahmashir Incident. In subsequent reports, the Labour Superintendent recounted that, at around 2 P.M., three Indian soldiers had gone to visit 'a certain prostitute in the Abadan Bazaar' in Ahmadabad, and apparently left without paying for the services rendered.[62] In the ensuing melee, locals confronted the soldiers, attacked them with stones and chased them out of the bazaar. While this disturbance seemed to be over by 4 P.M., other Indians, unrelated to the incident, were being harassed in the bazaar. Rumours were rampant among the Iranians, many of whom were in the streets of Ahmadabad because 19 December also happened to be ʿ*eyd-e qorban* (Festival of Sacrifice, a Muslim holiday) and thus one of the very rare breaks in the oil-worker calendar.

The second incident also took place in the bazaar. Some six Indian employees of the Company, who had been engaged in a bout of ʿ*araq* drinking, went into the streets and reportedly abused a local boy and some women passing by. According to Company reports, policemen, under the control of the Iranian municipal authorities, were called to the scene, but instead of quelling the disturbance, they exacerbated the situation by shouting 'Catch the Indians, they are insulting our womenfolk!' The ensuing unrest was described in a Company report as follows:

> The news that the Indians were doing this and that spread like wildfire, and the hooligans and the riff-raff, taking advantage of the situation, spread all sorts of news, and many self-styled leaders jumped into the 'field of action' and ran to the Indian residential area. The batch of policemen who had at first chased them were among the crowd, still shouting the same words. The Ahmedabad population heard all these stories related to them by clever [*corrected in handwriting:* 'rogues'] in their own fashion. The 2 o'clock incident of the soldiers had not quite lost its effect when this occurred. The mob had increased in size as it

reached the Indian quarters, and then all sorts of hangers-on rushed up and started the general loot of the Indian quarters.⁶³

Two scuffles in the bazaar had thus led inhabitants of Ahmadabad to cross the fences around their neighbourhood to attack and ransack the Indian Lines. Indians were forced out of their houses and chased by mobs. Some Indians took refuge on rooftops and in the Apprentice Training Shop, others barricaded themselves in The Artisans' Club. The police reportedly shot bullets into the air to disperse Indians who were defending their properties. Some thirty houses belonging to Indians were raided and looted, and 'at the end of an hour over 80 Indian employees of the Company had lost practically everything they possessed.'⁶⁴ By the end of the day, twelve people had been injured, seven Indians and five Iranians, two of whom died in hospital.

Shortly after the attack, a Sikh Guard took up positions to protect the Indian neighbourhood. Some Polish troops also showed up at the scene in two armoured cars, but reportedly did not intervene.⁶⁵ To calm down the agitated Indians, who were 'badly shaken' and 'no less frightened of the [Iranian] police than of the mob',⁶⁶ the Company promised to repair quarters and feed those now homeless. The Sikh Guard was retained to assure the Indians' safety. However, the Company also demanded that the Indians return to work as soon as possible, and threatened to 'deal suitably' with those who did not.⁶⁷ Two days after the incident, the Indians were back to work and the situation, the Company claimed, had returned to normal. The question such a claim begs, of course, is: what constituted 'normal'? What could have caused such animosity?

On the surface, the incident can be read as a case of religious–cultural intercommunal tension: Indians, probably Hindus, and certainly acting disrespectfully, had angered the Muslim sensitivities of people in Ahmadabad, possibly also dishonouring women or breaking other codes of conduct. The religious–cultural coding does appear to be prominent: the incident occurred on a holy day, it involved religiously unlawful behaviour (prostitution and alcohol consumption), and the attackers reportedly shouted slogans about (gendered) honour (*namus*). The incident started, as has often been the case in Iranian history, in the bazaar and spilled over from this traditional space into the modern spaces of Bahmashir.

However tempting, I will argue that it is wrong to succumb to an analysis that reduces the violence to something conditioned by culture and ethnicity, or even racism and sectarianism. While the violence was certainly coded culturally, the animosity was, I propose, rooted in social inequality and spatial coercion. Indeed, the records show that the looters in particular stole foodstuffs and furniture from the Indian Lines. Rather than an act of sectarian rage or nationalist fury, the ransacking of the Indian Lines thus represented a rare opportunity for desperately impoverished Iranians to gain immediate material advantages. In this respect, it is important to situate the Bahmashir Incident within the context of the Second World War.

Throughout 1941–42, attacks by armed robbers on Company personnel in Khuzestan increased, as did theft of Company property. In early December 1942, a secret memorandum warned that since 'the entry into Iran of Allied Forces, there has been a gradual and progressive deterioration of security throughout the country'.[68] The 1941 British occupation of southern Iran obviously had oil security as a key objective, and the Company lent its infrastructure to the war effort.[69] Fearing that employees would abandon Abadan, London issued an Order in Council to prevent British (including Indian) subjects from leaving jobs that were now considered essential to the national war effort. There were reports of low morale among employees.[70] At the same time, the extent of Company militarization meant that its security operations could at times hardly be distinguished from those of the British military. The official correspondence speaks volumes about this ambiguity of power.[71]

To project power more comprehensively and, ostensibly, to prevent sabotage, both British military authorities and the Company wished to make Khuzestan 'a special military zone' under martial law.[72] Any future Iranian military governor should, the Company stressed, be able to act completely independent of Tehran – in other words, under Company command. On the pretext of wartime exigencies and in a situation where Iranian central authority had all but broken down, the Company was already in the process of institutionalizing its own unilateral security measure: an identity card scheme that would give it total control over movement in Abadan, not only of employees but also of 'the Persian non-Company civilians'.[73] It seemed, however, as if the Company still needed one final excuse to enforce a special military zone. It came in the form of the Bahmashir Incident.

The war had, by 1942, intensified Abadan's socio-economic problems. In the first years of war, Company investment dropped drastically and the number of employees in Khuzestan fell from 51,000 in 1939 to 26,000 in 1942. As was the usual practice, workers were simply dismissed without warning, and left with no income to endure their already appalling conditions. Cutbacks coincided with a severe famine raging throughout Iran that was worsened by the war. Iranians flocked from across the country to Khuzestan in search of work, only to join the masses of unemployed in areas such as Ahmadabad. The shortage of materials even forced many to live under the open sky. The 1940s also saw several outbreaks of typhus and smallpox in Abadan's shanty towns, and an investigation in 1943–44 showed that 'malnutrition was very common'.[74] Due to food shortages, the Company had to institute a system of rationing, and since this system favoured Europeans, it generated discontent.

There thus seemed to be, among the people of Ahmadabad, plenty of material reasons and motivation for raiding the Indian Lines. In this sense, it can be classified as a bread riot. Nonetheless, whether intended or not, the Bahmashir Incident also sent a broader political signal to the rulers of Abadan. Even though Company reports contain no evidence of political demands or ideological slogans among the attackers, and even though the Company sought to dismiss the unrest as the work of criminals and hooligans, the language used in its reports ('agitators', 'clever rogues') insinuated the presence of a political enemy. It is worth noting that at least one of the scuffles that led to the attack on the Indian Lines started with the behaviour of Indian soldiers, who were part of an occupying British force in Iran.

While the existence of the Indian Lines underscores that subaltern agency in Company Abadan was more diverse than that presented in most Iranian labour movement narratives, Abadan was nonetheless a city marked and marred by colonial lines of socio-geographic demarcation. The Indian Lines symbolically represented a stage only one step removed from the luxuries of the British neighbourhood of Braim, and the attack on the Lines was therefore also an attack on the British. It was a transgression of the principle of reciprocal exclusivity, which Fanon describes vividly as the 'native's' wish of 'setting himself up in the settler's place'.[75] it was an act of motion across boundaries of movement, a violent trespassing of the Company-instituted geography of violent compartmentalization, and thus a challenge to the order enforced by the quasi-colonial rulers of Abadan.

Mending the Lines: Oil, War and Security

While the Iranian labour movement undoubtedly perceived the Company as nothing but an extension of British imperialism, the Company could also be seen in a more nuanced light: as a new form of economic imperialism that was rooted in the colonial empires, but that would continue to dominate and evolve in a post-colonial world. Such a nuanced light can appear through a critical reading of the correspondence between the Company, the British government and the British military, especially during a sensitive period such as the Second World War. Indeed, not only did Company policy sometimes differ from British policy; the Company often operated autonomously and contrary to British recommendations. This had a direct impact on the question of order and disorder in Khuzestan, and ultimately on the Company's failure to secure its foothold in Iran.

Kaveh Ehsani has previously warned against overstating the colonialist aspect of the Company, arguing instead that even though its claims to 'political impartiality were rather far-fetched', the Company 'nurtured little political appetite' and that it did not wish to become 'another East India Company'.[76] As Reidar Visser notes in a study of British companies in nearby Basra, 'profitability, rather than political concerns, appeared to be the guiding principle when these corporations established their territorial desiderata'.[77] In Abadan, Visser argues, the Company failed to undertake a 'thorough community-building project', like those seen in African mining company towns, simply because it was concerned only with 'the prospect of short-term economic benefit'.[78] Only when strikes restricted oil output in 1929 and 1946 did the Company agree, grudgingly, to make improvements in housing, education and working conditions. The Company was simply not in the business of empire building in the classic colonial sense. This also partly explains why the Company never took full advantage of the nascent Arab nationalist and separatist movements in Khuzestan to turn the Concession into a breakaway state on its own.[79]

For a more nuanced understanding of the nature of Company rule, it is instructive to look at its reaction to the Bahmashir Incident. Firstly, the Company held Abadan's chief of police personally responsible, reprimanding him for incompetence and demanding that he oversee a retrieval of the looted goods from Ahmadabad.[80] The very tone of the correspondence leaves no doubt that the Company considered itself a de facto authority. Secondly, the Company addressed higher authorities in Tehran, including the Iranian prime minister. This served a greater purpose: already on the day after the riots, the Company presented the Bahmashir Incident as final proof of the need to turn not just Abadan but all of Khuzestan into a special military zone.

As usual, the British representative in Tehran backed the Company demand, stating that 'previous experience' had shown 'that the imposition of severe penalties' and 'personal mutilation of offenders' were 'effective in engendering a respect to the laws and in achieving obedience to them'.[81] Even though he did not 'recommend' such severe measures, it was 'quite clear that until evildoers are brought to book and adequately punished no form of security in this area can be expected'.[82] He concluded that if the police were unable to handle the Bahmashir Incident, then they would also be incapable of acting against looting, which he felt 'could be expected certainly as a result of air raids or other forms of attack'.

The Company itself flat out called for a British military intervention in the Concession – possibly in the hope that such an intervention could further consolidate Company authority in Khuzestan. However, the military authorities disagreed with this crucial assessment. On 12 January 1943, the Headquarters reported to the Company:

> The disturbance on the 19 Dec. 42 [the Bahmashir Incident] was intercommunal and there is not the slightest evidence or any possibility that the disorder was occasioned by anti-British feeling or directed towards interfering with the work of the Refinery ... It is not a British military responsibility to prevent or deal with this sort of disorder. It is purely a matter for the Persian police.[83]

Indeed, the Headquarters concluded, the one battalion already at Abadan was sufficient for dealing with sabotage, and quelling 'civil disorder' was not part of its duty. The military instead called on the Company to enforce its own mechanisms of social control:

> The best way of preventing a recurrence of fighting and looting between Persians and Indians is for the [Company] to build a really strong fence around the Indian quarters. Up to the 19th Dec. the company had allowed a not very formidable fence to fall into dis-repair [sic] and Persians were in the habit of passing through this fence at any time they wanted.[84]

The Company and several British diplomats objected. As they had already argued immediately after the riots, 'improving fences' would not be sufficient, and they felt that the Bahmashir Incident had afforded 'proof [of] urgent need [in] declaring Abadan [a] Military Area'.[85] In this fashion, the Company directly linked internal security with that of external strategic concerns arising from the war, and thus prevailed with its demand for a heavy-handed military rule in Khuzestan. The Military Zone was established shortly after, and lasted for the duration of the war. In the end, the Company, albeit with British diplomatic backing, had succeeded in pushing through their own demands within Iranian bureaucracy.

This had more or less been the case for over three decades. The expansion of Company operations in the 1920s coincided with the Iranian central state's consolidation of power in Khuzestan, and this sometimes worked to Company advantage. In other words, the Company – precisely because Iran was not a colony – never attempted to thoroughly institute any of the organizations and services expected from paternalist corporations in colonial states. However, at the same time, the Company did take the liberty, buttressed by British global power and influence over Iranian politics, to unilaterally institute its own systems of spatial coercion and social control in Khuzestan. The war, and incidents such as that in Bahmashir, simply offered further tokens of justification.

All this notwithstanding, it seems that, by the time of the Bahmashir Incident, the Company had realized that mending fences, instituting martial law and calling for British military intervention could no longer secure its arbitrary rule over the Concession: the empire in whose shadow the Company exercised its dubious power was threatened and would soon crumble. In this sense, the Bahmashir Incident was one of many events leading up to the 1951 nationalization movement that would uproot the Company from Khuzestan.

Conclusion

Abadan was at once a frontier of capitalist company expansion, of British military and colonial reach and of centripetal processes towards consolidation of the Iranian nation state.[86] This particular combination of clashing interests and multiple actors and agencies makes it a remarkable arena for the study of historical change. It also makes the study of 'forgotten' events of violence such as the Bahmashir Incident ever more pertinent.

Recent literature teaches us to see oil as a commodity and artefact, not just in concrete physical or abstract macro-economic terms, but also on the social micro-scale: 'one needs to examine carefully the historical and cultural local contexts of oil', Michael Watts writes in his study of 'petro-violence'.[87] In a city such as Abadan, shaped by the forces of hydrocarbon capitalism and with the sole purpose of oil exportation, socio-economic problems and intercommunal tensions were intimately connected to the Company's nature as an autonomous entity operating in a tenuous space of exception.

Even during a global war in which the Company was under political pressure to continually supply the most strategically important substance for the mechanized British war effort, the Company's top 'mission' was still to secure its own business. To fulfil this mission, it would use any means available, whether buying off local strongmen or Iranian police, raising its own security forces, or compelling Britain, with vague threats of a drop in oil output, to intervene. In short, the Company was first and foremost a business enterprise, and the Concession should not be understood as a mere extension of British imperialism: it was the frontier of another form of imperialism that differed from the colonial legacy upon which it was founded. Company rule in Khuzestan was in this sense a precursor to the 'extractive enclaving' of contemporary multinational corporations in frontiers such as Angola and Nigeria.

These extractive enclaves are characterized by minimal corporate engagement with host societies and by privatized security, as well as by militarization, violent conflicts and rampant crime. While the present-day extractive enclave (particularly the offshore kind) is virtually disconnected from the national grid of the host country, in 1942 the Company was still dependent on restive local populations and problematic migrant labour, and was forced to take into account the increasingly nationalistic and uncooperative country within which it operated. While the British occupation of Iran further facilitated the Company's grip on Khuzestan, the Second World War also added significant strain to an already tense situation. All of these factors played into the Bahmashir Incident.

Since there is a direct link between the particular form of urbanization seen in Abadan and the violence that occurred both on a daily basis and in moments of 'unrest', it is important not to reduce these links to a struggle between a native labour movement (Iranian) and a foreign colonizer (the British). The presence of Indian labour disrupts such a simplistic model of analysis. This is also why the Bahmashir Incident is never mentioned in Iranian labour movement accounts or, by extension, in scholarly works: it was seemingly banal, it had no clear idealist agenda and it does not cast Iranian workers in the favourable role of freedom fighters. Compared with the well-studied incidents of labour unrest, the perpetrators of violence cannot be exonerated, so to speak, in the name of anti-British struggles.

Yet it is exactly the banality of the event that underscores the central role of violence in the urban politics of Abadan. Violence was not simply the instrument of the oppressor or the weapon of leftist agitators, but was omnipresent and multi-directional. For this reason, we also need to take into account the violence, such as the Bahmashir Incident, that did *not* carry a clear political programme. The Company's presence and operations engendered a space of exception in Khuzestan in which violence was explicitly business as usual: it upheld systems of coercion and differentiation aimed at optimizing industrial output; and it made intercommunal violence not only a possibility, but a latent element of an everyday life conditioned by a new breed of global hegemonic forces.

Notes

1. Bahmashir, today 'Bahmanshir', was an English corruption of Bahman-Ardashir, the Persian name of the river that flows past Abadan Island on the north side.
2. E.g., E. Abrahamian. 1988. 'The Strengths and Weaknesses of the Labour Movement in Iran, 1941–1953', in M. Bonine and N. Keddie (eds), *Continuity and Change in Modern Iran*, Albany, NY: SUNY Press, 211–31; K. Bayat. 2007. 'With or Without Workers in Reza Shah's Iran: Abadan, May 1929', in T. Atabaki (ed.), *The State and the Subaltern: Modernization, Society and the State in Turkey and Iran*, London and New York: I.B. Tauris, 111–21; S. Cronin. 2010. 'Popular Politics, the New State and the Birth of the Iranian Working Class: The 1929 Abadan Oil Refinery Strike', *Middle Eastern Studies* 46(5), 699–732; M.E. Dobe. 2008. *A Long Slow Tutelage in Western Ways of Work: Industrial Education and the Containment of Nationalism in Anglo-Iranian and ARAMCO, 1923–1963*, doctoral dissertation, New Brunswick: Rutgers, The State University of New Jersey; W.M. Floor. 1985. *Labour Unions, Law and Conditions in Iran (1900–1941)*, Durham: University of Durham; and H. Ladjevardi. 1985. *Labour Unions and Autocracy in Iran*, Syracuse, NY: Syracuse University Press. Cronin, Dobe and Floor have given brief attention to the Indian element in their respective works.
3. With its basis in materials from the BP Archive (BPA), the British National Archives (BNA) and the India Office Archives (IOA), this study admittedly suffers from a lack of Indian and Iranian perspectives on the Bahmashir Incident – perspectives that have, to my knowledge, never been recorded. To contextualize, the study instead draws on a wide range of secondary sources and comparative research that will appear from the footnotes. These materials in turn are also the basis for a broader research project on the history of Abadan. I would like to thank Drs Stephanie Cronin, Kaveh Ehsani, Ulrike Freitag, Touraj Atabaki, Don Watts and Kevan Harris, and in particular Dr Nelida Fuccaro, for their insightful feedback and critique.
4. This term was popularized by Abu-Lughod's pioneering sociological study, which analysed the city of Rabat as an entity containing two urban spaces divided by colonial rulers along ethnic lines of apartheid. See J.L. Abu-Lughod. 1981. *Urban Apartheid in Morocco*, Princeton, NJ: Princeton University Press.
5. J. Ferguson. 2005. 'Seeing Like an Oil Company: Space, Security, and Global Capital in Neoliberal Africa', *American Anthropologist* 107(3), 377–82.
6. Loosely inspired by the works of Carl Schmitt (via S. Legg. 2011. *Spatiality, Sovereignty and Carl Schmitt: Geographies of the Nomos*, London and New York: Routledge) and G. Agamben (2005. *State of Exception*, Chicago: University of Chicago Press), here the term is used specifically to indicate a territorial space in which a (foreign, non-state) entity that derives its legitimacy from an agreement with the nominal local authority (nation state) brings into question the sovereignty of that space. On the controversial history of Company–Iranian relations, refer to M. Elm. 1992. *Oil, Power and*

Principle: Iran's Oil Nationalisation and its Aftermath, Syracuse, NY: Syracuse University Press; and L.P. Elwell-Sutton. 1955. *Persian Oil: A Study in Power Politics*, London: Lawrence & Wishart.

7. M. Crinson. 1997. 'Abadan: Planning and Architecture under the Anglo-Iranian Oil Company', *Planning Perspectives* 12(3), 341–59; K. Ehsani. 2003. 'Social Engineering and the Contradictions of Modernization in Khuzestan's Company Towns: A Look at Abadan and Masjed-Soleyman', *International Review of Social History* 48(3), 361–99.
8. See, for example, S. Malesevic. 2010. *The Sociology of War and Violence*, Cambridge: Cambridge University Press; C. Tilly. 2003. *The Politics of Collective Violence*, Cambridge: Cambridge University Press.
9. On the direct relation between violence and oil industries, see R. Dufresne. 2004. 'The Opacity of Oil: Oil Corporations, Internal Violence, and International Law', *Journal of International Law and Politics* 36(2–3), 331–94; T. Dunning and L. Wirpsa. 2004. 'Oil and the Political Economy of Conflict in Columbia and Beyond: A Linkage Approach', *Geopolitics* 9(1), 81–108; M. Watts. 2001. 'Petro-Violence: Community, Extraction, and Political Ecology of a Mythic Commodity', in N. Peluso and M. Watts (eds), *Violent Environments*, Ithaca, NY: Cornell University Press, 189–212; and M. Watts. 2004. 'Resource Curse? Governmentality, Oil and Power in the Niger Delta, Nigeria', *Geopolitics* 9(1), 50–80.
10. BNA: PRO LAB13/515, 1942.
11. R.W. Ferrier. 1982. *The History of the British Petroleum Company, Vol. 1: The Developing Years, 1901–1932*, Cambridge: Cambridge University Press, 153–54.
12. Ibid., 6.
13. See, for example, Elwell-Sutton's accounts (*Persian Oil*, 102–3); on the connections between oil industry culture and racism, see also R. Vitalis. 2004. 'Aramco World: Business and Culture on the Arabian Oil Frontier', in A. Madawi and R. Vitalis (eds), *Counter-Narratives: History, Contemporary Society, and Politics in Saudi Arabia and Yemen*, New York: Palgrave Macmillan, 151–81.
14. Ibid.
15. Until the 1930s, modern notions of an Iranian national identity were still relatively weak among the illiterate rural masses of the geographical periphery. In Khuzestan, there were important divisions between rural and urban groups, between indigenous Khuzestanis (Arabs, Lors, Bakhtiaris, Behbahanis, etc.) and newcomers (Persians, Azeris), and between Shia and Sunni (migrants from the Persian Gulf). Sometimes the Company exploited these divisions. See for example Abrahamian, 'Strengths and Weaknesses', and R.C. Elling. 2015. 'A War of Clubs: Inter-Ethnic Clashes and the 1946 Oil Strike in Abadan', in N. Fuccaro (ed.), *Public Violence in Modern Middle Eastern Cities*, forthcoming. Stanford, CA: Stanford University Press. On ethnicity and minorities in Iran, see R.C. Elling. 2013. *Minorities in Iran: Nationalism and Ethnicity after Khomeini*, New York: Palgrave Macmillan.

16. BNA, FO 371/7818; Ferrier, *History of the British Petroleum Company*, 401, Table 10.1.
17. R. Visser. 2007. 'The Gibraltar That Never Was', paper presented to the British World Conference, Bristol, July 11–14, http://www.historiae.org/abadan.asp, 6.
18. Dobe, *A Long Slow Tutelage*, 5.
19. Crinson, 'Abadan: Planning and Architecture', 347. Today, the Indian influence is still very prevalent in Abadan: Indian loanwords are part of the local dialect, and Indian food is popular at home and in restaurants.
20. H. Yule. 1903. *Hobson-Jobson: A Glossary of Colloquial Anglo-Indian Words and Phrases, and of Kindred Terms, Etymological, Historical, Geographical and Discursive*, New edition, ed. William Brooke, London: J. Murray, entry: 'Cooly'. Also note that in Abadan, 'coolie' was sometimes used to signify all non-white labour. See for example the descriptions provided by Jewish employees of a Zionist company in Abadan, in Y. Shenhav. 2002. 'The Phenomenology of Colonialism and the Politics of "Difference": European Zionist Emissaries and Arab-Jews in Colonial Abadan', *Social Identities: Journal for the Study of Race, Nation and Culture* 8(4), 527 and 529.
21. See for example: U. Mahajani. 1977. 'Slavery, Indian Labour and British Colonialism', *Pacific Affairs* 50(2), 263–71.
22. M. Carter and K. Torabully. 2002. *Coolitude*, London: Anthem Press.
23. Government of India to APOC, 25 Nov. 1920, in BNA: FO371/6426.
24. Floor, *Labour Unions*, 28.
25. See, for example, Dobe, *A Long Slow Tutelage*, 30.
26. Cronin, 'Popular Politics, the New State'.
27. BNA: FO371/7818.
28. Ibid.
29. Ibid.; see also Floor, *Labour Unions*, 28–31.
30. Elwell-Sutton, *Persian Oil*, 68.
31. BNA: FO371/7818.
32. Floor, *Labour Unions*, 32.
33. Dobe, *A Long Slow Tutelage*, 31.
34. Ibid., 65, 68.
35. Cronin, 'Popular Politics, the New State', 715.
36. Minister, Tehran to Foreign Secretary, Government of India, 2 July 1924, in BNA: FO371/10126.
37. Manager, Strick, Scott & Co. to H.B.M.'s Consul for Arabistan, Mohammerah, 24 Sept. 1914, in BPA: ArcRef 71754.
38. Kennion, Mohammerah to Neilson, Tehran, 21 May 1915, in BPA: ArcRef 71754.
39. Note by Sir Hugh Barnes on Proposed Abadan Police Force, 30 July 1915, in BPA: ArcRef 71754.
40. BPA: ArcRef 71754.
41. Ferrier, *History of the British Petroleum Company*, 275, 402.
42. Quoted by Cronin, 'Popular Politics, the New State', 720.

43. Translation of an article from *Habl-ol-matin*, published in Calcutta on 2 Aug. 1927, from BPA: ArcRef 129909.
44. Mahmoud Khuzestani quoted in Bayat, 'With or Without Workers', 117.
45. Eftekhari in M.T. Tafreshi and K. Bayat. 1991. *Khaterat-e dowran-e separishode*, Tehran: Ferdows, 118.
46. The notion of the conniving Indian agent of British colonialism is known from literary masterpieces such as Simin Daneshvar's *Savushun* and Iraj Pezeshkzad's *Da'i Jân Nâpel'un*, and has existed in popular political mythology for decades.
47. Cronin, 'Popular Politics, the New State', 715.
48. J.H. Bamberg. 1994. *The History of the British Petroleum Company, Vol. 2: The Anglo-Iranian Years, 1928–1954*, Cambridge: Cambridge University Press, 34.
49. Ibid., 247.
50. See, for example, Tafreshi and Bayat, *Khaterat-e dowran-e*.
51. Crinson, 'Abadan: Planning and Architecture', 342.
52. Visser, 'The Gibraltar That Never Was', 6–7.
53. BPA quoted by Crinson, 'Abadan: Planning and Architecture', 350.
54. Ehsani, 'Social Engineering', 376.
55. On 'public space' in Abadan, see ibid., 393, note 55.
56. Even when the Company built the ethnically mixed neighbourhood of Bawarda in the 1940s – a project then presented as a progressive measure – this neighbourhood was ultimately inhabited mostly by Britons and a few British-educated Iranians and Indians.
57. Ferrier, *History of the British Petroleum Company*, 6.
58. Ehsani, 'Social Engineering', 393.
59. Ibid., 392.
60. R. Lawless and I. Seccombe. 1993. 'Impact of the Oil Industry on Urbanisation in the Persian Gulf Region', in H. Amirahmadi and S.S. El-Shakhs (eds), *Urban Development in the Muslim World*, New Brunswick, NJ: Center for Urban Policy Research, Rutgers University, 199.
61. G. C.-L. Low. 1996. *White Skins, Black Masks: Representation and Colonialism*, London: Routledge, 163.
62. BPA: ArcRef 68881, 5 Jan. 1943.
63. 'Report on the Bahmashir Incident', BPA: ArcRef 68881, 5 Jan. 1943.
64. BPA: ArcRef 68881, 22 Dec. 1942.
65. BNA: FO 248/1435, 21 Dec. 1942. The Polish regiment had been relocated to Abadan due to Second World War displacements and put in the service of the Company by the British occupying forces.
66. Pattinson to Rice, BPA: ArcRef 68881, 22 Dec. 1942.
67. 'Disturbances in the Artizans Lines', BPA: ArcRef 68881, 20 Dec. 1942.
68. BPA: ArcRef 43758, 4 Dec. 1942.
69. See Bamberg, *History of the British Petroleum Company*, 240.
70. For a description of life in wartime Abadan, see H. Longhurst. 1959. *Adventure in Oil: The Story of British Petroleum*, London: Sidgwick & Jackson

Ltd., Chapter 10; see also R.C. Elling. 2013. 'The World's Biggest Refinery and the Second World War: Khuzestan, Oil and Security', paper presented at Comparative Social Histories of Labour in the Oil Industry Conference, June 2013, Amsterdam.
71. See, for example, BPA: ArcRef 68881, 19 July 1943.
72. BPA ArcRef 68881, 9 Dec. 1942.
73. Pattinson to Rice, BP Archives 68881, 9 Dec. 1942.
74. BPA: ArcRef 25553, quoted in Bamberg, *History of the British Petroleum Company*, 248–49.
75. F. Fanon. (1961) 1963. *Wretched of the Earth*, tr. Constance Farrington, New York: Grove Press, 39.
76. Ehsani, 'Social Engineering', 365, note 10; and 382.
77. Visser, 'The Gibraltar That Never Was'.
78. Ibid.
79. See Elling, 'A War of Clubs'.
80. 'Disturbances in the Artizans Lines', BPA: ArcRef 68881, 20 Dec. 1942.
81. Pattinson to Rice, BP Archives 68881, 22 Dec. 1942.
82. Ibid.
83. GHQ PAIFORCE to HQ 12 IND DIV., BPA: ArcRef 68881, 12 Jan. 1943.
84. Ibid.
85. Pattinson to Sunbury, BPA: ArcRef 68881, 24 Dec. 1942.
86. For an example of the use of 'frontier' about the Persian Gulf oil industry, see the groundbreaking work of Vitalis, 'Aramco World'; about Khuzestan as a frontier, see Dobe, *A Long Slow Tutelage*.
87. Watts, 'Petro-Violence', 212.

· Chapter 10 ·

Reading Oil as Urban Violence
Kirkuk and Its Oil Conurbation, 1927–58

NELIDA FUCCARO

> You worked in darkness, groping about, with nothing but the roar of the monster, his blows upon your body, his spitting in your face, to tell you where he was. You worked at high tension, for there were bonuses offered ... No one could figure how much wealth that monster was wasting, but it must be thousands of dollars a minute.[1]
> – *Oil! A Novel*, Upton Sinclair

Upton Sinclair's personification of oil as a monster of wealth suddenly gushing out of the earth in his acclaimed novel *Oil!* introduces the reader to the sinister powers of oil both as a mineral substance and in its ability to violate the environment and human bodies. The history of the oil industry has a long pedigree as an 'incubator' for violence: first at the point of production — as epitomized by the destructive force of Sinclair's oil well in early twentieth-century California and then during the process of refinement, distribution and marketing.[2] As a substance, commodity and industry, oil has also been associated with dramatic urban change. Throughout the twentieth century, towns located in the vicinity of oil installations and serving the industry often became critical nodes of early modern life in their regions.[3]

With a focus on Kirkuk and its oil conurbation, this chapter engages in a particular reading of urban violence from the perspective of the development of the oil industry in Iraq during the Hashemite monarchy (1921–1958). As suggested by James Ferguson in his incisive critique of contemporary neo-global capitalism, oil enclaves constitute forms of spatialized order and disorder, potentially violent landscapes of power where corporate interests intermingle with mechanisms of government.⁴ Working from this premise, this article explores oil-related violence in the urban areas that became part of the industrial enclave developed by the Iraq Petroleum Company after 1931. It looks first at the relationship between oil, violence and British imperialism in Hashemite Iraq, introducing the local setting of Kirkuk and its oil conurbation. It then examines how forms of structural violence became embedded in the new urban geographies and disciplines of oil production. An examination of two episodes of labour unrest shows how these forms of violence became 'operational' as a result of the socio-economic and political dislocation brought to Kirkuk by the Second World War. Lastly, the chapter provides an assessment of the extent to which oil-related violence fits in with the turbulent urban landscape of monarchical Iraq.

Locating Oil, Violence and Imperialism in Iraq and Kirkuk

In Iraq, violence and the oil industry have generally been approached as a corollary of the history of the political struggles unfolding on the national stage or in the context of state building, development and the political economy of war. The state has been considered the violent actor par excellence, particularly the oil state that emerged after the takeover by the Baʿthists in 1968. That oil was a 'resource curse' in Baʿthist Iraq is illustrated by the role played by the national development plans of the 1970s in the evolution of a brutal security apparatus able to oppress the population and to wage war against its neighbours.[5] In contrast, before the 1958 Revolution, Iraq's oil industry was an integral part of an international cycle of energy production and distribution that in Timothy Mitchell's words was intimately bound up with the 'making and unmaking of democratic politics' at a global and imperial scale.[6] As such, the violent history of Iraqi oil during the monarchy has to be located at the intersection of the complex corporate, imperial, national and international politics that marked the development of oil production in the Middle East after the First World War.

Kirkuk's oil industry was developed and managed by the Iraq Petroleum Company (IPC), an enterprise with American, French and Italian shareholders but with close links to the British government through the participation of the Anglo-Iranian Oil Company, which had a majority share in IPC.[7] Since 1927, when substantial oil deposits were discovered in the Baba Gurgur oilfields, IPC flourished in a colonial and postcolonial setting, with Great Britain assisting the development of a docile and stable Iraqi government under the Hashemite monarchy. As elsewhere in the post-First World War era, the company and the imperial power had an occasionally uneasy if generally intimate relationship. Oil was a vital asset for the defence of British strategic and economic interests in Iraq. To this end, the High Commission's colonial expertise was often placed at the service of the company, and British officials often acted as 'go betweens' in negotiations involving IPC and the Iraqi government. Until the early 1930s, the British mandatory administration greatly encouraged the company to develop production, although the international cartel involved in the concession had an interest in slowing down the development of a large new oil supply.[8] After the termination of the mandate in 1932, since Great Britain retained vital economic and strategic interests in Iraq, the British government was instrumental in providing a timeline for the construction of the pipeline between Kirkuk and the Mediterranean. In the 1940s and 1950s, the British Embassy in Baghdad offered diplomatic and political assistance to IPC industrial operations in a context of mounting industrial unrest inspired by nationalism, anti-imperialism and communism.[9]

A focus on the Hashemite state, British imperialism and the international politics of oil development alone does not disclose the lifeworlds that oil created on the ground and the multiple histories of violence it generated. Such histories can indeed be seen as part and parcel of the 'urban' shift that occurred in Iraq during the monarchy. As urbanization proceeded apace in the 1940s and 1950s, expanding cities became the stages where popular politics, radical movements and intellectual effervescence engaged in a fierce battle with what Iraqi novelist Gha'ib Farman called Iraq's 'Black Regime', a Hashemite state that increasingly resorted to coercion and surveillance to control its people.[10] Oil became a constitutive part of Iraq's 'violent' urban landscapes as one of the industrial forces that triggered the development of new physical, political and ideological spaces of contention. In this respect, Kirkuk's oil conurbation was not an isolated enclave, but shared with other urban areas important political and social developments. IPC did not have the same degree of control over Iraq's oil regions as the Anglo-Iranian Oil Company had in south-western Iran or as the Arabian American Oil Company (Aramco) had in eastern Saudi Arabia in the same period. While IPC established its own security and intelligence bureaus in Kirkuk, the town and its hinterland were under the direct administration and jurisdiction of the government of Iraq. Again, unlike the oil centres of Abadan in Iran and Dhahran in Saudi Arabia, Kirkuk was not built de novo as a company town, but had a long history before the age of oil as an important Ottoman garrison town and administrative centre.

Reading Oil as Urban Violence   225

The transformative powers of oil in Kirkuk become apparent when considering the town's position in the new geographies of oil extraction and distribution. Kirkuk's role as the oil capital of Hashemite Iraq was defined by a network of parallel pipelines that linked the Baba Gurgur oilfields located on the outskirts of the town to oil terminals and refineries on the Syrian and Palestinian coasts. Kirkuk developed effectively as a 'pipeline town', the terminus of Iraq's modern 'river of wealth'. This epic image was popularized by the IPC in the propaganda film *The Third River*, which juxtaposed the flow of oil to the Mediterranean with that of the life-enhancing water of the Tigris and Euphrates rivers.[11]

Oil urbanization materialized in a variety of ways. In Kirkuk, a series of industrial and residential complexes mushroomed around the Baba Gurgur fields to the west and north-west of the town. Along the pipeline, the IPC built twelve mini company towns that functioned as pumping stations, four of which were located in Iraqi territory. K1 was part of the Kirkuk Fields, as it lay in the vicinity of Baba Gurgur; K2 was twenty-five miles away, while K3 was built in the upper Euphrates region at the intersection of the Haifa and Tripoli pipelines, not far from the border with Syria. Farther west, T1 (the first station on the Tripoli branch of the line) was the last IPC outpost in Iraq, some thirty-seven miles from Syrian territory.

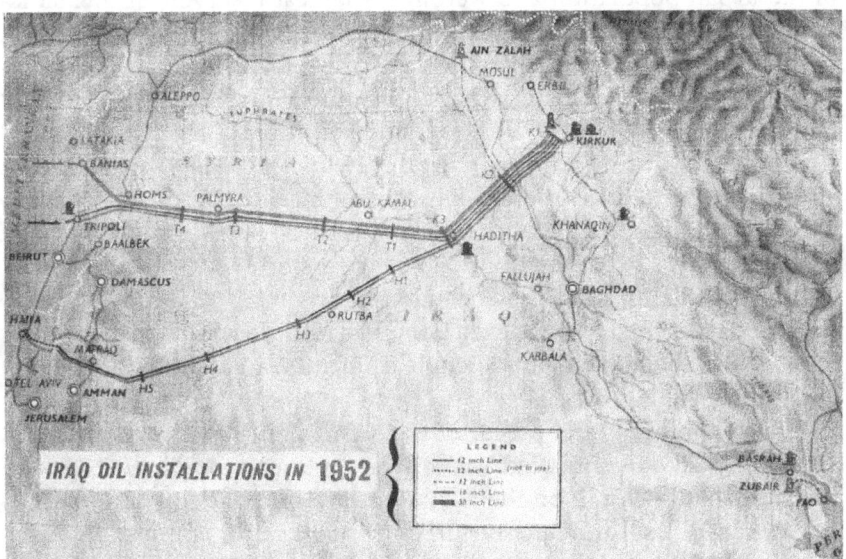

Figure 10.1. Kirkuk's pipelines and oil stations, 1952. *The Petroleum Times*, 8 August 1952.

Structuring Violence in IPC's Urban Domains

To penetrate the thick bituminous layers that have concealed the impact of oil at an urban and local level in the Hashemite era, we shall turn to some key elements of structural violence that are embedded in the spatial, institutional and disciplinary organization of the oil industry. Structural violence was an integral part of the history of Iraq's oil industry as an extractive enterprise.[12] It was a bloodless, subtle and invisible violence that was routinely and often surreptitiously exercised through legal and jurisdictional arrangements, unfair industrial relations, differential treatment of the workforce and the deployment of mechanisms of surveillance and control of space and people.[13]

Central to the creation of new landscapes of inequality were the differential processes of oil urbanization and suburbanization in Kirkuk town and along the pipeline. Since the early 1930s, the demand for labour led to the spontaneous development of new residential districts around the old town. Neighbourhoods such as Imam Qasim and al-Shurja provided the stage for the emergence of a dispossessed, turbulent and politically inclined suburban proletariat that included mainly Kurdish immigrants of rural extraction by the 1950s.[14] Growing class consciousness fuelled ethnic animosities, particularly between Kirkuk's Kurdish and Turkmen populations. By the 1950s, Kurds came to constitute a larger proportion of the urban population and were IPC's largest reservoir of menial labour. In contrast, the importance of the Turkmen community decreased, both demographically and politically.[15] The growth of Kirkuk's suburban areas reveals traumatic experiences of urban/rural migration, both individual and collective. With the intensification of the Kurds' armed struggle against the government in the 1940s and 1950s, the sustained violence that engulfed the city's Kurdish hinterland brought villagers, tribesmen and fighters to the city in search of both employment and shelter. Kirkuk's expanding Kurdish districts became the focus of strict police surveillance after the Second World War as the Ministry of the Interior established a special branch office in central Kirkuk to monitor intelligence, the movement of people from rural areas and the spread of communist ideas.[16]

The squalid sight and precarious economic and security situation of suburban Kirkuk contrasted with the glamorous industrial/residential complex that IPC built on the north-western outskirts of the town. Often awe inspiring to the poorer urban residents, this complex included the New Camp, the administrative headquarters of the company, which also accommodated the management of IPC, and the Arrapha estate, a residential area built after 1946 for local employees. Several small townships provided additional accommodation for IPC's European and Iraqi staff: New Baba and Camp no. 8, the latter located on the banks of the river Zab some twenty-two miles from the old town.[17]

Like the Bawarda and Braim districts in Abadan, the Arrapha estate was an exclusive and modern living space in the urban texture of Kirkuk.[18] Endowed with 'all mod cons', this oil camp provided the symbolic and ideal separation between old Kirkuk, the 'native city', and New Camp, the European mini company town. Typically, the estate was organized in a corporate hierarchy as the quality, size and layout of dwellings reflected salary scales, separating skilled from unskilled workers.[19] Celebrated in the Iraqi press as *Kirkuk al-Jadida* (New Kirkuk), Arrapha was the tangible outcome of IPC's 'material obligations' vis-à-vis the indigenous population, being one of the development projects devised by the company to defuse mounting labour discontent after the bloody strike of 1946.[20] Yet by the early 1950s, as the estate accommodated the largest proportion of local employees in the Kirkuk Fields, it had become the symbol of IPC's discriminatory housing and employment policies.[21]

Figure 10.2. Kurdish worker in Kirkuk oilfields, 1945.

The dangerous implications of isolating some of the oil population within the precincts of Kirkuk stemmed from the preferential treatment accorded to Christians and Armenians, who constituted the bulk of IPC's locally recruited clerical staff and benefited extensively from housing perks. Although in theory accommodation was also open to unskilled labour, the allocation of dwellings based on a point system disadvantaged menial workers, as they started from a considerably lower scale.[22] By 1953, as Arrapha had come to be perceived as IPC's Christian 'stronghold', resentment had escalated to the extent that members of other communities refused to live there. Many chose to take up residence in central Kirkuk, taking advantage of the home ownership scheme that allowed local employees to build or acquire a house in town with IPC subsidies.[23]

Along the pipeline, the pumping stations offered striking evidence of the success of IPC's industrial expansion. As miniature oil towns, they were man-made 'oases' of grey stone residential buildings with tree-lined avenues, gleaming silver tanks, oil depots, pumping houses, recreational facilities, administrative offices, schools and supermarkets. Like the pipeline, the oil stations were central to IPC's oil propaganda in Iraq and in the Middle East. *Iraq Petroleum*, the company's glossy magazine, celebrated them as the harbingers of a new industrial future and the prototypes of the industrial city of the twentieth century.[24] These stations were sought-after places of employment for local skilled labour. Sargon Joseph Hallaby, a Christian born in Kirkuk whose father worked in K3 during the Second World War as the manager of the station supermarket, recalls:

> Our living quarters, which were supplied by the company, were beautiful and we had three large bedrooms. The houses were built of local stone and everything was provided, such as furniture, linen, crockery and cutlery. We had hot water 24 hours a day and could shower whenever we wanted to. The homes were heated during the very cold winters. We lived very well there.[25]

Hallaby's upbeat recollection of life in K3 tells only one side of the story of the regime established by IPC in the oil stations. Inside the stations, the living conditions of daily-wage labourers were much better than those in the expanding urban sprawls of Kirkuk, Baghdad and Basra.[26] Yet the self-contained world of Iraq's oil compounds manifested the often elusive and intangible racism and classism that characterized IPC as a corporate enterprise. As a British Embassy official noted in 1948:

> It is difficult to make precise criticism of the workers' conditions. At the IPC stations they are for the most part well fed, and are for the most part housed in Nissen huts, which are far superior to the mud hovels in their villages ... But the relationship between management and labour is outwardly that of 'sahibs and niggers', and this aspect is accentuated by the luxury in which the management and British staff live, and their remoteness ... In brief, my impression was of what our Russian friends would call capitalism at its worst, and foreign capitalism at that.[27]

In the compartmentalized world of IPC's oil townships, the production of inequality eluded the simplistic binary logic of the company versus the indigenous workforce. For local Christians and Armenians, the privileged 'minority races' living in the luxury accommodation of the

IPC camps, the threat of violence and intimidation by labour activists, criminals and unskilled workers often materialized in the violation of their houses, thefts and physical attacks. In the Christian 'stronghold' of Arrapha in particular, the sparse layout of bungalows added to a continuous feeling of danger, as residents often complained to IPC management of insufficient police protection and the insecurity of modern houses.[28]

Different systems of labour recruitment in the oilfields around Kirkuk and in the stations also underscored the multiplicity of actors and relations of force that contributed to shape the violent contours of IPC's oil society. In the Kirkuk Fields, the company controlled directly the supply of labour with the assistance of Iraqi officials. Daily wage workers were generally employed at the gates of the oil installations, by recall or through the local labour office of the Ministry of Social Affairs.[29] Particularly before the strike of 1946, working conditions were pretty harsh as a result of the ready supply of labour and the absence of unions. As expressed in some of the underground literature, many workers were treated as a 'cheap commodity', often malnourished and unable (or barely able) to provide for their families.[30]

In the stations, which also functioned as recruitment centres for the work camps along the pipeline, a complex system of local clientelism trapped jobseekers in a vicious cycle of poverty and subordination. Often they resorted to local moneylenders to raise the funds to pay employment fees. In fact, the recruitment of labour was part of a system of supply of essential services that relied on a variety of local intermediaries. Until the early 1950s, Bedouin sheikhs functioned as the employment agents par excellence, mostly in connection with the policing duties they had exercised on behalf of the company since the construction of the pipeline. Tribal leaders distributed jobs to their followers and clients in exchange for a protection tax that was often collected on a monthly basis by their retainers, usually working as watchmen in and around the stations. Competition between tribal factions often caused brawls, and occasionally killings, as leaders demanded their fair share of recruits from villages and tribal constituencies.[31]

The heavy hand of tribal 'racketeering' also fell upon local suppliers of commodities other than labour. Emblematic is the case of a contractor in one of the stations along the Haifa branch of the pipeline who entered into competition with a local sheikh over a tender for the supply of meat. When the company accepted the contractor's tender, he was beaten up and robbed of all his sheep.[32] What the International Labour Organization defined as 'job trafficking' was also occasionally practised by local employees of the stations, as reported in 1952 when a number of clerks were accused of having sold employment to Bedouin workers. Wealthy contractors were also in a position to enter the lucrative job market of Iraq's oil stations. In 1952, Yasin Hajj Dawud, a landowner and merchant from the village of Haditha who managed catering and the provisions of foodstuffs to K2 and K3, was employing his protégées with little or no salary, as they were heavily indebted to him.[33]

The case of the Bedouin leaders suggests that the security systems supported by IPC played a large part in creating potentially violent oil landscapes in the stations. But the increasing association of the company with Iraq's post-colonial security regimes can partly explain the lingering industrial tensions in Kirkuk's oil conurbation. The IPC had no sovereign power of its own and limited means to enforce the discipline necessary to control the workforce and to protect the oilfields. So its links to the Iraqi government and the British Embassy, an important player in policing and internal security issues, were manifold and became most apparent in the Kirkuk Fields. Here, although IPC subsidized a large force of watchmen and had its own intelligence apparatus, the management was forced to rely on Kirkuk's municipal guards to patrol the installations and camps around the town.

In the inner city, the IPC was largely unaware of the geography of urban risk, as security was in the hands of the municipal police. As in the oil stations, IPC management sought 'special' police protection to restore order in times of unrest. The support of the Iraqi police extended to intelligence and surveillance, the pillars of the company's security regime since the beginning of oil operations in the late 1920s. As early as 1929, after the strike in Abadan, the company's recently established Intelligence Unit started to liaise with the Iraqi Criminal Investigation Department and the local police for first-hand information on the activities of workers and for the arrest, trial and punishment of suspects.[34] With no legal or jurisdictional authority over the workforce, IPC was only able to inflict punishment by victimization, usually through verbal threats or direct dismissal. Management and British officials used legal arguments to justify arbitrary layoffs, stressing that the Iraqi labour laws of 1936 and 1942 did not contain any provisions for the protection of casual labourers.[35]

The IPC solicited the use of force as a last resort when all possibilities of negotiation with strikers had been exhausted. Management was fully aware that the disciplinary powers of the police, courts and prisons created a dangerous liaison between the company and the government, which for the increasingly politicized labour and nationalist movement infringed on basic labour entitlements and human rights.[36] In this respect, after 1950 the centralization and bureaucratization of the company's security apparatus and the creation of the oil police helped to ease the pressure on IPC. Although subsidized by the company, this special force was placed directly under the Ministry of the Interior with a commander of police based in Kirkuk.[37] By the mid-1950s, as the system of IPC watchmen and guards was discontinued and the Iraqi government took official charge of protecting all oil installations, personnel and properties, industrial grievances were increasingly directed against the Hashemite regime and its pro-imperialist policies. This is suggested by a number of articles published in the illegal communist press that circulated in the Kirkuk Fields in 1956 in the aftermath of the Baghdad Pact. Unlike in much of the propaganda that preceded the 1946 strike, there was no mention of the company; but there was widespread condemnation of the reckless economic policies of the Development Board (established in 1950 to manage oil income) and of the corrupt government led by Prime Minister Nuri al-Saʿid.[38]

Unleashing Public Violence: Labour Agitation after the Second World War

As the key nodes of oil production on the network of pipelines, Kirkuk, the stations and the work camps were interconnected 'points of vulnerability', to use Timothy Mitchell's definition of oil installations in interwar Iraq.[39] This 'vulnerability', set in motion by the corporate, imperial and state interests that shaped the labour landscape of Kirkuk's oil conurbation, created almost endless possibilities for violence. As suggested in the previous section, IPC's employment policies, arbitrary dismissals and competition for the control of the workforce in the oil stations could trigger different forms of abusive behaviour. Physical violence materialized in the acrimony of daily interactions and encounters in living, working and industrial spaces: offices, houses, workshops, streets, gates and compounds. Yet although industrial crowds shared confrontational emotions and grievances, there was no outbreak of large-scale unrest until the end of the Second World War.

Workers often channelled their discontent through peaceful forms of protest, which attest to the intense and fast political socialization experienced by IPC's male (and generally young) employees. The silent and orderly work stoppages staged in seven oil stations in 1937 are a case in point. The stoppages spread from the Baba Gurgur fields and K1 to K2 and K3 and to some of the stations on the Haifa pipeline, involving technical staff, daily wage workers and even cooks and servants.[40] Iraq's brief war with Great Britain in May 1941 and the British military occupation of the country for the remainder of the Second World War further exposed the 'vulnerability' of Kirkuk's oil conurbation, setting the stage for the explosion of industrial conflict. In May 1941, following the coup by Rashid ʿAli al-Gaylani, IPC European personnel were interned in New Camp, and company properties were looted and vandalized. Sabotage also affected some of the stations, with reports of industrial machinery badly damaged.[41]

After British troops occupied Kirkuk, the imperative to protect the Baba Gurgur oilfields from German attacks brought a new security regime to the town. Local administrative officials effectively acted as colonial district commissioners, since the British occupation authorities granted them extensive executive powers under the Prevention of Crime Ordinance. While political activities were heavily censored, access to IPC camps and installations was closely monitored as British soldiers replaced IPC watchmen and municipal guards.[42] As in other urban areas of Iraq, the British occupation forces became the largest employer of native labour. The army hired large numbers of technicians and skilled workers who had previously been employed by the company, paid them high salaries and granted them considerable privileges.[43]

Figure 10.3. British Indian soldier guarding an oil well in Kirkuk Fields, 1945.

The war economy had far-reaching repercussions on the most vulnerable sections of the urban population. Profiteering and a sharp rise in the price of basic commodities brought considerable economic hardship. With a large number of residents below the subsistence level, microcriminality, theft, disease and psychological instability increased, and reduced activity in the oilfields hit unskilled labourers hard.[44] As the company started to distribute essential commodities such as sugar, wheat, rice and firewood at fixed prices to its employees, hungry and desperate jobseekers turned up daily in large numbers at the gates of the oil installations. They were refused employment on the grounds that either they were not needed or they were unfit for work as a result of their poor physical and mental condition.[45]

At the end of the war, as the British troops left Kirkuk, the relaxation of security and censorship unleashed unprecedented amounts of nationalist and communist propaganda. When the company stopped food subsidies to its employees, the prices of basic commodities and of housing rocketed, triggered by the increasing popularity of the town as the centre of the oil industry.[46] The close links between mounting underground activism and food scarcity are made explicit in a pamphlet circulating among IPC's Kurdish workers in early 1946, encouraging them to unionize. Using a collective voice, the pamphlet articulates in fairly simple terms their distress: 'We have been deprived of the wheat allotted to us, and many a night have we slept without food.'[47]

Blood was shed in July 1946 in Kirkuk town a month after police had fired upon a crowd of peaceful demonstrators marching towards the British Embassy in Baghdad. As in Baghdad, violence was the result of brutal police tactics of crowd control. It erupted quite suddenly, several days after the beginning of a strike that involved some five thousand workers. For the first time in the history of the Iraqi oil industry, IPC's workers came out with their demands: wage increases, housing and rent allowances, social security insurance against unemployment and injury, and the establishment of unions to prevent arbitrary dismissals.[48] Every evening large numbers of workers convened in a garden in West Kirkuk to listen to the briefs of their leaders who were involved in negotiations with the company. While few policemen were present on foot, a large force of mounted police surrounded a crowd of several hundred people on the evening of 12 July. After they were asked to disperse, the situation got out of hand and police opened fire indiscriminately. Several reports suggest that the security forces shot protesters while they were trying to escape, and their horses stampeded over the bodies of the dead and injured lying on the ground. Official figures reported five people killed and fourteen injured, including six policemen, while communist sources claimed that that number of fatalities was much higher.[49]

Iraq's progressive press published short accounts of the event, describing it as 'distressing and painful' and condemning the behaviour of the police in both Kirkuk and Baghdad.[50] While police inexperience in handling crowds partly accounts for the carnage, the British Embassy interpreted the violence as an outcome of the absence of 'any government machinery for handling differences between labour and employers'. In other words, ignoring the disproportionate force used by the police,

British officials blamed the bloodshed on the failure of the Iraqi labour laws to provide adequate protection to industrial workers.[51] Typically, in the aftermath of the event, both the embassy and IPC management dehumanized the protesters. They construed them as passive, illiterate and submissive, at the mercy of shrewd and manipulative activists (allegedly communists) who used coercion very effectively to further their cause. The magnitude of the scheming and deceit of 'ringleaders' and 'agitators' was used to justify police violence as the lesser of evils and as an appropriate response to the tactics of intimidation used by activists against workers and security forces. IPC management was particularly keen to stress this point, also emphasizing how, before the ill-fated 12 July, 'outside agitators' had routinely picketed oil camps and installations, using verbal and physical intimidation to force reluctant workers to join the strike.[52]

In marshalling evidence to suit particular visions of provocative crowd behaviour, official reports tended to gloss over the multi-layered nature of the violent confrontation between protesters and police. Fadhil al-ʿAzzawi provides lively insight into the 1946 incident in his novel *The Last of the Angels*, a nostalgic and partly autobiographical recollection of life in Kirkuk. He visualizes the crowd as a multitude of men, women and children suddenly frightened by rumours of the impending arrival of mounted policemen. 'Fear drove the workers to greater zeal and they shouted even louder...', al-ʿAzzawi writes, depicting acrimonious verbal battles between protesters and the police while the crowd surged back and forth as policemen started to charge the strikers who refused to disperse.[53]

Azzawi's depiction of verbal and physical violence is in contrast with his portrayal of the silent and submissive return of Kirkuk's workers to their jobs after the bloodshed: 'They avoided each others' eyes for fear their hearts' shame would show.'[54] This fictional representation of defeat, powerlessness and humiliation corroborates contemporary accounts of Kirkuk in the aftermath of the strike – a town stifled by an atmosphere of fear and intimidation under a strict surveillance regime. In the following years, plainclothes policemen often flooded Kirkuk's streets and public venues as a preventive measure against the resurgence of labour troubles and the spread of communist propaganda. IPC watchmen and the officers of the Central Investigation Department of the Ministry of the Interior became frontline security forces in the battle against political subversion. They conducted routine house-to-house searches that often led to the arrest, detention and maltreatment of activists. Further, after 1947, eighty policemen trained by the Iraqi government started to operate as the nucleus of the oil police.[55]

The security regime established in Kirkuk after 1946 readily explains the virtual absence of public unrest until the horrific explosion of intercommunal violence in 1959, an episode that belongs to the history of early revolutionary Iraq and was not strictly related to the oil industry. In 1948, while other Iraqi cities were shaken by the popular insurgence against the government known as *al-Wathba*, Kirkuk remained eerily calm, closely monitored by detachments of military police from Baghdad.[56] As the entanglement of oil and nationalist politics grew deeper, unrest moved to the oil stations, the more secluded nodes of IPC's 'vulnerability'. In the eyes of IPC's intelligence officers, the oil stations were less likely to be exposed to the danger of unionization than Kirkuk,[57] but between April and May 1948 they were proved wrong. For ten days militant workers took over K3, the largest and most important oil station located at the intersection of the Haifa and Tripoli branches of the pipeline. No acts of sabotage or vandalism against IPC properties were reported, and the British personnel were largely unscathed. At K3, police restraint prevented an escalation of violence similar to that in Kirkuk two years earlier. As a large force of armoured cars surrounded the protesters' quarters on the fourteenth day of the strike, they were forced to abandon the station and started a long and debilitating march to Baghdad to present their demands directly to the government.[58]

After the occupation of K3, protesters brought oil operations to a standstill and organized rosters to picket the station and the ferry across the river Euphrates to prevent infiltration by outsiders. The station's watchmen were disarmed and expelled, and only some were allowed to return after the issue of special permits signed by the strike leaders.[59] Orchestrated by the Iraq Communist Party, the strike was seemingly an orderly and disciplined movement reminiscent of the work stoppages of 1937. Typically, it relied on a number of committees to organize key activities such as meetings, communist indoctrination and negotiations with the company and security. In Hanna Batatu's words, K3 became 'a practical communist training ground' in preparation for the party's takeover of Iraq.[60]

The imposition of communist order in K3 can be read as an act of policing in reverse. The disciplining and organization of the workforce by indoctrination and the expulsion of 'undesirables' from the station were acts that aimed at cleansing both ideological and physical space. An operation such as the takeover of K3 that purported to create a *tabula rasa* required control of the means of both persuasion and coercion. Reports of rifles discharged in the air during inflammatory meetings suggest that some of the strikers were armed. Although the extent of the militarization of the movement is unclear, station patrollers often resorted to force to expel watchmen (normally carrying weapons), labourers and villagers, or to prevent them from re-entering the station. Intimidation and bullying were also used against the families of some of the Christian clerks who were unwilling to join the strike. The local Bedouin sheikh in control of security was prevented from taking action to protect his watchmen. Some reports suggest that strike leaders threatened and insulted him.[61] In the heavily armed tribal world surrounding the station, one can easily imagine that threats were effective only if backed by the display of adequate means of physical coercion.

Further, the anti-imperialist rhetoric of abuse that permeated communist teachings in K3 made the government and the company solely responsible for the exploitation of workers, while ignoring the presence of key violent actors such as tribal leaders as procurers of labour. In fact the strike, which had been preceded by months of protracted tribal violence around the station, was also precipitated by the increasingly extortionate demands of warring factions on the workforce. This became apparent in some interviews that the Ministry of Labour and Social Affairs conducted with protesters inside K3 during the occupation of the station.[62]

Conclusion

In spite of the often dehumanizing effects of local labour conditions, the powerless of Kirkuk's oil conurbation rarely resorted to outright physical violence to fight against Upton Sinclair's 'monster of wealth'. Acts of brutality were a prerogative of the few: police, watchmen, tribal sheikhs and activists. Structural and physical violence worked in a dialectical relationship. While the former was stored in the different milieus of oil production, the latter was ready to be 'performed' by the multitude of actors who gravitated around IPC's corporate enterprise. As elsewhere in urban Iraq, the conditions engendered by the British military occupation during the Second World War were key catalysts of unrest. The 1946 strike and the takeover of K3 in 1948 suggest the multiple manifestations, the rhetorical underpinnings and representations of industrial violence, and the different ways oil urbanization played out in the contested terrain of oil and national politics at a crucial juncture in Iraq's modern history.

In this respect, while Kirkuk and its oil enclave can be read as specific urban/industrial landscapes of power where order and disorder coexisted in a precarious balance, the violent history of the town and of its industrial conurbation reflected wider political and social struggles unfolding in the country. The company's reliance on the Iraqi police and intelligence (and during the war on the British army) was a key factor that contributed to popularize oil as an anti-imperialist and anti-government trope across monarchical Iraq. Yet while oil generated increasing resentment among labour and nationalist activists, students and workers, the outbreak of large-scale public violence in Kirkuk was quite exceptional if compared with other urban centres such as Basra and Baghdad. The contrasting and in many ways disconnected urban worlds of Kirkuk's oil enclave and the increasing efficiency of security regimes partly account for this. Kirkuk was a growing industrial town whose coexistence with an often politically fractious 'native city' beset by a difficult relationship with the central government determined the increasing securitization of public order, a fact that partly explains the absence of large-scale labour unrest after 1946 until the end of the monarchy. The oil stations were purpose-built compounds that enshrined a new vision of the urban/industrial future of Iraq. As such they became 'vulnerable' to labour mobilization as the microcosm of the order of difference championed by the oil industry. Yet, after the dramatic events of 1948 in K3 (that ended in a bitter defeat for the communist movement and the establishment of the oil police in 1950), there is no evidence to suggest that these locations became the stage of major industrial conflict.

Notes

The author wishes to thank the members of the DFG/AHRC research group on urban violence in the modern Middle East for their insights and comments that have helped to shape this article. I also want to express my gratitude to the staff of the British Petroleum archive at the University of Warwick, in particular Peter Housego and Joanne Burman, for their kindness, efficiency and support.

1. U. Sinclair. (1926) 2008. *Oil! A Novel*, London: Penguin Books, 26. The film *There Will Be Blood* (2007), directed by Paul Thomas Anderson, is loosely based on Sinclair's novel.
2. See M. Watts. 2001. 'Petro-Violence: Community, Extraction and the Political Ecology of a Mythic Commodity', in N.L. Peluso and M. Watts (eds), *Violent Environments*, Ithaca, NY: Cornell University Press, 189–212; idem. 2005. 'Righteous Oil? Human Rights, the Oil Complex and Corporate Social Responsibility', *Annual Review of Environment and Resources* 30, 9.1–9.35. For a discussion of oil violence in relation to environmental issues in Saudi Arabia, see T.C. Jones. 2010. *Desert Kingdom: How Oil and Water Forged Saudi Arabia*, Cambridge, MA: Harvard University Press, 179–216.
3. N. Fuccaro (ed.). 2013. *Histories of Oil and Urban Modernity in the Middle East*, thematic issue in *Comparative Studies of South Asia, Africa and the Middle East* 33(1), 1–88.

4. J. Ferguson. 2005. 'Seeing Like an Oil Company: Space, Security, and Global Capital in Neoliberal Africa', *American Anthropologist* 107(3), 377–82.
5. A. Alnasrawi. 1994. *The Economy of Iraq: Oil, Wars, Destruction of Development and Prospects, 1950–2010*, Westport, CT: Greenwood Press, 35–104. For a reflection on the meaning of Ba'thist violence, see S. al-Khalil. 1991. *Republic of Fear: Saddam's Iraq*, London: Hutchinson Radius, new edn, Introductory Note, xiii–xxxi.
6. T. Mitchell. 2011. *Carbon Democracy: Political Power in the Age of Oil*, London: Verso, 8.
7. Alongside IPC, two subsidiary companies operated in Iraq during the monarchy: the Mosul and Basra Petroleum Companies. For the early history of IPC in Iraq and the Levant states, see *Handbook of the Territories which Form the Theatre of Operations of the Iraq Petroleum Company Limited and its Associated Companies*, London: Iraq Petroleum Company, 1948, 1–17, 141.
8. After the original area of concession was expanded from 192 to 32,000 square miles in 1931, oil production increased from approximately 1 million tons in 1934 to 24 million tons in 1954, with a slump during the Second World War. British Petroleum Archive, University of Warwick, Coventry (hereinafter 'BP') 119015, *Guide to Kirkuk* (London: Iraq Petroleum Company, 1955). For the history of British involvement in Iraqi oil before and during the mandate, see P. Sluglett. 2007. *Britain in Iraq: Contriving King and Country*, London: I.B. Tauris, 65–75. The intricacies of IPC's and British oil politics in Kirkuk are also discussed in A. Bet-Shlimon. 2012. *Kirkuk, 1918–1968: Oil and the Politics of Identity in an Iraqi City*, Ph.D. dissertation, Cambridge, MA: Harvard University, 148–58.
9. J. Sassoon. 1987. *Economy Policy in Iraq, 1932–1950*, London: Cass, 247–53.
10. Although Baghdad, Basra and Mosul feature prominently in accounts of political violence and social unrest, little attention has been devoted to the history of Iraqi urban centres as the venues of public violence during the monarchy and soon after the 1958 revolution. Hanna Batatu's detailed discussion and almost graphic reconstruction of the bloody events of 1959 in Mosul and Kirkuk are an exception. See H. Batatu. 1978. *The Old Social Classes and Revolutionary Movements of Iraq*, Princeton, NJ: Princeton University Press, 866–89, 912–21. On Farman's novel *The Black Regime in Iraq*, see O. Bashkin. 2009. *The Other Iraq: Pluralism and Culture in Hashemite Iraq*, Stanford, CA: Stanford University Press, 103.
11. BP 143547 FILM, *The Third River*, 28 minutes, produced for the Iraq Petroleum Company Films by Film Centre, 1952, CD; BP 203649/001, 'Making "The Third River"', *Iraq Petroleum* 2(5), 1952, pp. 14–18. The film premiered in London in November 1952, and British and Arabic versions were shown in Britain and in the Arab world in the following years.
12. For an instructive example of the relationship between extractive enterprises and violence, see the case of the South African gold mines, in partic-

ular T. Dunbar Moodie. 1994. *Going for Gold: Men, Mines and Migration*, Berkeley: University of California Press, 180–210.
13. Johan Galtung and Paul Farmer's formulation of the concept of structural violence is quite useful in this context. They see the relationship between an unequal distribution of power and the production of inequality as constraining and disadvantaging human agency. Although this concept has been generally linked to contemporary violations of human rights, Farmer stresses the historically constructed nature of violent structures and institutions. See J. Galtung. 1969. 'Violence, Peace, and Peace Research', *Journal of Peace Research* 6(3), 167–91; and P. Farmer. 2004. 'An Anthropology of Structural Violence', *Current Anthropology* 45(3), 305–17.
14. N. al-Din Bayraqdar. 2011. *Karkuk bayna 'l-Haqiqa wa-l-Waqi': Dirasa ʿan Huquq al-Turkman fi 'l-ʿIraq bayna Haqq al-Wujud wa-l-Sira' hawla Madinat Karkuk*, Beirut: Dar al-ʿArabiyya li-l-Mawsuʿat, 158–59. For a detailed account of Kirkuk's demography and urban growth up to the 1960s, see Bet-Shlimon, *Kirkuk, 1918–1968*, 158–71.
15. At the beginning of the 1920s, Kirkuk's population of approximately 25,000 was 25 per cent Kurdish with a large majority of Turkmens. By 1959, out of a total of 120,000 residents, Kurds constituted more than one-third of the population, while the Turkmens had decreased to less than half. Language offers some indication of this demographic distribution. The 1957 census identified 40,000 Kurdish speakers and 45,000 Turkmen speakers living in the city. C.J. Edmonds. 1957. *Kurds, Turks and Arabs*, London: Oxford University Press, 265; Batatu, *The Old Social Classes*, 913; Bet-Shlimon, *Kirkuk, 1918–1968*, 167. In 1955, some 5,000 Iraqis were directly employed by IPC in the Kirkuk Fields, including clerical and technical staff and unskilled labourers. Regrettably, available figures do not provide the ethnic composition of the workforce. BP 39649, 'Personnel Statistics. Actual Strengths by Nationalities and Locations as at 31 December 1955'.
16. Bayraqdar, *Karkuk*, 159: National Archives of the United Kingdom, London (hereinafter NAUK) FO 624/176, minutes 734/1/49, 9 May 1949.
17. BP 127276, maps 'Iraq Petroleum Company – Kirkuk' in 'Notes for the Guidance of New Staff – Arriving/Settling in Kirkuk', 1949.
18. On Bawarda as a legacy of colonial urban planning, see M. Crinson. 1997. 'Abadan: Planning and Architecture under the Anglo-Iranian Oil Company', *Planning Perspectives* 12(3), 351–57.
19. A sketch of Kirkuk showing the old town, indigenous suburban areas and modern IPC developments on the west bank of the Khasa river is included in BP 65577, 'Pipelines Across the Desert', *The Sphere*, 26 July 1952, pp. 126–27; BP 49717, map 'Kirkuk Development. Proposed New Housing in the Arrapha Ridge Area', 1947.
20. BP 163897, translation of an article published in *al-Thawra* included in Memo, 8 December 1958. For an analysis of IPC's policies of local development in Kirkuk after 1946, see A. Bet-Shlimon. 2013. 'The Politics and Ideology of Urban Development in Iraq's Oil City: Kirkuk, 1946–1958', in

N. Fuccaro (ed.), *Histories of Oil and Urban Modernity in the Middle East*, 26–40.
21. In 1955, 450 of the 630 families that IPC housed in its Kirkuk camps lived in Arrapha. BP 119015, 'Personnel Services', in *Guide to Kirkuk* (London: Iraq Petroleum Company, 1955).
22. NAUK LAB 13/674, 'Visit to IPC, Kirkuk Fields, 15th–18th August, 1950', Iraq Labour Memorandum no. 4, August 1950, 8.
23. BP 135819, Memo Kirkuk Fields Officer to IPC Managing Director, 'Accommodation at Kirkuk', January 1953; Bet-Shlimon, 'The Politics and Ideology of Urban Development', 32.
24. 'Life in a Pipeline Station – Part I The General Scene/ Part II The Industrial Scene/ Part III The Social Scene', *Iraq Petroleum* 1(6/7/8), January/February/March 1952, pp. 4–9/4–7/16–21; 'Desert City of the 20th Century Parts I and II', *Iraq Petroleum* 6(3/4), October/November 1956, pp. 4–10/12–17.
25. http://www.migrationheritage.nsw.gov.au/exhibition/belongings/hallaby, accessed on 9 Feb. 2012.
26. NAUK, LAB 13/672, 'Note on Manpower Problem in Iraq', Labour Adviser to the Iraqi Government to Ministry of Labour and National Affairs London, 20 April 1952, p. 3.
27. NAUK FO 624/130, minutes by F. Wells, 7 April 1948.
28. BP 135819, 'Security of Houses in the Arrapha Estate', Memo Fields Manager Kirkuk to IPC Managing Director, 2 July 1949.
29. NAUK LAB 13/674, 'Visit to IPC, Kirkuk Fields, 15th–18th August, 1950', pp. 3–4.
30. BP 16246, 'The Miserable State of the Iraq Petroleum Company's Workmen at Kirkuk', pamphlet, 1946, in 'Secret Report on Iraq during the Year 1946' by A.J.B. Chapman, Land and Liaison Officer, Kirkuk Fields.
31. NAUK LAB 13/672, 'Notes of Labour Expert's visit to K3 & K2 on 11th to 15th Jan. 1952' by Labour Adviser to the Iraqi Government, p. 1; 'Note on Manpower Problem in Iraq', 20 April 1952, p. 1. BP 163120, IPC Employment and Liaison Officer to General Manager Tripoli, 8 May 1948, and Iraq Ministry of Social Affairs to Iraq Interior, 8 May 1948.
32. BP 163120, IPC Employment and Liaison Officer to General Manager Tripoli, 8 May 1948.
33. NAUK LAB 13/672, 'Notes of Labour Expert's visit to K3 & K2', pp. 1 and 4.
34. BP 162444, Extract private correspondence Turkish Petroleum Company General Manager Iraq to Mr Templeton, 11 July 1929; BP 161667, Précis of meeting between IPC Management Kirkuk Fields and Iraq Interior, 20 November 1949, p. 5.
35. NAUK LAB 13/674, 'Visit to IPC, Kirkuk Fields, 15th–18th August, 1950', p. 1.
36. On the key role that policing, surveillance, intimidation and censorship played in shaping government policy and leftist public discourse against the Hashemite government and the British, see Bashkin, *The Other Iraq*, 102–11.

37. On the oil police, see files BP 161667 and 161668, particularly 'A Survey of the Oil Police', November 1964, and 'Security and Protection of All Overseas Areas', 20 November 1963.
38. BP 163884, Translation of excerpts of articles in *al-Qaʿida*, 24 February 1956, in memo 10 May 1956.
39. Mitchell, *Carbon Democracy*, 103.
40. BP 68103, *Group memos IPC*, 26–30 June 1937.
41. BP 164175, 'Iraq during the Year 1941', n.a., pp. 4–5; H.S. Longrigg. 1969. *Oil in the Middle East: Its Discovery and Development*, London: Oxford University Press, 119.
42. NAUK, LAB 13/193 British Embassy to Foreign Office, 21 August 1946, pp. 1–2; BP 212109, 'Annual Report of the Fields Manager for 1941', p. 8; 'Annual Report of the Fields Manager for 1942', p. 14.
43. No numbers are available for Kirkuk, but in 1943, 57,000 Iraqis were on the Army payroll. NAUK LAB 13/193, British Embassy to Foreign Office, 3 January 1946; FO 371/52410, British Embassy to Foreign Office, 14 March 1946. BP 212110, 'Annual Report of the Fields Manager for 1942', p. 6.
44. BP 212110, 'Annual Reports of Fields Manager for 1942/1943/1944', pp. 8, 10/10, 14/12–15; BP 212111, 'Annual Report of Fields Manager for 1945', pp. 18–20.
45. BP 212110, 'Annual Report of the Fields Manager for 1943/1944', pp. 7, 12–14.
46. NAUK FO 371/52456, British Embassy to Foreign Office, 25 October 1946.
47. BP 162461, 'The Miserable State of the Iraq Petroleum Company's Workmen at Kirkuk', pamphlet, 1946.
48. NAUK FO 371/52456, British Embassy to Foreign Office, 19 July 1946.
49. NAUK FO 624/95, 'Conditions in Iraq', 16 August 1946, pp. 8–9; FO 371/52456, Telegram British Embassy to Foreign Office, 8 July 1946, and British Embassy to Foreign Office, 19 July 1946. Batatu, *The Old Social Classes*, 532–33. For the role played by the communist movement in the strike, see ibid., 622–24. The strike and communist activities are also discussed in Bet-Shlimon, *Kirkuk, 1918-1968*, 180–88.
50. 'al-Hadith al-Muʾsif fi Kirkuk. Bayan al-Hukuma Yukshif ʿan ʿAmaliha', 'Hadith Kirkuk al-ʿAlim', 'Itlaq al-Rassas ʿala l-Mutadhahirin', *al-Ahali*, 15, 16 and 18 July 1946.
51. FO 371/52456, Foreign Office minutes, 24, 25 and 26 July 1946.
52. FO 371/52456, British Embassy to Foreign Office, 19 July 1946; Foreign Office minutes 24 July 1946; minutes by P. Garran, 30 July 1946.
53. F. al-Azzawi. 2007. *The Last of the Angels*, transl. William M. Hutchins, Cairo: The American University in Cairo Press, 53–54. A short account of the incident based on some first-hand testimonies is also included in Batatu, *The Old Social Classes*, 623–24.
54. al-ʿAzzawi, *Last of the Angels*, 56.
55. NAUK FO 624/117, Secret Report, British Consulate Kirkuk, 29 October 1947. BP 163120, IPC Employment and Liaison Officer to General Manager

Tripoli, 8 May 1948; BP 161667, Précis of Meeting between IPC Management Kirkuk Fields and Iraqi Interior, 20 November 1949.
56. NAUK FO 624/138, Political Summaries for Kirkuk and Sulaymaniyya, February and March 1948.
57. BP 135819, Note from AP1 KK/37/51. In 1948, approximately 600 people were employed in K1, including occasional labourers. In 1950, the workforces of K2 and K3 were approximately 1,000 and 950 respectively, with the addition of 320 British and American technical staff between the two stations. These figures seem to include daily wage workers, although Batatu mentions some 3,000 workers and clerks in K3 in 1948. NAUK LAB 13/674, 'Visit to IPC, Kirkuk Fields, 15th–18th August, 1950', p. 2; LAB 13/672, 'Notes of Labour Expert's visit to K3 & K2 on 11th to 15th Jan. 1952', pp. 1–2; Batatu, *The Old Social Classes*, 625.
58. NAUK FO 371/ 68479, British Embassy to Foreign Office, 4 and 5 May 1948; Report by Vice Consul Kirkuk, 14 May 1948, in correspondence British Embassy to Foreign Office, 21 May 1948; Batatu, *The Old Social Classes*, 625–27.
59. NAUK FO 371/ 68479, Report by Vice Consul Kirkuk, 14 May 1948. BP 163120, IPC Manager Tripoli to Management London, 12 June 1948.
60. Batatu, *The Old Social Classes*, 625–26.
61. NAUK FO 371/ 68479, Report by Vice Consul Kirkuk, 14 May 1948.
62. BP 163120, Iraqi Ministry of Social Affairs to Interior, 3 May 1948; IPC Manager Tripoli to Management London, 12 June 1948. NAUK FO 624/138, Political Summary for Kirkuk and Sulaymaniyya, February 1948.

❖· Chapter 11 ·❖

Structural and Physical Violence in Saudi Arabian Oil Towns, 1953–56

CLAUDIA GHRAWI

In this chapter, I will discuss the different forms of violence that occurred in the course of labour protests in Saudi Arabian oil towns between 1953 and 1956. My focus lies on the three towns of Dhahran, Ras Tanura and Abqaiq, as they shared the common character of being newly built industrial towns whose purposes were the housing of the industrial labour force and the administration of the local oil industry. The three places materialized when oil production in Saudi Arabia's province of al-Hasa[1] first reached commercial quantities in 1938. With the end of World War II, Saudis from more distant parts of the Kingdom increasingly poured into the province seeking work with the oil industry, and the provisional oil exploration camps developed quickly into permanent industrial settlements. These early oil towns were of dual character, partly planned by the Arabian American Oil Company (Aramco) and partly wild-grown formations that were shaped by a steady influx of job seekers, local entrepreneurs and their families. In 1954, the population of Dhahran was 10,554, Ras Tanura 5,882 and Abqaiq 5,721.[2] As centres of the oil industry, they became nuclei of local development and were economic pacemakers in the young kingdom's transition into a centralized state whose political economy was increasingly based on oil rents.[3] Furthermore, the early oil towns generated a new type of political subject: oasis villagers, townspeople, and Bedouins were transformed into an industrial labour force that settled in a gradually urbanizing area. Young men from the al-Hasa province constituted the majority of the Saudi oil workers, among them many Shiites from the old local towns Qatif and Hofuf.[4] These specific characteristics must be taken into account when observing that in the mid twentieth century, the three oil towns grew into landscapes of episodic contention between Saudi oil workers, the oil company, and the Saudi Arabian government.

The four years of 1953–1956 were ones of recurring unrest. A general strike in autumn 1953 was followed by a number of boycotts and demonstrations in 1955 and 1956, which were only ended by harsh intervention by the state and the banning of all forms of labour protest in June 1956. The workers' protests are often interpreted in the context of capitalist industrialization and contemporary popular ideologies that nourished a growing political consciousness among the Saudi oil workers.[5] In his novel demystification of Aramco's oil operations in Saudi Arabia, Robert Vitalis argued that the workers' dissatisfaction was largely rooted in their discrimination by the company in regard to housing, salaries and status, and the prevalence of (U.S.-imported) racism in the company's dealings with its non-American employees.[6] Vitalis was the first scholar to describe the events discussed in this chapter in a comprehensive manner using primary sources in U.S. archives.[7] However, no attempt has so far been made to analyse the protests in the light of the evolving relationship between the Saudi oil workers and the newly constituted Saudi Arabian state.[8] In fact, the latter has largely been written out of the protests' history and is recognized solely in the form of intervening police or army troops. Yet, cases of oil-producing countries in which territorialized capital investment created privately secured oil enclaves isolated from a weakly governed hinterland[9] do not provide a universal pattern. Oil industrialization worked in different ways and created different outcomes depending on time and place. I will argue that in Saudi Arabia oil industrialization and state building operated *together* in institutionalizing structural and physical violence as a means of governing the growing industrial communities in Saudi Arabian oil towns, which the Saudi oil workers and the local population challenged and resisted.

As a theoretical approach rather than a conclusive model, I take recourse to the works of the sociologist Johan Galtung who defined 'structural violence' as a larger process (in contrast to 'direct' or 'physical' violence, which is a single event) that impedes the formation of consciousness and mobilization of the suppressed, and thus prohibits any effective struggle against exploitation.[10] Four mechanisms are assumed to work within this process: '*penetration,* implanting the topdog inside the underdog so to speak, combined with *segmentation,* giving the underdog only a very partial view of what goes on ... And *marginalization,* keeping the underdogs on the outside, combined with *fragmentation,* keeping the underdogs away from each other.'[11] I would further suggest that what Charles Tilly called 'threats of violence'[12] constitute a fifth mechanism of structural violence. Such threats became permanently in-built in the Saudi Arabian oil conurbation and their function was to ensure that the industrial communities complied with the order envisaged by the state and the oil company.

However, the relationship between Saudi rulers and subjects never functioned solely along lines of paternalism, violent suppression and obedience. There were 'spaces' for bargaining that were moulded and remoulded in conflicts, yet grew smaller with the expansion of state administration and the ongoing struggle for the consolidation of the Saudi monarchy. Structural and physical violence in Saudi Arabian oil towns marked the evolving relationship between the young Saudi Arabian state and its subjects in the very manner depicted by Michael Watts as 'petro-violence [that] elevated to the point where profound questions of state, nation, and citizens are posed by it and where structural violence is perpetuated in its name'.[13]

Governing Industrial Communities – Saudi Arabian Oil Towns in the Early 1950s

In the late 1940s and early 1950s, Saudi Arabia lacked an efficient state apparatus.[14] The building of a centralized administration and modern infrastructure, and the integration of the different parts of the country under the rule of the Al Sa'ud, accompanied a constant need for money and a strong dependence on oil revenues.[15] During its initial expansion, the Saudi oil industry relied massively on the local workforce, and in 1953 the number of Saudi oil workers exceeded 13,500. These men almost exclusively constituted the bottom of the Aramco workforce, the so-called general staff. In 1953 only little more than seven hundred Saudis were classified in the intermediate staff level. This professional rank consisted mainly of clerical and technical employees from Palestine, Pakistan or India. Not even a dozen Saudi employees (university graduates and company interpreters) belonged to the senior staff level, whose national composition was almost exclusively U.S. American.[16]

The company's formal classification of its employees in professional ranks meant their practical segregation along national and ethnic lines.[17] General, intermediate, and senior employees wore coloured badges that identified them as members of their respective ranks.[18] The three staff levels lived in separate camps distinguished by differing standards of accommodation and geographically divided by open lands, roads, fences, security gates and guard posts. The fenced and highly secured senior or 'American' camps with their neat bungalows, greenery and refined recreational areas stood in stark contrast to the general camps that were unfenced and, although Aramco had divided the land into parcels using a grit pattern, could grow with less restriction. Intermediate camps were located like buffer zones between general and senior camps. They were fenced like the American residential areas. As the sociologist Kaveh Ehsani has pointed out, this layout was typical for oil towns built in the first half of the twentieth century all over the Middle East, as it followed a common pattern 'dictated by the requirements of the oil industry'.[19] Segregation of professional ranks was intended to enforce the industrial hierarchy and to secure discipline.[20]

The oil company had created the physical constraints that perpetuated the envisioned social order and secured compliance with it. However, it was the task of the provincial governor, the amir of the al-Hasa province, to keep order in the three oil towns and among Aramco's Saudi workforce.[21] In addition, each Saudi community was administered by a local amir who had small police and security forces at his disposition in order to control the Saudi population in his administrative territories and to enforce Saudi law.[22]

The general camps in the three districts were crowded places that bustled with oil workers and folk that had no formal affiliation with the oil company. Although the oil company did not provide family housing for employees other than senior level, many Saudi workers brought

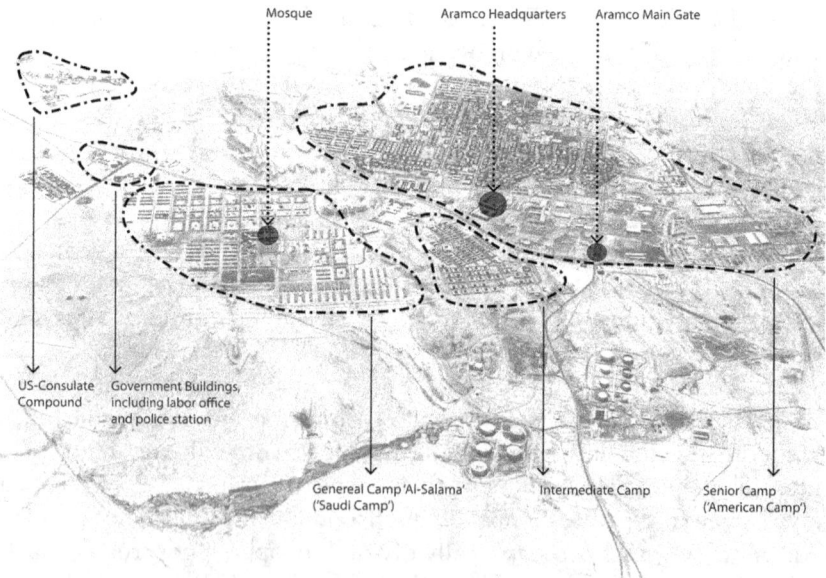

Figure 11.1. The spatial organization of Dhahran, 1965. Drawn by Melody Mosavat, based on an aerial photo by courtesy of J.P. Mandaville.

their families with them into the oil towns. They found shelter in shack conglomerations that grew at the edges of the general camps. Furthermore, the growing communities attracted all kinds of small-scale entrepreneurs and day labourers who ran grocery stores, repair shops and restaurants, or who worked for the company or one of its numerous contractors and then returned to their villages during the harvest season. It was also common for workers from more distant regions to share their limited space with friends or relatives who were looking for work with Aramco or elsewhere in the area. Many residents of the general camps commuted to their local homes on weekends. Before the company began to provide bus transportation for its Saudi employees in the mid-1950s, this meant several hours walking across desert and farmland, often barefoot, as many workers owned no shoes.[23]

The oil company provided accommodation for its Saudi employees in the form of palm huts (*barastis*), tents and brick barracks. General camps had no running water, sewage system or electricity. Their inhabitants used gas stoves for cooking and carried their water from wells.[24] After a strike by Saudi oil workers in 1945, the Saudi government urged the company to improve the accommodation of its Saudi employees.[25] Yet, whereas by the end of that decade intermediate workers were enjoying air-conditioned housing, running water and even a cinema,[26] the general camps remained in their adverse condition far into the 1950s.[27]

While most Americans and Saudis referred to the general camps as 'Saudi camps', the company coined and promoted the use of more 'natural' names:[28] 'al-Salama' for the general camp in Dhahran and 'Rahima' in Ras Tanura. By the mid-1950s, the general camp in Abqaiq was known as 'Madinat Abqaiq'.[29] Al-Salama gained municipal status in 1954;[30] Rahima followed in 1957.[31] Each camp featured a police station, a courthouse and a small jail, haphazardly erected shops, restaurants, coffee houses, sport fields and a large mosque. These mosques were visible landmarks that provided a certain degree of affiliation and pride among general camp residents.[32] Archival sources further document that the squares in front of the mosques served as gathering places where workers met for prayer and discussed labour issues, and where the local authorities punished criminals.

Although the power of the Saudi authorities formally extended into American residential areas, Saudi law was enforced within their fences only in very general terms. Yet, occasionally, the local authorities would decide to punish lawbreakers among general or intermediate workers or the local population at the company main gates, which served as entrances and exits to the three districts including senior camps and, in the case of Dhahran, to Aramco headquarters.[33] Corporal punishments were probably scheduled at the end of day shifts, so that workers on their way back to the general and intermediate camps could be forced to stop and watch the penalty. Severed body parts were displayed on the fences at each side of the gate as a reminder to the Saudi workforce and local communities to abide to the rules.[34] Such violent rituals,[35] in which Saudi law was intentionally executed on Aramco premises, were bound to obliterate the palpable boundaries between the legal and spatial 'terrains' of the oil company and those of the Saudi authorities. Particularly the provincial amir, Saʿud b. Jiluwi, became the visible power behind the control of the Saudi oil workers.[36]

It is, however, important to note that the Saudi authorities would often choose non-violent measures in their dealings with the Saudi oil workers. A local amir would for instance mediate conflicts through direct consultation with the workers, for example during meetings in one of the general camps' coffee houses,[37] or with a local shaykh who intervened on behalf of his people.[38] Yet, I would argue that, in the course of oil industrialization, local modes of rule went through a process of growing depersonalization that contributed to the social and political marginalization of the Saudi oil workers. The traditional ideal of leadership required that political power was based on a personal relationship between ruler and ruled, in which the latter had direct access to the king and his state officials.[39] But the needs of governing an increasingly industrialized and urbanized area, an expanding state administration and a growing number of state officials who competed for positions and influence rendered such traditional ideals at least partly impracticable. The Saudi government anticipated this development, as is reflected in a royal decree issued in 1952 that penalized any attempt to hinder ordinary citizens from delivering their demands directly to the king.[40]

Mobilizing the Saudi Workforce, 1953

The labour protests of 1953–1956 were initiated by the relatively small group of Saudi intermediate workers who in the course of the labour movement were able to mobilize the larger part of the Saudi workforce. Discontent in the intermediate rank had been rising for some time: the nationalization of the Iranian oil industry in 1951 and the Egyptian revolution of 1952 had sparked a new political consciousness among the better-trained workers, who felt it unjust that a foreign company should exploit the national soils and that Saudis still constituted the lowest-paid and worst-off layer of Aramco's workforce. Low wages and poor housing conditions concerned Saudi workers in particular.[41]

When, in May 1953, the Aramco management received a petition from 155 Saudi intermediate employees who demanded living allowances comparable to those granted to senior staff employees and better chances for Aramco's Saudi employees to rise to higher professional levels,[42] the company hoped to 'bring government pressure to bear to stop the movement'.[43] Several weeks passed and the workers received no further response than the company's reluctance to recognize their elected representatives from the three districts. However, the initiators of the protest did not remain inactive and started to mobilize the Saudi workforce in the three oil towns. Broadsides on the company bulletin boards in the general camps campaigned for the workers' cause. Mass meetings of workers were held in front of the mosque in al-Salama and in the nearby villages. These activities caused the company, on around 23 August, to alarm the provincial governor that the Saudi oil workers were planning to go on strike.[44] On 1 September, the workers directed a petition to Crown Prince Saʿud, signed by 6,500 Saudi intermediate and general employees from all three districts. The petition repeated the workers' demands and asked the crown prince to recognize their representatives.[45]

In late September, a Royal Committee was formed and sent to Dhahran to investigate the workers' cause in a series of meetings between the labour leaders and representatives of the local authorities and the oil company. While the members of the Royal Committee considered the workers' demands, some of the younger labour leaders, possibly after a disagreement with the company representatives, threatened that the workers were ready to employ acts of sabotage and vandalism against company installations in the pursuit of their aims.[46] This discord made Aramco hope that 'the ringleaders ... might have gone too far and that the Government might of its own volition take action to oppose the activities of the leaders'.[47] And indeed, in mid-October, the government intervened against the labour movement. Crown Prince Saʿud assigned full command over the Saudi military forces in the region to the director of the military airfield in Dhahran, Colonel Mohammad ʿAwartani, who had the reputation of being 'eager to advance himself in the eyes of the Royal family'.[48] ʿAwartani immediately moved fifteen hundred soldiers into the oil production area as reinforcement for the five hundred men that were permanently stationed in Dhahran.[49] On 14 and 15 October, after the increase in Saudi army troops in the area, the Royal Committee ordered the arrest of the labour representatives and four other activists from the three districts, and transferred them to a prison in Hofuf.[50] The following day, company and government officials reported 'sporadic meetings, beatings and disturbances in Aramco's labour camps and nearby Arab villages'.[51] In the afternoon, a group of between five hundred and two thousand workers gathered in front of the police station in al-Salama and then spilled out onto the road that led to Aramco's main gate, company headquarters and senior camp. The angry workers threw stones at passing vehicles, causing some minor damages and injuries. ʿAwartani's soldiers quickly arrived on the scene and dispersed the workers, but the incident caused the local authorities to install additional security around the labour camps.[52]

In response to the arrests of the labour leaders, Aramco's Saudi employees went on a general strike on 17 October. Labour activists gave speeches in the general camps and in their hometowns and villages to promote the strike among their co-workers.[53] For the following two weeks, up to two-thirds of the Saudi workforce stayed away from work. Meanwhile, the local police forces failed in their attempts to disperse meetings of workers held in the general camps and the local towns and villages. The strikers widely ignored the local amirs' orders to return to work, which, according to the American consul in Dhahran, was 'an unprecedented action'.[54] By 20 October, approximately one thousand alleged agitators had been arrested by the Saudi police forces, but when the latter still proved unable to end the strike, Colonel ʿAwartani proposed to send his troops into the labour camps to urge workers back to the oilfields or otherwise 'order them out of the area'.[55] Two days later, ʿAwartani and members of the Royal Committee, backed up by army forces, started to move through the general camps 'in all three districts block by block' and ordered the workers back to their jobs. Defiant workers were arrested for further investigation. On the following day, forty-five Aramco employees and eleven others, all Saudis, were deported from the oil operations area by train and under army escort, 'witnessed by a considerable crowd of Saudis who booed and jeered at the troops'.[56] In early November the strike was ended, and the majority of the Saudi troops were withdrawn from the area and replaced by *khawiya* (sing. *khawi*), who were stationed midway between Dhahran and Abqaiq and Dhahran and Ras Tanura.[57] The American consul interpreted the use of *khawiya*, personal armed retainers and bodyguards of the provincial amir,[58] as the provincial government's attempt 'to soften any resentment the strikers felt against the government's earlier use of the Army to maintain order'.[59]

The relative longevity of the strike and the resilience of the strikers in facing the state authorities can be explained by their ability to draw upon their local networks: merchants in the nearby towns granted extended credit to the workers, who were paid on a bi-weekly basis and otherwise would have quickly run out of money.[60] Strikers set up roadblocks in villages near the production sites to prevent company buses from moving contract workers to the oil installations.[61] Astonished about the well-organized strike, the American consul reported that 'meetings [of workers] occurred with apparent spontaneity, first in one place and then another. Speakers abruptly disappeared into the crowd at the approach of the police or other officials and few were positively identified'.[62] Hundreds of strikers fled from ʿAwartani's soldiers into the towns and villages in the area. In Qatif, one of the province's centres of the Shiite minority, people opened their homes and *husayniyyas*[63] for shelter.[64] Yet, all the written and oral testimony from participants in the strike and their descendants points to the fact that the labour activities comprised Sunnis as much as Shiites.[65]

Increasing the Threat of Violence, 1954

The lessons the Saudi government learned from the strike were twofold. On his first visit to Dhahran in January 1954, King Saʿud, who had followed his father on the throne in November 1953,[66] publicly announced improvements negotiated between the Royal Committee and Aramco on behalf of the welfare of the Saudi workers, including wage increases, greater efforts to promote the building of family houses with the help of company loans and the intention to expand transportation of workers to and from their workplaces.[67] Furthermore, the agreement contained some decisions that would help the provincial and local amirs to manage labour unrest in the future: the presence of non-employees in the labour camps was declared an undesirable situation and fences were to be erected around general camps.[68] Furthermore, a permanent Labour Committee, which consisted mainly of members of the Royal Committee set up during the 1953 protests, was established under the supervision of Amir Saʿud b. Jiluwi. Labour offices were opened in all three districts.[69] In the eyes of the American consul, this decision was most probably 'a recognition of the need of the Permanent [Labour] Committee for the police powers at the disposal of the Amirate in times of labor disturbances'.[70]

Another action taken by the Saudi government, which was probably connected to the labour protests, was initiated in early November 1953, shortly after the strike had ended. Around that time, Crown Prince Saʿud announced a five-year plan for the development of the Saudi armed forces in the framework of American military assistance.[71] On several occasions, the Saudi Minister of Defence and Civil Aviation, Prince Mishʿal b. ʿAbd al-ʿAziz b. Saʿud, substantiated the government's request for U.S. military aid with the 'desire to strengthen [the armed forces'] capability to deal with situations such as had recently arisen at Dhahran'.[72] The argument was obviously stressed to encourage the U.S. government to invest in the Saudi defence apparatus. However, it became a permanent element of the negotiations over U.S. military assistance. When, two months later, the minister forwarded comprehensive lists of required military equipment to Washington, his justifications became even more substantial:

> Prince Misha'al pointed out that the Saudi Government expected to initiate large-scale development projects in several sections of the country which would necessitate the assembling of large groups of workers. He maintained that an increase in Saudi armed forces was imperative in order to prevent possible trouble which would result from the assembling of these groups of workers throughout the country. He pointed out that it was entirely due to the sending of Saudi army units to Dhahran that it was possible to maintain order in the area during the recent strike.[73]

In April 1954, the Saudi government requested the purchase of sixty fully equipped armoured cars for the maintenance of internal security in the oil operations area, where five hundred infantrymen had just begun their training as security forces.[74] Rumours of a new strike by Saudi oil workers intensified again around May, when leaflets appeared in the three oil towns demanding the implementation of the improvements in transportation and housing that had been promised at the beginning of the year.[75] Aramco feared that this time the workers would attempt to sabotage the oil installations.[76] Apparently, the Saudi government shared Aramco's fear of a slowdown or even temporary stoppage of oil production, and intended to answer possible disorder immediately and with the utmost vigour. On 22 May, King Sa'ud gave Colonel 'Awartani a free hand to arrest 'troublemakers' without any prior consultation with the provincial amir. In a step similar to that carried out in 1953, additional troops were moved to the oil operations area and the number of Saudi soldiers in the region reached three thousand.[77] Up until September, no strike had materialized, but the Saudi government nonetheless ordered forty additional armoured cars, as they were 'needed urgently for training and use [by the] Saudi troops for quelling riots and civil disturbances in Dammam area which includes major Aramco installations'.[78]

Creating a Violent Space, 1955–1956

New unrest among the Saudi oil workers surfaced in April 1955. A petition signed by 3,231 Saudi intermediate and general staff employees was sent to the company management, demanding the extension of bus services to and from their workplaces and the provision of 'better quality buses "in keeping with the dignity" of Saudi workers'.[79] The workers underlined their demands with a boycott of the bus services that had been introduced by Aramco shortly before in Dhahran and Abqaiq.[80] The petition suggests that the workers' discontent with the transportation services was rooted in the lack of mobility and relative isolation of the workers who lived in the oil towns: apparently, no buses were running between the labour camps, and bus stops were situated at some distance from the living quarters, which meant that workers who wanted to use bus transportation had to undertake long walks in tough climatic conditions.[81]

As in 1953, the company chose to ignore the workers' demands and started investigations into who had organized the protest. Aramco further forwarded to the provincial government a comprehensive list of names and personal records of Saudi employees who had signed the petition.[82] Archival sources do not provide any information on how the amir proceeded with these Saudi employees. Instead they reveal that throughout the following weeks the Saudi police arrested seventy intermediate workers, mostly Palestinians, who were suspected of being members of subversive political organizations, and had them deported from the area.[83] The American officials in Dhahran later pondered that 'the Aramco employees' boycott of company buses ... may have played a part in alerting the government to subversive activities' among the oil workers.[84] At the end of May, Aramco was informed that one thousand Saudi Mujahidin, irregular forces of 'predominantly Najdi-Wahabi [origin] with minimum ties to eastern province or industrial labor element', were to be transferred from Riyadh and stationed at two camping sites strategically located between the three oil towns.[85] While nothing implies that the deportation of third-nation workers and the stationing of Saudi irregulars were direct responses to the boycott of company buses, it seems clear that the government feared the growth of a new unrest among Aramco's workforce, and therefore aimed at isolating the workers in the three districts from each other, and at preventing a probable fraternization between the security forces and the Saudi workers or the local population.[86]

In January 1956, violent protests among Saudi workers broke out in Abqaiq and Dhahran in response to the erection of fences around al-Salama and Madinat Abqaiq. The fencing in of the general camps corresponded with the decisions taken by Aramco and the Royal Committee in early 1954.[87] On 4 January, about two hundred workers and others called on the local Amirate in Abqaiq and complained that they regarded the erection of fences as a form of imprisonment and an attempt to isolate them from their families and friends. Nevertheless, the project was continued. On 7 January, a group of angry workers gathered at the fence construction site next to the Labour Office in Abqaiq and eventually started to tear down the already installed fence posts and Y-bars. They were dispersed by the local police. In an attempt to confer with the enraged workers, the director of the Labor Department, Amir Turki ʿUtaishan summoned five of the men to the Labour Office for private consultation. Meanwhile, more workers arrived in company buses, 'whose drivers were forced or cowed into diverting them to the Labor Office'. The workers then started to shout and jostle at ʿUtaishan and eventually got rough. ʿUtaishan was able to flee the place in his car. The unrest and vandalism, namely tearing down more fences and throwing stones at passing cars, lasted until the next day. On 8 January, hundreds of workers protested the erection of fences around general camps in front of the Labour Offices in Dhahran and Ras Tanura. Apparently, the mass protest was organized by activists who informed their co-workers at the bus stops in al-Salama and Rahima 'as they boarded the buses to go to work that they were to attend a mass meeting in front of the Labour Offices after 5:00 that evening'.[88] Aramco stopped the construction of fences the same evening after an intervention by the local amirs and ʿUtaishan, whom the company management later suspected of having unduly tolerated the disorder or even of having made common cause with the protesters.[89]

Crossing the Lines, June 1956

Throughout the first half of 1956, unrest in the three oil towns persisted. In April, the American consul reported: 'mounting labor problems and conflicting pressures ... have placed local officials, particularly Amir Abd al-Muhsin [b. Jiluwi, brother of Amir Saʿud b. Jiluwi][90] and Turki ibn ʿUtaishan, in a position where they find it difficult to cooperate fully with company management'.[91] Dissatisfaction among the oil workers took on an even more open political spin with the nationalization of the Suez Canal and the pending conflict between Israel and its Arab neighbours. In early summer 1956, a group of workers and young men from the local towns sent a petition to King Saʿud, asking him to stop military cooperation with the United States. The men were arrested, closely interrogated and eventually released on the condition that they would never again meddle in political questions.[92]

In this political climate, the oil workers became even more determined to push their demands forward: in a famous move during a visit by King Saʿud to the oil operations area at the beginning of June 1956, a group of workers repeatedly attempted to approach his car convoy to hand him a petition, and felt bitterly disregarded when the king did not stop or even bother to make enquiries about their request.[93] On the evening of 9 June, a group of several hundred workers marched from the Labour Office building near al-Salama to the company main gate, where they gathered to welcome the king on his way to a banquet at Aramco headquarters.[94] When Saʿud and his entourage arrived at the gate, the workers committed an open offence: instead of the usual greetings and celebration, they shouted the slogan '*fa-l-yasquta-l-istiʿmar*' (down with imperialism) and raised banners that read '*mazlumin*' (we have been wronged) and '*nurid huquqana*' (we want our rights).[95] The king proceeded to the planned banquet. Meanwhile, more and more people crowded outside the main gate, reaching a total of two thousand, and when Saʿud again passed the gate on his departure, they repeated their slogans and raised their banners. The king was later reported to have ordered his bodyguards to seize the banners before he continued his journey to Dammam, where he was confronted by another group of demonstrators.[96] After Saʿud had left Dhahran, the local police started to disperse the crowd by force, leaving many demonstrators wounded.[97] The American consul later commented:

> This type of disorderly demonstration and shouting of demands is unusual in the Eastern Province and unprecedented at a formal gathering for the King. The King is reported to be disturbed at its occurrence, and he was noticed to be unusually silent and unsmiling at the banquet given in his honor the following evening.[98]

Within forty-eight hours of the demonstration ending, a royal decree banned all forms of collective labour action as well as any attempt to organize a strike.[99]

Only a few days after the demonstrations in front of the Aramco main gate in Dhahran, another rumour alerted the Saudi authorities: Saudi general workers were supposedly planning to storm the intermediate camp in Ras Tanura and burn down the cinema, to which they had repeatedly been denied access. In the course of the second week of June, groups of Saudi general workers and non-employees 'forced their way into the theater and ... began throwing stones when they were refused admittance'.[100] As a response to these disturbances, the local amir and the provincial governor ordered additional police forces and *khawiya* to the gate of the intermediate camp. Nevertheless, in the late evening of 14 June, a group of several hundred workers 'forced their way into the camp, throwing stones and sticks'.[101] More policemen and *khawiya* were sent to Ras Tanura and finally quelled the unrest. The rioters were arrested and ten men publicly flogged the following day, receiving one hundred lashes each. The American consul later identified a number of the punished men as Shiites from Qatif who, he reported, had been mere members of the crowd and 'in no sense ringleaders'. At least two of the flogged died, one of them a thirteen-year-old boy from Qatif.[102]

In the afternoon of 16 June, Aramco's Saudi employees were summoned to the main gates in the three oil towns, where Labour Office representatives publicly proclaimed the government decision 'to expand benefits or meet the demands of workers in the fields of education, health, dossiers on workers, employment conditions, job standards, etc.'[103] However, this move did not succeed in suffocating the unrest among the Saudi workforce. A number of workers planned again to go on strike, whilst others hurried to leave the oil towns to find refuge in their hometowns and villages due to the prospect of new troubles.[104] The provincial government then started a province-wide arrest campaign. Suspected strikers were rounded up at their workplaces or in their homes. For those who had gone into hiding, family members were taken into custody. After the first round of arresting mainly Aramco employees, the authorities proceeded with the local population, presumably as a warning to potential subversives and those who had taken part in the workers' protests. Between three and five hundred detainees were brought to a place widely known as the Qasr al-ʿAbid (prison of slaves), where they were interrogated and tortured.[105]

The unrest and mass arrests of 1956 marked a temporary peak in the violent confrontation between oil workers, the local population and the state. The second half of the decade were years of relative tranquillity in which the oil company and government addressed, with mixed results, the most acute problems of the housing and status of the Saudi oil workers, while opposition against authoritarian rule and political and economic marginalization realigned itself outside the realms of direct confrontation with the government. In 1957, Aramco's housing loan scheme for its Saudi employees was expanded to include Rahima and Madinat Abqaiq.[106] Al-Salama was omitted from long-term planning and torn down in 1980/81.[107] Meanwhile, the presence of large Saudi security forces in the oil operations area became permanent.[108] New confrontations between oil workers, local population and the state erupted in the 1960s. The protests of 1953–1956 can be further, though by no means exclusively, understood as a prelude to Shiite opposition against a discriminating government, which would break through the surface of political conflict in the late 1970s.

Conclusion

Structural and physical violence in Saudi Arabian oil towns between 1953 and 1956 revealed and deepened emerging antagonisms between the Saudi Arabian government and the industrial and local population over modes of rule and control, and more general questions of welfare and citizenship. Despite its relative weakness in terms of organization and internal cohesion, the Saudi Arabian state played a decisive role in the protests of 1953–1956. The Saudi Arabian oil towns were not enclaves isolated from state rule, nor were company policies towards Saudi oil workers shaped outside the realms of government decisions. Yet, at this particular stage of Saudi history, the will and ability for the (traditional) allocation of resources from a paternalist ruler to his subjects were dissolving. At the same time, the Saudi state's policing capability still proved rather ineffective. What remained was keeping order among the Saudi oil workers and local population – if necessary by force.

Saudi authorities actively defended policies and patterns that eased the segmentation and marginalization of the Saudi workforce, most visible in the spatial segregation of the oil towns and the plan to erect fences around the general camps. Throughout the 1950s, state patronage of the oil workers remained half-hearted and achieved only limited results, and the conflict between the labour force and the company gradually developed into a conflict between the Saudi oil workers and the Saudi government. Saudi oil towns became manifestations of this conflict to the extent that the relationship between the Saudi government and the people was reflected in their organizational, spatial and discursive configurations. While the government increased the threat of violence in order to maintain compliance with repressive structures in the three oil towns, the oil workers mostly attacked physical constraints erected by the oil company and defended by the state authorities. The deepening antagonism between government and oil workers is illustrated, for instance, by the differing uses of company gates by both conflict parties. At these places of demarcation and control, the palpable boundaries between the foreign oil enterprise and the Saudi Arabian state were blurred to the point of obliteration. State authorities used the gates as places for disciplinary rituals and for the announcement of government decisions about relations between the Saudi labour force and the oil company. Quite understandably, the workers chose them as places of assembly and objects of seizure and conquest when targeting both the oil company and the state.

The resort to violence on a structural level became a central means of preventing any collective action by the oil workers. During the strike of 1953, the workers had proved rather effective in deploying their local networks and resources for the formation of a persistent opposition. Their social and geographical connections to the local towns and villages allowed them to mobilize their co-workers beyond the borders of their respective labour camps and to escape the police and military. This situation led the Saudi government to institutionalize a policy of control and force by establishing structures that aimed at preventing any effective mobilization of the oil workers. The permanent threat of violence in the form of a strong military presence in the oil production area developed into an intrinsic element of governing the growing industrial communities. The unison action of local Shiite and Sunni oil workers, who were mostly work-immigrants from more distant regions, is especially noteworthy, as it suggests that the harsh punishment of local Shiites by Saudi authorities intended to divide the labour movement and to cut it off from local support networks.

Physical violence by the protesters occurred at those stages of the conflict at which the dialogue between the conflicting parties broke down or at which the government increased the threat of violence in order to end negotiations on its own terms. The throwing of stones at buses and cars (means of transport reserved mainly for higher staff levels and state officials), the tearing down of fences, the storming of company gates and bodily attacks against security personnel can be comprehended as attacks against symbols of suppression and marginalization. They were furthermore attempts to continue negotiations when alternative modes of bargaining had failed. The series of failed negotiations, symbolic attacks and bodily violence[109] came into operation in all cases, although the protests against the fencing in of labour camps in 1955 show that the state authorities were occasionally willing to make concessions to the workers and thus to stop the fatal cycle of violence. Yet, the ability and will of state authorities to resolve conflicts through personal intervention was declining, and the use of 'effective' force took its place more often. As a result, individuals were perceived as mere objects of control or agents of systemic repression that needed to literally be overcome in the pursuit of a certain aim. Hence, the processes of state building, industrial and urban growth, and parallel administrative expansion produced an intrinsic logic of structural and physical violence that often replaced alternative modes of conflict resolution in the following decades.

Notes

This chapter is a result of the joint ZMO–SOAS programme 'Urban Violence in the Middle East between Empire and Nation State', financed by the German

DFG and the British AHRB. I would like to thank Ulrike Freitag, Nelida Fuccaro, Nora Lafi, Rasmus Elling, Fatemeh Masjedi, Nushin Atmaca and Amer Ghrawi for their valuable thoughts and comments on this chapter. I am especially grateful to Jim Mandaville for his tireless efforts in collecting maps and pictures, and for his critical and immensely helpful comments.

1. The provincial status of al-Hasa originated in Ottoman administration. When the provinces of the kingdom were reorganized in 1953, al-Hasa was added to the newly established Eastern Province. The seat of the provincial government was moved from the old town Hofuf to the new administrational centre Dammam. Depending on the time and context, I will refer either to al-Hasa or the Eastern Province.
2. I. Seccombe and R. Lawless. 1987. *Work Camps and Company Towns: Settlement Patterns and the Gulf Oil Industry*, University of Durham: Centre for Middle Eastern and Islamic Studies, 41.
3. For the impact of the oil industry on Saudi Arabian internal and foreign politics, see T. Al-Shaikh. 1988. *Al-Bitrul wa-'l-Siyasa fi-l-Mamlaka al-ʿal- ʿArabiyya al-Saʿudiyya*, London: Dar al-Safa li-l-Nashr wa-l-Tawziʿ. A comprehensive study of the role of the oil industry in the modernization process in Saudi Arabia, and especially al-Hasa, can be found in A. Thamir al-Ahmari. 2007. *Dawr Sharikat al-Zayt al-ʿArabiyya al-Amrikiyya (Aramku) fi Tanmiyat al-Mintaqa al-sharqiyya min al-Mamlaka al-ʿArabiyya al-Saʿudiyya*, Riyadh: ʿAbd al-Rahman b. ʿAbdallah Thamir al-Ahmari.
4. Saudi Arabian nationals constituted about 60 per cent of the Aramco workforce: R. Lebkirchner, G. Rentz and M. Steineke. 1960. *Aramco Handbook*, New York: Arabian American Oil Company, 161. About four-fifths of Aramco's Saudi workforce originated in al-Hasa and nearby areas: I. Al-Elawy. 1976. *The Influence of Oil upon Settlement in al-Hasa Oasis, Saudi Arabia*, doctoral thesis, University of Durham: Department of Geography, 249. There exists no official statistical data on the religious composition of Aramco's workforce in the early 1950s. Vidal estimated the ratio between Sunnis and Shiites in al-Hasa at 45:55 – F. Vidal. 1964. 'The Oasis of al-Hasa', doctoral thesis, Cambridge, MA: Harvard University, 73. Statistical information presented by Al-Elawy and Al-Shuaiby implies that, in the 1950s, Shiites were only slightly overrepresented in the Saudi Aramco workforce: Al-Elawy, *The Influence of Oil*, 249; A. Al-Shuaiby. 1976. *The Development of the Eastern Region with Particular Reference to Urban Settlement and Evolution in Eastern Saudi Arabia*, doctoral thesis, University of Durham: Faculty of Social Sciences, 257, 322, 354.
5. See, for example, H. Lackner. 1978. *A House Built on Sand: A Political Economy of Saudi Arabia*, London: Ithaca Press, 89–109; J. Buchan. 1982. 'Secular and Religious Opposition in Saudi Arabia', in T. Niblock (ed.), *State, Society and Economy in Saudi Arabia*, London: Croom Helm, 106–24; M. Abir. 1993. *Saudi Arabia: Government, Society and the Gulf Crisis*, New York and London: Routledge, 32–39.
6. R. Vitalis. 2007. *America's Kingdom: Mythmaking on the Saudi Oil Frontier*, Stanford, CA: Stanford University Press.

7. I have reviewed a large part of these sources and interpreted them anew in the light of secondary sources in Arabic and English, and of interviews held during field research in Saudi Arabia in 2012 and 2013.
8. For a relational understanding of collective violence in contentious politics, see C. Tilly. 2003. *The Politics of Collective Violence*, Cambridge: Cambridge University Press, 5–7, 20–21.
9. J. Ferguson. 2005. 'Seeing Like an Oil Company: Space, Security, and Global Capital in Neoliberal Africa', *American Anthropologist* 107(3), 380.
10. J. Galtung. 1990. 'Cultural Violence', *Journal of Peace Research* 27(3), 294. Italics from the original. For the development of the concept by Galtung and its critics, see K.M. Weigert. 2010. 'Structural Violence', in G. Fink (ed.), *Stress of War, Conflict and Disaster*, Amsterdam and Boston: Academic Press, 126–33.
11. Galtung, 'Cultural Violence', 294.
12. Such threats of violence mark the liminal space between structural and physical violence, and are usually applied by those whom Charles Tilly called 'violent specialists', i.e. military, police, executioners, etc. 'The genuinely effective specialist deploys *threats* of violence so persuasively that others comply before the damage begins.' Tilly, *The Politics of Collective Violence*, 36.
13. M. Watts. 2001. 'Petro-Violence: Community, Extraction, and Political Ecology of a Mythic Commodity', in N.L. Peluso and M. Watts (eds), *Violent Environments*, Ithaca, NY: Cornell University Press, 212. My own insertion.
14. R.K. Krimly. 1993. 'The Political Economy of Rentier States: A Case Study of Saudi Arabia in the Oil Era, 1950–1990', doctoral thesis, Ann Arbor: University of Michigan, 145–49.
15. U. Pfullmann. 1996. 'Politische Strategien Ibn Saʿuds Beim Aufbau des Dritten Saudischen Staates: Eine Historische Studie Unter Besonderer Berücksichtigung des Deutschen Archivmaterials', *Leipziger Beiträge zur Orientforschung* 8, Frankfurt am Main: Peter Lang, 415–18. Oil revenues exceeded the mark of 200 million US dollars in 1952: Al-Elawy, *The Influence of Oil*, 245.
16. Georgetown University Library Special Collections Research Center, William E. Mulligan Papers (hereafter: Mulligan Papers), Box 2, Folder 38, ARD, Chronological Files, March 1953, 'Distribution by Grade of Saudi Employees 1949–1953'.
17. C. Hicke. 1995. *American Perspectives of Aramco: The Saudi Arabian Oil Producing Company, 1930s to 1980s*, Berkeley: University of California, 506.
18. S.A. Al-ʿAwwami. 2012. *Al-Haraka al-Wataniyya Sharq al-Saʿudiyya 1373–1393 H/1953–1973 M: Al-Juzʾ Al-ʾAwwal*, Beirut: Riyad al-Rayyis al-Kutub wa-l-Nashr, 112.
19. K. Ehsani. 2003. 'Social Engineering and the Contradictions of Modernization in Khuzestan's Company Towns: A Look at Abadan and Masjed-Soleyman', *International Review of Social History* 48(3), 376.
20. Ibid., 379–81.
21. Interview in Riyadh, March 2012. Foreign observers usually drew connections between the temporary absentees of the provincial amir and outbreaks of unrest: Department of State Instruction, 29 December 1953,

National Archives and Records Administration, Washington, DC (hereafter: NARA) RG 59 886A.062/12-2953; Dhahran to State, 20 May 1954, enclosure 1, NARA RG 59 886A.062/5-2054.
22. The ruling amirs did not necessarily originate from the local elites, but were often appointed governors with family ties or proven loyalty to the Al-Saʿud, as in the case of the Amir of al-Hasa, Saʿud b. Jiluwi, who had inherited the office from his father, a cousin and loyal combatant of the King ʿAbd al-ʿAziz b. Saʿud: Krimly, 'The Political Economy of Rentier States', 146–47. The office of the local amir was usually hereditary within the most prominent local families who had already administered their respective communities prior to the founding of the present Saudi state: Vidal, 'The Oasis of al-Hasa', 70–71. A general idea of the state institutions concerned with public security in al-Hasa can be derived from J. ʿAli Bak. 1951. 'Hadithuna al-Shahri: Rihlati ila-l-Zahran wa-Shimal al-Mamlaka', *Al-Manhal* 5, 222–24. The daily routines of maintaining law and order in the three oil towns are described in: Hicke, *American Perspectives*, 411–12.
23. Interview in Dammam, May 2013.
24. Al-ʿAwwami, *Al-Haraka al-Wataniyya*, 112–13.
25. Dhahran to State, 28 July 1954, enclosure 2, NARA RG 59 890F.5045/7-2845.
26. Thamir al-Ahmari, *Dawr Sharikat al-Zayt al-ʿArabiyya al-Amrikiyya*, 165–66.
27. A former general oil worker and resident of Rahima who had started his employment with Aramco in 1957 described the prospect of escaping the adverse living conditions in the general camp as a strong motivation for him to obtain a better education and to rise to a higher staff level: Interview in Dhahran, May 2013.
28. Personal communication with J.P. Mandaville.
29. Interview in al-Khobar, May 2013.
30. J. Parsinnen and K. Talib. 1982. 'The Development of Dhahran (Saudi Camp) as a Community', in I. Serageldin and S. El-Sadek (eds), *The Arab City: Its Character and Islamic Cultural Heritage*, Arlington: Arab Urban Development Institute/Arab Towns Organization, 180.
31. Mulligan Papers, Box 3, Folder 1, ARD, Chronological Files, May–June 1960, 'Preliminary Report Baladiyah Election Rahima', 22 May 1960.
32. Information on who financed these mosques varies. While some claim that donations from workers and local business families had helped to build the mosques in the general camps, others state that they were paid for by the government or, as in the case of the early big mosque in al-Salama, by the King himself: Interview in al-Khobar, May 2013; personal communication with J.P. Mandaville.
33. Dhahran to Jidda, memorandum covering the period June 4 through 7 June 1947, NARA RG 84 125.66/Waldo E. Bailey/db.
34. Dhahran to State, 19 July 1946, NARA RG 59 890F.00/7-1946 CS/A; Personal communication from a former Aramco employee, March 2013; the practice is further described in a vast number of auto-biographical works like M.S. Cheney. 1958. *Big Oil Man From Arabia*, New York: Ballantine Books, 17–18; J. Arnold. 1964. *Golden Swords and Pots and Pans*, London:

Victor Gollanz Limited, 206–7; F. Basrawi. 2009. *Brownies and Kalashnikovs: A Saudi Woman's Memoir of American Arabia and Wartime Beirut*, Reading: South Street Press, 54–56; K. Bird. 2010. *Crossing Mandelbaum Gate: Coming of Age between the Arabs and Israelis, 1956–1978*, London: Simon & Schuster, 115–16.

35. See Tilly, *The Politics of Collective Violence*, 81–101.
36. References to the reputation of Sa'ud b. Jiluwi as the king's strongman who kept order among the Saudi workforce are legion. See, for example, N. Al-Sa'id. 1980. *Tarikh Al Sa'ud*, Beirut: Manshurat Ittihad Sha'b al-Jazira al-'Arabiyya, 151–52; A.K. Hamud. 1973. 'Sharikat Aramku wa-'l-'Amal: al-Thawra al-'Amal', in A. 'Attar (ed.), *Al-Haraka al-Taharruriyya fi-l-Hijaz wa-l-Najd 1901–1973*, Beirut: Ma'tuq Ikhwan, 65–68; Cheney, *Big Oil Man*, 68–69.
37. Al-Sa'id, *Tarikh Al Sa'ud*, 791-794; Dhahran to State, July 28, 1945, NARA RG 59 890F.5045/7-2845.
38. Interview with a grandson of the Shaykh of Safwa, Washington, DC, June 2012.
39. Krimly, *The Political Economy of Rentier States*, 146; J. Kostiner. 1993. *The Making of Saudi Arabia 1916–1936: From Chieftaincy to Monarchical State*, New York and Oxford: Oxford University Press, 190–91.
40. Jidda to State, 10 October 1952, NARA RG 59 786A.34/7-1052.
41. Jidda to State, 5 February 1951, NARA RG 59 886A.01/1-2651; Dhahran to State, 30 August 1951, NARA RG 59 886A.06/8-3051; Thamir al-Ahmari, *Dawr Sharikat al-Zayt al-'Arabiyya al-Amrikiyya*, 180.
42. Dhahran to State, 4 November 1953, NARA RG 59 886A.062/11-453.
43. Jidda to State, 29 September 1953, NARA RG 59 886A.2553/9-2953.
44. Dhahran to State, 4 November 1953, NARA RG 59 886A.062/11-453.
45. Dhahran to State, 4 November 1953, enclosure D, NARA RG 59 886A.062/11-453.
46. Al-'Awwami, *Al-Haraka al-Wataniyya*, 95–96, 100; Dhahran to State, 4 November 1953, NARA RG 59 886.A.062/11-453.
47. Jidda to State, 11 October 1953, NARA RG 59 886A.2553/10-1153.
48. Dhahran to State, 20 May 1954, enclosure 2, NARA RG 59 886A.062/5-2054.
49. Dhahran to State, 4 November 1953, NARA RG 59 886A.062/11-453.
50. Dhahran to State, 5 November 1953, NARA RG 59 886A.062/11-553.
51. Dhahran to State, 4 November 1953, NARA RG 59 886A.062/11-453.
52. Dhahran to State, 16 October 1953, NARA RG 59 886A.062/10-1653. According to Al-'Awwami, the buses were company buses used by Americans to travel to al-Khobar and Dammam for their weekend shopping: Al-'Awwami, *Al-Haraka al-Wataniyya*, 101, 114.
53. Al-'Awwami, *Al-Haraka al-Wataniyya*, 104; Interview in Dhahran, May 2013.
54. Dhahran to State, 4 November 1953, NARA RG 59 886A.062/11-453.
55. Dhahran to State, 20 October 1953, NARA RG 59 886A.062/10-2053.
56. Dhahran to State, 4 November 1953, NARA RG 59 886A.062/11-453.
57. Dhahran to State, 4 November 1953, NARA RG 59 886A.062/11-453.

58. Dhahran to State, enclosure to A-130, 3 June 1968, NARA RG 59 POL 18 Saud. It is possible, that the report confuses the mentioned *khawiya* with Mujahidin, the non-uniformed Bedouin irregular militia, as it mentions that the forces in question were sent from the central region of Najd.
59. Dhahran to State, 4 November 1953, NARA RG 59 886A.062/11-453. For the traditional role of the *khawiya* in al-Hasa, see Vidal, 'The Oasis of al-Hasa', 73.
60. State to Dhahran, 29 December 1953, NARA RG 59 886A.062/12-2953.
61. The use of contract workers, presumably Indians and Pakistanis, to maintain oil production at a high level seems to have led to rising resentment among Saudi workers towards third-nation workers: Hamud, 'Sharikat Aramku wa al-ʿAmal', 57.
62. Dhahran to State, 4 November 1953, NARA RG 59 886A.062/11-453. My own insertion.
63. Congregation halls for Shia commemorative ceremonies, which take a central role during Muharram festivities.
64. Al-ʿAwwami, *Al-Haraka al-Wataniyya*, 104.
65. Ibid.; Interviews in Dhahran, Dammam and Darin, May 2013.
66. King ʿAbd al-ʿAziz had died on 9 November 1953.
67. Jidda to State, 23 January 1954, NARA RG 59 886A.062/1-2354.
68. Jidda to State, 23 January 1954, enclosure 1, NARA RG 59 886A.062/1-2354.
69. This step meant a reorganization of the Labour Office in Dammam, a government institution that mediated conflicts between Saudi workers and companies in Eastern Province. Quite contrary to the interest of the government, the local labour offices would play a central role in organizing labour activities in the coming one-and-a-half decades.
70. Dhahran to State, 8 February 1954, NARA RG 59 886A.062/2-854. My own insertion.
71. Jidda to State, 4 November 1953, NARA RG 59 786A.5/11-353.
72. Jidda to State, 4 November 1953, NARA RG 59 786A.5/11-453. My own insertion.
73. Jidda to State, 29 December 1953, NARA RG 59 786A.5/12-2953.
74. State to Jidda, 5 June 1954, NARA RG 59 786A.5 MSP/6-554; Jidda to State, 22 June 1954, NARA RG 59 786A.5MSP/6-2154.
75. Dhahran to State, 20 May 1954, NARA RG 59 886A.062/5-1954.
76. Dhahran to State, 20 May 1954, NARA RG 59 886A.062/5-2054.
77. Dhahran to State, 23 May 1954, NARA RG 59 886A.062/5-2354.
78. Jidda to State, 1 September 1954, NARA RG 59, 786A.5 MSP/9-154. My own insertion. Some of the military equipment was probably also used in the Buraimi dispute between Saudi Arabia and Great Britain.
79. Dhahran to State, 19 May 1955, NARA RG 59 886A.2553/5-1955.
80. Ibid.
81. Dhahran to State, 17 June 1955, NARA RG 59 886A.2553/6-1755.
82. Dhahran to State, 19 May 1955, NARA RG 59 886A.2553/5-1955.
83. Dhahran to State 17 May 1955, NARA RG 59 886A.2553/5-1755; Dhahran to State, 10 May 1955, NARA RG 59 886A.2553/5-1055.

84. Jidda to State, 31 May 1955, NARA RG 59 786A.52/5-3155.
85. Dhahran to State, 29 May 1955, NARA RG 59 886A.2553/5-2655. My own insertion.
86. The year 1955 had witnessed an unsuccessful attempt by members of the Saudi military in Taʾif to overthrow the rule of King Saʿud: Jidda to State, 26 July 1955, NARA RG 59 786A.52/7-2655. The Saudi government was further troubled by the activities of several subversive political groups from inside and outside the country who openly attacked the present regime: Jidda to State, 31 May 1955, NARA RG 59 786A.52/5-3155.
87. Dhahran to State, 14 January 1956, NARA RG 59 886A.2553/1-1456.
88. Dhahran to State, 21 January 1956, memorandum to file in confidential by T.C. Barger, 30 January 1956, NARA 886A.06/1-3056 CS/HHH.
89. Dhahran to State, 14 January 1956, NARA RG 59 886A.2553/1-1456.
90. Amir Saʿud b. Jiluwi repeatedly left Saudi Arabia for medical treatment in the United States and Europe. During his long absences, his brother, ʿAbd al-Muhsin b. Jiluwi, took over the office of the provincial governor.
91. Dhahran to State, 17 April 1956, NARA RG 59 786A.11/4-1756. My own insertion.
92. Hamud, 'Sharikat Aramku wa-l-ʿAmal', 57–62.
93. Ibid., 62–63.
94. Dhahran to State, 13 June 1956, NARA RG 59 786A.11/6-1356.
95. Hamud, 'Sharikat Aramku wa-l-ʿAmal', 62.
96. Dhahran to State, 13 June 1956, NARA RG 59 786A.11/6-1356; Dhahran to State, 14 July 1956, NARA 886A.062/7-1456. Apparently, the demonstrators in Dammam had also staged a protest in front of the Amirate building, the seat of the provincial government: interview in Dhahran, 17 May 2013.
97. Hamud, 'Sharikat Aramku wa-l-ʿAmal', 63.
98. Dhahran to State, 13 June 1956, NARA RG 59 786A.11/6-1356.
99. Dhahran to State, 30 June 1956, enclosure 1, NARA RG 59 886A.062/6-3056.
100. Dhahran to State, 20 June 1956, NARA RG 59 886A.062/6-2056.
101. Ibid.
102. Dhahran to State, 14 July 1956, NARA RG 59 886A.062/7-1456.
103. Dhahran to State, 20 June 1956, NARA RG 59 886A.062/6-2056.
104. Ibid.
105. Hamud, 'Sharikat Aramku wa-l-ʿAmal', 65–68; Dhahran to State, 14 July 1956, NARA RG 59 886A.062/7-1456.
106. Thamir al-Ahmari, *Al-Haraka al-Wataniyya*, 183.
107. T. Parssinen and K. Talib. 1982. 'A Traditional Community and Modernization: Saudi Camp, Dhahran', *Journal of Architectural Education* 35, 14–17.
108. Troops of the government-loyal White Army (National Guard) were permanently stationed at the road leading from Dammam to al-Khobar via Dhahran: Dhahran to State, weekly summary A-144, 8 January 1964, NARA RG 59 POL 2 SAUD.
109. This is an adaptation of Charles Tilly's 'Typology of Interpersonal Violence': Tilly, *The Politics of Collective Violence*, 14–16.

⸎· Afterword ·⸎

Urban Injustice, Urban Violence and the Revolution
Reflections on Cairo

KHALED ADHAM

Revolutions are like deep tectonic shifts. They result from the sudden release of human energies that create a violent, seismic tidal wave of change, their energies rollicking headily towards the prevailing, dominant political powers and organizational structures – and when successful, causing their replacement in a relatively short period of time. The early signs of these impending ruptures are scattered coyly in the occasional surface eruptions or in the acceleration of motion in the various interrelated tectonic social, economic and political plates. True, the manner, form and time of these sudden, deep tectonic shifts are impossible to predict. But that they will occur is almost certain, particularly when social injustice prevails and there is a social momentum to turn things around. Moreover, these sudden energy eruptions are not only played out in the brick and mortar urban spaces of the city, but going further, I will argue that their precursors, their surface eruptions and indeed their causes are to be found to a large extent in the spatiality of social injustice. The events of the Egyptian revolution of 25 January 2011, therefore, have to be situated in the context of the spatiality of injustice.

The emphasis that the Egyptian January revolution is directly linked to the systemic violence inherent in the urban practices of the past few decades does not mean that issues related to the spatiality of injustice or class struggle were the only driving forces triggering the revolution. What was striking to participants and observers of the Egyptian revolution, particularly during the first eighteen days, was the sense of unity exhibited on Midan al-Tahrir among the different social, economic, religious and political groups, manifested in the improvised medical care, the communal food supplies and the scene of the Copts performing a mass for the revolutions' martyrs protected by a ring of Muslims.[1] In fact, many of the capitalist Egyptian bourgeoisie felt as alienated as the other classes and social groups had under the former Mubarak regime, and therefore participated in the uprising: did they not suffer from the same corruption, bribery, nepotism and absence of law enforcement in matters related to the protection and expansion of their private property? Moreover, economic inequalities are not, of course, unique to Egypt. During the January uprising, someone commented that if inequality is the cause of the revolution, then the United States is next.[2]

While in this chapter the focus is on how the social injustice inherent in the recent urban practices was a prominent factor in triggering the uprising, I will argue that it is still too early to pinpoint with certainty other causes of and reasons for its outbreak. Today, we are not far enough away from it to be able to be relatively unaffected by the frenzied enthusiasm or disenchantment of those who saw it through.[3] I believe that Hegel was correct when he wrote, in the preface to his *Philosophy of Right*, that 'the owl of Minerva spreads its wings only with the falling of the dusk', by which he meant that philosophy, true wisdom, symbolized by the Roman goddess of wisdom, Minerva, understands reality only after the event.[4] I contend that the time has not yet come when deep questions about the January revolution can be answered; that today we are not yet in a position to see these memorable events in their true perspective, and so not yet able to pass judgment on them. For I believe we are still in the middle of an ongoing revolution. So at this historical juncture, for our initial understanding of what has happened and what is happening from an urban, spatial perspective, it is instructive to look at Cairo's pre-revolution urban spatial practices, to search for the signs and occasional surface eruptions, to rummage about for the urban spatial causes and to investigate the actual unfolding of revolutionary events in the city's urban spaces.

Urban Injustice, Violence and Revolution

It might be appropriate to begin this chapter by first pointing out how I understand the relationship between the words 'injustice', 'violence' and 'revolution'. In its lexical meaning, injustice refers to the violation of the rights of others.[5] In spatial terms, it is a violation of the 'right to the city', to use the words of the Marxist and social theorist Henri Lefebvre.[6] Violation, on the other hand, is an act of infringement and transgression: to violate is to disrespectfully transgress physical, symbolic, administrative or judicial boundaries. The spatiality of injustice is a spatiality that violates, transgresses, the right to the city.

Violence, like its related linguistic form 'violation', is also a form of transgression. Violence is commonly understood as physical aggression and transgression. In its lexical meaning, it refers to the use of physical force with the intention of causing either personal injury or physical damage. But violence is not only the visible form of transgression, of crime and terror, civil unrest or war performed by a clearly identified agent. This is subjective violence, Slavoj Žižek tells us.[7] According to him, there is a second type of violence that he terms 'systemic' violence: the catastrophic consequences of the smooth, surreptitious, transgressive functioning of economic and political systems.[8] It is this form of violence that I am interested in here. Thus, revolutions can be viewed as moments of violations from both sides. A revolutionary is indeed violating, transgressing, the dominant regime's established order. Thus, revolutions are violence against violence; they are violations against systemic violence, against the contours of the background that generates such revolutionary outbursts. Having laid this out, I now want to look at the early spatial violations and urban surface eruptions against the contours of authority that prefigured the revolution.

Urban Signs and Precursors

Urban and political historians are beginning to ask when and where the first signs and symptoms of a budding revolutionary spirit against the authority of the former Egyptian regime became manifest in the public realm; however, as stated above, it is too difficult at this point to have clear answers to these questions. During the past decade and despite all the visible signs of public contestations against the former Mubarak regime, most observers had no inkling that something of this magnitude might happen. Even those who believed that change was imminent did not, in their wildest dreams, think about its eventual scenario. Now, looking back at the earlier urban signs and events, one realizes that, not unlike the warning written on rear-view mirrors of automobiles, it was indeed closer than what we thought.

The social urban historian Richard Sennett offers an interesting entry point for looking back at how authorities begin to disintegrate. Sennett tells us that the root Latin meaning of *auctoritas*, from which authority is derived, is protector, the guardian who cares for those who cannot care for themselves or the advisor of those who are uncertain.[9] Authority in this root sense, concludes Sennett, is about much more than sheer domination and far from being a humiliating figure of oppression. I will argue that during the past few decades numerous local and national events proved to Egyptians that the former Mubarak regime was failing to provide the protection and care expected from it as ruler, and it was hence losing its authority in the eyes of the majority even before the outburst of the revolution. Thus we find even today that, for Egyptians, authority is understood to mean an oppressive, humiliating, violent force that cares only for those within its immediate orbit.

Although discontent with the authorities began to appear in various manifestations in the public sphere, street protests remained the most visible signs and precursors of the revolution.[10] In an article published in the New York Times, the late Anthony Shadid wrote that a popular Egyptian novel, *Utopia*, which is set in a future Cairo, quotes a character explaining an uprising.[11] 'As the saying goes, "the rock endured many blows, but only shattered at the fiftieth". It's not the fiftieth blow that did that, but all the previous ones.'[12] During the period between 2004 and 2010, an estimated 2 million people from all walks of life took to the streets in demonstrations, strikes, gatherings and sit-ins to protest against the government. True, some of these public discontents were spontaneous, erupting in response to a specific event perceived as a failure of public policy, such as the outburst of violence in the wake of the 2008 rockslide on Muqattam Hills that killed more than three hundred people, the 2006 sinking of the Al-Salam Boccaccio 98 that drowned more than thirteen hundred people, and the 2002 blaze on board a train that killed nearly four hundred people.

The majority of these public contestations, however, were planned in advance to protest against laws and procedures governing economic and political decision making as well as against police brutality and violence, reflecting a growing degree of political consciousness.[13] Using data collected from the Land Centre for Human Rights, Joel Beinin tells us that there were nearly two thousand street protests between the years 2004 and 2008, a surge compared with the data that had been collected four years earlier, which estimated around seven hundred protests.[14] In fact, adding the number of protests in 2009 and 2010, the total figure of protests since 1998 comfortably crosses the three thousand mark. These numerous surface eruptions of discontent in a sense prefigured the January revolution; they were the forty-nine stones thrown at the regime, to use the words of the fictional character quoted by Shadid above. They were also the unplanned rehearsals leading up to the big drama.[15]

Rehearsals in Urban Spaces

Some of the early stones thrown, worth mentioning here, are the demonstrations organized by the Sixth of April Youth Movement, one of the leading youth groups that started the January uprising. Rather than focusing on downtown Cairo or in front of high-profile buildings like many other earlier political demonstrations, such as those organized by the Kefaya Movement, every one of these organized protests started in a different location around the city, usually a small public space in a residential neighbourhood or an informal settlement. These urban locations were strategically selected to be far removed from the customary public spaces of demonstrations familiar to security forces; they were also densely populated areas so that the demonstrators could reach out to a wide audience. Prior to every staging, the organizers calculated the time that it would take the participants to complete the different parts of the route. Its termination point was carefully chosen, usually near a transportation hub from where the demonstrators could easily disperse before the arrival of the security forces. An example of this type of demonstration is the one organized in November 2010 in the district of Imbaba, Giza.[16] Blowing whistles, waving flags and carrying signs condemning the killers of the blogger Khaled Said, around two hundred activists demonstrated in al-Qawmiyya al-ʿArabiyya Street, a relatively broad street in the densely populated neighbourhood of Ard al-Gamaʿi-yya. The demonstrators traversed the street, from al-Buhi Square to the Cairo Ring Road, in what an earlier rehearsal calculated would take around forty minutes. The termination of the street was the Cairo Ring Road, where some of the collective had parked their private vehicles, while others were dispatched in public transportation, long before the security forces took any notice. Let me briefly describe how these rehearsals worked out spatially on the day of the uprising.[17]

Like earlier protests, the organizers of the 25 January demonstration set up an operations room to discuss and plan the details, including innovative mechanisms of protesting aimed at overcoming the methods that the security police always used to pre-empt demonstrations and protests.[18] One of the security methods for clamping down on earlier demonstrations was to arrest activists the day before the protest. 'This is why', says Ahmed Maher, one of the main founders of the Sixth of April Movement, 'a small committee was formed, with only the members of this committee being aware of the details of the protests, especially regarding the locations where protests were scheduled to set off from.'[19] Maher tells us that the committee organized cells of between thirty and fifty activists; each cell was to meet at a preselected spot in Cairo known

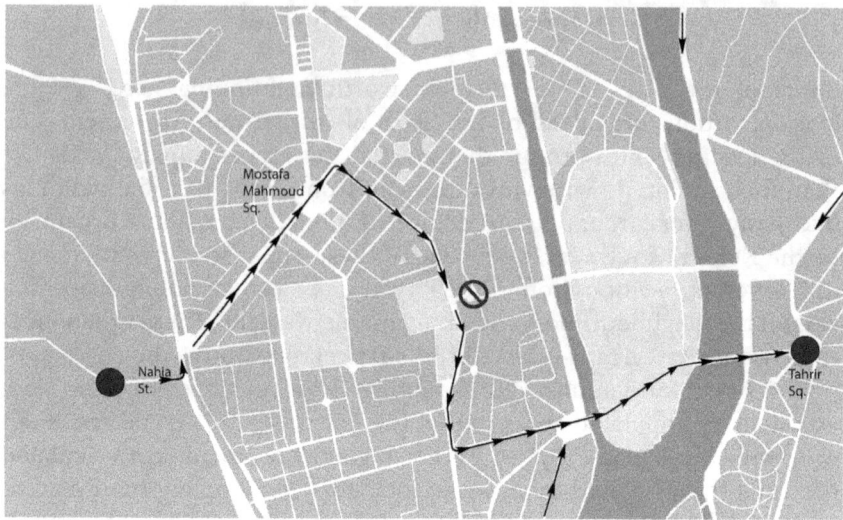

Figure 12.1. The route of the main demonstration to Midan al-Tahrir on 25 January 2011.

in advance to only a few people in each cell, who would later direct the other cell activists to that place.

While the organizers selected several squares around the metropolis as their initial urban spaces of contestation, a decision was taken to proceed to Midan al-Tahrir as the final converging place for all demonstrations coming from different parts of the metropolis, but only if demonstrators reached a large number.[20] In the Giza area, the strategically located Mustafa Mahmud Square was selected as the first meeting place for demonstrators. In addition to the square being in the heart of a relatively affluent neighbourhood, hence more visible to the media and the more influential members of the general public, it was also close to four densely populated 'informal areas' (i.e. neighbourhoods that developed piecemeal without formal planning), where the organizers greatly relied on mobilizing their youth, namely, Bulaq al-Dakrur, ʿArd Al-Liwaʾ, Mit ʿUqba and Imbaba. One of the major cells was to set off the demonstration from the neighbourhood of Bulaq al-Dakrur, specifically, from Nahiyya Street. Following the usual procedure, the walk to the square from Nahiyya Street was rehearsed and the options for overcoming some of the route difficulties were discussed. For example, a railway separated Nahiyya Street from Gamaʿat al-Duwwal al-ʿArabiyya Street, which leads directly to the square, leaving two options for making the necessary crossing: a flyover and a pedestrian bridge. The pedestrian bridge was narrow, rendering it not only very difficult to move the hoped for number of demonstrators, but also more vulnerable to police blockage. The flyover was therefore selected, and a plan to block the incoming vehicular traffic to allow the protestors to cross was executed on the day of the demonstration.

Another problem was the difficulty of assembling the demonstrators in busy Nahiyya Street, which was always full of traffic and street vendors. To overcome this problem, the Nahiyya cell was divided into several subcells; each one congregated in one of the narrow alleys perpendicular to Nahiyya Street. As the furthest subcell moved eastward towards the crossing point, other subcells successively joined the demonstration. This strategy, which the organizers dubbed the 'Snowball Strategy', was devised throughout the demonstration trajectory until reaching Mustafa Mahmud Square. Not only did the strategy solve the problem of street density, it also gave the appearance of a rapidly enlarging crowd, which indeed acted as a catalyst on the psyche of the non-activists, inducing more people to join. An estimated five thousand demonstrators set off along Nahiyya Street, many more than the organizers had anticipated. When the crowd reached the square in Muhandisin, the total number had more than quadrupled. For the organizers, the crowd was considered large enough to proceed to Midan al-Tahrir. The 5 km march to Midan al-Tahrir first moved through al-Batal Ahmad ʿAbd al-ʿAziz Street until it reached Sixth of October Bridge. At this juncture, a decision was taken to avoid the bridge, even though it was the shortest route to Midan al-Tahrir, because it would have been too easy for the security apparatus to block and trap the demonstrators on top of the long, wide bridge. Instead and with the Snowball Strategy in mind, the demonstrators continued on to the more residential and dense areas of Tahrir Street, then over the narrower Qasr al-Nil Bridge and finally to Midan al-Tahrir where they converged with the other demonstrations coming from different parts of the city. The demonstrators' entry to Midan al-Tahrir marked the beginning of violent clashes, which erupted in the evening and continued throughout the following eighteen days in Midan al-Tahrir and other parts of Cairo, as well as in major urban spaces of other cities around the country, with more than eight hundred people killed and six thousand injured. Moreover, violent confrontations between demonstrators and organs of the interim authorities have continued intermittently since then, with more deaths and injuries. Although Midan al-Tahrir was transformed after the revolution to become the nation's *shaʿbi*, the vernacular for parliament, confrontations with the new authority spread to other urban spaces around the city, such as nearby Muhammad Mahmud Street, and in front of the governmental TV building and across the city in ʿAbbasiyya Square, where the Supreme Military Council's headquarters are located. Moreover, at one point, two diametrically opposed political positions, revolutionary and counterrevolutionary, became associated in the minds of people with two urban spaces, Midan al-Tahrir and Roxi Square, respectively.

Rehearsing Community: Street Celebrations

No doubt the earlier demonstrations that took place between 2004 and 2010 built spatial expertise, bravery and momentum for the January uprising. But these rehearsals were not limited to street protests; street celebrations, too, played a pivotal, complex role in the preparation for and the unfolding of the revolution. On several occasions in the past few years, millions of Egyptians have taken to the streets to celebrate their national football team's international achievements. Like street protests, these spontaneous, grand public gatherings were very important signs – precursors and unconscious preparations for the revolution. There is a connection between sports celebrations and the revolution that can be analysed at three different levels: first, there is the obvious, direct level connecting the forms and magnitudes of the celebrations of both types of events, particularly between the ones following Mubarak's resignation and those following the winning of international football games and tournaments.

There is also a second level, namely the similarities of their participants and of how these national street celebrations influenced the way they would later protest. In addition to showing them the power of collective energies, therefore, these celebrations functioned as rehearsals of collective action and influenced the street protests at a very pragmatic level. For example, many commentators are now beginning to acknowledge the key role played in the revolution by the organized soccer fans, known locally as 'Ultras'. Consisting of a mix of well-educated university graduates, workers and youths from many social levels in Egypt, the Ultras offered a platform for the revolutionaries to use their networks and organizational skills, particularly during the early days of the revolution. One video uploaded onto YouTube just a few days before the uprising reassured those intending to join the demonstrations that they need not be scared of the security forces, because they would be protected by the Ultras, who had experience of clashing with the police. According to Muhammad Bashir, from the first day of the demonstrations Ultras appeared most prominently on Qasr al-ʿAyni Street, then increased their activities on the subsequent days throughout the city, particularly in the neighbourhoods of Bulaq al-Dakrur, Giza and Shubra.[21] Moreover, ʿAmr

Figure 12.2. Street celebrations in 2010 for the national football team's winning of the African Cup of Nations.

'Izz tells us that many members of the Ultras heroically defended the frontlines of demonstrations during various clashes, from the famous Qasr al-Nil Confrontation on the Friday of Rage to the Battle of the Camel.[22] In short, Ultras played an important role in mobilizing a substantial number of demonstrators, in transferring and using their skills in and techniques of confronting the police forces, and in providing security amidst the ensuing lootings on 28 January when the police forces withdrew from the streets.[23]

Finally, there is a third, more hidden level connecting sports celebrations and the revolution. During these rare moments of collective jubilation and when social norms and behaviours are temporarily suspended, these street celebrations reveal to their participants their own deep longing and desire for unity and community, as opposed to individualism and the market. To put it differently, these events help to forge among the participants a shared sense of co-being and belonging, whose disappearance from contemporary public life is often lamented.

The most common explanation for the disappearance of the sense of belonging, and for the rise of individualism and other manifestations of social malaise, is to blame them on Egypt's economic and political reorientation in 1974 towards what is known as *Infitah*, or open-door economic policies (the policies of systemic violence).[24] Infitah is usually understood to mean the opening of virtually all doors to the importation of foreign goods and capital, and the gradual withdrawal of the state from an active role in the economy. This new political economy had all manner of social, political and indeed urban consequences. Economists and sociologists have often argued that, prior to the introduction of these policies, people's sense of loyalty and of belonging to the homeland was strong. Egyptians were committed to a project of national revival, had a strong feeling of community and were in general optimistic about the future. For its critics, the shift towards a consumer culture in the post-Infitah era resulted in a fragmented, decentred self, consisting of a multiplicity of consuming, desiring machines. In short, Infitah was responsible for the fragmentation of collective social life, the growing inequality in income distribution and the rising pessimism about the future for the majority of Egyptians.

My argument is that if political action assumes a connection between the emotions and the intellect, then, by reattaching the fragmented individual to the memory of the group, to the innate nostalgia for belonging to a larger community, these street celebrations intermittently exposed emotional bonds that were at once manifestations of discontent and rehearsals for the upcoming drama.[25] How this economic regime that produced social inequalities and divisions worked to reorganize and restructure Egyptian cities, creating a spatiality of injustice, is my main observation on the urban causes of the revolution.

Spatiality of Injustice and Systemic Violence

I will argue that since the days of Infitah, the subsequent authorities in Egypt were implicated through corruption or connections in establishing the contours of systemic violence by supplying a new class of neo-capitalists with the necessary power to monopolize a large segment of the economy. I will argue that the normal workings of the urban system, from housing and land markets to the strategies of developers and planners, tended towards a redistribution of resources in favour of the rich and more politically powerful. Therefore, a monopolistic capitalism and urban oligarchy consisting of an alliance between government and neo-capitalists characterizes much of the political economy of Cairo's recent urban history.

This urban oligarchy, which operated in recent times under the global economic mantra of neo-liberalism, was largely responsible for polarizing society into the haves and the have-nots. Salwa Ismail tells us that today it is estimated that around a thousand families maintain control of vast areas of the economy.[26] In the meantime, more than three-quarters of Egyptian households have a daily income of less than $1 (U.S.). It is striking how the unevenness and inequalities of wealth distribution were mirrored in the recent spatial expansions of the city of Cairo. The estimate is that the total area of all the luxurious housing comprises more than 250,000 acres, five times the area that comprised all of Cairo in the early 1970s.[27] The result has been a jumbled urbanity, an uncomfortable coexistence of enclaves of affluence amid mass squalor, a sharp rise of more than one hundred gated communities with a few thousand residents each, amid another hundred squatter communities with some 6 million inhabitants. Let me illustrate how corruption and connections were implicated in the systemic violence of land robberies since the real estate boom of the 1990s by first looking at one example of a mega project, namely Dreamland.[28]

In the rush for land that followed the privatization bonanza of the 1990s, Ahmed Bahgat, the chairman of the Bahgat Group and the progenitor of this project, managed to secure a 2,000-acre stretch along the Cairo–Oases desert road, a few kilometres west of the great pyramids of Giza. Bahgat is an industrialist who started building his empire by assembling Korean television sets and other electrical appliances. Timothy Mitchell tells us that the company expanded and, with a suspicious deal linked to senior military officers, began using military factories to build its own products. While the value of the land, which was originally

Figure 12.3. Dreamland.

a quarry, was estimated at less than 2 EGP per square metre at the time Bahgat bought it, just a few months later this went up to 200 EGP. This dramatic increase in land value was enough to make the land collateral for a huge bank loan, which Bahgat used to finance the construction of Dreamland. It is not clear how he managed to purchase this large tract, why the land value went up so much or why the National Bank of Egypt secured the loan and initially became a partner in developing the project. Rumours circulating at that time linked him to high officials in the former presidential offices. One of the architects who worked in the early stages of the project informed me that when Bahgat came to check and approve the final drawings, he arrived along with his partner and her husband, General Gamal.[29] It was only after the January revolution that I discovered that General Gamal was none other than Mubarak's secretary, Gamal ʿAbd al-ʿAziz who died recently in jail after being imprisoned for corruption scandals involving an estimated 1 billion USD. Needless to say, this was not an isolated instance of corruption and nepotism; similar scandals surround many other real estate megaprojects around the country.

But perhaps the most glaring evidence of the systemic violence in Cairo's recent urban history and its presumed future came with the so-called Cairo Vision Plan 2050, officially dropped after the revolution. Commissioned in 2006 by the former Egyptian Cabinet, and prepared by the General Organization for Physical Development, a department of the Egyptian Ministry of Housing, Utilities and Urban Development, Cairo 2050 was a study to develop a visionary master plan for Cairo's future.[30] Starting in 2008, a series of images and maps from it began to leak. Interestingly, throughout Cairo's history, master plans have always been proposed during a political transitional period: the end of one political regime and the beginning of another.[31]

True, the stated goals and objectives of Cairo Vision 2050 were not unlike those proposed in previous master plans for the city to address its more than half-a-century-old urban problems and ills. What may distinguish this vision most from earlier master plans is the magnitude of interventions and of the dislocations of people. Many critics of the proposal rightly found it irking to see the vision displacing so many people in favour of increasing tourism and elite spaces.[32] Nowhere in the official report do we find a clear scenario of where the masses of people who live in degraded, informal areas, and who would have been displaced by this proposed plan, would have ended up living. Take for example Manshiyyat Nasir, one of the oldest informal settlements in Cairo. The report shows a new district composed of terraced villas replacing the existing squalor. But the report fails to show where the current residents, estimated at around eight hundred thousand, would have been relocated. Or go further north, to the vast expanse of cemeteries located just across the major highway from Manshiyyat Nasir, known as the City of the Dead. Home to a small population living between tombs and mausoleums, this dead/living city was to have been transformed into a large park, serving as a pretty view for the stepped villas that were proposed to replace Manshiyyat Nasir. Once again, nowhere in the report were the displaced people counted or considered.

And finally, consider the proposed Khufu Axis, a new proposed boulevard that would have linked Sphinx Square in the Muhandisin area with the Great Pyramid of Giza. The proposed avenue cut through the poor neighbourhood of Bulaq in Giza, displacing what I have estimated to be more than half a million residents. The report shows images of a 10-lane avenue lined with trees and a lush green median, and flanked by glitzy high-rise buildings. Once more, mention of where the displaced would have been be relocated is omitted. The mere fact that almost all the proposed developments in the plan would have displaced residents is striking, and gives the impression, which was voiced in opposition circles when the report began to leak, that this vision was only for the upper class, who are increasingly turning their backs on the lower classes.[33]

Figure 12.4. The transformation of Manshiyyat Nasir into an upscale district in the first draft of Cairo Vision 2050.

The vision deliberately engineered the removal from the city centre of many of the dispossessed people who live in degraded areas. No doubt, if executed, violence would have been required or would have erupted, because the state and the private sector would have had to expropriate much land, old neighbourhoods and informal settlements to make space for these spectacular projects. It is also important to note that this vision was preceded in the previous two decades by a radical transformation in upper-class lifestyles – a new way of life based on highways, automobiles, gated communities, malls and golf clubs. For many observers, therefore, the vision was the epitome of the workings of the neoliberal urban economic regime on the city, of its spatial injustice and of inequality.[34]

Reflections

The chain of ideas triggered by the Egyptian revolution, therefore, has the universal message of social justice and freedom that takes us beyond Egypt, as it began to question the socio-economic order of global capitalism. This is attested by the apparent connection between Midan al-Tahrir and the later protests in several cities around the globe. Thus we find the Marxist geographer David Harvey asking whether it is the Arab Spring or the Autumn of Capitalism.[35] I believe, however, that in the days ahead researchers will begin to explore other possible urban and spatial triggering factors. For example, many of the analyses of the Egyptian January revolution have rightly revolved around its temporal connections with the Tunisian revolt. But no one has yet paid attention to the indirect spatial role played by the Gulf Arabs. I do not mean the role played by al-Jazeera Satellite Channel. No doubt, comparisons and contrasts between urban Cairo and cities in the Gulf states have in recent years forcefully entered cultural and political discourses. Wa'il Ghunim, one of the spearheads of the revolution, was living in Dubai and on several occasions compared its thriving urbanity to the degrading condition of Cairo. In fact, I have argued elsewhere that Cairo Vision 2050 was in part a response to a political condition created by the feeling that there has been a shift in power and influence in the Arab world. As the journalist Thomas Friedman put it: 'For decades it was the big, central Arab powers that set the tone for the Arab world and led innovation. But today the region is being led from the outer edges. It's the little guys that are doing the most interesting stuff, and it's the big guys that will be left behind if they don't wake up.'[36] Cairo Vision 2050 was a response to this feeling of a waning Egypt and a waxing Gulf; it was the ruling elite's attempt to exhibit Cairo as if it were waking up to the new Gulf reality.

But the felt injustice of residential segregation and socio-spatial inequalities has also reawakened, reinvented and renewed the meaning of public spaces as spaces of socio-political contestation. I would like to highlight four observations about the urban characteristics of these protests and contestations. First, the January revolution was primarily an urban movement. Millions of people who live in different regions in Egypt gradually prepared this highly complex drama. But it was ultimately on the streets and squares of cities around the country that the collective challenge against the former regime really materialized. Second, as a result of these earlier protests, the public spaces of cities developed either as spaces of violent confrontations and contestations or as depoliticized places, controlled by the instruments of authority. Third, nearly one-third of these numerous surface eruptions took place in Cairo, reflecting not only the urban nature of the movement, but also the centralization of the country and the capital's domination over the other cities and provinces in the country.

Finally, although the less densely populated suburbs and new desert developments on the fringes of Cairo constitute over double the surface area of the built-up city, demonstrations never took off from their public spaces. Rather, demonstrations were always organized in the urban spaces of either the formal or the informal areas of the metropolis. True, urban proximity to the city centre, visibility to the media, population density and the socio-spatial background of most of the participants – who belonged mainly to the urban youth of the lower-middle, middle and upper-middle classes and who predominantly lived in the formal and informal sections of the city – may account for the urban geography of the early 'rehearsals' and the later contestations during the January uprising. But I will further argue that the geographic distribution of protests and its final culmination in Midan al-Tahrir mirrors the spatialization of politics and the political power of urban theatricalities.

The Urban Theatre of Violence

Jacques Derrida once suggested that the act of political revolution is theatrical.[37] The eighteen days of the Egyptian revolution in Midan al-Tahrir indeed contained all the elements of a theatrical drama. To many observers around the world, the ensuing events seemed like a spectacular reality show in an open-air theatre filled with cameras, volunteers, spectators, smiles, cries, blood, music, suspense, action and a grand finale when former president Hosni Mubarak resigned on 11 February 2011. And the protesters on Midan al-Tahrir clearly understood the spectacular power of this particular urban theatre. In the words of one Egyptian activist describing Midan al-Tahrir events: 'The authority's spectacle was confronted by the revolution's spectacle. We understood the lesson, and the square was the theatre: splendid, colourful, music. We produced, directed, and participated in the biggest spectacular show in history. And the whole world watched us'.[38] The inviolability of Midan al-Tahrir during and in the aftermath of the January uprising has indeed been striking. The visibility of the revolution was contingent on the capacity of the revolutionaries, through their collective actions during the eighteen days, to appropriate the urban space of Midan al-Tahrir as the space of hegemonic production of visibility. Moreover, during the subsequent months its urban space has witnessed numerous attempts by various struggling political forces to reoccupy it. But why has Midan al-Tahrir and not any other urban space in the city become the most contentious urban space in the nation, the theatre par excellence of resistance and revolutionary dramas?

In a very prophetic book published in 2010, Asef Bayat gives us some clues to the significant characteristics of these urban theatres of contention.[39] Based on his observations, I will suggest two sets of characteristics that answer this question: first, there are physical and practical characteristics of the urban space related mainly to size, features and

Figure 12.5. Midan al-Tahrir as an urban theatre during the revolution.

location; and second, there are symbolic associations, reinvigorated by past iterations of protest, national events and signification evoked by buildings enclosing the urban theatre. From a physical point of view, Midan al-Tahrir is a large urban space that can accommodate thousands of protestors.[40] It has a central location within the metropolis, which facilitates access to it from all directions and helps to disseminate news outwards, as such events attract attention from both the media and city residents. Indeed, the space hosts diverse organizations: headquarters of the press and television stations, embassies, hotels where tourists and journalists usually reside, as well as mass transportation networks. Moreover, the square is close to what the general public perceives as the seat of the government (the cabinet, several ministry buildings including the Interior Ministry, and the main administrative building of the government). From a practical point of view, the enclosed urban space of the square has, first, several entrances/exits where protestors can easily flee from the police and, second, many shops and residential blocks where revolutionary fugitives can find respite or sanctuary.

In addition to these physical and practical characteristics, history has lent the square intricate symbolic significances to Egyptians, either embedded in the pantheon of the enclosing buildings or stored in the memory of the place from past iterations of national events, such as funerals, protests and celebrations. Like a palimpsest, the square is composed of layers of meanings overlaid on top of each other. The residue of most prior layers is still visible in some of the buildings that have survived the erasure of successive civic and political orders or in the forms and street patterns that replaced them. And new layers are inscribed with new meanings that are constantly being reconfigured and reconstructed within the web of prior and emerging national and international significations. More than any other urban space in the city, and more than just a backdrop, Midan al-Tahrir functions symbolically in inspiring and igniting national and patriotic feelings needed for a historic event of this magnitude. Interestingly, by occupying the square, the revolutionaries disrupted the former regime's plans to introduce changes to the square in Cairo Vision 2050 that would have deprived it of its cultural and political symbolic significance.[41]

Parting Thoughts

'In a revolution, as in a novel, the most difficult part to invent is the end.'[42]

– Alexis de Tocqueville

On 25 January 2011, the demonstrators gathered in Nahiyya Street in Bulaq to march to Mustafa Mahmud Square on their way to Midan al-Tahrir. They were chanting for social justice and freedom, though not cognizant that they were demonstrating on the same street that the Cairo Vision 2050 would remove and reinvent as Khufu Axis. Ironically, they were protesting against the violence of eviction that would have been imposed by expropriation to make the new urban geography of Khufu Axis out of the wreckage of the old neighbourhood of Bulaq. The Nahiyya demonstration was, coincidentally, a visible protest against the subterranean violence embedded in the very structure of this urban space. I have argued that the unjust urban and spatial outcomes of the past few decades arose from inherently unjust processes operating in an urban milieu preloaded with the systemic violence of distributional injustices. What binds violence, spatial injustice and urban spaces together is often more than the visible discrete events that appear to disrupt these spaces. While urban violence and protests erupt in certain spaces because of social, physical, or symbolic spatial logics, violence, I argue, is a latent spatio-temporal actualization in the city's urban spaces, specifically when no egalitarian social or spatial tendencies prevail.

When I was concluding a draft of this chapter nearly a year and a half ago, Egyptians were going to the polls to choose their next president. Today, late October 2013, as I am editing its final version, the trial of the ousted 'next president' is about to begin after tumultuous years of urban violence, with no clear end in sight. Much of the talk coming from the interim government revolves around a new road map for democracy and social justice. Will the result of this democratic roadmap process be the end of the ensuing urban violence, let alone the spatial injustices and systemic urban violence associated with the former political urban economy? It is not certain how events will unfold in the next few months and years. What is certain is that, unless the future authority addresses the spatiality of social injustice, acts of disruption, protest and another revolutionary wave will continue to bring the hidden violence into view in the urban spaces of the city.

Notes

1. I deliberately use the Arabic word *midan* instead of the English translation 'square'. In the everyday language of Cairenese, *midan* refers to the urban space of Tahrir. While the lexical meaning of 'square' is a plaza or piazza, *midan* maintains a more pliable form, at once connoting a plaza, a roundabout, a racecourse, a field or a range.

2. P. Garofalo. 2011. 'Income Inequality in the US Is Worse than Egypt', *Think Progress*, 31 January 2011. Viewed on 18 November 2011 at http://thinkprogress.org/politics/2011/01/31/141611/income-inequality-egypt/?mobile=nc.
3. Most historical writings tell us something not only about their explicit subject matter, but also about the time when they were written. My first draft of this chapter was written in November 2011; my first revised version of it was submitted to the editors in June 2012; and my final version was completed in November 2013. During this period, much urban violence went on in various cities of Egypt. Since my first draft, except a few commentaries, I have resisted any significant alteration of the text to reflect on some recent developments. Much of the text expresses my views and underlying arguments following the memorable events of 25 January 2011. It reflects, among other things, a certain cautious optimism that I and perhaps many others have felt towards the events. It also reflects some particular views that may not be widely accepted today, such as the role played by the football fans in the revolution. If I were to write on the same subject today, however, I would write about the urban violence episodes in much the same way. My examination could be expanded to include other urban spaces from around the city.
4. G.W.F. Hegel. 1942. *Hegel's Philosophy of Right*, trans. T.M. Knox, Oxford: Clarendon, 13.
5. Oxford Dictionary, *Revised and Illustrated Oxford Dictionary*, Oxford: University of Oxford Press, 931.
6. H. Lefebvre. 1996. *Writings on Cities*, trans. E. Kofman and E. Lebas, London: Blackwell.
7. S. Žižek. 2008. *Violence*, New York: Picador, 1.
8. Žižek, *Violence*, 2.
9. R. Sennett. 1990. *The Conscience of the Eye*, New York: Norton, 36.
10. It is interesting to note that when the controls and constraints on the public spaces of the city became too stifling, particularly for political contestations, parallel signs of the impending storm began to also emerge in other spaces: the cyberspace of the Internet, the literary space of the novel and the reel space of films.
11. A. Shadid. 2011. 'The Old Order Stifles the Birth of a New Egypt', *New York Times*, 22 November, viewed on 23 November 2011 at http://www.nytimes.com/2011/11/23/world/middleeast/vestiges-of-hosni-mubaraks-order-stifle-birth-of-new-egypt.html?pagewanted=all.
12. A. Tawfik. 2011. *Utopia*, trans. C. Rossetti, Doha: Bloomsbury Qatar Foundation, 153.
13. R. Springborg. 2009. 'Protest against a Hybrid State', in N. Hopkins (ed.), *Political and Social Protest in Egypt*, Cairo Papers in Social Science 29(2/3), Cairo: American University in Cairo Press, 9–11.
14. J. Beinin. 2011. 'A Workers' Social Movement on the Margin of the Global Neoliberal Order, Egypt 2004–2009', in J. Beinin and F. Vairel (eds), *Social

    Movements, Mobilization and Contestation in the Middle East and North Africa, Stanford, CA: Stanford University Press, 181–201.
15. The demands during the early protests echoed those used during the uprising: from calling for an improvement in wages and working conditions, to asking for the reduction of certain fees and living expenses, to demanding better urban living environments; from protesting for political freedom and against laws and procedures governing political decision making to protesting against police brutality – for example, the demonstration against the killing of the blogger Khalid Said in June 2010 and the demonstration by the Kefaya Movement against what they called the 'Torture Factory', situated in the Egyptian Interior Ministry's compound five years earlier.
16. ʿA. Izz. 2011. 'Shahid ʿala 'l-Thawra', A. Mansour interview with ʿA. Izz on Al-Jazeera Satellite Channel. Viewed on 27 June 2011 at http://www.youtube.com/watch?v=LF9rcz-Ar-8.
17. In addition to two personal communications with direct eyewitnesses, there are two main primary sources for my reconstruction of the events that took place before and during the 25 January uprising: first, an interview with ʿAmr ʿIzz on Al-Jazeera Satellite Channel (Note 16 above), and second, an interview with Ahmed Maher in Al-Sharq al-Awsat newspaper: E. Fadl. 2011. 'Al-Sharq al-Awsat Talks to Egypt's April 6 Youth Movement Founder Ahmed Maher', 10 February. Viewed on 18 March 2012 at http://www.aawsat.net/2011/02/article55247577.
18. This day was picked as the protest date because it marked the annual Police Day celebration in Egypt. Since its establishment in 2008, the Sixth of April Youth Movement always protested on this date to mock the holiday, despite losing the element of surprise. While it is true that this organized event was planned as one in a series of other protests throughout that year leading to the 2012 presidential elections, events in Tunisia a few weeks earlier gave the organizers a different feel.
19. Fadl, 'Al-Sharq Al-Awsat Talks to Egypt's April 6 Youth Movement Founder Ahmed Maher'.
20. In fact, the organizers did not anticipate this large turn out of people, so they originally considered Mustafa Mahmud Square to be their most likely final destination.
21. M.G. Bashir. 2011. *Kitab al-Ultras*, Cairo: Dar Diwan, 65–75.
22. ʿIzz, *Shahid ʿala 'l-Thawra*.
23. There is a twist of irony in the role played by sports fans in the revolution. It is usually argued that the former regime used sports, and football in particular, to distract and disengage people from real politics. But, apparently, even if true, this worked against the regime, as the success of the uprising owed much to football fans' contribution.
24. G. Amin. 2000. *Whatever Happened to the Egyptians?* Cairo: American University of Cairo Press.
25. This point is greatly influenced by Mestrovic. See S. Mestrovic. 1996. *Postemotional Society*, London: Sage.

26. S. Ismail, 2011. 'A Private Estate Called Egypt', *The Guardian*, 6 February. Viewed on 29 March 2011 at http://www.guardian.co.uk/commentisfree/2011/feb/06/private-estate-egypt-mubarak-cronies.
27. K. Adham. 2005. 'Globalization, Neoliberalism and New Spaces of Capital in Cairo', in *Traditional Dwellings and Settlement Review* 17(1), 19–32.
28. Adham, 'Globalization, Neoliberalism and New Spaces', 26–31.
29. My interview with Arch. Mustafa Hussam, Cairo, 18 July 2005.
30. D. Sims. 2010. *Understanding Cairo*, Cairo: American University in Cairo Press, 88.
31. In fact, realizing this pattern, I took it as a sign of a coming change in a research paper presented at a Beirut Conference a few weeks prior to the revolution.
32. N. Berg. 2010. 'Cairo 2050 Plan Makes Big Shifts in City', *Planetizen*, 23 December, viewed on 9 November 2011 at http://www.planetizen.com/node/47385.
33. E. Cordts. 2010. 'Cairo 2050: Ambitious Plans, Threatened Population', *Mondiaal Nieuws*, 5 February. Viewed on 8 October 2010 at http://www.mo.be/node/24962.
34. E. Denis. 2006. 'Cairo as Neoliberal Capital?', in D. Singerman and P. Amar (eds), *Cairo Cosmopolitan*. Cairo: American University of Cairo Press, 47–71.
35. See the round table discussion, 'The Meaning of Maghreb?', held during the International Conference 'Decolonization – New Emancipatory Struggles', in Zagreb, Croatia on 18 May 2011. Viewed on 16 January 2012 at http://www.youtube.com/watch?v=TN-O09WhKko.
36. T. Friedman. 2001. 'The Fast Eat the Slow', *New York Times*, 2 February. Viewed on 29 April 2012 at http://www.nytimes.com/2001/02/02/opinion/foreign-affairs-the-fast-eat-the-slow.html.
37. J. Derrida. 1997. 'The Theatre of Cruelty and the Closure of Representation', in T. Murray (ed.) *Mimesis, Masochism and Mime: The Politics of Theatricality in Contemporary French Thought*. Ann Arbor: University of Michigan Press, 53.
38. A. 'Abd al-Fattah. 2011. 'Al-Hilm Awwalan', *Al-Shorouk*, 25 June. Viewed on 25 June 2011 at http://www.shorouknews.com/columns/view.aspx?cdate=24062011&id=cd2f555b-e375-479c-a878-1d40b05af52c.
39. A. Bayat. 2010. *Life As Politics*, Stanford, CA: Stanford University Press.
40. I have estimated Midan al-Tahrir's full capacity at around a quarter of a million people. Of course, the number could rise if demonstrators spilled out into the surrounding streets.
41. It is significant that Cairo Vision 2050 revealed the intention of the former government to introduce changes that might have deprived the square of its cultural and political symbolic centrality by relocating the Egyptian Museum to the Giza Plateau and moving most of the governmental agencies to New Cairo, including the main administrative building known locally as *al-Mugamma* and the surrounding ministry and parliament buildings. The

proposed flight was preceded by the American University's move to its new campus in New Cairo.
42. A. de Tocqueville. 2007. *The Recollections of Alexis de Tocqueville,* trans. A.T. de Mattos, New York: Macmillan, 71.

Contributors

Khaled Adham is associate professor at the United Arab Emirates University. His publications and current research activities are focused on the impact of late capitalism on the architectural and urban transformations of Cairo, Doha and Dubai.

Rasmus Christian Elling has a Ph.D. in Iranian studies and is assistant professor at the University of Copenhagen, Denmark, where he teaches the sociology and history of the Middle East. He is the author of *Minorities in Iran: Nationalism and Ethnicity after Khomeini* (2013).

Ulrike Freitag is a historian of the modern Middle East with a special interest in urban history and the Arabian Peninsula in its global context. She directs Zentrum Moderner Orient, and teaches at Freie Universität, Berlin. She is author of *Indian Ocean Migrants and State Formation in Hadhramaut* (2003).

Nelida Fuccaro is reader in modern Middle Eastern history at the School of Oriental and African Studies, University of London. She has recently published *Histories of City and State in the Persian Gulf: Manama since 1800* (2009) and edited a volume of *Comparative Studies in South Asia, Africa and the Middle East* entitled 'Histories of Oil and Urban Modernity in the Middle East' (2013).

Claudia Ghrawi holds an MA in history and political sciences, and studied Arabic in Damascus and Berlin. She works as a research fellow at the Zentrum Moderner Orient and is a Ph.D. student at the Freie Universität, Berlin.

Hanan Hammad is a social and cultural historian of the modern Middle East with a focus on gender, sexuality and urban history. She is an assistant professor of history at Texas Christian University. Her recent publications include "Regulating Sexuality: The Colonial-National Struggle over Prostitution after the British Invasion of Egypt," in Marilyn Booth and Anthony Gorman (ed.), *The Long 1890s in Egypt, Colonial Quiescence, Subterranean Resistance* (Edinburgh: University of Edinburgh Press, 2014) and "Relocating a common past and the making of East-centric modernity: Islamic and secular nationalism(s) in Egypt and Iran" in Afshin Marashi and Kamran Aghale (ed.), *Rethinking Iranian Nationalism* (Austin: University of Texas Press, 2014).

Feras Krimsti is researcher at Zentrum Moderner Orient, Berlin. His work focuses on the Arabic-speaking domains of the Ottoman Empire. He has published *Die Unruhen von 1850 in Aleppo – Gewalt im urbanen Raum* (2014).

Nora Lafi is researcher at Zentrum Moderner Orient, Berlin. She is a historian of the Ottoman Empire with a focus on urban studies. She co-edited *The City in the Ottoman Empire: Migration and the Making of Urban Modernity* (2010).

Noémi Lévy-Aksu is assistant professor at Boğaziçi University (Istanbul), Department of History. Her main research interests are urban history, public order, and legal transformations in the late Ottoman Empire, and she has recently published *Ordre et désordres dans l'Istanbul ottomane, 1879–1909* (2013).

Fatemeh Masjedi holds a BA in Iranian history from Tehran Teachers' Training University. She received her MA in American history from Illinois State University, and is currently a Ph.D. fellow at Zentrum Moderner Orient, Berlin. Her research project is on Tabriz between political violence, imperial violence, and socio-political struggle during 1906–1920.

Roberto Mazza is assistant professor of history at Western Illinois University, and research associate at the School of Oriental and African Studies, University of London. He is the author of *Jerusalem from the Ottomans to the British* (2009), and co-editor of *Jerusalem in World War One: The Palestine Diary of a European Consul* (2011).

Reza Masoudi Nejad is an urbanist, currently an Alexander von Humboldt Research Fellow at Zentrum Moderner Orient, Berlin. He received a Ph.D. from University College London in 2009 on the spatial dynamics of religious processions in Iranian cities.

Florian Riedler is a historian of the nineteenth-century Ottoman Empire, focusing on social and urban history. He is a research fellow at Zentrum Moderner Orient and a member of the competence network 'Phantom Borders in East Central Europe'.

Selected Bibliography

Note: This is a consolidated bibliography, and excludes the archival, internet and journalistic sources quoted by individual authors.

Abcarius, M.F. 1946. *Palestine through the Fog of Propaganda*, London: Hutchinson & Co.
Abir, M. 1993. *Saudi Arabia: Government, Society and the Gulf Crisis*, New York and London: Routledge.
Abrahamian, E. 1988. 'The Strengths and Weaknesses of the Labour Movement in Iran, 1941–1953' in M.E. Bonine and N.R. Keddie (eds), *Continuity and Change in Modern Iran*, Albany, NY: SUNY Press, 211–32.
Abu Lughod, J. 1969. 'Varieties of Urban Experience: Contrast, Coexistence and Coalescence in Cairo', in I.M. Lapidus (ed.), *Middle Eastern Cities*, Berkeley and Los Angeles: University of California Press, 159–87.
———. 1981. *Urban Apartheid in Morocco*, Princeton, NJ: Princeton University Press.
Adham, K. 2005 'Globalization, Neoliberalism, and New Spaces of Capital in Cairo', *Traditional Dwellings and Settlement Review* 17(1), 19–32.
———. 2014. 'Modes of Urban Diffusion', in S. Wippel et al. (eds), *Under Construction: Logics of Urbanism in the Gulf Region*, London: Ashgate, 133–46.
Agamben, G. 2005. *State of Exception*, Chicago: University of Chicago Press.
Ajimer, G. 2000. 'The Idiom of Violence in Imaginary and Discourse', in G.Ajimer and J. Abbink (eds), *Meanings of Violence: A Cross-Cultural Perspective*, Oxford and New York: Berg, 1–21.
'Alawi, M.M. al-. 2010. *Fitnat Jidda: Riwaya*. Beirut: al-Kaukab.
'Ali Bak. J. 1951. 'Hadithuna al-Shahri: Rihlati ila-l-Zahran wa-Shimal al-Mamlaka', *Al-Manhal* 5, 222–24.
Ali Bey el-Abbasi. 1816. *The Travels of Ali Bey*, vol. 2, London: Longmans.
Alnasrawi, A. 1994. *The Economy of Iraq: Oil, Wars, Destruction of Development and Prospects, 1950–2010*, Westport, CT: Greenwood Press.
Alyot, H. 1947. *Türkiye'de Zabıta*. Ankara: Kanaat Basımevi.
Ambroise-Rendu, A.-C. 2004. *Petits Récits des Désordres Ordinaires. Les Faits Divers dans la Presse Française des Débuts de la Troisième République à la Grande Guerre*. Paris: Éditions Seli Arslan.
Amin, G. 2000. *Whatever Happened to the Egyptians?* Cairo: American University in Cairo Press.
André, R. 1968. 'Quartiers et Mouvements Populaires au Caire', in P.M. Holt (ed.), *Political and Social Change in Modern Egypt*, London: Oxford University Press, 104–16.

d'Antigny, J.F.L.C.C. de Damas. 1799. *Rapport Fait au Gouvernement Français des Evénements qui se Sont Passés en Egypte depuis la Conclusion du Traité d'el-A'rych jusqu'à la Fin de Prairial An 8*, Cairo: Imprimerie Nationale.

Arnold, J. 1964. *Golden Swords and Pots and Pans*, London: Victor Gollanz Limited.

Ashbee, C.R. (ed.). 1921. *Jerusalem 1918–1920, Being the Records of the Pro-Jerusalem Council during the Period of the British Military Administration*, London: John Murray.

———. 1923. *A Palestine Notebook 1919–1923*, London: William Heinemann.

Atamian, S. 1955. *The Armenian Community: The Historical Development of a Social and Ideological Conflict*, New York: Philosophical Library.

Avcı, Y. 2011. 'Jerusalem and Jaffa in the Late Ottoman Period: The Concession Hunting Struggle for Public Works Projects', in Y. Ben-Bassat and E. Ginio (eds), *Late Ottoman Palestine*, London: I.B. Tauris, 81–102.

'Awwami, S.A. Al-. 2012. *Al-Haraka al-Wataniyya Sharq al-Sa'udiyya 1373–1393 H/1953–1973 M: Al-Juz' Al-'Awwal*, Beirut: Riyad al-Rayyis al-Kutub wa-l-Nashr, 112.

Aymes, M. 2010. *'Un Grand Progrès – sur le Papier'. Histoire Provinciale des Réformes Ottomanes à Chypre au XIXe siècle.* Paris and Leuven: Peeters Publishers.

Ayoub, M. 1987. 'Ashura', in E. Yarshater (ed.), *Encyclopaedia Iranica*, Vol. II, London and Boston, MA: Routledge & K. Paul, 874–76.

Azzawi, F. al-. 2007. *The Last of the Angels*, transl. William M. Hutchins, Cairo: The American University in Cairo Press.

Badrawi, M. 2000. *Political Violence in Egypt (1910–1925): Secret Societies, Plots and Assassinations*, Richmond, VA: Curzon.

Baer, G. 2009. 'Popular Revolt in Ottoman Cairo', *Der Islam* 54(2), 213–42.

Bamberg, J.H. 1994. *The History of the British Petroleum Company, Vol. 2: The Anglo-Iranian Years, 1928–1954*, Cambridge: Cambridge University Press.

Banani, A., and E. Abrahamian (ed.). 1978. *State and Society in Iran*, Chestnut Hill, MA: Society for Iranian Studies.

Bank, C. 2012. 'Al-Thawra al-Suriyya...Ikhtilat al-Dam bi-'l-Fann', *Deutsche Welle*, 27 March, retrieved 23 September 2013 from http://dw.de/p/14Sm2.

Barbaro, G., et al. 2010. 'Narrative Most Noble Vincentio d'Alessandri', in *Travels to Tana and Persia, and A Narrative of Italian Travels in Persia in the 15th and 16th Centuries*, Cambridge: Cambridge University Press.

Barendse, R. 2009. *Arabian Seas 1700–1763*, vol. 1, Leiden and Boston, MA: Brill.

Bashir, M.G. 2011. *Kitab al-Ultras*, Cairo: Dar Diwan.

Bashkin, O. 2009. *The Other Iraq: Pluralism and Culture in Hashemite Iraq*, Stanford, CA: Stanford University Press.

Basrawi, F. 2009. *Brownies and Kalashnikovs: A Saudi Woman's Memoir of American Arabia and Wartime Beirut*, Reading: South Street Press.

Batatu, H. 1978. *The Old Social Classes and Revolutionary Movements of Iraq*, Princeton, NJ: Princeton University Press.

Bayat, A. 1997. *Street Politics: Poor People's Movements in Iran*, New York: University of Columbia Press.
——. 2010. *Life As Politics*, Stanford, CA: Stanford University Press.
——. 2013. 'Post-Islamism at Large', in A. Bayat (ed.), *Post-Islamism: The Changing Faces of Political Islam*, Oxford: Oxford University Press, 3–34.
——. 2013. 'The Making of Post-Islamist Iran', in A. Bayat (ed.), *Post-Islamism: The Changing Faces of Political Islam*, Oxford: Oxford University Press, 35–70.
Bayat, K. 2007. 'With or Without Workers in Reza Shah's Iran: Abadan, May 1929', in T. Atabaki (ed.), *The State and the Subaltern: Modernization, Society and the State in Turkey and Iran*. London and New York: I.B. Tauris, 111–22.
Bayraqdar, N. 2011. *Karkuk bayna 'l-Haqiqa wa-l-Waqiʿ: Dirasah ʿan Huquq al-Turkman fi 'l-ʿIraq bayna Haqq al-Wujud wa-l-Siraʿ ḥawla Madinat Karkuk*, Beirut: Dar al-ʿArabiyya li-l-Mawsuʿat.
Behar, C., and A. Duben. 1991. *Istanbul Households: Marriage, Family and Fertility, 1880–1940*. Cambridge: Cambridge University Press.
Beinin, J. 2011. 'A Workers' Social Movement on the Margin of the Global Neoliberal Order, Egypt 2004–2009', in J. Beinin and F. Vairel (eds), *Social Movements, Mobilization and Contestation in the Middle East and North Africa*, Stanford, CA: Stanford University Press, 181–201.
Benbassa, E. 1986. '1901'de İzmir'de Cereyan Etmiş bir Kan İftirası Vak'ası', *Tarih ve Toplum* 30, 44–50.
Bennafla, K. 2013. 'Avant-propos', in K. Bennafla (ed.), *Villes Arabes: Conflits et Protestations*, Paris: L'Harmattan, 9–16.
Bentwich, N. 1923. *England in Palestine*, London: Kegan Paul.
Benvenisti, M., and S. Tamari. 2006. 'Jerusalem, between Urban Area and Apparition', in P. Misselwitz and T. Rieniets (eds), *City of Collision: Jerusalem and the Principles of Conflict Urbanism*, Boston, MA: Birkhäuser, 33–47.
Berg, N. 2010. 'Cairo 2050 Plan Makes Big Shifts in City', *Planetizen*, 23 December, retrieved 9 November 2011 from http://www.planetizen.com/node/47385.
Berridge, W.J. 2011. 'Object Lessons in Violence: The Rationalities and Irrationalities of Urban Struggle during the Egyptian Revolution of 1919', *Journal of Colonialism and Colonial History* 12(3).
Bet-Shlimon, A. 2012. *Kirkuk, 1918–1968: Oil and the Politics of Identity in an Iraqi City*, Ph.D. dissertation, Cambridge, MA: Harvard University.
——. 2013. 'The Politics and Ideology of Urban Development in Iraq's Oil City: Kirkuk, 1946–1958', in N. Fuccaro (ed.), *Histories of Oil and Urban Modernity in the Middle East*, thematic issue in *Comparative Studies of South Asia, Africa and the Middle East* 33(1), 26–40.
Bird, K. 2010. *Crossing Mandelbaum Gate: Coming of Age between the Arabs and Israelis, 1956–1978*, London: Simon & Schuster.
Birken, A. 1976. *Die Provinzen des Osmanischen Reichs*, Wiesbaden: Reichert.

Bocquet, D. 2012. 'Henri Lefebvre und der Begriff der Urbanisierung ohne Urbanität: Deutung eines missverstandenen Begriffs aus heutiger Sicht', *Informationen zur Modernen Stadtgeschichte* 2012(2), 41–47.
Bodman, H.L. 1963. *Political Factions in Aleppo, 1760–1826*, Chapel Hill: University of North Carolina Press.
Bosworth, C.E., C. Hillenbrand and L.P. Elwell-Sutton (eds). 1983. *Qajar Iran: Political, Social and Cultural Change, 1800–1925*, Edinburgh: Edinburgh University Press.
Brown, R.D. 2003. 'Microhistory and the Post-Modern Challenge', *Journal of the Early Republic* 23(1), 1–20.
Brubaker, R., and D. Laitin. 1998. 'Ethnic and Nationalist Violence', *Annual Review of Sociology* 24, 423–52.
Bruce, J. 1790. *Travels to Discover the Source of the Nile, in the Years 1768, 1769, 1770, 1771, 1772, and 1773*, vol. 1, Edinburgh: J. Ruthven.
Buchan, J. 1982. 'Secular and Religious Opposition in Saudi Arabia', in T. Niblock (ed.), *State, Society and Economy in Saudi Arabia*, London: Croom Helm, 106–24.
Burckhardt, J.L. 1829. *Travels in Arabia*, London: Henry Colbourn.
Burke III, E. 1986. 'Towards a History of Urban Collective Action in the Middle East: Continuities and Change 1750–1980', in K. Brown et al. (eds), *État, Ville et Mouvements Sociaux au Maghreb et au Moyen-Orient: Urban Crisis and Social Movement in the Middle East*, Paris: Editions L'Harmattan, 42–56.
Burton, R.F. 1893. *Personal Narrative of a Pilgrimage to Al-Madinah & Meccah*, vol. 2, London: Tylston & Edwards.
Büssow, J. 2011. *Hamidian Palestine: Politics and Society in the District of Jerusalem 1872–1908*, Leiden: Koninklijke Brill.
———. 2011. 'Street Politics in Damascus: Kinship and Other Social Categories as Bases of Political Action, 1830–1841', *History of the Family* 16, 108–25.
Butler, J. 1999. *Gender Trouble: Feminism and the Subversion of Identity*, New York: Routledge.
Cahen, C. 1958, 1959. 'Mouvements Populaires et Autonomisme Urbain dans l'Asie Musulmane du Moyen Age', *Arabica* 5(3), 225–50; 6(1), 25–56; 6(3), 233–65.
Calmard, J. 1996. 'The Consolidation of Safavid Shi'ism: Folklore and Popular Religion', in C. Melville (ed.), *Safavid Persia: The History and Politics of an Islamic Society*, London: I.B. Tauris, 139–90.
Campos, M. 2011. *Ottoman Brothers: Muslims, Christians and Jews in Early Twentieth-Century Palestine*, Stanford, CA: Stanford University Press.
Carter, J.R.L. 1979. *Leading Merchant Families of Saudi Arabia*, London: Scorpion Publications.
Carter, M., and K. Torabully. 2002. *Coolitude*, London: Anthem Press.
Chardin, J. 1671. *Le Couronnement De Soleïmaan Troisième Roy de Perse, et ce qui s'est Passé de plus Memorable dans les deux Premières Années de son*

Regne, Paris: Barbin – with a translation in Farsi: 1993. *Safarnameh-ye Shardan: Matn-e Kamel*, Tehran: Tus.

Cheney, M.S. 1958. *Big Oil Man from Arabia*, New York: Ballantine Books.

Cole, J. 1989. 'Of Crowds and Empires: Afro-Asian Riots and European Expansion, 1857–1882', *Comparative Studies in Society and History* 31, 106–33.

———. 2008. *Napoleon's Egypt: Invading the Middle East*, New York: Palgrave.

Cordts, E. 2010. 'Cairo 2050: Ambitious Plans, Threatened Population', *Mondiaal Nieuws*, 5 February. Viewed on 8 October 2010 at http://www.mo.be/node/24962.

Coronil, F., and J. Skurski. 2006. 'States of Violence and the Violence of States', in F. Coronil and J. Skurski (eds), *States of Violence*, Ann Arbor: University of Michigan Press, 1–31.

Crinson, M. 1997. 'Abadan: Planning and Architecture under the Anglo-Iranian Oil Company', *Planning Perspectives* 12(3), 341–59.

Cronin, S.M. (ed.). 2003. *The Making of Modern Iran: State and Society under Riza Shah (1921–1941)*, Routledge Curzon/BIPS Persian Studies Series, New York and London: Routledge Curzon.

———. 2010. 'Popular Politics, the New State and the Birth of the Iranian Working Class: The 1929 Abadan Oil Refinery Strike', *Middle Eastern Studies* 46(5), 699–732.

Dabashi, H. 2011. *The Green Movement in Iran*, New Brunswick: Transaction Publishers.

Dadrian, V.N. 1995. *The History of the Armenian Genocide: Ethnic Conflict from the Balkans to Anatolia to the Caucasus*, Providence, RI and Oxford: Berghahn Books.

Daghir, Sh. (ed.). 2009. *Way idhan lastu bi-ifranj*, Beirut: Dār al-Fārābī.

Daguenet, R.J. 1997. *Histoire de la Mer Rouge de Lesseps à Nos Jours*, Paris and Montreal: L'Harmattan.

Dahlan, A.Z. 1887–88. *Khulasat al-Kalam fi Bayan Umara' al-Balad al-Haram*. Cairo.

Dasnabedian, H. 1988. *Histoire de la Fédération Révolutionaire Arménienne Dachnaktsoutioun, 1890–1924*, Milan: Oemme.

David, J.-C. 1990. 'L'Espace des Chrétiens à Alep. Ségrégation et Mixité, Stratégies Communautaires (1750–1850)', *Revue du Monde Musulman et de la Méditerranée* 55(1), 150–70.

———. 2008. 'Aleppo: From the Ottoman Metropolis to the Syrian City', in S.K. Jayyusi (ed.), *The City in the Islamic World*, vol. 1, Leiden: Brill, 329–56.

Davison, R. 1954. 'Turkish Attitudes Concerning Christian–Muslim Equality in the Nineteenth Century', *The American Historical Review* 59(4), 844–64.

Denis, E. 2006. 'Cairo as Neoliberal Capital?', in D. Singerman and P. Amar (eds), *Cairo Cosmopolitan*. Cairo: American University in Cairo Press, 47–71.

Deringil, S. 1998. *The Well-Protected Domains, Ideology and the Legitimation of Power in the Ottoman Empire, 1876–1909*. London and New York: I.B. Tauris.

Derrida, J. 1997. 'The Theatre of Cruelty and the Closure of Representation', in T. Murray (ed.) *Mimesis, Masochism and Mime: The Politics of Theatricality in Contemporary French Thought*. Ann Arbor: University of Michigan Press, 40–59.

Didier, C. (1854) 1985. *Sojourn with the Grand Sharif of Makkah*, Cambridge: Oleander Press.

Dobe, M.E. 2008. *A Long Slow Tutelage in Western Ways of Work: Industrial Education and the Containment of Nationalism in Anglo-Iranian and ARAMCO, 1923–1963*, Ph.D. dissertation, New Brunswick: Rutgers, The State University of New Jersey.

Dubois, C. 2002. 'The Red Sea Ports during the Revolution in Transportation, 1800–1914', in L. Fawaz and C. Bayly (eds), *Modernity and Culture from the Mediterranean to the Indian Ocean*, New York: Columbia University Press, 58–74.

Dufresne, R. 2004. 'The Opacity of Oil: Oil Corporations, Internal Violence, and International Law', in *Journal of International Law and Politics* 36(2–3), 331–94.

Dunbar Moodie, T. 1994. *Going for Gold: Men, Mines and Migration*, Berkeley: University of California Press.

Dunning, T., and L. Wirpsa. 2004. 'Oil and the Political Economy of Conflict in Columbia and Beyond: A Linkage Approach', *Geopolitics* 9(1), 81–108.

Early, E.A. 1993. *Baladi Women of Cairo: Playing with an Egg and a Stone*, Boulder, CO: Lynne Rienner Publishers.

Edmonds, C.J. 1957. *Kurds, Turks and Arabs*, London: Oxford University Press.

Ehsani, K. 2003. 'Social Engineering and the Contradictions of Modernization in Khuzestan's Company Towns: A Look at Abadan and Masjed-Soleyman', *International Review of Social History* 48(3), 361–99.

Elawy, I. al-. 1976. *The Influence of Oil upon Settlement in al-Hasa Oasis, Saudi Arabia*, doctoral thesis, University of Durham: Department of Geography.

Eldem, E. 2007. '26 Ağustos 1896 "Banka Vakası" ve 1896 "Ermeni Olayları"', *Tarih ve Toplum Yeni Yaklaşımlar* 5, 113–46.

Elias, N. 1976. *Über den Prozess der Zivilisation*, vol. 1, Frankfurt: Suhrkamp.

Elling, R.C. 2013. *Minorities in Iran: Nationalism and Ethnicity after Khomeini*, New York: Palgrave Macmillan.

———. 2013. 'The World's Biggest Refinery and the Second World War: Khuzestan, Oil and Security', paper presented at Comparative Histories of Labour in the Oil Industry Conference, Amsterdam, 13–16 June. Amsterdam: International Institute for Social History.

———. 2015. 'War of Clubs: Inter-Ethnic Clashes and the 1946 Oil Strike in Abadan', in Nelida Fuccaro (ed.), *Public Violence in Modern Middle Eastern Cities*, Stanford: Stanford University Press.

Elm, M. 1992. *Oil, Power and Principle: Iran's Oil Nationalisation and its Aftermath*, Syracuse, NY: Syracuse University Press.

Elsheshtawy, Y. 2004. *Planning Middle Eastern Cities: An Urban Kaleidoscope in a Globalising World*, London and New York: Routledge.

Elwell-Sutton, L.P. 1955. *Persian Oil: A Study in Power Politics*, London: Lawrence & Wishart.
Emmett, C. 2009. 'The Siting of Churches and Mosques as an Indicator of Christian–Muslim Relations', *Islam and Christian–Muslim Relations* 20(4), 451–76.
Ergin, O.N. 1995. *Mecelle-i Umur-ı Belediyye*, vol. 1. Istanbul: Büyükşehir Belediyesi Yayınları.
Ergut, F. 2004. *Modern Devlet ve Polis, Osmanlı'dan Cumhuriyet'e Toplumsal Denetimin Diyalektiği*. Istanbul: İletişim.
Fabrizio, D. 2006. *Fascino d'Oriente*, Genoa: Marietti.
Fadl, E. 2011. 'Al-Sharq al-Awsat Talks to Egypt's April 6 Youth Movement Founder Ahmed Maher', 10 February 2011. Retrieved 18 March 2012 from http://www.aawsat.net/2011/02/article55247577.
Fahmy, K. 1999. 'The Anatomy of Justice: Forensic Medicine and Criminal Law in Nineteenth-Century Egypt', *Islamic Law and Society* 6(2), 224–71.
Falls, C. (ed.). 1930. *Military Operations Egypt & Palestine*, London: HMSO.
Falsafi, N.A. 1985. *Zendegani-ye Shah ʿAbbas Avval*, Tehran: ʿIlmi.
Fanon, F. (1961) 1963. *The Wretched of the Earth*, transl. C. Farrington, New York: Grove Press.
Faqihi, A.A. 1978. *Al-e Buya va Awzaʿ-i Zaman-e Ishan: Ba Nimudari-ye Zendegi-ye Mardom dar an ʿAsr* [Buyids and the Condition of their Era], Tehran: Entesharat-e Saba.
Farmer, P. 2004. 'An Anthropology of Structural Violence', *Current Anthropology* 45(3), 305–17.
Ferguson, J. 2005. 'Seeing Like an Oil Company: Space, Security, and Global Capital in Neoliberal Africa', *American Anthropologist* 107(3), 377–82.
Ferrier, R.W. 1982. *The History of the British Petroleum Company, Vol. 1: The Developing Years, 1901–1932*, Cambridge: Cambridge University Press.
Field, M. *The Merchants: The Big Business Families of Saudi Arabia and the Gulf States*, New York: The Overlook Press, 14–21.
Fishman, L. 2005. 'The 1911 Haram-al-Sharif Incident: Palestinian Notables versus the Ottoman Administration', *Journal of Palestine Studies* 34(3), 6–22.
Floor, W.M. 1985. *Labour Unions, Law and Conditions in Iran (1900–1941)*, Durham, NC: University of Durham.
———. 1987. *Justarhaʾi az Tarikh-e Ejtemaʿi-ye Iran dar ʿAsr-e Qajar* [The Inquests of Social History of Iran in the Qajar Era], Tehran: Tus.
———. 1998. *A Fiscal History of Iran in the Safavid and Qajar Periods, 1500–1925*, New York: Bibliotheca Persica Press.
Friedman, T. 2001. 'The Fast Eat the Slow', *New York Times*, 2 February. Retrieved 29 April 2012 from http://www.nytimes.com/2001/02/02/opinion/foreign-affairs-the-fast-eat-the-slow.html.
Freitag, U. 2011. 'The City and the Stranger: Jeddah in the Nineteenth Century', in U. Freitag et al., *The City in the Ottoman Empire: Migration and the Making of Urban Modernity*, London and New York: Routledge, 218–27.

———. 2012. 'Helpless Representatives of the Great Powers? Western Consuls in Jeddah, 1830s to 1914', in *Journal of Imperial and Commonwealth Studies* 40(3), 357–81.
Frumkin, G. 1954. *Derekh Shofet bi-Yerushalayim*, Tel Aviv: Dvir.
Fuccaro, N. (ed.). 2013. *Histories of Oil and Urban Modernity in the Middle East*, thematic issue in *Comparative Studies of South Asia, Africa and the Middle East* 33(1), 1–88.
Galtung, J. 1969. 'Violence, Peace, and Peace Research', *Journal of Peace Research* 6(3), 167–91.
———. 1990. 'Cultural Violence', *Journal of Peace Research* 27(3), 291–305.
Garofalo, P. 2011. 'Income Inequality in the US Is Worse than Egypt', *Think Progress*, 31 January. Retrieved 18 November 2011 from http://thinkprogress.org/politics/2011/01/31/141611/income-inequality-egypt/?mobile=nc.
Gasper, M. 2009. *The Power of Representation: Publics, Peasants, and Islam in Egypt*, Stanford, CA: Stanford University Press.
Gavin, R.J. 1975. *Aden under British Rule*, London: Hurst, 22–38.
Gennep, A. van. 1960. *The Rites of Passage*, London: Routledge & K. Paul.
Georghallides, G.S. 1985. *Cyprus and the Governorship of Sir Ronald Storrs*, Nicosia: Cyprus Research Centre.
Ghobashy, M. El-. 2012. 'The Praxis of the Egyptian Revolution', *Middle East Research and Information Project* 258(1–7), retrieved 13 September 2013 from http://www.merip.org/mer/mer258/praxis-egyptian-revolution.
Giesl, W. 1927. *Zwei Jahrzehnte im Nahen Orient*, Berlin: Verlag für Kulturpolitik.
Ginzburg, C. 1993. 'Microhistory: Two or Three Things I Know about It', *Critical Inquiry* 20(1), 10–35.
Glassman, J. 2011. *War of Words, War of Stones: Racial Thought and Violence in Colonial Zanzibar*, Bloomington: Indiana University Press.
Gossman, P.A. 1999. *Riots and Victims*, Boulder, CO: Westview Press.
Gupta, A. Das. 2001. 'The Maritime Merchant and Indian History', in A. Das Gupta, *The World of the Indian Merchant 1500–1800*, Delhi: Oxford University Press, 23–33.
Haddad, G. 1970. 'A Project for the Independence of Egypt', *Journal of the Oriental Society* 90(2), 169–83.
Haddad, R.M. 1970. *Syrian Christians in a Muslim Society: An Interpretation*, Princeton, NJ: Princeton University Press.
Hadrawi, A. b. M. al-. 2002. *Al-Jawahir al-Muʿadda fi fadaʾil Judda*, Cairo.
Halabi, E. 2007. 'The Transformation of the Prophet Moses Festival in Jerusalem, 1917–1937: From Local and Islamic to Modern and Nationalist Celebrations', Ph.D. dissertation, Toronto: University of Toronto.
Hammad, H. 2011. 'Between Egyptian "National Purity" and Local Flexibility: Prostitution in al-Mahalla al-Kubra in the First Half of the Twentieth Century', *Journal of Social History* 44(3), 751–83.
Hamud, A.K. 1973. 'Sharikat Aramku wa-l-ʿAmal: al-Thawra al-ʿAmal', in A. ʿAttar (ed.), *Al-Haraka al-Taharruriyya fi-l-Hijaz wa-l-Najd 1901–1973*, Beirut: Maʿtuq Ikhwan.

Hanssen, J. 2005. *Fin de Siècle Beirut: The Making of an Ottoman Provincial Capital*. Oxford: Oxford University Press.

Harel, Y. 1998. 'Jewish–Christian Relations in Aleppo as Background for the Jewish Response to the Events of October 1850', *International Journal of Middle East Studies* 30, 77–96.

Harvey, D. 2003. 'The Right to the City', *International Journal of Urban and Regional Research* 27(4), 939–41.

———. 2012. *Rebel Cities: From the Right to the City to the Urban Revolution*, London and New York: Verso.

Hashemi, N., and D. Postel (eds). 2010. *The People Reloaded: The Green Movement and the Struggle for Iran's Future*, Brooklyn: Melville House.

Hegel, G.W.F. 1942. *Hegel's Philosophy of Right*, trans. T.M. Knox, Oxford: Clarendon.

Heyberger, B. 2003. 'Alep, Capitale Chrétienne (XVIIe–XIXe siècle)', in B. Heyberger (ed.), *Chrétiens du Monde Arabe. Un Archipel en Terre d'Islam*, Paris: Autrement, 49–67.

Hicke, C. 1995. *American Perspectives of Aramco: The Saudi Arabian Oil Producing Company, 1930s to 1980s*, Berkeley: University of California.

Hourcade, B. 2008. 'The Demography of Cities and the Expansion of Urban Space', in P. Sluglett (ed.), *The Urban Social History of the Middle East, 1750–1950*, 154–81.

Hughes, G. 1991. *Swearing: A Social History of Foul Language, Oaths and Profanity in English*, Oxford: Blackwell.

Humphrey, C. 2012. 'Odessa: Pogroms in a Cosmopolitan City', in C. Humphrey and V. Skvirskaja (eds), *Post-Cosmopolitan Cities*, New York: Berghahn Books, 17–64.

Hüseyin Nâzım Paşa, H.N. 1993. *Ermeni Olayları Tarihi*, Ankara: T.C. Başbakanlık Devlet Arşivleri Genel Müdürlüğü, 2 vols.

Hussain, A.J. 2005. 'The Mourning of History and the History of Mourning: The Evolution of Ritual Commemoration of the Battle of Karbala', *Comparative Studies of South Asia, Africa and the Middle East* 25, 78–88.

Hyaman, B. 1994. 'British Planners in Palestine 1918–1936', Ph.D. dissertation, London: London School of Economics.

Iraq Petroleum Company. 1948. *Handbook of the Territories, which Form the Theatre of Operations of the Iraq Petroleum Company Limited and its Associated Companies*, London: Iraq Petroleum Company.

Ismail, S. 2011. 'A Private Estate Called Egypt', *The Guardian*, 6 February. Retrieved 29 March 2011 from http://www.guardian.co.uk/commentisfree/2011/feb/06/private-estate-egypt-mubarak-cronies.

Izz, ʿA. 2011. 'Shahid ʿala 'l-Thawra', A. Mansour interview with ʿA. Izz on Al-Jazeera Satellite Channel. Retrieved 27 June 2011 from http://www.youtube.com/watch?v=LF9rcz-Ar-8.

Jabarti, al-. 1879–80. *ʿAjaʾib al-Athar fi 'l-Tarajim wa-l-Akhbar*, vol. 4, Cairo: Bulaq (republished 1997, Cairo: Madbuli).

Jacobson, A. 2011. *From Empire to Empire: Jerusalem between Ottoman and British Rule*, Syracuse, NY: Syracuse University Press.

Jawhariyyeh, W. 2004. *Al-Quds al-Intidabiyya fi 'l-Mudhakarat al-Jawhariyya*, S. Tamari and I. Nassar (eds), Beirut: Mu'assasat al-Dirasat al-Filastiniyya.

Jones, T.C. 2010. *Desert Kingdom: How Oil and Water Forged Saudi Arabia*, Cambridge, MA: Harvard University Press.

Kabili, Wahib. 2004. *Al-Hirafiyun fi Madinat Jidda fi 'l-Qarn al-Rabiʿ ʿAshar al-Hijri*, 3rd ed., Jeddah.

Kashani-Sabet, F. 2002. *Frontier Fictions: Shaping the Iranian Nation, 1804–1946*, London: I.B. Tauris.

Katouzian, H. 2003. *Iranian History and Politics: The Dialectic of State and Society*, London: Routledge Curzon.

Khalil, S. al-. 1991. *Republic of Fear: Saddam's Iraq*, London: Hutchinson Radius.

Khalili, L. 2013. 'Thinking about Violence', *International Journal of Middle East Studies* 45, 791–812.

Kieser, H.-L. 2000. *Der verpasste Friede: Mission, Ethnie und Staat in den Ostprovinzen der Türkei 1839–1938*, Zurich: Chronos.

Kılıçdağı, O. 2010. 'The Armenian Community of Constantinople in the Late Ottoman Empire', in R.G. Hovannisian and S. Payaslian (eds), *Armenian Constantinople*, Costa Mesa: Mazda, 229–42.

Kimche, D. 1972. 'The Opening of the Red Sea to European Ships in the Late Eighteenth Century', in *Middle Eastern Studies* 8(1) 63–71.

King, A. 1989. 'Culture, Space and Representation: Problems of Methodology in Urban Studies', in Research Project 'Urbanism and Islam' and The Middle Eastern Culture Center in Japan (eds), *Proceedings of the International Conference on Urbanism and Islam (ICUIT)*, Supplement, Tokyo, 339–74.

Kırlı, C. 2000. *The Struggle over Space: Coffeehouses of Ottoman Istanbul, 1780–1845*, Ph.D. dissertation. Binghampton: State University of New York.

Kléber, J.-B. 1988. *Kléber en Egypte (1798–1800)*, vol. 1, Cairo: Imprimerie de l'Institut Français d'Archéologie Orientale.

Kostiner, J. 1993. *The Making of Saudi Arabia 1916–1936: From Chieftaincy to Monarchical State*, New York and Oxford: Oxford University Press.

Krimly, R.K. 1993. 'The Political Economy of Rentier States: A Case Study of Saudi Arabia in the Oil Era, 1950–1990', doctoral thesis, Ann Arbor: University of Michigan.

Krimsti, F. 2014. *Die Unruhen von 1850 in Aleppo. Gewalt im urbanen Raum*, Berlin: Klaus Schwarz.

Kuroki, H. 1999. 'The 1850 Aleppo Disturbance Reconsidered', in Institut für Orientalistik (ed.), *Acta Viennensia Ottomanica. Akten des 13. CIEPO-Symposiums vom 21. bis 25. September 1998 in Wien*, Vienna: Selbstverlag des Instituts für Orientalistik, 221–33.

———. 2003. 'Mobility of Non-Muslims in Mid-Nineteenth-Century Aleppo', in H. Kuroki (ed.), *The Influence of Human Mobility in Muslim Societies*, London: Routledge, 117–50.

Kushner, D. 1984. 'Intercommunal Strife in Palestine during the Late Ottoman Period', *Asian and African Studies* 18, 187–204.

Lackner, H. 1978. *A House Built on Sand: A Political Economy of Saudi Arabia*, London: Ithaca Press.

Ladjevardi, H. 1985. *Labour Unions and Autocracy in Iran*. Syracuse, NY: Syracuse University Press.
Lafi, N. 2011. *Esprit Civique et Organisation Citadine dans l'Empire Ottoman*, Aix-en-Provence: Université de Provence.
Lambton, A.K.S. 1953. *Landlord and Peasant in Persia: A Study of Land Tenure and Land Revenue Administration*, London, New York and Toronto: Oxford University Press.
Laurens, H. 1999. *La Question de Palestine*, vol. 1, Paris: Fayard.
Lawless, R., and I Seccombe. 1993. 'Impact of the Oil Industry on Urbanisation in the Persian Gulf Region', in H. Amirahmadi and S.S. el-Shakhs (eds), *Urban Development in the Muslim World*, New Brunswick, NJ: Centre for Urban Policy Research, Rutgers University, 183–212.
Lebkirchner, R., G. Rentz and M. Steineke. 1960. *Aramco Handbook*, New York: Arabian American Oil Company, 161.
Lefebvre, H. 1974. *La Production de l'Espace*, Paris: Anthropos.
———. 1996. *Writings on Cities*, transl. E. Kofman and E. Lebas, London: Blackwell.
Legg, Stephen (ed.). 2011. *Spatiality, Sovereignty and Carl Schmitt: Geographies of the Nomos*, London and New York: Routledge.
Lévy-Aksu, N. 2008. 'Une Institution en Formation: la Police Ottomane à l'Époque d'Abdülhamid II', *European Journal of Turkish Studies* 8, retrieved from http://ejts.revues.org/index2463.html.
———. 2008. 'Yakından Korunan Düzen: Abdülhamid Devrinden İkinci Meşrutiyet Dönemine Bekçi Örneği', in N. Lévy and A. Toumarkine (eds), *Osmanlı'da Asayiş, Suç ve Ceza. 18.–20. Yüzyıllar*, Istanbul: Tarih Vakfı, 55–67.
———. 2011. 'Criminality and Public Disorders: Some Reflexions on Violence and its Perception in Late 19th Century Istanbul', Rethinking Urban Violence in Middle Eastern Cities Conference, 8–10 December. Berlin: Zentrum Moderner Orient.
———. 2013. 'Troubles Fêtes: Les Perceptions Policières de Pâques et du Ramadan à Istanbul au tournant des XIXe et XXe Siècles', in N. Clayer and E. Kaynar (eds), *Penser, Agir et Vivre dans l'Empire Ottoman*. Leuven: Peeters, 321–38.
Lewy, G. 2005. *The Armenian Massacres in Ottoman Turkey: A Disputed Genocide*, Salt Lake City: University of Utah Press.
Linz, D., E. Donnerstein, B. J. Shafer, K. C. Land, P. L. McCall and A. C. Graesser. 1995. 'Discrepancies between the Legal Code and Community Standards for Sex and Violence: An Empirical Challenge to Traditional Assumptions in Obscenity Law', *Law & Society Review* 29(1), 127–68.
Livingston, J. 1994. 'Shaykh Bakri and Bonaparte', *Studia Islamica* 80, 125–43.
Lodhi, A.Q., and C. Tilly. 1973. 'Urbanization, Crime and Collective Violence in 19th-Century France', *American Journal of Sociology* 79(2), 296–318.
Longhurst, H. 1959. *Adventure in Oil: The Story of British Petroleum*, London: Sidgwick & Jackson Ltd.
Longrigg, H.S. 1969. *Oil in the Middle East: Its Discovery and Development*, London: Oxford University Press.

Low, G. C.-L. 1996. *White Skins, Black Masks: Representation and Colonialism*, London: Routledge.
Löw, M. 2008. *Die Eigenlogik der Städte*, Frankfurt: Suhrkamp.
Maghrabi, ʿA. 1994. *Aʿlām Jidda*, vol. 3, 2nd ed., Jeddah.
Mahajani, U. 1977. 'Slavery, Indian Labour and British Colonialism', *Pacific Affairs* 50(2), 263–71.
Makdisi, U. 2000. *The Culture of Sectarianism: Community, History, and Violence in Nineteenth-Century Ottoman Lebanon*, Berkeley: University of California Press.
———. 2002. 'Rethinking Ottoman Imperialism: Modernity, Violence and the Cultural Logic of Ottoman Reform', in J. Hanssen, T. Philipp and S. Weber (eds), *The Empire in the City: Arab Provincial Capitals in the Late Ottoman Empire*, Beirut and Würzburg: Ergon Verlag, 29–48.
Malesevic, S. 2010. *The Sociology of War and Violence*, Cambridge: Cambridge University Press.
Mamarbaschi, J. 1855. *Les Syriens Catholiques et leur Patriarche Mgr Ant. Samhiri*, Paris: Aux Bureaux de l'Univers.
Maʿoz, M. 1966. 'Syrian Urban Politics in the Tanzimat Period between 1840 and 1861', *Bulletin of the School of Oriental and African Studies* 29, 277–301.
———. 1968. *Ottoman Reform in Syria and Palestine, 1840–1861: The Impact of the Tanzimat on Politics and Society*, Oxford: Clarendon Press.
Martin, D., and B. Miller. 2003. 'Space and Contentious Politics', *Mobilization* 8(2), 143–56.
Masters, B. 1990. 'The 1850 Events in Aleppo: An Aftershock of Syria's Incorporation into the Capitalist World System', *International Journal of Middle East Studies* 22, 3–20.
———. 2001. *Christians and Jews in the Ottoman Arab World: The Roots of Sectarianism*, Cambridge: Cambridge University Press.
———. 2010. 'The Establishment of the Melkite Catholic *Millet* in 1848 and the Politics of Identity in Tanzimat Syria', in P. Sluglett and S. Weber (eds), *Syria and Bilad al-Sham under Ottoman Rule: Essays in Honour of Abdul-Karim Rafeq*, Leiden: Brill, 455–73.
Mazza, R. 2009. *Jerusalem from the Ottomans to the British*, London: I.B. Tauris.
——— (ed.). 2011. *Jerusalem in World War One*, London: I.B. Tauris.
Mazzaoui, M.M. 1979. 'Shiʿism and Ashura in South Lebanon', in P.J. Chelkowski (ed.), *Taʾziyeh, Ritual and Drama in Iran*, New York: New York University Press, 228–37.
Melson, R. 1982. 'A Theoretical Inquiry into the Armenian Massacres of 1894–1896', *Comparative Studies in Society and History* 24(3), 481–509.
Mengin, F. 1823. *Histoire de l'Égypte sous le Gouvernement de Mohammed-Aly ou Récit des Événemens [sic] Politiques et Militaires qui Ont Eu Lieu depuis le Départ des Français jusqu'en 1823*, vol. 2, Paris: A. Bertrand.
Mergel T. 2002. 'Überlegungen zu einer Kulturgeschichte der Politik', *Geschichte und Gesellschaft* 28, 574–606.
Mestrovic, S. 1996. *Postemotional Society*, London: Sage.

Ministry of Finance of Egypt, Statistical Department. 1909. *Population Censuses Conducted in Egypt 1907*, Cairo: Government Press.
Mıntzuri, H. 1993. *İstanbul Anıları, 1897–1940*, Istanbul: Tarih Vakfı, 7.
Mirjafari, H. 1979. 'The Haydari–Niʿmati Conflicts in Iran', *Iranian Studies* 12, 135–62.
———. 1984. 'Heydari va Neʿmati', *Ayandeh* 9, 741–54.
Misri, K. al-, 1931. *Qanun al-ʿUqubat al-Ahli Mudhayyal bi-Ahkam al-Mahakim al-Ahliyya li-Ghatyat 1930*, Cairo: al-Maktaba al-Tujariyya al-Kubra.
Mitchell, T. 2011. *Carbon Democracy: Political Power in the Age of Oil*, London: Verso.
Moghadam, F.E. 1996. *From Land Reform to Revolution: The Political Economy of Agricultural Development in Iran 1962–1979*, London: I.B. Tauris.
Morris, B. 2001. *Righteous Victims*, New York: Vintage Books.
Nakash, Y. 1993. 'An Attempt to Trace the Origin of the Rituals of ʿAshura'', *Die Welt des Islams* 33(2), New Series, 161–81.
Napoli, P. 2003. *Naissance de la Police Moderne. Pouvoir, Norme, Société*. Paris: La Découverte.
Nasser, N.I. 2004. *Al-Rafd wa-l-Ihtijaj fi 'l-Mujtama' al-Masri fi 'l-ʿAsr al-ʿUthmani*, Cairo: Cairo University Press.
Niebuhr, C. 1772. *Beschreibung von Arabien: Aus eigenen Beobachtungen und im Land selbst gesammelten Nachrichten.* Copenhagen and Leipzig: Möller für Breitkopf.
———. 1774. *Reisebeschreibung nach Arabien und Anderen Umliegenden Ländern*, vol. 1, Copenhagen: Hofbuchdruckerei Nikolas Möller.
Nirenberg, D. 1996. *Communities of Violence: Persecution of Minorities in the Middle Ages*, Princeton, NJ: Princeton University Press.
Niyazi, H. (1329) 1913. *Polis Dersleri.* Dersaadet.
Ochsenwald, W. 1977. 'The Jidda Massacre of 1858', *Middle Eastern Studies* 13(3), 314–26.
———. 1982. 'The Commercial History of the Hijaz Vilayet, 1840–1908', *Arabian Studies* 6, 57–76.
———. 1984. *Religion, Society, and the State in Arabia: The Hijaz under Ottoman Control, 1840–1908*, Columbus: The Ohio State University Press.
Onley, J. 2007. *The Arabian Frontier of the British Raj*, Oxford: Oxford University Press.
Osmanoğlu, A.E. 2004. *Hicaz eyaletinin teşekkülü (1841–1864)*, MA thesis, Istanbul: Marmara University.
Oxford Dictionary. Revised and Illustrated Oxford Dictionary. 2010. Oxford: University of Oxford Press.
Pappé, I. 2005. *The Modern Middle East*, London: Routledge.
———. 2010. *The Rise and Fall of a Palestinian Dynasty*, Berkeley: University of California Press.
Parsinnen, J., and K. Talib. 1982. 'The Development of Dhahran (Saudi Camp) as a Community', in I. Serageldin and S. El-Sadek (eds), *The Arab City: Its*

Character and Islamic Cultural Heritage, Arlington: Arab Urban Development Institute/Arab Towns Organization, 177–83.
———. 1982. 'A Traditional Community and Modernization: Saudi Camp, Dhahran', *Journal of Architectural Education* 35, 14–17.
Pearlman, W. 2011. *Violence, Nonviolence, and the Palestinian National Movement*, Cambridge: Cambridge University Press.
Perry, J.R. 1999. 'Toward a Theory of Iranian Urban Moieties: The Haydariyyah and Niʿmatiyyah Revisited', *Iranian Studies* 32, 51–70.
Pétriat, P. 2010. 'Fitna Djeddah, les Hadramis dans l'Èmeute du 15 Juin 1858', unpublished Mémoire de Master 2, Paris: Université Paris 1.
———. 2013. 'Notables et Rebelles, Les Grands Marchands Hadramis de Djedda au Milieu du XIXe Siècle', *Arabian Humanities* 1, retrieved 13 December 2013 from http://cy.revues.org/1923.
———. 2013. 'Les Grandes Familles Marchandes Hadramies de Djedda, 1850–1950', unpublished Ph.D. dissertation, Paris: Université Paris 1.
Pfullmann, U. 1996. 'Politische Strategien Ibn Saʿuds Beim Aufbau des Dritten Saudischen Staates: Eine Historische Studie Unter Besonderer Berücksichtigung des Deutschen Archivmaterials', *Leipziger Beiträge zur Orientforschung* 8, Frankfurt: Peter Lang.
Philip, T., and M. Perlmann (trans.). 1994. ʿ*Abd al-Rahman al-Jabarti's History of Egypt*, vol. 3, Stuttgart: Steiner.
Poisson, S. 2013. 'Les Mobilisations Discrètes des Mouvements Environnementalistes au Caire', *Confluences Méditerranée* 85(2), 129–40.
Porath, Y. 1974. *The Emergence of the Palestinian-Arab National Movement 1918–1929*, London: Frank Cass.
Qarʾali, B. (ed.). 1933. *Ahamm hawadith Halab fi 'l-nisf al-awwal min al-Qarn al-Tasiʿ ʿAshar*, Cairo: al-Matbaʿa al-Suriyya.
Quataert, D. 1983. 'The Port Worker Guilds and the Istanbul Quay Company', in D. Quataert (ed.), *Social Disintegration and Popular Resistance in the Ottoman Empire, 1881–1908*. New York: New York University Press, 95–120.
Qushaqji, Y. (ed.). 1985–1994. *Akhbar Halab kama katabaha Naʿʿum Bakhkhash*, 4 vols, Aleppo: Matbaʿat al-Ihsan.
Rafeq, A.K. 1988. 'The Social and Economic Structure of Bab al-Musalla (al-Midan), Damascus, 1825–1875', in G.N. Atiyeh and I.M. Oweiss (eds), *Arab Civilization: Challenges and Responses. Studies in Honor of Constantine K. Zurayk*, New York: State University of New York Press, 272–311.
Rahimi, B. 2004. *Between Carnival and Mourning: The Muharram Rituals and the Emergence of the Early Modern Iranian Public Sphere in the Safavi Period, 1590–1641 C.E.*, Ph.D. dissertation. Florence: European University Institute.
Ramadan, M. 1986. *Dawr al-Azhar fi 'l-Hayat al-Misriyya Ibbana 'l-Hamla al-Faransiyya*, Cairo: s. ed.
Rambert, L. 1926. *Notes et Impressions de Turquie. L'Empire Ottoman sous Abdul-Hamid II, 1895–1905*, Geneva: Atar.

Raymond, A. 1968. 'Quartiers et mouvements populaires au Caire', in P.M. Holdt (ed.), *Political and Social Change in Modern Egypt*, London: Oxford University Press, 104–16.
———. 2002. 'A Divided Sea', in L. Fawaz and C. Bayly (eds), *Modernity and Culture from the Mediterranean to the Indian Ocean*, New York: Columbia University Press, 46–57.
———. 2002. 'An Expanding Community: The Christians of Aleppo in the Ottoman Era (16th–18th centuries)', in A. Raymond (ed.), *Arab Cities in the Ottoman Period: Cairo, Syria and the Maghreb*, Aldershot: Ashgate, 83–100.
———. 2002. 'Islamic City, Arab City: Orientalist Myths and Recent Views', in A. Raymond (ed.), *Arab Cities in the Ottoman Period: Cairo, Syria and the Maghreb*, Aldershot: Ashgate, 1–16.
———. 2010. 'Aux Origines du Plan d'Alep par Rousseau: Le plan de Vincent Germain de 1811', in P. Sluglett and S. Weber (eds), *Syria and Bilad al-Sham under Ottoman Rule: Essays in Honour of Abdul-Karim Rafeq*, Leiden: Brill, 499–512.
Reinhard, W. 2000. *Geschichte der Staatsgewalt: Eine Vergleichende Verfassungsgeschichte Europas von den Anfängen bis zur Gegenwart*, 2nd ed., Munich: C.H. Beck.
Riches, D. 1986. 'The Phenomenon of Violence', in D. Riches (ed.), *The Anthropology of Violence*, Oxford: Basil Blackwell, 1–27.
Riedler, F. 2011. 'Armenian Labour Migration to Istanbul and the Migration Crisis of the 1890s', in U. Freitag, M. Fuhrmann, N. Lafi and F. Riedler (eds), *The City in the Ottoman Empire: Migration and the Making of Urban Modernity*, London: Routledge, 160–76.
Robson, L. 2011. *Colonialism and Christianity in Mandate Palestine*, Austin: University of Texas Press.
Roche d'Héricourt, C.-E.-X. 1841. *Voyage sur la Côte Orientale de la Mer Rouge, dans le Pays d'Adel et le Royaume de Choa*, Paris: Bertrand.
Rubin, A. 2011. *Ottoman Nizamiye Court, Law and Modernity*. New York: Palgrave Macmillan.
Ruiz, M.M. 2005. 'Virginity Violated: Sexual Assault and Respectability in Mid- to Late Nineteenth-Century Egypt', *Comparative Studies of South Asia, Africa and the Middle East* 25(1), 214–27.
Rüppell, E. 1838. *Reise in Abyssinien*, vol. 1, Frankfurt: Siegmund Schmerber.
Ryzova, L. 2009. 'Efendification: The Rise of Middle Class Culture in Modern Egypt', Oxford: Ph.D. dissertation, University of Oxford.
Sa'id, N. Al-. 1980. *Tarikh Al Sa'ud*, Beirut: Manshurat Ittihad Sha'b al-Jazira al-'Arabiyya.
Şakır, Z. 1943. *Yarım Asır Evvel bizi İdare Edenler*, vol. 2. Istanbul: Anadolu Türk Kitap Deposu.
Salibi, K., and Y.K. Khoury (eds). 1995. *The Missionary Herald: Reports from Ottoman Syria, 1819–1870*, 5 vols, Amman: Royal Institute for Inter-Faith Studies.
Sassoon, J. 1987. *Economy Policy in Iraq, 1932–1950*, London: Cass.

Saupp, N. 1989. *Das Deutsche Reich und die Armenische Frage 1878–1914*, Ph.D. dissertation. Cologne: University of Cologne.
Savitch, H.V. 2005. 'An Anatomy of Urban Terror: Lessons from Jerusalem and Elsewhere', *Urban Studies* 42(3), 361–95.
Scheu, J. 2011. 'Dangerous Classes: Tracing Back an Epistemological Fear', *Distinktion: Scandinavian Journal of Social Theory* 12(2), 115–34.
Seccombe, I., and R. Lawless. 1987. *Work Camps and Company Towns: Settlement Patterns and the Gulf Oil Industry*, University of Durham: Centre for Middle Eastern and Islamic Studies.
Segev, T. 2001. *One Palestine Complete*, New York: Henry Holt.
Sennett, R. 1990. *The Conscience of the Eye*, New York: Norton.
Sewell, W.H. Jr. 1992. 'A Theory of Structure: Duality, Agency, and Transformation', *American Journal of Sociology* 98(1), 1–29.
———. 2001. 'Space in Contentious Politics', in R. Aminzade et al. (eds), *Silence and Voice in the Study of Contentious Politics*, Cambridge: Cambridge University Press, 51–88.
Shadid, A. 2011. 'The Old Order Stifles the Birth of a New Egypt', *New York Times*, 22 November, retrieved 23 November 2011 from http://www.nytimes.com/2011/11/23/world/middleeast/verstiges-of-hosni-mubaraks-order-stifle-birth-of-new-egypt.html?pagewanted=all.
Shaikh, T. al-. 1988. *Al-Bitrul wa-l-Siyasa fi-l-Mamlaka al-ʿArabiyya al-Saʿudiyya*. London: Dar al-Safa li-l-Nashr wa-l-Tawziʿ.
Shakry, O. El. 2008. 'Peasants, Crime, and Tea in Interwar Egypt', *ISIM Review* 21(Spring), 44–45.
Shamy, S. (ed.). 2009. *Publics, Politics, and Participation: Locating the Public Sphere in the Middle East and North Africa*, New York: Social Sciences Research Council.
Shenhav, Y. 2002. 'The Phenomenology of Colonialism and the Politics of "Difference": European Zionist Emissaries and Arab-Jews in Colonial Abadan', *Social Identities: Journal for the Study of Race, Nation and Culture* 8(4), 521–44.
Sherman, A.J. 1997. *Mandate Days*, Slovenia: Thames and Hudson.
Shuaiby, A. al-. 1976. 'The Development of the Eastern Region with Particular Reference to Urban Settlement and Evolution in Eastern Saudi Arabia', doctoral thesis, University of Durham: Faculty of Social Sciences.
Sievers, P. von. 1988. 'Rural Uprisings as Political Movements in Colonial Algeria, 1851–1914', in E. Burke III, E. Abrahamian and I.M. Lapidus (eds), *Islam, Politics, and Social Movements*, Berkeley and Los Angeles: University of California Press, 39–59.
Sims, D. 2010. *Understanding Cairo*, Cairo: American University in Cairo Press.
Sinclair, U. (1926) 2008. *Oil!*, London: Penguin Books.
Sluglett, P. 2007. *Britain in Iraq: Contriving King and Country*, London: I.B. Tauris.
Smith, S.A. 1998. 'The Social Meanings of Swearing: Workers and Bad Language in Late Imperial and Early Soviet Russia', *Past & Present* 160(1), 167–202.

Société des Géographes (ed.). 1825. *Dictionnaire Géographique Universel*, vol. 2, Paris: Kilian.
Spafford, B.V. 1977. *Our Jerusalem*, New York: Arno Press.
Springborg, R. 2009. 'Protest against a Hybrid State', in N. Hopkins (ed.), *Political and Social Protest in Egypt*, Cairo Papers in Social Science 29(2/3), Cairo: American University in Cairo Press.
Storrs, R. 1937. *The Memoirs of Sir Ronald Storrs*, New York: G.P. Putnam's Sons.
Swanson, Glen W. 1972 'The Ottoman Police', *Journal of Contemporary History* 7(1/2), 243–60.
Tafreshi, M.T., and K. Bayat. 1991. *Khaterat-e Dowran-e Separi-shode*, Tehran: Ferdows.
Tamari, S. (ed.). 2000. 'My Last Days as an Ottoman Subject', *Jerusalem Quarterly* 9, 28–34.
———. 2006. 'City of Riffraff: Crowds, Public Space, and New Urban Sensibilities in War-Time Jerusalem 1917–1921', in P. Misselwitz and T. Rieniets (eds), *City of Collision: Jerusalem and the Principles of Conflict Urbanism*, Boston, MA: Birkhäuser, 23–48.
———. 2011. *A Soldier's Diary and the Erasure of Palestine's Ottoman Past*, Berkeley: University of California Press.
Tamdoğan-Abel, I. 2004. 'Le Quartier (*mahalle*) de l'Époque Ottomane à la Turquie Contemporaine', *Anatolia Moderna* 10, 123–25.
Tamisier, M. 1840. *Voyages en Arabie, Séjour dans le Hedjaz, Campagnes d'Assir*, vol. 1, Paris: Louis Desessart.
Tarrow, S. 1996. 'The People's Two Rythms: Charles Tilly and the Study of Contentious Politics', *Comparative Studies in Society and History* 38(3), 586–600.
Tavernier, J.B. 1684. *Collections of Travels Through Turkey into Persia, and the East-Indies, Giving an Account of the Present State of Those Countries: Being the Travels of Monsieur Tavernier, Bernier, and Other Great Men: Adorned with Many Copper Plates*, London: Moses Pitt.
Tawfik, A. 2011. *Utopia*, transl. C. Rossetti, Doha: Bloomsbury Qatar Foundation.
Taymur, A. (Pasha). 1956. *Al-Amthal al-ʿAmmyya Mashruha wa-Murataba ʿala al-Harf al-Awwal min al-Mathal*, 2nd ed., Cairo: Matabiʿ Dar al-Kitab al-ʿArabi.
Ter Minassian, A. 1996. 'Nationalism and Socialism in the Armenian Revolutionary Movement (1887–1912)', in R.G. Suny (ed.), *Transcaucasia, Nationalism, and Social Change: Essays in the History of Armenia, Azerbaijan, and Georgia. Revised Edition*, Ann Arbor: University of Michigan Press, 151–60.
Thamir al-Ahmari, A. 2007. *Dawr Sharikat al-Zayt al-ʿArabiyya al-Amrikiyya (Aramku) fi Tanmiyat al-Mintaqa al-sharqiyya min al-Mamlaka al-ʿArabiyya al-Saʿudiyya*, Riyadh: ʿAbd al-Rahman b. ʿAbdallah Thamir al-Ahmari.
Thompson, E.P. 1971. 'The Moral Economy of the English Crowd in the Eighteenth Century', *Past & Present* 50, 76–136.

Tilly, C. 1993. 'Contentious Repertoires in Great Britain, 1758–1834', *Social Science History* 17(2), 253–80.
——. 2003. *The Politics of Collective Violence*, Cambridge: Cambridge University Press.
Tilly, C. and Tarrow, S. 2007. *Contentious Politics*, Boulder, CO: Paradigm.
Tocqueville, A. de. 2007. *The Recollections of Alexis de Tocqueville*, trans. A.T. de Mattos, New York: Macmillan.
Toledano, E. 1982. *The Ottoman Slave Trade and its Suppression: 1840–1890*, Princeton, NJ: Princeton University Press.
Tonkiss, F. 2005. *Space, the City and Social Theory*, Cambridge: Polity Press.
Toprak, Z. 2000. 'Osmanlı Devleti'nde Sayısallaşma ya da Çagdaş İstatistiğin Doğuşu', in Ş. Pamuk and H. İnalcık (eds), *Osmanlı Devleti'nde Bilgi ve İstatistik*. Ankara: Başbakanlık Devlet İstatistik Enstitüsü, 95–112.
Tuastad, D. 2013. 'From Football Riot to Revolution: The Political Role of Football in the Arab World', *Soccer & Society* 14(1), 1–13.
Tucker, J. 1985. *Women in Nineteenth-Century Egypt*, Cambridge: Cambridge University Press.
Turk, N. 1950. *Chronique d'Egypte (1798–1804)*, ed. and trans. G. Wiet, Cairo: Imprimerie de l'Institut Francais d'Archeologie Orientale, 205.
Turner, V. 1969. *The Ritual Process: Structure and Anti-Structure*. London: Routledge & K. Paul
Tuscherer, M. 1993. 'Le Commerce en Mer Rouge Au Alentours de 1700: Flux, Espaces et Temps', in R. Gyselen (ed.), *Circulation des Monnaies, des Marchandises et des Biens*, vol. 5, Bures-sur-Yvette: Peeters Publishers, 159–78.
——. 2002. 'Trade and Port Cities in the Red Sea–Gulf of Aden Region in the Sixteenth and Seventeenth Century', in L. Fawaz and C. Bayly (eds), *Modernity and Culture: From the Mediterranean to the India Ocean*, New York: Columbia University Press, 28–45.
ʿUmar, ʿA. 1978. *ʿAbd al-Rahman al-Jabarti wa-Nicolas Turk: Dirasa Muqarana*, Beirut: Jamiʿat al-Arabiyya.
Valentia, G. Viscount. 1806. *Voyages and Travels to India, Ceylon, the Red Sea, Abyssinia, and Egypt in the Years 1802, 1803, 1804, 1805, and 1806*, vol. 3, London.
Vassiliev, A. 1998. *The History of Saudi Arabia*, London: Saqi.
Veer, P. van der. 1996. 'Riots and Rituals: The Construction of Violence and Public Space in Hindu Nationalism', in P.R. Brass (ed.), *Riots and Pogroms*, New York and London: Macmillan Press, 154–76.
Verheij, J. 1999. 'Die Armenischen Massaker von 1894–1896. Anatomie und Hintergründe einer Krise', in H.-L. Kieser (ed.), *Die Armenische Frage und die Schweiz (1896–1923)*, Zurich: Chronos, 69–129.
Vidal, F. 1964. 'The Oasis of al-Hasa', doctoral thesis, Cambridge, MA: Harvard University.
Visser, R. 2006. 'Britain in Basra: Past Experiences and Current Challenges', retrieved 11 July 2014 from http://www.historiae.org/cosmopolitanism.asp.

———. 2007. 'The Gibraltar That Never Was', British World Conference, Bristol, July 11–14, retrieved from http://www.historiae.org/abadan.asp.
Vitalis, R. 2004. 'Aramco World: Business and Culture on the Arabian Oil Frontier', in M. al-Rasheed and R. Vitalis (eds), *Counter-Narratives: History, Contemporary Society, and Politics in Saudi Arabia and Yemen*, New York: Palgrave Macmillan, 151–82.
———. 2007. *America's Kingdom: Mythmaking on the Saudi Oil Frontier*, Stanford, CA: Stanford University Press.
Vratzian, S. (ed.). 1990. *Bank Ottoman: Memoirs of Armen Garo*, Detroit: Topouzian.
Vrolijk, A. 2002. 'No Conscripts for the *Nizâm*: The 1850 Events in Aleppo as Reflected in Documents from Syrian and Dutch Archives', *Journal of Turkish Studies* 26(2), 311–38.
Wallach, Y. 2006. 'The 1920s Street-Naming Campaign and the British Reshaping of Jerusalem', Second World Congress for Middle Eastern Studies (WOCMES-2), Amman, 1–16 June. Amman: Royal Institute of Inter-Faith Studies.
———. 2008. 'Reading in Conflict: Public Text in Modern Jerusalem', Ph.D. dissertation, London: Birkbeck College.
Wasserstein, B. 1991. *The British in Palestine*, Oxford: Blackwell.
Watenpaugh, K.D. 2006. *Being Modern in the Middle East: Revolution, Nationalism, Colonialism, and the Arab Middle Class*, Princeton, NJ: Princeton University Press.
Watts, Michael. 2001. 'Petro-Violence: Community, Extraction, and Political Ecology of a Mythic Commodity', in N.L. Peluso and M. Watts (eds), *Violent Environments*, Ithaca, NY: Cornell University Press, 189–212.
———. 2003. 'Economies of Violence: More Oil, More Blood', *Economic and Political Weekly* 38(48), 5089–99.
———. 2004. 'Resource Curse? Governmentality, Oil and Power in the Niger Delta, Nigeria', *Geopolitics* 9(1), 50–80.
———. 2005. 'Righteous Oil? Human Rights, the Oil Complex and Corporate Social Responsibility', *Annual Review of Environment and Resources* 30, 9.1–9.35.
Wavell, A.P. 1946. *Allenby: Soldier and Statesman*, London: George G. Harrap.
Weigert, K.M. 2010. 'Structural Violence', in G. Fink (ed.), *Stress of War, Conflict and Disaster*, Amsterdam and Boston, MA: Academic Press, 126–33.
Weller, R.P., and S.E. Guggenheim (eds). 1982. *Power and Protest in the Countryside: Studies of Rural Unrest in Asia, Europe, and Latin America*. Durham, NC: Duke University Press.
Wellsted, J.R. (1837) 1978. *Travels in Arabia*, vol. 2, Graz: Akademische Druck- und Verlagsanstalt.
Winton, A. 2004. 'Urban Violence: A Guide to the Literature', *Environment & Urbanization* 16(2), 165–84.
Wyszomirski, M.J. 1975. 'Communal Violence: The Armenians and the Copts as Case Studies', *World Politics* 27(3), 430–55.

Yule, H. 1903. *Hobson-Jobson: A Glossary of Colloquial Anglo-Indian Words and Phrases, and of Kindred Terms, Etymological, Historical, Geographical and Discursive.* New ed., ed. William Brooke. London: J. Murray (Available online: http://dsal.uchicago.edu/dictionaries/hobsonjobson/).

Zayed, D., and S. El Madany. 2011. 'Egypt Vigilantes Defend Home as Police Disappears', *Reuters*, January 29, retrieved 13 September 2013 from http://www.reuters.com/article/2011/01/29/us-egypt-vigilante-trib-idUSTRE70S3AZ20110129.

Zemon Davis, N. 1973. 'The Rites of Violence: Religious Riot in Sixteenth-Century France', *Past & Present* 59, 51–91.

Zepter, J., C. Walbiner and M. Braune (eds). 2011. *Ulrich Jasper Seetzen. Tagebuch des Aufenthalts in Aleppo, 1803–1805,* Hildesheim, Zurich and New York: Olms.

Žižek, S. 2008. *Violence,* New York: Picador.

Zubaida, S. 2008. 'Urban Social Movements, 1750–1950', in P. Sluglett (ed.), *The Urban Social History of the Middle East 1750–1950,* Syracuse and New York: Syracuse University Press, 224–53.

Index

Abadan, 18, 197–220, 224, 227, 230
ʿAbdallah Agha, 115, 122–23, 125
Abdülaziz (Ottoman sultan 1861–1876), 168
Abdülhamid II (Ottoman sultan 1876–1909), 52, 54–55, 58, 62–63, 66, 67n8, 68n17, 172, 178
Abqaiq, 243, 247, 250, 253–54, 256
Aden, 114, 125
Africa
    African Cup of Nations, 273
    mining company towns, 213
    North Africa, 3–4
    See also slaves (and slavery)
ahl al-balad (*ahali, ahali 'l-balad, ahali 'l-balda*), 39, 144–45, 149, 157
ahl al-dhimma (and *dhimmi*), 126, 128
Ahmadabad, 197, 207–13
Ahmad Taymur Pasha, 75
Ahmad-zadeh, 98, 101–3
ʿAkkash mosque (Jeddah), 120–21
al-Ahsa. *See* al-Hasa
Aleppo, 16–17, 141–63
Alexandria, 4–5, 176
Alfi, Mohammed Bey, 39–41
al-Hasa (province in Saudi Arabia), 243, 246, 259n1, 259n3–4, 261n22, 263n59
ʿAli, Muhammad (Pasha, ruler of Egypt 1803–1848), 113–15, 118
al-Khobar, 262n52, 264n108
al-Mahalla al-Kubra, 15, 70, 72–73
Al Saʿud, 245, 251–52, 261n22
al-Shayhk Yabraq (fortress in Aleppo), 141

America, 3, 223, 245–47, 251, 254
    consulate (Dhahran), 250–51, 253–56
ʿamma, 39, 44, 81
ʿAmudi, Shaykh al-, 123, 125–26
Anatolia, 164–69, 171, 175–76
anti-imperialism, 123, 127, 224, 236–37, 255
Anglo-Iranian Oil Company, 197–216, 223–24
Arabia/Arabian Peninsula, 41, 114, 128. *See also* Saudi Arabia
Arab-Israeli conflict, 187, 191, 254
Aramco (Arabian American Oil Company), 224, 243–58
Armenakan (Armenian revolutionary group), 168
Armenia
    Abadan, Armenians in, 200
    Aleppo, Armenians in, 16–17, 146, 172
    Istanbul, Armenians in, 17, 62, 65, 164–76
    Jeddah, Armenians in, 114
    Khuzestan, Armenians in, 200, 205
    Kirkuk, Armenians in, 227–29
    See also nationalism; Patriarch (patriarchate)
army. *See under individual nation or empire*
arrest, 4, 37–38, 61, 111, 125, 141, 174, 205, 230, 234, 249–50, 252–54, 256, 269
artisans, 43–44, 123, 129, 151, 200, 203, 208
    Artisans' Club, 208–10

Arutin, Bulus (Maronite Bishop of Aleppo), 143, 149
Ashbee, Charles, 184
ashraf, 43
   naqib al-ashraf, 33, 39, 44
Ashura, 92–95, 98–99, 104–7
Associations, 10, 12, 187
   Christian-Muslim/Muslim-Christian, 183, 188, 190, 192n21
Athens, 176
ʿAttar, Shaykh al-, 43
aʿyan. *See* notables

Babinsi, ʿAbdallah (*mütesellim* of Aleppo), 141
bachelor (*bekar*), 59, 64, 68n16
Baghdad, 92, 116, 224, 228, 233, 235, 237, 238n10
Bahmanshir, 197–98, 206, 208–16, 217n1, 217n3
   Bahmanshir Incident, 209–12
Bahrain, 5
Ba ʿIshn (family), 113, 120
Bakri, Shaykh al-, 33–37, 41–44
Bakhkhash, Naʿʿum (Syrian Catholic teacher in Aleppo), 143, 155
Balfour Declaration, 179, 183, 186–87
bank(s), 10, 72, 276
   Ottoman Bank, 165, 167, 169–73
bargain, 11, 19, 245, 258
Basra, 202, 213, 228, 237, 238n10
bazaar (market), 16, 31, 71, 118, 120–23, 130, 137n86, 189, 197, 207, 209–10
Bedouin(s), 124, 127, 146, 229–30, 243, 263n58
bombs (and bombardments), 11, 41–45, 127, 170, 174
Bonaparte, Napoleon, 29, 32–33, 37, 114
border(s), 45, 97–100, 107–8, 114, 169, 187, 207, 225, 258
Borton, Bill (first British governor of Jerusalem), 180, 182–83

boycott, 12, 115, 244, 253
Braim (neighbourhood of Abadan), 207–8, 212, 227
Britain (Great Britain), 12, 114–16, 200, 215, 223–24, 231
   Abadan, British in, 197–216
   anti-British sentiments and actions, 122–29, 197, 206, 214, 216
   British-Indian, 201–2, 205, 209, 212, 232 (military/soldiers); 189, 204 (police); 202, 204, 211 (subjects in Persia)
   Cairo (and Egypt), British in, 15, 31, 33, 36–39, 44
   consuls (and consulates), 202 (Ahwaz); 143 (Aleppo); 204 (Bushehr); 174 (Istanbul); 111, 114–16, 122–24, 128, 130–31 (Jeddah)
   diplomats, 214 (Abadan); 183–84 (Cairo); 199, 213 (Tehran)
   East India Company, 213 (Iraq); 114–15 (Jeddah)
   embassy (and ambassador), 224, 228, 230, 233, 235 (Baghdad); 143, 173 (Istanbul); 125 (Jeddah)
   Empire, 198, 201
   government, 112, 125, 198, 201, 212, 223–24
   governor, 180, 182–84 (Jerusalem)
   imperialism, 198, 205–6, 212, 216; 223–24 (Iraq)
   Jeddah, British in, 111–31
   Jerusalem, British in, 179–91
   Kirkuk, British in, 222–37
   military, 198, 200, 214–15 (Abadan); 202 (Basra); 205, 209–12, 216 (Iran); 122 (Jeddah); 179–83 (Jerusalem); 231–33, 236–37 (Kirkuk)
   soldiers, 189, 232 (Kirkuk)
British Petroleum Company, 197, 199
Bulaq. *See under* Cairo

Burckhardt, Johann Ludwig, 121, 135n35
bus, 247, 253–54
Bushehr, 98, 204

Cairo, 3–8, 14, 19–20, 29–47, 124, 183–84, 265–82
    Bulaq, 43, 270, 272, 277, 282
    Cairo Vision 2050, 276–78, 281–82
    Manshiyyat Nasir, 276–77
    Midan al-Tahrir (*see* Tahrir Square (Midan al-Tahrir))
Canning, Stratford, 143
capitalism (and capitalist), 9, 148, 198–99, 215, 222, 228, 244, 266, 274, 278
capitulations, 114–15
car, 81, 83, 206, 210, 235, 252, 254–55, 258
caravan, 116, 130
caravanserai, 40, 120–21, 135n35
cemetery, 94–95, 98, 104, 117, 120, 131
censorship, 2, 52, 58–59, 61–63, 74–75, 232–33
census
    Aleppo, 162n52
    Cairo, 72
    Istanbul, 14, 68n16
    Kirkuk, 150, 161n43, 239n15
centralization, 1, 5, 10–11, 19, 56–57, 100–101, 114, 230, 243, 245, 279
Christians (and Christian Churches), 181
    in Abadan, 200, 205
    in Aleppo, 17, 142–58
    anti-Christian sentiments and actions, 16–17, 141–49, 154–58 (Aleppo); 40–41 (Cairo); 11, 151, 158 (Damascus); 17, 64, 171 (Istanbul); 15–16, 111, 123–26 (Jeddah)
    Armenian (arman), 200 (Abadan); 16–17, 146, 172 (Aleppo); 17, 62, 65, 164–76 (Istanbul); 114 (Jeddah); 200, 205 (Khuzestan); 227–29 (Kirkuk)
    Christian-Muslim/Muslim-Christian Associations (*see* associations)
    Coptic, 40, 43, 266 (Cairo)
    Greek Orthodox (rum), 146, 150 (Aleppo); 61–63, 159 (Constantinople); 143–44, 154–55 (Damascus); 181 (Jerusalem)
    in Istanbul, 17
    Jacobite Syrian (suryan), 146 (Aleppo)
    in Jeddah, 114–15, 117, 129, 131, 138n88
    in Jerusalem, 17, 180, 183–84, 186–91
    in Kirkuk, 227–29, 236
    Maronite, 143, 146 (Aleppo)
    Roman Catholic, 155, 160n23, 161n44 (Aleppo)
    Syriac/Syrian Catholic, 143, 146, 148–49, 155 (Aleppo); 40, 43 (Cairo)
churches (as buildings/structures), in Aleppo, 141, 146, 148–49, 154–55, 157
    in Istanbul, 169, 173
    in Jerusalem, 187
cinema, 207, 247, 255
coffee houses, 12, 78, 118, 120, 122, 130, 247–48
colonialism, 47, 147, 198, 200–201, 206–9, 212–13, 215–16, 223–24, 232
    administration, 35
    anti-colonialism, 208
    Egypt, 57, 72, 74
communalism, 180–81, 186–87
Communism (and Communists), 224, 226, 231, 233–37
confessional (and confessionalism), 1, 13, 141–42, 144, 147, 149–51, 154, 157. *See also* sectarian

312 Index

confessionalization, 17–18, 180, 184–86, 190
conflict, 7–13, 19–21, 30, 33, 38, 45, 61–65, 71–74, 98, 100, 103, 115, 122–23, 142, 154, 165, 173, 175–76, 179, 181, 185–91, 216, 232, 237, 245, 248, 254–58
    mediation, 80, 86, 148, 263n69
    resolution/settlement, 19, 21, 55, 62–63, 65, 258
    social, 53, 61–63, 71–72
    See also contention
Constantinople, 63, 124–25, 170, 173. See also Istanbul
consuls (and consulates). See under America; Britain; Europe; France
contention (and contentious politics), 1–2, 9–14, 18–21, 45, 47, 114–15, 144, 155, 186, 199, 224, 244, 280. See also conflict
Copts (and Coptic), 40, 43, 266
councils, 32, 35, 114, 122, 211, 272
courts (and courthouses),
    Egyptian, 70–83
    in Jerusalem, 183
    Ottoman, 56, 60, 128, 174
    in Saudi Arabia, 247
    shariʿa, 146
criminals (and criminality/criminal activity), 5, 14–15, 52–53, 57, 60, 72, 75, 82–83, 86, 126, 212, 229–30, 232, 247
crowd, 12, 36, 172, 188, 231, 233–34, 250–51, 255–56, 271
    urban, 15–16, 33, 112, 163n68, 168–69
    violent, 6, 33, 39–44, 61–62, 122–23, 127–30, 209
    See also mob
cursing (and swearing), 70–86
customs, 113, 115–21, 123, 125, 129–31, 175

Dahlan, 126–27, 137n86
Damascus, 5, 141, 187

Greek Orthodox Patriarchate in Damascus, 143–44, 150, 154–55, 159n8
Massacre of the Christians in 1860, 151, 158, 158n6, 159n9
Dammam, 252, 255, 259n1, 262n52, 263n69, 264n96, 264n108
Dashnak, 167, 169–71, 173
Delhi, 125, 201
demonstrations, 4–5, 20, 165, 167–69, 171, 173–75, 189, 244, 255, 268–73, 279, 282. See also protest
demonstrators, 233, 255, 269–71, 273, 282. See also protestors
deportation, 203, 253
Dezful, 15–16, 91–92, 94–108
Dhahran, 224, 243, 246–55
    American consulate, 250–51, 253–56
dhimmi, 126, 128
diplomacy (and diplomats), 65, 122, 124, 129, 171–72, 198–99, 203
discrimination, 17, 173, 227, 244, 256
disease, 208, 232
disorder, 14, 31, 36, 52–57, 65–66, 189, 203, 207–8, 213–14, 222, 236, 252, 254–55
Diyarbakır, 141, 167
drinking, 204, 209
dual city, 18, 198
Dumas, Thomas Alexandre (French general), 43

East India Company
    in Iraq, 213
    in Jeddah, 114–15
Edward VII (King of the United Kingdom, Emperor of India 1901–1910), 131
Effendiyya, 15, 83
Egypt, 13–15, 30, 33, 37, 44, 70–86, 112–16, 124, 126, 130, 155, 182, 184, 189, 265–82
    Egyptian Revolution of 25 January 2011, 5–6, 19–20, 265–82

Egyptian Revolution of 23 July
1952, 248
government, 74, 77, 268, 271,
274, 281–82, 285n41
empire. *See individual empires*
England, 11, 115–16, 120, 124, 128,
143. *See also* Britain
Europe, 2, 4, 16, 21, 40, 61, 111, 113,
124, 126–27, 156, 169–72, 186,
199–200, 202, 207–8, 212, 227,
232
    aggression, 127, 170
    anti-European sentiments and
actions, 127, 142 (*see also
under* Britain; Christians;
France)
    commercial expansion, 114, 129,
170
    consuls (and representatives),
126–27, 130, 142, 147 (*see
also under* Britain; France)
    governments, 124 (*see also
under* Britain; France)
    imperialism, 14, 40, 114 (*see also
under* Britain; France)
    powers, 1, 14, 16, 111, 116, 124,
142, 166–67, 170–71 (*see also*
Great Powers)
    trade, 111
execution, 42, 111, 125–28, 260n12
    public, 125–27, 130, 137n86
expansion
    commercial, 112, 114
    company, 214–15
    imperial, 1, 114
    industrial, 199, 228, 245, 258
    state, 21, 245, 258
    urban, 2, 7, 13, 17, 72–73, 118,
200–201, 206, 226, 258, 275
Ezbekiyye Square (Cairo), 32, 34, 38,
40–41, 43, 45

faction(s) (and factionalism), 1, 4,
30–45, 157, 229, 239
    urban, 6, 14–15, 21, 29, 41
    violence (*see* violence)

Fehmi, Hasan, 60
fire, 5, 61, 167, 174, 189, 233
firefighter(s), 59, 64, 68n29
fitna, 111, 126
flag, 94, 98, 102, 116, 122, 127, 128,
130, 188, 269
force(s), 30, 36, 54, 60, 65, 128, 141,
189, 194n41, 215–16, 222, 224,
230–31, 235, 253, 263n58, 265,
268, 280
    military/armed, 35, 54, 62,
100–101, 124, 129, 166, 170,
182, 211–12, 232, 249–52,
256, 264n108
    police force(s), 5, 14, 52, 54–58,
62, 124, 187, 189, 203–4, 233,
246, 250, 255, 273
    security, 215, 233–34, 246,
252–53, 256, 269, 272
    threat of, 20
    use of, 5, 7, 19, 128–29, 166, 188,
230, 233–34, 236, 255, 258,
267
France, 11, 53, 64, 124, 171, 182, 223
    anti-French sentiments and
actions, 29–47
    consuls (and consulates), 111,
114, 120, 123, 126, 128, 131
(Jeddah), 188 (Jerusalem)
    government, 33, 50n43, 112, 125
    military (army/soldiers/troops),
29–47, 114
    occupation of Egypt, 14, 29–47
frontier, 41, 199, 209, 215–16

gang(s), 6, 31–33, 39–42, 45, 55, 60,
98, 171–73, 175
gathering(s), 12, 130, 168, 247, 255,
268, 272
geostrategy, 30, 32–33
Germain, Vincent, 151
governance, 6, 14, 31, 37, 45, 184
    urban, 20, 33, 35
government, 4–7, 11–16, 19, 21, 57,
184, 192n18, 233
    local, 96, 114, 126

municipal/urban, 17, 32
offices (see under office(s))
See also individual nations and empires
Great Britain. See Britain
Great Powers, 11, 133n16, 167 (see also Europe: powers)
Greek Orthodox Patriarchate in Damascus, 143–44, 150, 154–55, 159n8
Green Movement (Iran), 3–4
guilds, 31, 39, 43, 113, 130
Gujarati, 115, 134n21, 201
Gulf, 114, 218n15, 278

Hadhramawt, Hadhrami, 111, 113, 122–26, 129, 132n2
hajj. See pilgrimage
Hamadan, 98
Haram al-Sharif, 180–81, 187, 189, 191n8
Haydarpaşa, 53, 61
Hegel, Georg Friedrich Wilhelm, 266
Heydari (and Heydari-Neʿmati), 15, 91–108
Hijaz, 112–13, 116, 124–26, 131
    Hijazi fighters in Cairo, 41, 43, 45
Hindus, 204, 210
hinterland, 8, 14, 18, 198, 224, 226, 244
Hofuf, 243, 249, 259n1
hooligans, 209, 212
Hunchak, 167–69
Husayni, Musa Kazim al- (mayor of Istanbul, 1918–1920), 183, 188
husayniyya, 251

Ibrahim Agha (qaʿimmaqam of Jeddah), 122
imperialism. See under Britain; Europe
India, 43, 125, 128, 201, 203, 217n3
    British-Indian military, police, subjects (see under Britain)
    East India Company, 213 (Iraq); 114–15 (Jeddah)
    government, 200–202, 204
    in Iran, 18, 101, 197–216, 217n3, 219n19, 220n56
    in Jeddah, 113–15, 117, 122, 124–25, 128–30
    labourers, 197–216, 217n2, 245, 263n61
    'Indian Lines' (Bahmashir), 197, 206, 208, 210–12
    merchants, 113–15, 122
    pilgrims, 124–25
    soldiers, 209, 212, 232
Indian Mutiny, 125
Indian Ocean, 112, 115
industrialization, 2, 6, 18, 71–72, 199, 244, 248
industry, 4, 9, 13, 18, 20, 199–201, 206, 216, 224, 228, 230–32, 246, 257
    discipline, 8, 199, 203, 223, 230, 246
    oil (see oil)
    town (and city/conurbation), 8, 18, 197, 223, 225–26, 236–37, 243–45, 248, 258
    workers (and employees), 15, 234, 243, 253
Infitah, 273–74
injustice, 13, 205, 266, 282
    social, 19–20, 265–66, 282
    spatial, 265, 274, 278–79, 282
insecurity. See security
insurrection (and insurgents), 14, 19, 30, 41, 43–44, 141–42, 144, 150–51, 154, 157, 235
International Labour Organization, 229
international politics, 16, 29–30, 32, 36, 38, 111, 122, 223–24
intervention
    diplomatic, 122, 170
    foreign, 166, 181, 187, 205, 214
    military, 61–62, 214–15
    police, 55–56, 65
    political, 42, 114, 254

state, 15, 80, 86, 146, 244, 258, 276
Iran, 13, 91–108, 197–216
 Anglo-Iranian Oil Company, 197–216, 223–24
 labour movement, 197, 212, 216
 land reform, 16, 102, 104, 110n19
 leftists, 197, 204, 216, 240n36
 nationalists, 197, 204, 206
 police, 205, 210, 215
 prime minister, 100, 102, 213
 public, 199, 203, 208
 state, 4, 198, 203, 205–6, 211, 214–15
 urban society, 91–93, 96
 workers, 199–207, 209, 211–13, 216
Iranian Labour Party (*Hezb-e Zahmatkeshan*), 102–3
Iraq, 92, 114, 199, 222–37
 Communist Party (*see* Communism)
 government, 19, 224, 226, 230–31, 233–37, 240n36
 Hashemite Monarchy, 222–25, 237
 labour laws (1936, 1942), 230, 234
 oil industry, 18, 223, 226, 231, 233–34, 237
 workers/labourers in Iran, 199–200, 205
Iraq Petroleum Company (IPC), 223–36, 239n15, 240n21
Isfahan, 93
Islam, 1, 50n43, 93, 112, 126–28, 143–45, 151
Islamic Revolution, 3
Istanbul, 8, 14, 17, 50n43, 52–66, 68n16, 112, 114, 142, 155, 157, 164–76, 181. *See also* Constantinople

Jabarti, ʿAbd al-Rahman al-, 32–33, 35–36, 38–39, 41–44

jail. *See* prison
Jawhar
 Hasan b. Ibrahim, 122
 Salih, 122–23, 128
Jeddah, 15–16, 111–31, 141
Jerusalem, 8, 17, 179–91
Jews
 in Aleppo, 143–44, 148, 150, 161n43
 in Cairo, 41
 in Istanbul, 61–63, 173
 in Jeddah, 114
 in Jerusalem, 184, 186–90
 in Khuzestan, 200, 205
Jiluwi
 ʿAbd al-Muhsin, 254, 264n90
 Saʿud b., (*amir* of al-Hasa) 248, 251, 254, 261n22, 262n36, 264n90
judge
 in Cairo, 71, 80–85
 in Jeddah, 113

Kefaya Movement, 269, 284n15
khan (as building)
 in Istanbul, 164, 171, 174, 178n34
 in Jeddah, 121, 135n3
khawi (pl. *khawiya*), 250, 255–56, 263n58
Khorramshahr (formerly Mohammerah), 200, 204
Khuri, Khalil al-, 156
Khuzestan, 91, 197–216, 218n15
Kirkuk, 18, 222–37
 1946 strike, 227, 229, 231, 233–35
 labour unrest in K3 (IPC), 235–36
 New Camp (IPC), 226–27, 232
 oil conurbation, 18, 20, 222–24, 230–32, 236
 oil stations (IPC), 225, 228, 230–31, 235, 237
 pipeline, 224–26, 228–29, 231, 235

316   *Index*

Kléber, Jean-Baptiste (French general), 36, 39, 43, 48n13, 49n27, 49n37
Kurds
    in Aleppo, 146
    in Eastern Anatolia, 166
    in Istanbul, 64–65, 171, 175
    in Kirkuk, 226–27, 233, 239n15
    militia, 166, 171

labour, 17, 197–216, 222–37, 243–58
    activists, 205, 229, 250, 255
    camps, 249–51, 253, 258
    force, 18–19, 243, 257 (*see also* workforce)
    hierarchy, 199–200, 204–7
    Indian (*see* India: labourers)
    laws, 200 (in India 1920); 230, 234 (in Iraq 1936 and 1942)
    migrants (and migration), 169, 175, 199–201, 216
    mobilization, 237, 244, 258
    movement, 197, 212, 216, 248–49, 258
    office, 229, 251, 253–56, 263n69
    protest (strike, struggle, unrest), 19, 72, 202–3, 206, 216, 223, 237, 243–44, 248, 251
    as punishment, 70, 84, 86n2
    recruitment, 199, 201, 203, 229
    skilled (or specialized), 200, 203, 228
    unskilled (or menial), 199–201, 226–27, 232
    See also work
labourers, 129, 173, 179–216, 228, 230, 232, 236, 242n57, 247. *See also* workers
law, 60, 75, 78–82, 86, 122, 126, 129, 206, 209–10, 213, 246–48, 266, 268
    enforcement, 11, 203
    Islamic, 122, 128
    martial, 182, 189, 211, 215
    rule of law, 2
Laz, 171

liminality, 205, 260n12
looting, 6, 40–43, 141, 150, 152–54, 162n52, 164, 167, 188–89, 210, 213–14, 232, 273

Maghreb and Maghrebinians/Maghribi, 39, 41, 43–44, 113, 119–20
mahalla (and mahalleh), 94, 96–97, 149
Maher, Ahmed, 269
Mahmud II (Ottoman sultan 1808–1839), 54, 57
Mahruqi, Sayyid Ahmad al-, 39
Mamluk(s), 33, 44
    soldiers, 41, 49n37
map(s)
    Aleppo, 151, 154
    Cairo, 29–30, 34–37, 39, 42, 45–47, 276
    Dezful, 97, 99, 106
    Istanbul, 59
    Jeddah, 116, 118–21
market. *See* bazaar
Marseille, 171, 176
massacre, 2
    Amritsar 1919, 202
    Cairo 1800, 40
    Damascus 1860, 11, 151, 158
    Istanbul 1895–1896, 17, 164, 164–76
    Jeddah 1858, 16, 111, 123, 130–31, 138n90
Mecca, 70, 112–14, 116, 124–29, 133n11
    revolt of 1855–1856, 125–126
Medina, 70, 113–14
merchants (*tujjar*), 41, 111–18, 121–31, 151, 154, 171, 230, 250
microhistory, 142, 156, 158, 163n62
Middle East, 1–4, 8, 21, 71, 83, 127–28, 198, 223, 228, 246
    cities, 3, 6, 12, 20–21, 45–47
    history, 2, 8, 10, 13, 45
migrant(s) (and migration). *See under* labour; workers

militarization, 211, 216, 235
military. *See under individual nations or empires*
minister(s) (and ministry/ministries). *See under individual nations or empires*
minority/minorities, 142, 165, 200, 228
Misr Spinning and Weaving Company, 72
mission(s) (and missionaries), 145–47, 173, 175
mob, 32, 39, 41, 61–63, 116, 123, 170–71, 174, 186, 189, 209–10. *See also* crowd
mobilization, 4, 6, 9–14, 16, 18–20, 39, 41, 49n34, 50n43, 62, 100, 126–27, 130, 175–76, 181, 186, 208, 237, 244, 248–49, 258, 270, 273
modern, 40, 54, 66, 72, 77, 82, 91, 95, 130, 147, 169, 198, 207–8, 218n15, 222, 225, 236, 245
    cities/urban space, 6, 9, 20, 107–8, 164, 197, 210, 227, 229
    Middle East, 2, 21
    state, 5–7, 10–11, 14, 19, 21, 100–101
modernity, 12, 18, 20, 185, 188, 199
modernization, 1, 4, 6, 11, 13, 20–21, 64, 66, 91, 100–101, 105, 147, 181
Mohammad Reza Shah (ruler of Iran, 1941–1979), 100, 103
Mohammerah (now Khorramshahr), 200, 204
Mosaddeq, Mohammad (Prime Minister of Iran 1951–1953), 100, 102–3, 110n19
mosque(s), 12, 94, 120–21, 182, 247, 249, 261n32,
Mount Lebanon, 141
movement(s), 4–5, 32, 150, 168, 209, 213, 224, 235, 279
    communist, 235, 237
    Green movement (in Iran), 3–4
    labour, 197, 212, 216, 248–49, 258

    nationalist, 180, 183, 187, 198, 204, 206, 213, 215, 230
    popular, 36
    Sixth of April Youth Movement (Egypt), 269
    social, 12, 29, 100–103,
Mubarak, Husni (president of Egypt 1981–2011), 6, 266–68, 272, 276, 279
Muharram, 92–96, 98, 100, 104
    procession, 15–16, 91–95, 98, 101, 104, 107
    rituals, 91–92, 94, 101–2, 104, 107
muhtasib. *See under* Ottoman
Muhtasib, ʿAbdallah al-, 126
municipality, 3, 13, 207
Muslim-Christian Associations. *See under* associations
Mustafa Zarif Pasha (*vali* of Aleppo), 141. *See also* Ottoman: *wali/vali*

Nablus, 141
Namık Pasha (*wali* of Hijaz), 127, 133n11, 136n58. *See also* Ottoman: *wali/vali*
Nashid Pasha (*wali* of Hijaz), 130. *See also* Ottoman: *wali/vali*
Nasif, ʿAbdallah, 123–24
Nasif Pasha, 37–38, 40
nationalism, 12, 18
    Arab, 213
    Armenian, 17, 165, 167–68, 175–76
    Iranian, 100, 197–99, 201, 204, 206, 208, 211, 216
    Iraqi, 224, 230, 233, 235, 237
    Palestinian, 180, 183, 185–86, 188
nationalization
    of oil industry in Iran, 100, 102–3, 197, 215, 248
    of the Suez Canal, 254
Nebi Musa Riots (Jerusalem 1920), 17, 179–91
Neʿmati, 15, 91–108

newspapers, 52, 58–66, 188, 205. *See also* press
Niebuhr, Carsten, 116–18, 121
night, 32, 40, 55, 58–59, 61, 126, 145, 182, 189, 233
notables (aʿyan)
    in Aleppo, 12, 14, 16–17, 144
    in Cairo, 31–33, 35–37, 40–45, 82
    in Istanbul, 53, 59, 61–63
    in Jeddah, 112, 122–25, 128–29
    in Jerusalem, 181, 183, 188
    in Mecca, 127
Nuri al-Saʿid (Prime Minister of Iraq, 7 non-continuous terms between 1930–1958), 231
Nuri Pasha (*qaʾimmaqam* of Jeddah), 130

obscenities (and obscene language), 71–86
occupation, 170–71, 235–36
    British occupation, 114 (Aden); 182, 187 (Jerusalem); 211, 216 (Iran); 231–32 (Iraq)
    Egyptian occupation of Aleppo, 155
    French occupation of Egypt, 14, 29–33, 35–37, 45
oil, 197–216, 222–37, 243–58
    city/conurbation/town, 6–7, 14, 18–20, 222–26, 228, 230–32, 236, 243–57
    companies (*see* Anglo-Iranian Oil Company; Aramco; British Petroleum Company; Iraq Petroleum Company)
    development, 19, 224
    frontier (*see* frontier)
    industrialization, 18, 244, 248
    industry, 18–19, 63, 100, 102–3, 110n20, 199–200, 222–23, 226, 233, 235, 237, 243, 245–46, 248 (*see also under* Iraq)
    installations, 222, 229, 231, 233, 250, 252
    Iraq Petroleum Company (*see under* Iraq)
    rents, revenues, 100, 243, 245
    stations, 225, 228, 230–31, 235, 237
    workers (*see under* labour; workers; workforce)
Ottoman
    authorities, 11, 31, 40, 48n9, 49n34, 50n43, 57, 61–62, 65, 111–15, 118–20, 122–26, 128–30, 136n51, 136n58, 137n86, 141, 148, 164–68, 170, 172–76
    barracks, 61, 118–20, 131
    court (*see* court)
    Empire, 12–13, 54, 115–16, 125, 127, 131, 141–43, 147, 168–69, 180–81
    governor (*see* Ottoman: *wali/vali* (provincial governor))
    military (army/soldiers/ troops), 37–41, 43, 49n37, 124, 144–45, 166–68, 170, 172, 174–75
    Ministry of Police (Zaptiye Nezareti), 54, 56–57, 62, 65
    reform (*see* Tanzimat)
    wali/vali (provincial governor), 141, 155, 157 (Aleppo); 116 (Baghdad); 116 (Egypt); 113–14, 116–17, 122, 124–28, 130–31, 133n11, 136n58 (Hijaz, in Jeddah); 17, 181–82 (Jerusalem); 116 (Tripoli)

Palestine, 179–91, 199, 225
    nationalism (*see under* nationalism (and nationalists))
    in Saudi Arabia, 245, 253
Patriarch (and patriarchate)
    Armenian, 146, 168–69, 173
    Greek Orthodox, 63, 143–44, 150, 154–55, 159n9
patronage, 4, 12, 31, 42, 94, 144, 257
peasants, 82, 165–67

Index 319

Persia, 12, 113, 197, 202–6, 211, 214 (*see also* Iran)
petition, 12, 48n5, 64, 146, 155, 168–69, 249, 252–55
pilgrim(s), 112, 114, 118, 124, 125, 187, 189
pilgrimage, 92, 187
    hajj, 70, 112, 124–25
police, 4, 14, 19, 52–66, 70, 75–77, 84, 113, 117, 167–69, 172, 174–75, 187, 189, 203–5, 209–10, 213–15, 226, 229–31, 233–37, 244, 251, 253–56, 258, 268–69, 271–73, 281
    force(s), 5, 14, 52, 54–58, 62, 124, 187, 189, 203–4, 233, 246, 250, 255, 273
    Ottoman Ministry of Police (Zaptiye Nezareti), 54, 56–57, 62, 65
    reports, 55, 62, 64, 67n7, 80, 84
    station, 5–6, 54–56, 70, 76, 120, 172, 247, 250
    violence (*see* violence)
politics, 2, 10, 15, 18, 53, 131, 148, 157, 169, 198–99, 215, 223, 235, 279
    contentious, 2, 9–11, 13, 18, 21
    international, 29, 36, 38, 223–24
    local, 44, 129, 180, 183, 184
    state (and national), 190, 236
    street, 157, 163n68
    urban, 12, 17, 148, 156, 181, 216
port, 16, 53
    of Istanbul, 61, 63–65
    of Jeddah, 15–16, 111–31, 141
porters (*hammal*), 53, 59, 64–65, 68nn28–29, 70, 170, 173, 175
Poussielègue, 35
press, 10, 14, 52–53, 58–60, 63, 75, 206, 227, 231, 233, 281. *See also* newspapers
prison, 37, 41, 60, 63, 70, 75, 77–80, 83–84, 86, 125, 174, 230, 247, 249, 254, 256, 276
procession(s), 5, 12, 130, 182, 187–89

Muharram (*see under* Muharram)
profanity (and profane language), 71–72, 74–76, 84–85
Pro-Jerusalem Society. *See under* Jerusalem
prophets, 43, 92, 113, 184–85, 187
protection, 37, 65, 114–16, 126, 128, 142, 208, 229–30, 234, 266, 268
    police, 64, 229–30
protest, 2–8, 10, 12, 18, 64, 72, 74, 167–69, 202–3, 243–58, 268–72, 278–82. *See also* demonstrations
protestors, 5, 7, 141, 168–69, 233–36, 254, 258, 271, 279, 281. *See also* demonstrators
public, 5, 42, 52–53, 60, 66, 70–86, 111, 130, 164, 171, 199, 203, 270, 281
    act, 2, 4, 15, 32, 38–39, 70–86, 92, 123, 126, 130–31, 141, 168–69, 172, 188, 234–35, 251, 256, 267–68, 272
    decency (and morality), 42, 72–86, 100
    disorder (and unrest), 14, 52
    executions (*see* execution)
    life, 84, 273
    order, 14–15, 32, 53–65, 72–73, 75–76, 186, 237
    places, 77, 94, 121
    services, 73, 185
    space, 5, 10, 130, 202, 207, 269, 279, 283n10
    sphere, 2, 73–74, 76–77, 267
    violence (*see* violence: public)
publicity, 52, 58, 62, 66
Pullen, Captain, 122, 124–25, 128–29
punishment, 37, 44, 70, 79, 111, 124, 128, 230, 247, 258

qa'immaqam. *See under* Ottoman
Qajar Empire, 1, 12–13, 15, 93–94, 96
Qatif, 243, 251, 256

quarantine, 118, 120, 131
quarter(s), 76, 208, 210, 214, 228, 235, 253
    city/urban, 6, 10, 12–13, 15, 40–45, 94–108, 113, 121, 126, 130–31, 141–46, 149–58, 165–68, 173, 176, 184

racism, 199, 204, 210, 228, 244
railway, 84, 175, 270
rape, 41–42, 189
Ras Tanura, 243, 247, 250, 254–56
Red Sea, 15, 111–2, 115, 119, 126
reform(s), 12–13, 16, 18, 20, 54, 57, 82, 102, 104, 131, 167–69, 184
    Ottoman reform (*see* Tanzimat)
repression, 6, 14, 19, 30, 37, 44–45, 57, 66, 202, 258
resources, 6–7, 10–11, 19–20, 30, 57, 73, 77, 114, 198, 223, 257–58, 274
revolts, 54, 145, 166, 278
    Arab Revolt in Palestine (1936–1939), 186
    First Cairo Revolt Oct. 1798, 29, 35–37
    in Jeddah (1858), 111, 116, 125
    in Mecca (1855–1856), 125–26
    Second Cairo Revolt 3 March 1800, 14, 29–32, 37–47
    See also uprising
revolution(s), 12, 44, 265
    Egyptian (*see under* Egypt)
    in Iraq 1958, 223
    Islamic, 3
    Young Turk Revolution 1908, 12, 55, 57, 59–60, 66 (*see also under* Young Turks)
revolutionaries
    Armenian, 167–69, 175–76
    Egyptian, 267, 272, 280–82
    French, 5, 9, 33, 35, 44
Reza Shah (ruler of Iran 1925–1941), 98, 100, 199, 205
rights, 4, 64–65, 71, 73, 82, 93, 142, 168, 205, 255, 266
    human, 230, 239n13, 268
    to the city, 22n11, 71, 76, 266–67
riots (rioters and rioting), 6, 11, 16, 45, 61–63, 66, 72, 130, 141–42, 146, 148, 150–51, 163n69, 186, 206, 208, 252, 256, 281
    Bahmanshir Riots (*see* Bahmanshir Incident)
    bread (and food riots), 11, 137n75, 212
    Nebi Musa Riots (*see* Nebi Musa Riots)
rite, 92, 104–5, 146, 160
ritual (and ritualization), 2, 7–8, 12, 15–16, 18, 20, 128, 257
    murder, 62–63
    religious, 91–110 (*see also* Muharram)
    violence, 137, 181, 248
roads, 73, 77, 101, 103, 121, 187, 207–8, 245, 250, 264, 269, 275, 282
Rousseau, Jean-Baptiste, 151
rural, 6, 8, 10, 54, 82, 146, 198, 218, 226
    migration (*see* labour: migrants; workers migrants)
ruralization, 8
Russia, 88n41, 101, 111, 168–69, 171, 228

sabotage, 211, 214, 232, 235, 249, 252
Safavids, 92–93
Sarsi, 43
Sasun (region in SE Anatolia), 166, 168
Saʿud, Mishʿal b. ʿAbd al-ʿAziz b., 251–52
Saʿud b. ʿAbd al-ʿAziz Al Saud (King of Saudi Arabia 1953–1964), 249, 251, 254–55
Saudi Arabia, 13, 19, 224, 243–64
Sava Moscudi. *See* Toma
scale(s), 5, 10, 13, 15, 42, 44, 53, 63, 66, 112, 125, 129, 164–67, 173–74, 179, 189, 199, 215, 223, 231
    entanglement of, 29–33, 35–36, 39, 45, 47

sectarian (and sectarianism), 43, 141–42, 145, 147–49, 156, 158–59n6, 160n18, 210, 185, 204, 210–11
   sectarian violence, 7, 16, 40–41, 45
   See also confessionalism
security (and insecurity), 5, 32, 40, 52–59, 61, 65–66, 94, 114, 126, 131, 148, 170, 182, 201, 203, 206, 211–16, 223–41, 245–46, 250–58, 261, 269, 271–73
Seetzen, Ulrich Jasper, 145
segregation, 2, 7, 180, 185, 208, 245–46, 257, 279
Shadid, Anthony, 268
Shah, 93–94
   ʿAbbas I (Safavid ruler 1587–1629), 92
   Mohammad Reza, 100, 103
   Neʿmatollah Vali (Sufi master, 1330–1431), 92–93
   Reza, 98, 100, 199, 205
Shahada, Dimitri, 143, 159n9, 159n15
shanty town, 207–8, 212. See also slum
Sharifs of Mecca, 113–14, 116–17, 119, 123
Sharif ʿAbdallah, 127
Sharqawi, 33
shaykh, 32–33, 36–37, 43, 125, 248
   al-sada, 123
   al-tujjar, 113
shiʿa (shiʿi, Shiites), 15, 92–93, 218n15, 243, 251, 256, 258–59n4, 263n63
Sikhs, 201–3, 210
Sixth of April Youth Movement (Egypt), 268, 284n18
slaves (and slavery), 43, 116, 123–24, 129, 134, 201, 256
slum, 73, 79–80. See also shanty town
Snouck Hurgronje, Christiaan, 130

soldiers, 31, 38, 45, 48n5, 77, 249–52. See also under individual nations and empires
space of exception, 198, 206, 215–16
spies (and spying), 31, 33, 36, 52, 54, 172
state, 10, 14, 16, 19–21, 52–58, 60–66, 70–86, 91, 93, 129, 149, 165–67, 170, 175, 198, 203, 205–6, 213, 215, 223, 231, 244–45, 250, 256–58, 274, 278
   administration, 5–6, 14–15, 56, 83, 245, 248
   centralization/modernization, 10–12, 66, 100–101, 214, 223, 243
   nation, 1–7, 11–13, 15, 18–19, 215, 217n6
   oil, 223
   policing, 6, 20, 22, 257
   security, 56, 261n22
   violence, 7–8, 11, 15, 38, 166, 172, 223
statistics, 53, 56–57, 59, 173
Storrs, Ronald (British governor of Jerusalem), 180, 183–85, 189, 192n19, 192n23. See also British: governor
strike, 12, 72, 197, 202–3, 205–6, 213, 227, 229–31, 233–36, 241n49, 244, 247, 249–52, 255–57, 268
students, 3–4, 127, 168, 170, 237
   madrasa/religious/softa, 168, 171
subaltern, 11, 20–21, 197, 202, 212, 217
Sublime Porte, 146, 165, 167–69, 171, 173, 175. See also Ottoman: administration; Ottoman: government; Ottoman: authorities
Suez Canal, 112, 254
Sufis (and Sufism), 91, 93
sultan (Ottoman), 54, 66, 126, 154–55, 160, 165–70, 172, 184
sunni, 93, 165, 218, 251, 258–59
suq. See bazaar

surveillance, 19–20, 54–56, 66, 224, 226, 230, 234, 240n36
symbols, 16–17, 20, 36, 39–40, 45, 54, 67, 155, 157, 161, 167, 170, 184–85, 188, 205, 212, 227, 266–67, 281–82, 285n41
    symbolic acts (symbolic politics), 21, 24n51, 32–33, 89–139, 258
    See also under violence
synagogue, 61
Syria, 4, 7–8, 11, 24, 40, 43, 115, 142–43, 146, 148, 155, 181, 188, 225. *See also under* Christians

Tabriz, 93, 199
Tahrir Square (Midan al-Tahrir), 3, 7, 265, 270–72, 278–82, 285
Tamisier, Maurice, 118, 121, 129
Tanzimat, 1, 12–13, 20, 54–56, 62, 114, 142, 147–49, 155, 157–58, 165
    Hatt-ı Şerif of Gülhane, 148
    Hatt-ı Hümayun, 181
taxation (and taxes), 8, 44, 115–16, 141, 148, 150, 157, 165–66, 229
Tehran, 3, 199, 203, 211, 213
terror (and terrorism, terrorist), 14, 41, 44–45, 144, 168–69, 172, 176, 267
Tocqueville, Alexis de, 281
Toma (or Thoma) Sava & Co. (Greek merchant firm), Sava Moscudi, 115, 121, 123
torture, 4, 7, 256, 284n15
trade, 10, 16, 111–12, 115–16, 118, 129, 183, 198, 201
traders. *See* merchants
train, 250, 268
transformation, 2, 9, 12–13, 15, 17, 58, 61–62, 66–68, 72, 91–110, 114, 142, 179, 277–78
transportation, 185–86, 247, 251–53, 269, 281. *See also individual modes of transportation*

tribes (and tribesmen), 165, 199, 202, 226
Tripoli (Lebanon), 225, 235
Tripoli (Libya), 116
troops. *See* military
Turk, Nicolas, 35, 38–39
Turkey, 13, 66
Turkmens (in Kirkuk), 226, 239n15
Turks, 39, 58, 111, 146, 166, 175, 177n15. *See also* Ottoman; Young Turks
Tunis, 5
Tunisia, 4, 6, 8, 278, 284

ultras, 272–73
ʿUmar Makram (naqib al-ashraf in Cairo), 33, 35, 37, 39–40, 44
uprising(s), 111, 126–27, 131, 137n80, 164, 166–67
    in Aleppo 1850, 141–63
    Arab, 3–9, 266–80
    Iranian, 3–7
    urban, 23n27
urbanization, 2, 6, 8–9, 14, 24, 71–72, 80, 85, 216, 224–26, 236
    oil, 14, 19, 225–26, 236
ʿUtaishan, Turki ibn, 253–4

vali. *See* Ottoman: *wali/vali* (provincial governor)
vandalism, 232, 235, 249, 254
Varna, 176
vice-consul (British vice-consulate), 111, 114, 122, 128, 130. *See also under* Britain
violence
    bodily, 258
    communal, 7, 16–18, 53, 58, 61, 139–94, 187, 216, 235 (*see also* sectarian)
    factional, 14, 29–33, 35, 41–45, 229, 236
    gendered, 70–86
    physical, 18–20, 65, 73, 231, 234, 236, 243–45, 257–58, 260

police, 234
public, 2, 124–26, 164, 231, 237–38n19
sectarian, 7, 16, 40–41, 45
state, 8, 10–11, 38
structural, structured, 18–19, 179–72, 184, 187, 190, 223, 226, 239, 244–45
subjective, 267
symbolic, 6–7, 12, 15–17, 20–21, 24n51, 32–33, 45, 91–138, 161n40, 167, 170, 184–85, 258
systemic, 265, 267, 273–76, 282
theatres of, 10, 12, 39, 280
threats of, 19–20, 65, 71, 76, 112, 170, 176, 181, 187, 190, 208, 210, 215, 229, 236, 244, 249, 257–58, 260n12

wali. See Ottoman: *wali/vali* (provincial governor)
waqf, 121
war, 2, 40–41, 144, 208, 223, 267
  Crimean War (1853–1856), 168
  First World War (1914–1918), 1, 14, 182, 186–87, 223–24
  holy war (*jihad*), 40
  Russo-Turkish War (1877–1878), 165, 168
  Second World War (1939–1945), 18–19, 100, 198, 200, 209, 211–12, 214–16, 220n65, 223, 226, 228, 231–33, 236–37, 243
Wellsted, J.R., 121
Werry, Nathaniel William (British consul in Aleppo), 143
wikala, 40, 121
woman (women), 70–71, 76–86, 169, 185, 209–10, 234

work, 65, 71, 86n2, 129, 154–55, 157, 168, 199–200, 202–3, 210–12, 214
  camps, 229, 231, 235, 243–44, 247, 250, 254, 258
  See also labour
workers, 41, 44, 53, 63–65, 73, 76, 83, 101, 123, 169, 172, 174–76, 199–207, 209, 211, 216, 227–37, 242n57, 244–58, 261n27, 261n32, 263n61, 263n69, 272
  migrant, 17, 170, 174, 176, 201
  oil, 19, 206, 209, 243–49, 252, 254, 256–58, 261n27
workforce, 19, 72, 199–200, 203, 205–6, 226, 228, 230–31, 235–36, 239n15, 242n57, 245–46, 248–50, 253, 256–57, 259n4, 262n36
working class, 15, 59, 63, 72–74, 79–80, 82, 101, 170
World War I. *See* war: First World War (1914–1918)
World War II. *See* war: Second World War (1939–1945)

Yedi Sekiz Hasan Paşa, 55
Yemen, 116
Yıldız Palace, 55–56
Young Turks, 53, 57, 60, 67n7
Young Turk Revolution, 12, 55, 57, 59–60, 66
youth(s), 3–4, 6, 59, 269–70, 272, 279
Yusr, Faraj, 113, 122–24, 128

Zionism, 183, 185–86, 192n21
  anti-Zionism, 183
  Zionists, 17, 179, 181, 186–90, 219n20
Zionist Commission, 180, 183, 190
Zohrab (British Consul in Jeddah), 131

www.ingramcontent.com/pod-product-compliance
Lightning Source LLC
Chambersburg PA
CBHW072144100526
44589CB00015B/2080